PASSIONATE
LIBERATOR

PASSIONATE LIBERATOR

Theodore Dwight Weld
and the Dilemma of Reform

Robert H. Abzug

New York   Oxford
OXFORD UNIVERSITY PRESS
1980

Copyright © 1980 by Oxford University Press

Library of Congress Cataloging in Publication Data
Abzug, Robert H
  Passionate liberator.

  Bibliography: p. 359
  Includes index.
    1. Weld, Theodore Dwight, 1803–1895. 2.
Slavery in the United States—Anti-slavery move-
ments.   3.   United States—Social conditions—To
1865.   4. Abolitionists—United States—Biography.
5.   Social reformers—United States. I. Title.
E449.W46A29   326′.092′4 [B]   80-11819
ISBN 0-19-502771-X

Printed in the United States of America

for
my father and mother,
Seymour and Frances Abzug

Men, like planets, have both a visible and an invisible history. The astronomer threads the darkness with strict deduction, accounting so for every visible arc in the wanderer's orbit; and the narrator of human actions, if he did his work with the same completeness, would have to thread the hidden pathways of feeling and thought which lead up to every moment of action, and to those moments of intense suffering which take the quality of action—like the cry of Prometheus, whose chained anguish seems a greater energy than the sea and sky he invokes and the deity he defies.

George Eliot, *Daniel Deronda*

Preface

Theodore Dwight Weld is one of the most extraordinary little-known men in American history. During the 1830s, when militant abolitionism burst upon the scene as an infant and highly controversial crusade, Weld was among its most effective advocates. His impassioned oratory converted thousands to the slave's cause. His pamphlets, most notably *American Slavery As It Is*, reached a wider audience than the work of any other antislavery writer save Harriet Beecher Stowe. Mrs. Stowe herself credited much of the inspiration and evidence for *Uncle Tom's Cabin* to *American Slavery As It Is*. As an organizer and leader within the movement, Weld fostered an *elan* among his comrades of incalculable importance in the early lean years of abolitionist agitation. In short, he was a reformer's reformer.

Yet for reasons this book explores in some detail, Weld repudiated the life of antislavery activism fully seventeen years before the Civil War. Thus, by the time abolitionists reaped a harvest of belated praise, he had been long forgotten by all but his comrades from the early years. Nor has history been significantly kinder. Weld remains virtually unknown to anyone outside the historical profession, and even those scholars who first uncovered evidence of his vast contribution to the abolitionist cause erred in making a very complicated man into an unbelievable, two-dimensional Christian hero.

If this book presents a more "human" Weld, it is by no means in the spirit of iconoclasm. Rather I have tried to understand the odd mix of personal and philosophical motivations which made this man a reformer, which compelled him to live as a moral gadfly on the borders of the American mainstream. And I have attemped to explore the deep self-searching which caused him finally to reject reform as a vocation.

Most of all, I have wished to capture the passionate, almost epic quality of Weld's ninety-one year odyssey across nineteenth-century American history. Here was a man who lived life with an almost frightening intensity, an energy held in check only by an even more powerful propensity for self-scrutiny. Such pietistic zeal shaped both his public career and his more private cravings. It deeply colored his romance and marriage to the feminist Angelina Grimké. In general, it made of his life a constant quest for faith and truth. If some of the paths he followed seem to us odd or quixotic, it is no judgment on the spirit in which they were taken. For Weld's life was a brave one, brave in its common heroism and in its silent inner anguish.

This study could not have been written without the help of a number of persons and institutions. First I wish to thank the staffs of the research libraries listed in the bibliography, as well as those of the Doe Library at University of California, Berkeley, and Widener Library at Harvard University. Special thanks are due to Bill Joyce and John Dann for their aid as I perused the Weld and Birney collections at the William Clements Library. I also wish to mention the generosity of Ellen C. Peterson, who shared with me the results of her own research into late nineteenth-century Hyde Park.

I also gratefully acknowledge the generous support of the Ford Foundation, the Mabelle McLeod Lewis Memorial Fund, and especially the Danforth Foundation. All helped to finance the graduate work which led to this book. The University of Texas at

Preface

Austin, through its University Research Institute, provided a timely grant to expedite preparation of the book manuscript.

Finally, I wish to recognize numerous persons whose support and advice at various stages have improved this study. Kathy Berkeley, Marianne Carroll, Ruthy Graf, Daniel Walker Howe, Ginna Ingram, Bill Katkov, and Ernest Lee Tuveson all gave helpful readings. Of particular importance were the detailed comments of Michael Madigan, Stephen Maizlish, and Henry F. May.

The psychoanalytic sensibilities that inform some parts of this book were sharpened with the aid of Dr. Irving Berg, Joanne R. Wile, L.C.S.W., and the members of Dr. Joseph Afterman's seminar in psychoanalysis and history at the San Francisco Psychoanalytic Institute. I wish also to thank Susan Dickman, George Forgie, Lawrence Friedman, and Howard Miller for perceptive readings of various chapters. Thanks, too, go to Drew McCoy, Lorri Mills, and Penne Restad for their aid in the last stages of preparation. Susan Rabiner, Shelley Reinhardt, and everyone at Oxford University Press have at all stages been extremely helpful.

Most of all, I wish to acknowledge my debt to Kenneth M. Stampp, whose guidance and friendship I have enjoyed for some years. This work has, of course, benefited greatly from his suggestions. However, I thank him even more for the constancy of his caring and support in good and lean years, and for the inspiration of his example.

Austin, Texas   R.H.A.
May 1980

Contents

PASSIONATE
LIBERATOR

Theodore Dwight Weld, age c. 38
(*W. P. Garrison and F. J. Garrison*, William Lloyd Garrison, *1805–187*

I

Tornado Boyhood

I was a tempestuous boy.
Theodore Dwight Weld to his grandchild.

*Men can do nothing without the make-
believe of a beginning.*
George Eliot, *Daniel Deronda*

On a day in late May, 1836, as the Erie Canal packet boat *Oneida*
plodded past Schenectady toward Troy, Theodore Dwight Weld
sat huddled in its crowded cabin scrawling a letter to a fellow
abolitionist. Weld was at the height of his fame as an antislavery
orator. The previous year he had swept across Ohio, courting
mobs and converting great numbers to the cause. Now in New
York State, he had already scored triumphs in Rochester and
Utica and hoped for the same in Troy. He had yet to taste defeat. His letter complained of the laziness of most abolitionists
when it came to the hard work of making converts. They loved
to attend self-congratulatory celebrations or to preach the abolition gospel close to home, he charged. But who would join him
in more dangerous country? Who would help him in upstate
New York?[1]

Weld's challenge was in good part boast, for he had come to
see himself as an embodiment of the rough virtues of the hinterland West. Studiously avoiding the least refinement of dress or
appearance, he chose to make himself indistinguishable from the
most ordinary of men. At thirty-two, unkempt locks flying in all
directions, his muscular body clothed in homespun, he fancied

himself a "backwoodsman untamed." Two months earlier, he had declined a speaking invitation from the Boston Female Anti-Slavery Society. "My bearish proportions have never been licked into *City Shape*," he claimed, "and are quite too uncombed and shaggy for 'Boston notions.' . . . A *stump* is my throne my parish my home—My element the *everydayisms* of plain common life." Turning down another invitation from the East, he stated simply: "I was made to stand about among the yeomanry."[2]

Judged by his beginnings, Weld was not quite what he claimed to be. The son of a prominent Congregational minister and scion of several illustrious New England families, raised in a well-ordered Connecticut town, he was hardly a backwoodsman. Nor did he lead a yeoman's life. He was unmarried, owned little or no property, and had no ties to any particular locale or community; he lived outside the web of responsibilities that defined the common man's life. His homes were the packet boats and stagecoaches that conveyed him from town to town, and the spare rooms of friends who housed him wherever he preached antislavery.

In any case, Weld's concerns were hardly with the "everydayisms" of life. He had committed himself to an extraordinary earthly cause—abolishing slavery in America—and to the cosmic mission of preparing the world for Christ's Second Coming. Indeed, he had dubbed his homespun suit a "John the Baptist attire." Like John, he seemed to be crying in the wilderness; most Americans saw Weld either as a fanatic or a common criminal.[3]

His assumption of the yeoman's person, however, was no simple ruse. Like the journalist Walter Whitman, who in his poetry burst forth as "Walt Whitman, one of the roughs," Weld had found it necessary to invent a new self so that he might plunge headlong toward a fancied destiny. His romantic persona, this image of the rootless prophet from everywhere and from nowhere in particular, combined the trappings of an American Everyman with those of a primitive Christian. Moreover, his guise struck responsive chords wherever he spoke. No abolitionist of the 1830s, save William Lloyd Garrison, became more famous or more notorious. Garrison himself called his comrade "the lion-hearted, invincible Weld."[4]

Yet public success seemed only to accentuate a strain of inner torment. Evidence of it appeared everywhere—in Weld's wild and illegible handwriting, in a brooding dreaminess, and in cyclical bouts of overexertion and physical collapse. Most of all, etched into his face was what one friend called a "deep, wild gloom." Such signs bore enigmatic but compelling testimony to an unresolved and tortured past. Weld might mythologize his life, he might paint himself into the landscape of a millennial future; in short, he might try to remake his self in full view of the world. However, he could not shake the haunting presence of inner battles as yet unwon.[5]

Weld's triumphs before antislavery audiences allowed him to delay direct confrontation with his hidden demons, and, as he cruised aboard the *Oneida* toward Troy, he had no reason to believe that victories would not continue to come to him. Yet lying in wait at Troy was an opposition so potent that it not only dealt Theodore his first public defeat, but so shattered his romantic sense of self that it set in motion a slow and painful reevaluation of his entire life.

Sometime in early 1877, at the age of seventy-three, Theodore decided to pay a last visit to his childhood home. He had long since abandoned his homespun suit and itinerant life. Now, dressing instead in waistcoat and vest, he lived among Boston's reform elite as an educator and family man. And all around him signs of death were crowding in. Obituaries recited, one by one, the names of his old antislavery comrades. Angelina Grimké, his wife for almost forty years and herself once a vital reformer, lay half-paralyzed by stroke. Weld himself, though in good health, displayed sure signs of his age—the white whiskers of his grand patriarchal beard had begun to turn yellow and now framed a creased and mottled face. Only his eyes preserved a glimmer of the young rebel. They would guide him back to the battlefields of an admittedly "tempestuous" youth.[6]

So in the summer of 1877 Weld and his daughter Sissy boarded a train in Boston and journeyed southeast to the little town of Hampton, Connecticut. He had chosen for a companion the most adoring of his three children. Now thirty-three and married, Sissy still relished being her father's little girl. She had already blessed him with a grandchild, and now hoped to pass on to this next generation Theodore's earliest memories. By contrast, Weld's two sons had kept their distance—Stuart with rebellious reserve and Theodore, Jr. behind the curtain of insanity.

As father and daughter approached Hampton, they could see a typical New England village surrounded by modest farms with rolling fields set off by low stone fences. In contrast with her Boston of commerce and industry, of bustle and streetcars and hordes of immigrant strangers, Sissy saw Hampton as the incarnation of a past and golden age. Here townspeople had known each other and the other's place in society; farmers, craftsmen, and women in the home had provided the essentials of life; and the pace of everyday existence had been tied to the tasks of farming and the cycles of nature rather than to the mechanical clock of city life.

Sissy did know that life in her father's youth could be harsh, that nature might punctuate her normal rhythms with bitter winters, lengthy droughts, or epidemic disease. However, her upbringing in liberal Christianity precluded an understanding of the dark spiritual universe in which most of Hampton's inhabitants lived. Townsfolk in the late eighteenth and early nineteenth century found the commonplaces of life steeped in awesome meanings, in judgments, and in warnings. They sought constantly to second-guess the fates that might bring death or hardship. Most interpreted happenings through a mixture of Protestant Bible theology and more naturalistic folk belief. "The majority of my townsmen," commented a Connecticut Yankee of Weld's generation, ". . . knew something of the dream-book and palmistry, and of the influence of the moon (especially when first seen, after the change, over the right shoulder), not only on weather and vegetation, but on the world of humanity. They also understood full well, what troubles were betokened by the howling of a dog, the blossoming of a flower out of due season, or the beginning of a journey or a job of work on Tuesday or Friday."[7]

For that minority of Hampton's citizens who belonged to the First Congregational Church, Calvinism's theology cast individual lives and community actions into a more highly structured cosmic drama. While the things of everyday life were not neglected, simple pleasures and struggles meant relatively little except as confirmations or as countercurrents of a person's hopes for salvation or a town's ripeness for God's blessing or punishment. Man stood depraved and as nothing before the Lord's power. A few would be saved—these were God's Saints and New England Congregationalists believed that they constituted the visible church of Saints—but most men faced damnation. Nonetheless Calvinists believed that God had commanded all men to do His will and had chosen His elect to shepherd the world toward the prophesied end of days and thousand-year reign of Christ.[8]

Perhaps that is why no landmark loomed larger on the horizon than the white steeple of Hampton's Congregational Church that, even at a distance, dominated the landscape. It had been the church of Theodore's father, the Reverend Ludovicus Weld. Sissy, with her penchant for genealogy, must have been stirred by this physical symbol of the family's connection to New England Puritanism. She knew the story of Thomas Welde, who had landed at Boston in 1632 as one of the first generation of Yankee Saints; that he had been the original pastor of Roxbury Church, a founding overseer of Harvard College, and an ardent defender of the godly Commonwealth against the disruptive heresies of Anne Hutchinson (whom Sissy also proudly claimed as part of her family genealogy). She had traced the Welds back to their mythic origins among the Irish kings and forward from Thomas through a long roster of ministers and other notables. Sissy had also studied the lineage of Elizabeth Clark, Theodore's mother, whose family boasted such luminaries as Solomon Stoddard, Jonathan Edwards, Timothy Dwight, and the devilish Aaron Burr.[9]

One can only guess as to Theodore's feelings upon seeing

again the church of his youth. Early in life he had rebelled against the familial and theological traditions it symbolized and as part of that rebellion had endured an agonizing relationship with his father. If such turbulent memories loomed up in his mind, he did not relate them to his daughter. Rather he entertained her with more innocent recollections of the Sabbath—sitting silently in the family pew, squirming as Ludovicus delivered long and learned sermons and, on cold days, waiting impatiently for the hand and foot stoves to be passed from brother to brother.[10]

The drama of Theodore's childhood transpired more at home than at church, however, and it was to the now abandoned Weld farm that father and daughter directed their carriage. More than eighty years earlier, Ludovicus had traveled the same road to inspect his new home and sixty acres. He was twenty-six when Hampton's church called upon him to be their minister and was ordained on October 17, 1792. He had followed a traditional path to the ministry. Preparing at Andover Academy and graduating from Harvard in 1789, he then studied the way of the church with his father, the Reverend Ezra Weld of Braintree, Massachusetts. Ludovicus preached first at Epping, New Hampshire, but declined a permanent appointment there in favor of Hampton's offer.[11]

The young minister came as a stranger to Connecticut, but soon he was a familiar figure at the gatherings of Windham County's best families. Tall and handsome, his demeanor marked by a certain stern graciousness, Weld was clearly a most eligible bachelor. It was not long before he met Elizabeth Clark of neighboring Lebanon. "Pretty Betty," as she was called, was more than beautiful. She was an intelligent and apparently somewhat eccentric woman. Those of her letters that survive exude a poetic sensibility and most of all, a warm if troubled piety. She complemented the new minister almost perfectly. In any case, the match seemed to be fated by the currents of Windham County society. Elizabeth's older brother had married a daughter of Weld's predecessor, Samuel Moseley. Moseley himself had chosen a wife from the Clark family. Ludovicus and Elizabeth were married in 1795.[12]

Nor was it long before they started a family. Lewis arrived within a year of the marriage. Charles Huntington was born in 1799, to be followed by Ezra Greenleaf in 1801. A little more than two years later, on November 23, 1803, came Theodore Dwight. Finally, almost six years later, the Welds were blessed with a daughter, Cornelia Elizabeth. They comprised a household marked by energy and motion.

Now, as Theodore and Sissy approached the house, all was still. We have only the daughter's account of their visit, but she had learned in advance much about what had occurred in her father's years there. From the chaos of experience Theodore had forged a repertoire of tales and entertainments that he had recounted over the years at dinner table and fireside. These stories, psychically bowdlerized, invented, and reshaped into a personal myth, hardly represented an objective account of Weld's youth. Rather, taken as a whole, they were a subjective representation of how, consciously and unconsciously, the little boy Thoda (as he was called by the family) had experienced his world and what meaning those early experiences had for him later in life. Luckily, in an unpublished "Memories of Theodore Dwight Weld," Sissy wrote an account of their journey peppered with these stories. She thus preserved highly imperfect but compelling clues to the nature of Weld's childhood.*

---

* What follows in the text is an interpretation of a childhood based almost entirely upon the memories of a man in his seventies as filtered through the mind and pen of his loving daughter. One might rightly wonder whether such evidence can be the stuff of good history. For an objective reconstruction of events, it is certainly well-nigh useless. Nonetheless, I have seen fit to make use of these remembrances for a number of reasons. First, they constitute virtually the only body of material that deals directly with Weld's early years. Second, after having lived with Weld and his world for some time, I have come to the conclusion that Sissy's transcriptions are reasonably accurate representations of Weld's own memories of his childhood if not of his childhood itself.

Most important, however, no matter how useless they are as a guide to actual events, they can be useful tools in coming to an understanding of the subjective meaning of Weld's childhood to himself. Still, it is a tricky business to attempt to interpret such tales. I have followed Freud in think-

Sissy noticed her father quiver as he entered the house and led her to the room in which he had been born. She already knew that for the first six months of life, little Thoda had suffered from chronic spasms. All feared that he was close to death. Indeed, the dark prophecy of his doctor uncle—"Betty's baby had better die, for if he lives he'll be a fool"—survived to amuse the daughter. The infant suffered no apparent damage, but the struggle of those early months left its own sort of legacy in a particularly strong bond between mother and son, as well as a sense of specialness growing out of the retelling of the birth story itself.[13]

Little Thoda needed all the motherly love and sense of self he could muster to survive in the busy Weld household. He might be favored as the baby, but he was still the smallest of four brothers. In addition, the household was swollen by Elizabeth's servants and clusters of Ludovicus's ministerial students, sometimes as many as six at a time, who boarded with the family. It was a world of noise and motion, of chores and meals and little time for rest. Rather than retiring from the fray, Thoda responded with an energetic precocity and a propensity for getting attention by any means available. For instance, whenever a

---

ing of them as "screen memories," concoctions of the mind that condense, synthesize, and distort real and important events and relationships of childhood into stories that serve a dual function. They both preserve conscious reminders of crucial people and happenings, and at the same time smooth over the more troubling or even traumatic meanings of childhood and divert them from remaining consciously troubling by the use of changed endings, symbolic representations, and other alterations. Like the tips of icebergs, they appear above the surface of consciousness as relatively harmless and nostalgic monuments of the past, while submerging out of easy view a mass of dangerous emotions below. The psychoanalytic uses of this concept and a more precise clinical definition can be found in "Screen Memories" (1899), in Sigmund Freud, *Collected Papers*, V, (New York, 1957, ed. Strachey), 47–69.

My purpose in this chapter is not to present a definitive psychoanalysis of Weld, but rather to evoke the live issues of his childhood through the judicious and sensitive use of psychoanalytic insight. Some may think I have used the evidence too cautiously, while others will continue to see an edifice built upon too unreliable a foundation. My own intent has been to be responsive to what I know about Weld and his life while still listening closely to his stories and letting them lead me into a murky world that, of necessity, defies normal historical analysis and description.

thunderstorm came up, he would run outside and whoop and holler "like a wild indian" to gain notice, even though, and perhaps because, his mother might "tingle" his legs as "punishment." He learned to read and write early and by the age of three was attending school. At school he bid for friendship by playing pranks. Theodore told how his classmates once "put him up" to stowing a frozen chicken in the teacher's desk; when he was caught and told to pluck the bird, little Thoda responded by blowing the plucked feathers all over the schoolmaster's back.[14]

So many brothers in the same household bred a predictable mixture of camaraderie and conflict. As the youngest, Thoda learned the ways of a boy's world from his seniors. Weld now showed his daughter the fireplace where the brothers roasted pigs' tails and the well they had stocked with speckled trout in hopes of catching one in a bucket of water. He walked with her through fields marked by recollections of childhood games. The old man remembered less about the keen rivalries endemic in such a family, but he did recount one story that no doubt stood for a myriad of petty conflicts between the brothers. As three-year-old Thoda and his brother Greenleaf were sitting on the back doorstep having their evening bread and milk, they began to argue violently. Thoda finally answered his brother's verbal aggressions with a telling swat on the head with his pewter mug, knocking Greenleaf to the ground unconscious. In part a story of triumph, it is a triumph tinctured with guilt. In later years Theodore attributed his strict sense of self-control to the episode, remarking that whenever he became excited the image of his pale and helpless brother came before him.[15]

From these tales emerges a composite portrait of little Thoda in his first three or four years—made to feel special, indulged as the baby and as a survivor of an early disorder, but also struggling urgently and defiantly to make a place for himself in a busy and highly competitive household. Of great importance for his future was the fact that he had found one method of gaining love and attention particularly successful—that of performing for others through practical jokes or wild antics. It was a trait that in its more positive aspects contributed to his success as an orator. It was also a part of his character that, when later labeled by Weld himself as mere "vanity," caused endless hours of tortured self-recrimination and self-doubt. After all, his boisterous nature and need to call attention to himself clashed directly with his family's pious Protestantism, in which few sins were more serious than those of vanity and pride.

But when did this headstrong and energetic little boy begin to feel the anxious inner questioning of piety that would become so much a part of his adult character and, in the end, his reformer's conscience? Certainly the religious culture in which Thoda was raised emphasized both moral responsibility and introspective searching as part of a long road to salvation. Even before the child might begin to understand the details of Orthodox theology, he was imbued with rituals and language of church and home worship, which made God's presence and power a matter of everyday consciousness. As Thoda learned more about his family's place in society, he also became accustomed to thinking of himself as one who would someday influence or even lead society.

The presence of such religious and social imperatives, however, could not entirely dictate the nature of Theodore's confrontation with God and the world. Any culture produces its timeservers and its rebels, those who fit comfortably in the mainstream and those who eagerly explore the borders. The Weld household alone produced sons whose eventual places in society, though all true to tradition, varied widely. Lewis and Greenleaf easily found niches among the moral and social elite, the former as an educator of the deaf and the latter as a doctor. Charles, sickly since childhood and possessed of a poetic nature, failed at a number of professions but in the end defined his life through an intense, highly personal search for religious truth and godlike perfection. Theodore made his way along a course somewhere in among the examples of his older brothers. Basically strong, assertive, and committed to an important role in society, he also displayed an uncertainty about his place in the universe that accentuated inner searching and combined with his sense of social responsibility to produce a zeal for reform unmatched in the family since Thomas Welde's commitment to revolutionary Puritanism.[16]

The process by which little Thoda eventually became a moral gadfly to church and to society was a long and complex one, but it had much to do with the development of his sense of disorientation and self-doubt. One early and important event in this regard was the arrival of a sister, Cornelia Elizabeth, when the boy was five years old. As Weld told the story years later, he had been so bored by the sight of the newborn infant that he quickly ran away to play with his dog. The boy's indifference is hard to believe. If not at the moment of birth, then in the ensuing weeks and months, he must have felt deep rage and despair at being replaced as the baby of the family. Any child would have felt some jealousy, and Thoda's close relationship with his mother and long reign as the youngest child virtually guaranteed a more intense reaction.[17]

Striking if indirect evidence of these feelings appeared in a memory that came to Weld as he and Sissy stood in the empty birth room. He recalled that it was in this very room that he had read Jane Porter's *Thaddeus of Warsaw,* an immensely popular romantic novel of the period. He remembered crying over the fate of the hero, leaning out of the window and sobbing, "Poor Thaddeus, O Poor Thaddeus!" Curiously, the most poignant scene of this long-forgotten work is that of Thaddeus's mother dying in her son's arms amidst a siege on the family castle, and of Thaddeus being pulled away by a comrade before he could give her a proper burial. It seems likely that little Thoda and later the adult Weld preserved in this memory the emotions the boy felt at the time of Cornelia's birth, the emotions he felt when stunned by the "loss" of his mother. His anchor at home had been loosed and with it his place in the world.[18]

Weld had drawn his own lesson from the memory. "Yet when only a boy," he told Sissy, "I accustomed myself never to become so deeply absorbed in any novel that I could not at will lay it down instantly." As an adult he would adopt the same self-control when it came to women. His closest friends even chided him about his wariness toward love and marriage, an attitude that may have had much to do with his "loss" at age five. The storminess of his final capitulation to Angelina Grimké at age thirty-five also displayed an unusually deep fear that if he revealed his true emotions he would be rejected.[19]

Shock over the perceived loss of his mother's affections, however, defined only one important reaction to Cornelia's birth. Swallowing whatever anger he felt toward the infant, the little boy became his mother's helper and developed a close attachment to his baby sister, an attachment that would later blossom into a relationship of deep and mutual loving care. Indeed, Theodore's relationship with Cornelia would become a model for a number of safe, "sisterly" connections with women that would precede his marriage.

In any case, Cornelia's arrival coincided in Thoda's life with the time when most little boys turn to their fathers for love and direction as they begin to imagine a place for themselves in the world of adults. Yet he would find it difficult to seek out Ludovicus's attention. He might admire him from a distance, be awed by the attention and respect his sermons commanded, but he rarely had the sense that he could get very close to Ludovicus or that his father wished to be close to him. After all, so many others, brothers and students, blocked the way. Letters from son to father in Theodore's youth indicated all too painfully how neglected the son felt, and a seemingly innocent memory reported to Sissy as the pair walked through the kitchen of the old house gives us an almost "geographical" sense of the emotional distance little Thoda must have felt. The old man pointed to a worn spot on the wainscotting that framed the room and explained that his mother would rap on it to notify Ludovicus, ensconced in his upstairs study, that callers were waiting.[20]

The image of the minister hidden away in his study was probably true to the literal as well as the emotional experience of the boy. Ludovicus's responsibilities to the church and to his ministerial students were time-consuming and exhausting and left him little time for his youngest son. Besides, a debilitating nervous condition, which would plague the senior Weld throughout his life, may have already begun to erode his energy and patience. Whatever the realities of his father's life, it was not hard for the little boy to interpret lack of time and preoccupation with other matters as simple lack of love.

These feelings of estrangement were compounded by the fact that the one role Ludovicus seemed comfortable and willing to play in the boy's life was the traditional one of judge and enforcing authority. One memory in particular, evoked as Weld and Sissy entered another empty room, revealed a rather unpretty side of Thoda's upbringing. As a child, so he told his daughter, he had cut some fine lines in a row of green cheeses. The cheeses dried and the hair-thin slits of his penknife grew to gaping fissures. Asked by his parents if he had cut them, Thoda had answered no. He was summarily sent to this very room in which father and daughter now stood, there to live for a week in solitary confinement and with nothing to eat but bread and water. Weld pointed out the pillasters beneath the mantelpiece; he had counted them over and over again to relieve the boredom of his imprisonment.[21]

In the old man's version, he insisted that he had forgotten about the slits when he denied culpability and only later remembered his original act. Just as likely, he had been afraid to admit his guilt and perhaps had felt even righteously defiant enough to lie. Whatever the relationship of the memory to the "facts," this story is marked most of all by loneliness and hurt. Significantly, the old man drew no moral from the tale. It stood without embellishment as a symbol of a strain of distrust in his father's sense of justice and exercise of authority. Later in life, this ambivalence about authority and sense of having known what it is like to be a victim would cause Theodore to avoid positions that placed him under the direct control of others; it would also help sensitize him to the psychological plight of those trapped by the ultimate abuse of power—slavery.

Yet we may assume that when little Thoda asked himself why he deserved such a fate—not only the specific punishment of solitary confinement, but more generally the arrival of Cornelia and the distance of his father in a time of need—he may have spent as much time blaming himself as his parents. Perhaps God was punishing him for his fight with Greenleaf or for generally rivalrous feelings toward his brothers and new sister; maybe his stunts at school and antics at home had been to blame. Whatever the variety of sins imagined, mixed in with the boy's anger was no doubt a strong dose of guilt.

That is, at least, one way of explaining the extraordinary fact that soon after his fifth year little Thoda suddenly turned into an energetic religionist. By the time he was seven he had read the entire Bible, finishing it, as he later remembered, in a burning fever. His mother now became for him the fount of moral outrage and piety. He listened closely to her woeful tales of Hagar, the Clark family slave, and would later trace his hatred of slavery to these stories. More generally, a pietistic ideal of woman began to form around his mother and the stories of famous women missionaries they studied together. One story in particular made a lasting impression on him, that of the missionary who preached the Gospel to a barbarian king and army. "I remember reading it at my mothers knee when a child," he would later recount to Angelina Grimké, "and the majesty of her enkindled spirit so ravished my young heart that ever since I have turned instinctively towards her at the thought of womanhood in its glory." He would win his mother's heart by being as pious as the missionary and would, in the future, measure women by the standards of both mother and the female preacher in the story.[22]

Clearly his turn to religion was also an attempt to come closer to his father, to be like him, and to win his love. However, a combination of Thoda's defiant streak and Ludovicus's hidebound orthodoxy gave such efforts an ironic twist. According to a story Theodore loved to tell his children, he would barrage his father with challenging questions about Scripture. Once the minister became so enraged by such interrogation that he slammed down the Bible and shouted, "Shut up your mouth you little infidel!" No doubt a combining of many incidents, this tale symbolized in Theodore's mind a basic fact about his relationship to Ludovicus—he could only rouse his father by raising the specter of heresy. Then his father would listen, if only to condemn. As Weld grew to manhood, the memory of himself in this role may have preserved a lively sense of his basic stance toward all human authority. He would win notice as a renegade.[23]

At school Thoda underwent a similar transformation. Still calling attention to himself through remarkable acts, he changed from cut-up to saint. Theodore told how, when he was six, a new black student entered his common school. The teacher made little Jerry sit apart from the rest of the class and humiliated him after his recitations. When Thoda asked to have his seat put next to Jerry's, the teacher replied, "Why, are you a nigger too?" The class then chorused, "Theodore Weld is a nigger!"[24]

Later in life Theodore was fond of using this tale to prove his early commitment to black rights. We have no way to judge its accuracy in the most literal sense; however, we may see in the seemingly ironic identification of Weld as a "nigger" yet another aspect of Thoda's emotional life. In truth he was something of a "nigger" at school, though the more accurate description was "minister's son." Especially after he began to play the part with saintly relish, the boy bore the brunt of being the most defenseless representative of Hampton's self-proclaimed Congregational elite. Most of his peers grew up in families that resented those in the church. They liked to believe, according to William Andrus Alcott, that ministers were possessed of a certain "native imbecility" and that those, like Theodore, who "took to learning" were somehow "weak in the attic." It did not help matters that in post-Revolutionary America, when most churches had been disestablished, the Orthodox Church in Connecticut had remained part of the official establishment. Ludovicus still wore the ceremonial dress of the Standing Order, and school children were still required to bow and curtsy as he passed the school ground. Impotent to attack the minister himself, many children found an easy target in his son. Indeed, Weld would attribute his ability to face personal attack and unpopularity with a degree of equanimity to early training at the school yard.[25]

The fact that Thoda often courted the taunts of his classmates indicated that whatever hurt he experienced was tempered by a certain heroic satisfaction and even some delight. He felt special as well as isolated and took solace in being a soul set apart. In fact, in most ways he prospered and grew into a vigorous youth. He excelled at school despite the taunts of other students. At home, he impressed his family by a continuing passion for religion and an energetic commitment to the family farm. By age twelve he had taken over management of all hundred planted acres.

It was, indeed, in the fields that young Theodore, unburdened by the pressures of school and family, could be most himself. There he might take care of his heifer, run with his dog, and explode with energy—leaping, jumping, and swinging from tree limbs. During these hours in the fields the darker side of Theodore's aloneness also found expression, for he could not escape the inner questioning and self-recrimination that lay just below the surface of his almost muscular confidence. Thus his play sometimes turned toward self-destructiveness. "Before I was ten years old," he would later write, "in a number of instances, I almost killed myself by reckless daring, broke one of my hands and a bone in one foot, have dislocated bones at least four times, cut off the chords of one finger, had one of my eyes literally hooked out of its socket. . . ." Such a "tornado boyhood," he intimated, possessed "all the ghastliness and gashings of a dissecting room." He would later interpret this "keen relish" for recklessness as a "powerful temptation *presumptiously* to venture and thus tempt God." Perhaps in every reprieve lay proof that, whatever the doubts of this outwardly successful but inwardly troubled boy, at least God loved and cared for him. Yet no single test seemed good enough, no sign could assuage the fears within.[26]

In this inner doubt may lie the origin of certain "*mental* defects," as Weld later called them, that plagued his adult life.

Most of all, his memory would fail. He couldn't remember what day it was or even what month; often he couldn't remember the names or even his connections with those who would approach him with warmth and familiarity. "I very often swing like a pendulum," he admitted when age thirty-four, "in a dreamy totally abstracted revery, dont hear questions that are asked me, and sometimes I am told that I go on making a sort of inarticulate nasal um, um, um, um, as a sort of unconscious mechanical assent to some one talking to me and keep this up for five minutes perhaps without knowing or even hearing a single word he has said." One can easily imagine young Theodore alone in the fields or even among his family, lost in this same dreamy state, taken with inner battles and oblivious to the world and people around him.[27]

Yet not all his fantasies in the field were morbid reveries. One in particular would prepare him to enter society on his own terms. He dreamed of becoming a great orator. As the aging Weld and Sissy walked down the road leading from the house, they encountered a fifteen-foot-high boulder in their path. It was the rock, he told her, that he had mounted to make his first orations, swaying invisible multitudes as he scanned the woods and fields. Here he could emulate his father or even better him at his own tasks. Not entirely coincidentally, Theodore also remembered that it was at the foot of the great rock that, when a boy, he had courted his first "girl friend." Later, as a famous orator, he would find the public rostrum—with audiences in his control and at a distance—a safe place from which to court attention and love.[28]

At age fifteen Theodore had walked down this road and had passed this rock on his way to Andover Academy. At Andover he was to prepare for college and eventually for the ministry, the career he and his family assumed was his destiny. With such intelligence, talent for public speaking, passion for religion, and with such a long family tradition in the ministry, who could doubt that the troubled but energetic boy would follow in Ludovicus's footsteps?

Weld's deepest and as yet unconscious feelings about that fate, however, were perhaps revealed best in what he told Sissy was his first memory. He pictured himself lying in the grass near his father's door, filled with thoughts of God. Late in life he made this scene symbolic of an enduring and unwavering religious faith. However, in the memory it is a faith practiced just outside his minister-father's house; we may see it as indicative of the fact that Theodore's spiritual cravings could not find succor within his father's church.[29]

This presented a poignant dilemma for a minister's son. If Theodore felt unloved by his father and his father was God's representative on earth, how then could he feel secure about the more cosmic love of salvation? The search for a proper home for his faith, indeed the search for faith itself, would take a lifetime. The aging Theodore Weld, who now led his daughter down the path and back to Boston, had finally come home. Almost sixty years earlier, young Weld had no way of knowing that his departure for Andover down the same path would begin not a career in the ministry, but rather a spiritual odyssey.

II

Andover and Escape

Despite inner ambivalences and a troubled relationship to his father, Theodore would probably have become a minister had time and events not changed the fortunes of the Congregational Church. In the 1780s, when Ludovicus had gone to Andover to prepare for Harvard, he might still look forward to joining a ministry fairly secure in its place of public leadership. It was a sunny time to begin preaching in New England, some of whose Orthodox clergy had been in the forefront of the revolutionary movement. Ludovicus Weld must have felt special kinship to the new Republic, having been raised among the Adamses in Braintree; his father, the Reverend Ezra Weld, had been John Adams's minister. In any case, the Orthodox clergy in general had viewed the Revolution as a sign of Christian rebirth, one which might even herald the millennial day.[1]

By 1792, the year Ludovicus Weld came to Hampton, signs of trouble had already begun to appear. Deism was having a brief vogue; Unitarianism increasingly threatened Orthodoxy all over New England; Baptist congregations were churching the previously unchurched; and democratic ideals were beginning to undercut the deferential assumptions of Congregational power. Still, in Connecticut, the "land of steady habits," the so-called Standing Order seemed secure. But between 1792 and 1819, the year Theodore packed his bags and set off for Andover, the power and position of Orthodoxy had deteriorated seriously. Many ministers detected abroad in the land what one had described, some years before, as a "cold, contemptuous indifference toward every moral and religious subject." Lending credence to Orthodox fears was the fact that in 1818, democratic forces in Connecticut finally managed to disestablish the church.[2]

Ludovicus confronted symptoms of this decline in Hampton. Since 1775 the town had witnessed the growth of a sturdy Baptist congregation. Some decades later a new dissenting group appeared; one can only guess Weld's reaction to their self-consciously primitive rite of washing each other's feet and rolling on the floor to express humility before Christ. His own church records reveal troubled times. They are peppered with references to punishments meted out for swearing, cheating, and heresy. By 1815 the elder Weld had even considered making special trips to each family in his congregation to encourage church attendance, curb use of profanity, and generally reaffirm the presence of the church.[3]

Ludovicus's sermons of the period indicate how much he blamed the democratic ascendancy since Jefferson's election to the presidency in 1800 for the church's problems. He attacked "uneducated" ministers of the dissenting sects and through transparent veils cried out against democratic tendencies that threatened tradition and true freedom. His text was Jeremiah; the subject, false prophets: "When men of corrupt principles and licentious lives, secure general confidence, we have just occasion for alarm." In references to the French Revolution, Weld indulged in standard Federalist rhetoric that made Jeffersonians into domestic Jacobins:

> Their [France's] destroyers were those very persons who styled themselves "The Friends of the People," who pretended to be deeply concerned for their interest, and exceedingly desirous of alleviating their burdens, of breaking the shackles of tyranny, and of introducing them to permanent peace and *rational liberty*. Such, *most evidently*, were the principal instruments of their ruin.[4]

Not surprisingly, little Thoda's vision of society was constructed from the vocabulary and emotional sense of his father's defensive posture. A childhood tale from age three attests to the intense and sometimes humorous results of such an education. One Dr. Chapman, a pillar of the Standing Order, came to visit Ludovicus and left his gold-headed cane in the hall. The boy began examining the object, only to be reprimanded by Chapman. Shaking his fist with hurt and anger, Thoda blurted out, "You're a Jacobin!" It was the strongest curse that he knew. Though the child eventually got his epithets straight and even graduated to new issues and enemies, he never completely lost the apocalyptic sensibility imbued in him by his father's rhetoric.[5]

In any case, he found no relief from the Federalist-Orthodox view of the world at Andover. By the time Theodore arrived in 1819, it had become a bastion of traditional New England religion. The Unitarian takeover at Harvard in 1805 had forced Calvinists to relocate. After complicated negotiations among various factions, they decided that Andover, a small town north of Boston, would become a new center of opposition "not only to Atheists and Infidels, but to Jews, Mahometans, Arians, Pelagians, Antinomians, Arminians, Socinians, Unitarians, and Universalists, and to all other heresies and errors, ancient or modern, which may be opposed to the gospel of CHRIST, or hazardous to the souls of men." Much of the time Andover theologians also argued among themselves, battling over the relative merits of Hopkinsian or Old Calvinist doctrine.[6]

Students not only faced the task of mastering the details of these debates, but doing so amidst a grueling day-to-day existence. Most had little money. Rooms on campus were small, drafty hovels. Dining halls and lecture rooms remained unheated even in the dead of New England winter. In this bleak setting, students were expected to work day and night. "I have quartos around me to frighten a very timid man out of his senses," wrote one lad in 1819. He also described a typical day:

> By rising at the six o'clock bell he will hardly find time to set his room in order, and attend to his private devotions, before the

bell at seven calls him to prayer in the chapel. From the chapel he must go immediately to the hall and by the time breakfast is ended, it is eight o'clock, when study hours commence and continue till twelve. Study hours again from half past one to three. Then recitation, prayer, and supper, makes it six in the afternoon. Study hours again from seven to nine leave just time enough for evening devotion before sleep.

Perhaps it is a bit too heroic, this epistle to a lady friend. Yet the note of despair with which it ends seems genuine enough: "For my own part I expect to become an outlaw; for I will not be so much confined. Few means are wanting to enable us to become great men; but the opportunity to kill oneself with study is rather too good."[7]

Theodore did not kill himself at Andover; he only became blind. Taking hold of his studies with an energy previously reserved for ploughing fields or leaping streams, he spent long evenings deciphering barely legible books in dim light. Then, nerves rattled by such concentration, he regularly ran the mile up and down Andover hill before retiring. This breathless routine weakened him and led to a blinding inflammation of the eyes, one that forced him to leave school after little more than a year.[8]

The curious mixture of zeal and self-destructiveness evident in Theodore's brief career at Andover was, of course, highly reminiscent of his boyhood exploits and mishaps in the fields. But in this case such energies seemed to have had more pointed purpose. No doubt part of him wished to excel at his father's old school in hopes of earning Ludovicus's love and respect. Yet working himself blind was also a way to escape the fate all agreed was his. While Weld could not yet admit to himself that the ministry was not for him, perhaps he unconsciously pursued blindness as the only way out of a trap.

The case for psychological roots to Weld's blindness becomes compelling if we look at the course of his convalescence. When he returned home in late 1820, the most optimistic predictions of attending physicians saw recovery taking seven years or more, and only if Weld followed a strict regimen of no exercise, no study, and limited exposure to light. Accordingly, he was confined to a dark room. Freed from Andover but now in a new prison, he managed to regain his sight within a few months. Blindness had served its purpose. Yet even after having been released from his dismal cure, Theodore must have been something of a caged tiger, still largely immobilized by doctor's orders and forced each day to face the real or imagined judgments of Ludovicus's failed expectations. He yearned to break loose from Hampton.[9]

An opportunity soon arose when one doctor, noting his quick recovery, suggested travel as a final cure. The family could not afford to pay his expenses, but Weld had an idea. At Andover one of his teachers had tutored him in mnemonics—the art and science of memory—in an attempt to counter his dreamy forgetfulness. Theodore was sure that he could support himself as he traveled by lecturing on the subject. Ludovicus, skeptical about the worth of mnemonics and even more doubtful of his son's ability to earn enough to support himself, tried to discourage the project. Finally father and son agreed upon a trial run; Theodore set out one morning for neighboring Colchester, delivered his lecture, and returned to Hampton with twenty dollars after expenses. His father could not argue with such success.[10]

For over two years, though still a teenager, Weld traveled the country lecturing on mnemonics. He crossed Connecticut and then penetrated upstate New York, where his itinerary included stops in Albany, Monticello, Niagara, Poughkeepsie, Rochester, and a number of small towns enroute. At each stop he followed the same procedure. He had placards advertising the talks posted a week in advance. For his first lecture, admission was free; Weld then invited the audience to subscribe for an additional four talks, including in the price of admission a symbolic chart that was indispensable in learning his particular system of memory. He enjoyed large and warm audiences and, after a brief trip home, set out for the states of the upper South.[11]

In many ways the lecture tour was a turning point in Weld's life. He tested oratorical skills that would propel him to fame and notoriety, and came to find deep satisfaction in the adulation of crowds. The mnemonics adventure also marked his first extended step toward living beyond the domain of family. Not that he did not miss those in Hampton. The Welds' "fugitive boy" wrote to his mother for news of brothers, sister, aunts, and uncles. Elizabeth responded with warm and generous chronicles. And Theodore chided his father for ignoring him. This did not prevent the son from asking for fatherly advice about his travels, but even when an answer came it must have seemed disappointing. For instance, hoping for an endorsement of the plan, he asked for the minister's thoughts on his projected southern journey. Ludovicus replied that a decision could only be made on pecuniary grounds, and that he had "no data on which to found an opinion." All that he could offer Theodore was Polonial wisdom: "O my dear son, be prudent, be wise, meek, modest, humble." He also hoped that his son's mind might be "more and more impressed with the importance of eternal things." For Ludovicus, that probably meant returning to Andover.[12]

Most important, however, was the fact that mnemonics lecturing thrust Theodore outside the narrow confines of Hampton and the cultural world of New England. It was true that much of the time he boarded with relatives and that a number of speaking engagements were arranged through the Weld family's personal and professional contacts, that, in short, his forays in the countryside followed a network of connections that were an extension of Hampton. Nonetheless Weld undertook his adventure in the spirit of escape and may well have shared the feelings of another New Englander, Thomas Wentworth Higginson, about his own youthful flight from home. "[I]t must have been that there was left over from the American Revolution something of the popular feeling then inspired," wrote Higginson, "for without aid or guidance I was democratic in impulse; longed to know something of all sorts and conditions of men and . . . to place myself in sympathy with all."[13]

Judging from his later adoption of the yeoman persona, Weld's exposure to "all sorts and conditions of men" on the mnemonics tour was of incalculable importance to the later turnings of his life. He saw a society built not on a dismal defense of the past, but rather on the energy of optimism. He saw a people not isolated by outmoded notions of deference and elitism, but instead infused with the spirit of democracy. At least these were the romantic constructions Weld would soon place on the world of common Americans. He was still some distance from taking the equally romantic step of clothing himself in symbolic homespun and becoming one of them. But he had learned enough to begin to sense that the world of the future was not that of his father, and to begin to feel that in pursuing the Orthodox ministry as a career, he might find himself, in words Erik Erikson used to describe another, "fatally overcommitted to what he [was] not."[14]

III

Conversion

We had heard of the revival at Utica—hope our friends there will be sharers. We hope and pray too that our dear Theodore may not be left to witness, to wonder, and perish.

Elizabeth Weld to Theodore Dwight Weld,
February, 1826.

Theodore returned home in 1824 more confident of his personal powers but also in something of a spiritual quandary. As a mnemonics lecturer he had demonstrated an energy and personal magnetism that marked him for success in 1820s America. His venturesomeness reflected the very spirit of the young nation. Yet as a child of Ludovicus Weld, he could not forget the timeless mission of the Puritan Saint. To Weld the Christian, the mnemonics tour had merely staved off contemplation of the graver, intertwined issues of salvation and calling. As a troubled cousin wrote to him some years later, a life without faith and a fit occupation became "but a miserable round of expedients to banish reflection, to get rid of that time which is a burden, and to lose in the labyrinths of business or drown in the cup of pleasure the *remembrance* of a hell." One could, he warned, "invoke the oblivion of a temporary sleep"; but in the end "there must come a time of *fearful awakening*." These might have been Theodore's words and worries in 1824.[1]

In spite of its worldly rewards, then, public speaking per se was hardly the right calling for a young man with such a special and pious sense of self. It was this fact that kept Weld's eyes on the ministry. Still, he felt unsure of his fitness for the job. Ludovicus's cries of heresy, the breakdown at Andover, and a general malaise gnawed at him. How could he not suspect that these were signs from God? Besides, the very tenor of ministerial education and life as he had seen it seemed at war with his basic temperament. The speaking tour had given him a taste of what he really loved—the freedom of the road and the adulation of crowds. A ministry might afford the opportunity to deliver sermons, but it would also confine him to one town and wed him to the petty details of church administration.

Nonetheless coming home would most probably have meant renewed efforts at Andover or a fresh start at Yale had Ludovicus and Elizabeth not made the fateful decision to move west to upstate New York. Life for the senior Welds in Hampton had begun to become undone. Now in his fifties, Ludovicus complained of "feeble" health. At times of epidemic and other moments of extraordinary responsibility, he found himself weakened to a "state of debility." Nor did the congregation offer him support; they clearly wished for the services of a younger, more vital man.[2]

Meanwhile, the Weld sons were coming of age and leaving the Hampton orbit. Lewis, who had planned to become a minister, instead chose a career in the education of the deaf. In 1822 he accepted a principalship in Philadelphia. Finishing Yale that same year, Charles went to Andover to study theology. All the while, Theodore was lecturing on mnemonics. Humiliated by ill health and a neglectful congregation, separated from much of the family, Ludovicus resigned his pulpit in 1824.[3]

In New York the Welds would at least be close to members of Elizabeth's family, who had migrated years earlier. Ludovicus procured a ministry-at-large from the Presbyterian Church and purchased a small farm in Fabius township, some sixteen miles southeast of Syracuse and forty miles southwest of Utica.[4]

His father's retirement opened a new world for Theodore. By following the family, he found himself in one of the most rapidly developing regions of the country. As late as the 1790s, western New York had been a wilderness dotted by frontier outposts. Soon, however, substantial numbers of New Englanders abandoned towns in Massachusetts, Connecticut, and Vermont to make new lives across the border. Farmers, merchants, investors, lawyers, mechanics, and adventurers all plunged into the business of building livelihoods and communities. By the time the Welds arrived in 1825, New York's progress had come to be epitomized by the new and magnificent Erie Canal. More important for Theodore, the very dynamism and youth of the region had encouraged religious experimentation and enthusiasm. Some even called it the "burned-over district," so intense were the holy fires of revival that periodically swept from town to town. Here he would find a faith as expansive as his energies and a calling befitting his sense of mission.

Once having helped his parents move to their Fabius farm, Theodore spent most of his time in Utica and especially in the circle of Erastus Clark. Clark, Elizabeth Weld's older brother, became something of a second father to the young man for reasons not hard to understand. Compared to the now feeble Ludovicus, Erastus Clark was the embodiment of energy and daring. In 1791, at the age of twenty-eight, he had left a promising legal career in Connecticut to seek a new life on the frontier. He settled in Old Fort Schuyler, gained fame as a lawyer and politician, and won additional notice as the man who picked the city's new name of Utica. Clark held various civic posts, was named a founding trustee of Hamilton College, and served two terms in the state legislature. He also became an active member of the First Presbyterian Church, while his first wife, Sophia Porter Clark, founded the local Female Missionary Society.[5]

Theodore must have found attractive his bold personality as well as his accomplishments. Clark was both Puritan and Yankee. "No man was less indulgent to his own appetites," wrote one friend, "or more self-denying in his pleasures and personal gratifications." In his judgment of others, he flaunted a frankness that often appeared "ill-timed and excessive." Or as his eulogist put it, "what others *thought* he *spoke*." Clark did display a sense of humor, though its peculiar bent can only be described as tribal. For instance, if one asked him how to make a Dutchman out of a Yankee, he would reply: "Break his jaw and knock his brains out." How to make a Yankee out of a Dutchman? "Can't do it, sir; ain't stock enough!" Clark's energy, pugnacity, and wit made him a legend in the universe of Utica and a colorful model for his nephew.[6]

It was probably through the Clarks that Weld met William Kirkland, a tutor at Hamilton College and descendant of the school's founder. The two became fast friends. Kirkland even allowed Weld to live in his suite at the college, where he could take advantage of class offerings without actually being enrolled. Despite this marginal status, he became something of a leader among the students. However, Theodore was marking time at Hamilton, consciously thinking his future lay in study for the ministry, yet in no hurry to get on with it.[7]

Weld's friendship with Kirkland was soon overshadowed by a more deeply spiritual attachment. For some time his Aunt Sophia had been telling him stories about a family friend named Charles Stuart, who was principal of a local academy. She warned him that in "looks, dress, manners, whole air and bearing," Stuart was a bit peculiar. "Strangers stare at him and some think him a lunatic," she admitted. However, she insisted that he was in fact "a perfect being," the most saintly person she had ever met.[8]

One day, at Sophia's suggestion, Stuart visited Weld's quarters. Theodore answered the door and was confronted by the outstretched arms of a sweet-faced man sporting a scotch-plaid frock and elbow-length cape. They shook with both hands and sat down to talk for the rest of the day and night. Many years later, after their frendship had come to an awkward end, Theodore told an idealized version of their first meeting. "Out the man came," he remembered. "His soul of love, tenderness, purity, fidelity, moral courage, sublime elevation, his sense of right and justice, and his deep reverent love for God and love of man."

"He alone," Weld remarked, "filled out my ideal of a perfect character."⁹

It was not only Stuart's perfect character that intrigued Weld, but also the saga of his life. This boy from a small town in Connecticut, one who thirsted for adventure, must have gaped as his new friend told of his life spread over three continents. He had been born in Jamaica, West Indies, in 1783, the son of a British officer. His parents were devout Presbyterians; in particular, Charles's mother implanted high notions of piety in the young lad's mind. Following his father's cues first, he enlisted in the army of the British East India Company. However, the harsh realities of colonial army life soon conflicted with his humane, religious sensibility. Once, after the Vellore Mutiny of 1806, Stuart refused to lead a night attack on unarmed Indians; he claimed such a raid was butchery. Those who presided at his court-martial were convinced that he had suffered from "a touch of the sun," and he was sent home rather than to the stockade.¹⁰

Charles returned to India after a decent interval, and served nine more years before another incident finally forced him out of the service. The new colonel of his regiment had decreed that all staff dinners were to be held on Sunday. Stuart, a devout observer of the Sabbath, flatly refused to attend and rebuked the officer to his face for breaking God's commandment. It was the first volley of a private war that ended in Stuart's forced resignation. From India he migrated to Canada and then to Utica, New York, where he soon made a reputation as the most humble of Christians.¹¹

Stories about him abounded. The Vernons, who were relatives of Weld and who rented a room to Stuart, told of the time Stuart rushed into the house from below zero winds and without his overcoat. It turned out that he had come across a poor man on the road who had no wrap, had quickly bestowed his own upon the man, and had scurried home. Weld loved to tell another Stuart story: "I remember that once at my father's he took up a missionary box and read its motto, 'He that giveth let him do it with simplicity' and said 'Beautiful motto!' then put down the box and put *nothing* in it! 'Just like him' I tho't he will not be *seen giving*, but the box was shortly after amply replenished and we all knew, where it must have come from."[12]

Such stories would indicate that young Theodore was attracted to Stuart primarily as an exemplar of piety, and that their relationship was characterized only by awe and distance. Nothing could be further from the truth. In fact, in all but the sexual sense, Theodore and Charles became the most intimate of lovers. "His hold upon my heart went to the foundations of my nature," Weld would reveal over a decade later. "Many a time I have wept on his neck from *very love to him*. . . ." "[L]et *Sun-rise* be our time of heart meeting," Stuart once proposed, so that though separated physically, their souls might take flight in "the spontaneous Swell mutually, of seeking to bear each other and those we love to the footstool of the Glorious Majesty!" He dreamed of a "friendship that shall never die—nay, I wrong it— that shall grow with brightening life for ever. . . ."[13]

The age allowed men to prize such relationships without guilt, perhaps because the taboos against homosexuality, at least for the pious Christian, were so clearly drawn. Even frankly physical attractions could be rejoiced in freely. For instance, Henry Ward Beecher openly reminisced about his love for Constantine Newell—"He was the most beautiful thing I had ever seen"—and even named a child in his honor. Weld's and Stuart's passions were less physical, more a meeting of Christian souls. Besides, the difference in their ages encouraged Stuart to take on the role of aid and protector as well as spiritual lover. "If in want of a *fathers* or a *brothers*, or a *friends* assistance," he once wrote, "won't your heart *always* tell you in full *confidence of love* that as God may preserve and endow me, you have a *father* and *a brother* and *friend* in C. Stuart."[14]

In fact, it may well have been Stuart's willingness to grant Weld such unconditional fatherly love that opened the young man's heart to passion. He never thought to expect such from the judgmental Ludovicus. And it was Stuart's further gift to offer himself to Theodore full well knowing the darkness that lay just below the surface of his friend's cocksure demeanor. Indeed, Charles had named the sickness, had described Weld's "deep wild gloom" and "moveless severity" at their first meeting, and had chosen to love him despite all. In Charles, Theodore had found a father of mercy in a world of judges.[15]

Still, in Charles's love Theodore could only find a respite from his gloom, a secret weeping spot to relieve the burden of his pride. He paraded before the world as a natural orator and leader of men. Like his uncle, Erastus Clark, he was stern with himself and unreserved in his judgment of others. And, in place of a faith of his own, he clung to the trappings of Orthodoxy. He mouthed the proper pieties, was the son of a minister, and someday would be a minister himself (all agreed). However, as of 1825, Theodore had not yet experienced the wonder of conversion, that traditional portal to religious maturity and salvation. Nor was he sure that he ever would. "Spiritual pride is the most secret of all sins," Jonathan Edwards had written. "The heart is so deceitful and unsearchable in nothing in the world, as it is in this matter. . . ." Edwards had merely echoed a central premise of Puritan self-scrutiny, one whose lesson was not lost on young Weld.[16]

In the late fall of 1825, Erastus Clark, on his death bed, counselled his nephew: "Theodore it is a great thing to die, think of it." His uncle's passing must have reminded him that death lay in wait with every stage ride, in every epidemic, literally at every waking and sleeping. Would he be ready? Like Bunyan's Christian he asked, "What shall I do to be saved?" As yet he had found no answer.[17]

Though conflict with his minister-father and the pressures of family tradition lent special intensity to Theodore's religious quandary, he was by no means alone in his yearnings. Many among the New England families who had settled in New York's "burned-over district," particularly those of Presbyterian and Congregationalist background, felt acutely uneasy in their new surroundings. They, like Weld, confronted a dynamic society in which Orthodoxy seemed more and more irrelevant. They as a community, inspired and burdened by a sense of having been chosen to hasten the Second Coming of Christ, found themselves hard put to implement a mission whose terms had been formulated in colonial New England, but whose necessary field of battle was post-Revolutionary New York State. The burden of anxiety fell most harshly on the young; after all, their parents had been revolutionaries and pioneers. How could they make a place for themselves of equal greatness while saddled with a generally pessimistic, undemocratic faith in a land of egalitarian optimism? However, for both young and old the mission seemed to have been stymied; the world had spun out of control.[18]

In searching for explanations, some Orthodox minds turned to nostalgia. In the New England towns of their memories, they argued, order, restraint, piety, and deference had ruled men's lives. They had been happy under "the dominion of the Celestial King," argued the Reverend William Weeks of Utica in 1825, whose wisdom brought "the greatest equity and mildness, and imposed no restraints upon the inhabitants, but such as were necessary for their own and the general good."[19] The very geography of this memory, as in Timothy Dwight's "Greenfield Hill," exuded moral symmetry:

> The place, with east and western sides,
> A wide and verdant street divides:
> And here the houses fac'd the day,
> And there the lawns in beauty lay.
> There, turret-crown'd, and central stood
> A neat, and solemn house of God.
> Across the way, beneath the shade,
> Two elms with sober silence spread.
> The Preacher liv'd.[20]

Such mythic visions were hardly the whole truth of town life, even in the seventeenth century. But whatever truth such images suggested contrasted sharply with the realities of early nineteenth-century America as seen through Orthodox eyes. The American Revolution, once viewed as a great step in the advancement of the millennial day, now appeared also as the breeder of a licentious and anti-Christian brand of freedom. William Weeks, a "burned-over district" minister, attempted to allegorize what had happened, and in doing so shed light on a deep-seated ambivalence in the Orthodox-Federalist interpretation of the Revolution. His *Pilgrim's Progress in the Nineteenth Century*, which appeared originally in the *Utica Christian Repository* of 1825, told how the "black tyrant," implacable foe of the "Celestial King," had managed to convince the people "that the wholesome restraints they were under, were intolerable, and too grievous to be submitted to." They revolted, but "instead of being highly exalted, and becoming as gods, which he promised them," Weeks continued, "they have debased themselves to the lowest depth of degradation, and have become the vilest of creatures. And instead of enjoying greater liberty, they are now the veriest slaves in the universe."[21]

It was not that Weeks and those like him wished to turn back the clock to colonial times, to reject the Revolution. Rather, he and others whose moral universe depended on order and hierarchy were profoundly shaken by the questioning of every order that the Revolution provoked, and the sometimes reckless energy it unleashed. They who had championed the revolt against England, who had prospered in its aftermath, now wondered whether simple liberty and material progress had not begun to lead American society toward a spiritual City of Destruction, into a "Vortex of Dissipation."[22]

Such a vision of America in the 1820s called into question the millennial promise of the Revolution and convinced some that man could do little by positive effort to hasten the Second Coming. Dreams of converting the world paled before the sense that only God's timely intercession would bring on the prophesied end of days. "[T]he great mass of mankind," one writer speculated, ". . . will have reached a high pitch of wickedness, and will perhaps have nearly swallowed up the true church of Christ, and have begun their song of triumph at its anticipated speedy extinction . . . when the Lord will suddenly appear for the deliverance of his people and the dismay and overthrow of his enemies."[23]

Those, however, who clung to the hope that men's energies could make a difference, that the conversion of all humanity and the unification of Christianity would bring man to the brink of the Millennium, refused to settle for such a gloomy version of history's end. They saw irreligion and corruption in society not as the sign of imminent apocalypse, but rather as a godly judgment on the elect themselves. They, the visible Saints, who should have led society along paths of righteousness, had themselves displayed "a covetous spirit"; had neglected the Sabbath; had failed to educate their children properly; had failed to exercise discipline "on the alleged ground that it [was] repugnant to brotherly love and charity"; and had excused, justified, and even imitated "the fashionable indulgences of the present day. . . ." The problem was not so much that society was corrupt, but that the elect themselves had become caught in the worldly mire. "In looking over a promiscuous assembly," charged one critic from within, "a stranger would be at a loss to distinguish Christians. . . ."[24] The Saints were in danger of losing their purpose, their mission, their identity.

Such self-rebuke had been preached periodically among the Puritans and their descendants ever since the sons of the founders looked around and felt themselves lost in the shadow of their fathers. The Mathers, Jonathan Edwards, Timothy Dwight— all had preached some form of the so-called jeremiad, restating the choice of communal desolation or regeneration in each successive age of crisis. It was perhaps inevitable that a people who had created for themselves such a special place in cosmic history would continually bemoan their fate in a land that from the beginning had placed a special value on change and expansion, and whose religious and social pluralisms had steadily built a resistance to clerical domination. The jeremiad, then, served a dual purpose. It did squarely confront the community of Saints with their failures. However, in reminding them of their broken covenant with God, it also reminded them that they were still special. Now, in the nineteenth century, stripped of legally established authority and overwhelmed by the secular energies of the day, the Saints sought a new version of the covenant, a new definition of their special place in the world.[25]

Between the seeking and the finding, however, lay much misery, the misery of Theodore Weld's "deep wild gloom" writ large. No longer quite sure of their place in the universe, they found it harder to experience that wonder of conversion at the core of Protestantism. As neo-Edwardsian theologians continued to spin out complicated webs of doctrine intended to unite man and God, many found themselves tripped and caught in the fine strands of word and logic, and humiliated by their paralysis. The church, which should have brought them to the warmth of communion, too often left too many souls cold and desolate.[26]

The situation seemed all the more galling as they watched members of their own churches turn to Unitarian and Universalist heresies, or witnessed the phenomenal rise of Baptist and Methodist churches across the nation. Proud Presbyterians and Congregationalists could be shocked by the doctrinal errors of liberal Christianity and repulsed by what they considered to be the fanatic, almost diabolical revival practices of the democratic sects. After all, they wished to retain the integrity of Puritanism's fusion of intellect and heart, which justified their position at the top of a hierarchy of grace and granted them the task of showing the world the true path to God. But who could not envy others' successes, and who could not feel duty-bound to enter the fray?

Accordingly, Presbyterian and Congregationalist churches put aside doctrinal differences and joined forces in the Plan of Union of 1801, a move that enabled them to marshal Bible, tract, and missionary societies from both traditions to win souls in the West and across the world. In Connecticut, the Reverend Lyman Beecher began to promote revivals after Orthodoxy's disestablishment in 1818; in doing so, he promulgated, along with Nathaniel Taylor of Yale, a "New Haven Theology," which offered hope for salvation to all men if they would only return to the church. As for the "burned-over district," its Presbyterian community witnessed major revivals in 1800, 1815, 1819, and 1821.[27]

Such activity harnessed and directed the energies of a great number of people, renewing in them a sense of mission and Christian identity. But to some young and serious souls like Theodore, the flurry produced confusion. They could feel, if not entirely verbalize and understand, grave contradictions between what they saw and what they had been taught. The ideal of insular, small town universes hardly squared with the expansive reality of western life. Existing social hierarchies implied a doctrine of limited election, yet the revivals exhorted all men to seek saving grace. Both revival and missionary campaigns suggested a largely mobile, oratorical role for the ministry, yet seminaries continued to bury would-be preachers in a debilitating avalanche of classical study and complicated theology. Most of all, while the energies of men were transforming the world, Calvinist doctrine continued to cast grave doubt on the individual's native moral sense. And so preachers and missionaries did their best, but all the while with the knowledge that there was a limit to human effectiveness. Salvation remained the free gift of God offered only to some men, revivals of religion the showering of Holy Grace at God's whim. The Lord was largely unknowable, and men could only pray that their best efforts would be rewarded. No matter their fondest hopes, they knew that in the final analysis they had to sit uneasily and wait for the end, bound in what Charles Grandison Finney called Orthodoxy's theological "strait-jacket."[28]

To witness Charles Finney's preaching was to confront more than a man. So perfectly did he wed idea to word, word to motion, and silence to sound that at times he could seem the very incarnation of the struggle for salvation. Six feet two inches tall, with wispy blond hair, he appeared to focus his power in what Weld called "those great staring eyes." There "never was a man," Weld insisted, "whose soul looked out through his face as [Fin-

Charles Grandison Finney (*Ohio Historical Society*)

ney's] did." Henry B. Stanton, an antislavery comrade of Weld, once described a typical Finney performance:

> While depicting the glories or the terrors of the world to come, he trod the pulpit like a giant. His action was dramatic. He painted in vivid colors. . . . His gestures were appropriate, forcible, and graceful. As he would stand with his face towards the side gallery, and then involuntarily wheel around, the audience in that part of the house towards which he threw his arm would dodge as if he were hurling something at them. In describing the sliding of a sinner to perdition, he would lift his long finger towards the ceiling and slowly bring it down till it pointed to the area in front of the pulpit, when half his hearers in the rear of the house would rise unconsciously to their feet to see him descend into the pit below.[29]

It was perhaps fitting that this man who would bring faith to thousands in the "burned-over district" had remained virtually untouched by religious education until he approached age thirty. Born in Warren, Connecticut, in 1792, Finney soon moved with his family to the wilderness of Oneida County, New York. His parents were not religious and the few itinerant preachers who passed through frontier New York made little impression on the boy. Meanwhile, young Finney excelled in more secular realms, first teaching school and then becoming a lawyer. In his late twenties he moved to Adams, New York, where he practiced with a local lawyer.[30]

Despite his worldly success and lack of religious training, inner discontent made him crave the satisfactions of faith. Fortunately, the town of Adams had a Presbyterian church and an educated minister, the Reverend George W. Gale. Finney hoped finally to be instructed properly in Christianity. However, Gale's discourses disappointed him. The minister "seemed to take it for granted," recalled Finney, "that his hearers were theologians. . . ." Meanwhile, he had begun to read the Bible. It fascinated him but also troubled him as he became painfully aware that he was "by no means in a state of mind to get to heaven. . . ."[31]

Tantalized by the Bible yet disappointed by Gale and his

church, Finney became bitter and began to cynically attack the prayer meetings of the Adams congregation. "You have prayed enough since I have attended these meetings to have prayed the devil out of Adams, . . ." he charged. "But here you are praying on, and complaining still." Nonetheless, he persisted in studying the Bible for another two years. Slowly pressure built within until finally Finney felt he was at a crossroads. Soon after, in the fall of 1821, as the lawyer was making his way to the office, an inner voice asked, "Will you accept [salvation] today?" "Yes," he replied, "I will accept it today, or I will die in the attempt."[32]

So began one of the most famous accounts of a conversion in the annals of American religion. Written down long after the event, pruned and shaped to meet the conscious and unconscious needs of the evangelist, Finney's version of his own religious experience nonetheless provides us with a rough sense of the transcendence involved in his communion with God. It also gives us some insight into the revolutionary possibilities inherent in this moment, for it became the basis of Finney's challenge to Orthodoxy in its own church.[33]

Instead of continuing to work, he headed for the woods north of the village. A fall chill blew through the trees, scattering red and yellow leaves to the ground. He tried to pray, but his heart remained cold. The least stirring of leaves distracted him; imaginary prying eyes haunted him. Nervousness turned to despair; "it was too late;" his knees became too weak to rest upon. Sensing something approaching, he turned around to see a "vision" of his prideful heart. "What! Such a degraded sinner as I am, on my knees confessing my sins to the great and holy God," he cried; "and ashamed to have an human being, and a sinner like myself, find me on my knees endeavoring to make my peace with my offended God." He broke down.[34]

Just then in a flood of light the Spirit brought him a passage from Scripture: "Then shall ye go and pray unto me, and I will hearken unto you. Then shall ye seek me and find me, when ye shall search for me with all your heart." Finney pledged, "Lord, I take thee at thy word." The Spirit continued speaking; as the words flowed he "fastened upon them with the grasp of a drowning man." Finally he trekked home, having promised God that if converted, he would preach the Gospel.[35]

At his office, unable to work, devoid of appetite, he began to sing a sacred song. Tears flowed instead of words—"It seemed as if my heart was all liquid. . . ." His colleague then returned from lunch and they spent the afternoon doing menial work. At dark his partner left and, as the door closed, Finney's feelings "seemed to rise and flow out." His heart was "all liquid" again. Wishing to pour his soul out to God, he rushed into the darkness of a back room. There Jesus appeared before him in spectral light, forcing him to his knees without a word. He "wept like a child" and confessed.[36]

After a timeless moment at the feet of Christ, Finney returned to the front office. A sudden bolt from the Holy Spirit shook him. "I could feel the impression," he remembered, "like a wave of electricity, going through and through me. Indeed it seemed to come in waves and waves of liquid love; for I could not express it in any other way. It seemed like the very breath of God. I can recollect distinctly that it seemed to fan me, like immense wings. . . . I wept aloud with joy and love. . . . These waves came over me, and over me, and over me, one after the other, until I recollect I cried out, 'I shall die if these waves continue to pass over me.' "[37]

As he told it, the next morning a client appeared in his office to remind him that he was to try his case at ten o'clock. "I have a retainer from the Lord Jesus Christ to plead his case," Finney replied, "and I cannot plead yours." The lawyer had become an evangelist.[38]

Wishing to become an educated preacher of the Gospel, he returned to Gale for doctrinal guidance and clarification. However, by now the young lawyer had studied the Bible and spoken to God; things that had once confused him now seemed clear. He found himself at odds with the minister most of all on the issue of salvation and on that stickiest of all questions: Who were the Christians? Orthodox doctrine held that Christ, in dying on the cross, had absolved an elite elect of their earthly sins and automatically insured them of salvation. Those not of the elect had no chance for grace. It was all up to God, and God's ways were unknowable. Man, therefore, had no power to effect his own salvation. Various aspects of Puritan covenant theology tried to bridge gaps between the absolute unknowability of salvation and the natural human tendency to worry about such an issue. Signs of salvation might be found in holy behavior or religious experiences. But one could not know for sure, and as the standards for power, success, and virtue changed in post-Revolutionary America, the old signs became less and less meaningful.

Finney cut through this discouraging morass by applying common sense and democratic values to his own transforming experience. He could not accept that Christ died for only some men, or that his death insured salvation for any one man. The voice of the Spirit indicated to him that the crucifixion allowed all men to be saved; each individual might secure saving grace by repenting of his sins and giving himself to God.[39] This was not the Arminian "good works" road to salvation.[40] Finney's approach required complete self-abasement, a full negation of any supposed good in one's life before infusion of the Holy Spirit could take place. The doctrine was reminiscent of Cotton Mather's view of conversion, which developed in contradistinction to Arminian tendencies.[41] It also bore striking emotional resemblance to the main thrust of Jonathan Edwards's recreation of man's nothingness before the power of God.[42] However, whereas Mather and Edwards granted God most of the power in the conversion process, Finney stressed the importance of human means.

Finney's stubbornness on these points dismayed Gale, who stung the young convert by asking that he never reveal his having studied with the minister.[43] Finney, for his part, came to identify men such as Gale as "cold" professors of religion who, by their unwillingness to offer hope and proper means, discouraged men from repenting and thus actually did the Devil's work. As symbolized by Gale, Orthodoxy became to the evangelist not the last best hope of Christianity, but rather a misguided theology and a roadblock in the way of men's conversions. He did not automatically count as godly those already in the church, nor did he abandon those considered by Orthodoxy to be beyond hope. Like the first generation of Puritans and the New Lights of the Great Awakening, he saw his task as shaking the church to its foundations and repeopling it with the truly saved.

Toward that end Finney managed to procure a license to preach from the local presbytery. He convinced a number of other ministers that new means were needed to promote a revival of religion, and in 1825 and 1826 he swept across the "burned-over district" with unprecedented force. In its wake, the Finney revival left hundreds of souls reborn and not a few stupefied and outraged.

"[I]t is a fact not to be denied or concealed that sound learning, eminent talents and persuasive eloquence, have all been thrown into the shade before the blazing coruscations of the *wandering meteors* which have shot athwart our moral system. . . ."[44] This was a Unitarian's estimate of Finney and his helpers. An Orthodox layman in Troy, one who had watched his church fall under the sway of Finneyite Nathaniel Sydney Smith Beman, urged all who would listen to treat the evangelist with "but little more ceremony than an acknowledged outlaw."[45] Even Lyman Beecher, who was utilizing revivalism to strengthen the hand of Connecticut's Orthodoxy, feared that the New York revival would "roll back the wheels of time to semi-barbarism."[46] All had their reasons for attacking Finney. Unitarians used him as an easy target to counter Presbyterian charges of heresy. Conservative Orthodox critics deplored his doctrinal deviations. For his part, Beecher found Finney an embarrassment in the revival camp and wished to dissociate himself from the doings in Oneida County.[47]

There was, however, an uncanny harmony in these laments from men who rarely agreed on anything at all. The phrases "shot athwart our moral system," "an acknowledged outlaw," or "semi-barbarism" implied a challenge to something more than mere doctrine. By mocking the traditional modes of discovering and disseminating religious truth, Finney had posed a threat to general peace and order. "The importance of truth in religion," Beecher complained, "as that which brightens our moral atmosphere, and makes our day, is perhaps more frequently admitted than *the importance of order*. Truth and order are viewed as if so distinct, as to possess almost nothing in common. What is this, but to mistake them? They are near relations, and almost inseparable intimates!"[48] To Beecher and others the Finney revival was a frontal attack on social order.

Nor did such charges miss the mark. Finney *did* attack the orderly processes of religion as defined by Orthodoxy, at least as they manifested themselves in the hierarchies, rituals, language, and institutions of the church. He attacked them because he sensed that they, as much as any particular belief, discouraged many from seeking God. For instance, when sermonizing, Finney eschewed theological vocabulary in favor of words all could understand, using phrases and examples from everyday life. He dressed in a business suit rather than in clerical garb, thus undercutting traditional symbols of hierarchy within the church. He aimed his sermons toward one goal—to make the stakes of salvation burn in the minds of his listeners. Accordingly, a staid Presbyterian church found itself transformed from a meeting house for sober discourses to an excited arena for conversion. Conversion, which once had been open to a select few, now could be attained by all who would plumb the depths of their souls. Religious experiences, which had once been seen as private dialogues between God and man, now took place in public settings, men and women realizing and confessing their sinfulness before all who would listen. Not only did the scenes within church walls change, but the very definition of "church" expanded. Finney and his helpers pursued sinners in the streets, in stores, at factories; they sometimes even followed them home.[49]

Critics of the revival were particularly stung by the denunciatory spirit alive in revival preachers and their followers. They stood horrified as Finneyite ministers attacked so-called cold professors of religion by name; as young converts shouted, "You old, grey headed sinner, you deserved to be in hell long ago"; in short, as zealots assumed that they were entitled to judge established and venerated members of the community.[50] The situation was almost unavoidable. These previously unconverted souls, many of them youths, women, and others frustrated by the old ways of doing things, had finally found a justification for unleashing anger that had lain just below the now torn garb of custom and decorum. To the new Christians of the revival, intoxicated by a heady mixture of joyful communion and almost lusty vengefulness, those who stood in their way were literally doing the work of the Devil.

Weld raged when he first heard of Finney's tactics from students and professors at Hamilton. How could a legitimate minister, he remembered asking, preach in such a "terrific Jupiter Tonans sort of style?" What had happened to reason and tradition? "My father," he recalled telling his student friends, "was a real minister of the Gospel, grave and courteous, and an honor to the profession. This man is not a minister, and I will never acknowledge him as such."[51]

Weld later learned that the evangelist had "frightened" his cousin and that Aunt Sophia had fallen under his sway. Therefore, when his aunt asked him to visit one weekend in order to hear Finney preach, he approached the invitation with mixed emotions. He had no stomach for witnessing what he thought of as Finney's rantings; yet his aunt was Erastus Clark's widow and, in the spring of 1826, it was still less than six months since his death. He would go, but he assured his friends that he would stand fast before the evangelist's blasts. Anger gripped him all the way to Utica, and by the time Theodore arrived he decided not to hear Finney after all.[52]

Sophia had different plans; she knew her nephew well, understood his religious cravings, and hoped that he would be sparked to the work of saving souls. She convinced him to attend at least morning services, when the regular minister preached, and to decide later about hearing Finney's afternoon sermon. She then consulted with the minister and the evangelist and had them exchange preaching times. Finney, aware of Weld's views and also of his influence among Hamilton's students, welcomed the opportunity to "slay" this sinner.[53]

At church, Sophia carefully maneuvered Weld into the middle of the pew so as to make a quick exit impossible. The regular minister began the service, but soon stepped down. Finney rose, announced his text, "One Sinner destroyeth much good," and stared directly at Theodore. With inexorable logic he showed how one individual's sinning ways could destroy a multitude of souls. "And yes! you'll go to college," he cried, "and use all your influence against the Lord's work." Weld squirmed and tried to leave, but Sophia whispered, "*you'll break my heart* if you go!" He resigned himself to an hour of unremitting fire. "He just held me up on his toasting-fork before that audience," Weld recalled.[54]

The next day Theodore encountered Finney at a local store. The evangelist had come to preach salvation to the customers; instead, for almost an hour, he fell victim to Weld's abuse. A crowd gathered inside and outside the store to witness the tirade. Finally Finney interjected a chastening question. "Mr. Weld are you the son of a minister of Christ," he asked, "and is this the way for you to behave?" Stunned by embarrassment, Weld fired a final volley and fled. "He just t[oo]k my feeling and show[ed] it to me—t[oo]k it and show[ed] it to me," he remembered years later.[55]

He could remove himself from Finney's physical presence, but not from the memory of words that cut through layers of pretense. "I was so ashamed I could not live," he recalled. He decided to go to see Finney and to apologize. The evangelist came down the stairs, squinted in the dim light, but could not see that it was Weld till he reached the bottom of the stairs. "Ah," he exclaimed, "is it not enough? Have you followed a minister of the Lord Jesus to his own door to abuse him?" "Mr. Finney," Theodore murmured, "I have come for a very different purpose,

I—" and Finney threw his arms around Weld's neck, "dragged [him] into the parlor, and down on his knees, sobbing and praying and sobbing and praying."[56]

The ice had begun to break and melt, but so far Theodore had allowed himself only an apology for rudeness; outwardly he still despised Finney. That night his aunt asked him to lead the family in prayer. Weld took the opportunity to barrage them with a "most blasphemous strain of vituperation." Offended by his tantrum, the Clarks snuffed out the lights and went to bed. Theodore continued raging in his room. All night he paced the floor, then lay prostrate, then paced again. Eventually his anger turned inward, so guilty did he feel about his row with Finney. He realized that he was the sinner. Daybreak found him still pacing, when suddenly an invisible force crushed him to the floor and a voice called upon him to repent. He lay there until Sophia came to his room and found him on the floor "calling himself a thousand fools." The following evening he rose in meeting to confess his sins and vanity and to pledge himself to Finney's crusade.[57]

Elizabeth Weld had hoped that the Utica revival would touch her son, that he would not be left to "witness, to wonder, and perish." On April 25, 1826, a cousin brought her "the best news from Utica," that Theodore had been converted and that he and Charles Stuart would enter revival work. Ludovicus's reaction was not recorded, though whatever joy he may have felt was probably tempered by a dislike of Finney and the thought that revival work would keep his son from returning to school.[58]

As for Theodore, conversion meant more than the indescribable infusion of saving grace. He had finally found release for feelings of unworthiness and guilt about his pride that lay pent up within him for years. In public confession he was able to break through his isolation from others and say, in so many words, I am a sinner like you. In doing so as part of a popular religious movement, he was also attempting to say to those around him from whom he felt separated by the barriers of social position, that emotionally at least he was one of them. It is in the revival that we begin to see Theodore move toward his yeoman persona.

The conversion also marked a choice between the religious sensibility of his real father and that of Finney, in a sense his spiritual father. Theodore was well aware of this from the beginning and desperately tried to hide behind the decorum of Ludovicus Weld's tradition. It was Finney's genius to bring into both consciousness and action a Theodore hidden behind the proud Weld name, one trapped by its demands, yet longing for release. When Theodore finally embraced God through the evangelist, he could begin to reject familial expectations and to shape a place in the world more in keeping with his own talents and cravings.

If Weld's conversion was in one sense a rebellion against family, it was on a grander scale the reconciliation of his life to the heroic tradition of Thomas Welde, whose mission to establish New England spanned continents and aimed to shake societies and universes. In the Finney revival and its millennial promise to convert the world, in this mighty renewal of the Puritan's cosmic dream, Theodore had found a cause and a calling as glorious as those of his ancestors, certainly great enough to satisfy his own heroic sense of self.

In this spirit he thrust himself into revival work. As Finney's most talented and trusted lieutenant, he made the rounds of New York's towns and cities, assisting in the awakening of sinners and leading anxious hearts to the joys of conversion. He also led attacks on the revival's opponents, mostly of his father's generation, with what he would later describe, with some remorse, as "the unhallowed feeling of a political partizan." After all, like so many other converts, he had a score to settle with his father and his father's church.[59]

Revival work was exhausting, however, and in 1827 Theodore and his brother Charles shipped off to Labrador on a fishing vessel to restore their health. On the voyage he reimmersed himself in nature—facing ocean storms, passing rocky isles covered with birds' eggs, and watching flocks of wild ducks move like clouds across the sky. Years later he still remembered sitting on deck at midnight, reading the small print of books by the light of the aurora borealis. Those carpets of stars, shimmering in the black infinity of the universe, aptly mirrored the brilliant and dimensionless glow of rebirth that had so recently begun to burn in Theodore's heart.[60]

IV

Physiology
and Armageddon

Late in the winter of 1827, as the fishing vessel that had conveyed him to Labrador returned to Boston, Theodore may have taken time to consider how his life had been so recently transformed. The winter past he had been a talented, energetic, but deeply troubled soul; he had appeared before the world cloaked behind a cocksure manner and the easy security of family tradition. Yet that very tradition demanded that he find a proper calling in life, and here he had been stymied. His encounter with Finney had changed all that. Now, at the age of twenty-three, he was the most talented protegé and trusted aide of the evangelist and engaged in work worthy of his loftiest dreams—the conversion of the world.

It was probably in the service of this mission that Weld lingered in Boston for several weeks before returning to the "burned-over district." There, in the cradle of New England Puritanism, he conversed several times with the Reverend Lyman Beecher, who had only recently moved from his Connecticut pulpit to Boston's Hanover Street Church. We have no way of knowing exactly what transpired in the meetings between Finney's young lieutenant and one of the evangelist's most vocal critics. However, we do know that it was a crucial and awkward time for Beecher and Finney in their relation to each other. Beecher, though highly critical of Finney's "New Measures" and perhaps personally threatened by the westerner's meteoric rise, nonetheless recognized in his fellow revivalist a potential ally.[1]

For his part, Finney had begun to question the eccentricities of his more extreme followers. Under the tutelage of Samuel Aiken, in whose church Weld had been excoriated by the evangelist, he had read Jonathan Edwards's commentaries on the Great Awakening and had taken seriously Edwards's misgivings about uncontrolled religious enthusiasm. Besides, the Oneida revival had been in some sense the eruption of a long-festering sore. Now, after the poison of hidden resentment and frustration had been partially drained, a slow if fitful reconciliation among Christians could begin.[2]

In fact, Weld was meeting with Beecher in the months before a planned conference at New Lebanon, New York, one which had as its goal the resolution of differences between the two camps. It made sense that those who shared the goal of converting the world to Christ should not long remain enemies. Though the New Lebanon conference itself was a failure, a scene from Weld's stay in Boston reflected at least the dream of Christian harmony. Years later Weld remembered that he and Beecher had taken time out from their conversations to accompany the missionary Judd and his band of helpers to their ship in Boston harbor. Whatever the differences between eastern and western revivalists, they could join together in support of Christian endeavors in distant and exotic lands.[3]

At home in America, in addition to common goals, there were good practical reasons for reconciliation among basically like-minded Christians. Simply stated, their vision of America's future as part of a millennial mission represented just one of a number of competing ideas concerning the proper course of the new society. Indeed, the 1820s were preeminently exciting years precisely because the shape of America's future had not yet been set. The generation that came to maturity in this decade had been left the task of making good on the Revolutionary promise bequeathed to them by the founding fathers—to translate general principles of democracy and republican virtue into an ongoing political and social order.

Even as the founding fathers, however, sometimes differed sharply as to what the Revolution had meant, succeeding generations often disagreed on the question of what exactly America should become. They debated issues of democratic rule, expansionism, economic growth, and the use of governmental power. So too did Americans disagree about the proper role of religious institutions and power in a land imbued with Christianity but also committed to religious toleration and separation of church and state. On this last question Beecher and Finney stood together, for they both were religious activists who sought ways of creating what amounted to a Christian republic in America. Through revivals and the efforts of moral reform societies, they hoped to recruit public sentiment on the side of a godly social order without resort to an established church. Thus temperance societies would promote sobriety and sabbatarian societies would win public support for prohibition of mail delivery and other public services on Sundays. Men and women would voluntarily come to see the wisdom of God's order in both their private and public lives.[4]

Such campaigns, whether conducted with the sometimes uncontrolled zeal of the Oneida revival or with more orderly attempts to gain public confidence and power, met with suspicion and downright hostility from much of the population. Unitarians, freethinkers, and members of other denominations feared that moral reform societies and the more coercive aspects of revivalism came close to violating, in spirit at least, guarantees of religious toleration and separation of church and state. Some thought them to be harbingers of an attempt to reestablish Orthodoxy as an official church. In short, those who opposed the revival and its related social movements often did so as jealous guardians of hard-won religious and social freedom.[5]

It was around very different concepts of freedom, then, that the battle lines were drawn. The opposition understood the concept of freedom in the tradition of the Bill of Rights; that is, one was constitutionally protected against infringement of basic rights and against the intrusion of others' moral and religious convictions. Weld and others in the revival camp, of course, did not feel that their zealous advocacy of religion and reform infringed on other's rights. In fact, they saw it as a proper exercise of their own right of freedom of speech.

More important to men like Weld was the concept of Christian freedom—the freedom *to do* God's will. This positive freedom meant liberation from the slavery of doing wrong. Thus one might have the perfect constitutional right to drink to excess, yet by exercising that right find oneself enslaved to alcohol. One might be perfectly free to ignore the Bible and to lead a life uninformed by the quest for or the presence of saving grace. To the Christian, however, this would be no freedom at all, but rather slavery to Satanic darkness. Christian freedom meant ultimately the wonder of basking in the light and warmth of a changed heart, and the ability to act in the world according to the dictates of that feeling.

Nor was the freedom they sought only of personal significance. While some in America saw the rush of events around them as simple progress and growth, Christians were inclined to decipher prophetic signs of, in Lyman Beecher's words, the "*great commotions and distress of nations* [that] will exist, antecedent to the spiritual, universal reign of Christ on earth."[6] Weld himself called it the "age of action," a time in which God and the Devil faced each other with ever-heightening will and ingenuity.[7] Many believed America to be the future site of Armageddon, that ultimate battle between the forces of God and his fallen angel. Jonathan Edwards had predicted that the Millennium might begin in the New World; now, in the 1820s, ministers revived his prediction to bolster their own expectations.[8] Thus the proper ordering of individual lives and society, momentous in its own right, took on cosmic meaning when linked to the Second Coming of Christ.

Finneyite commitment to the millennial view of American

destiny put young activists like Weld in an ambiguous position as regarded Orthodoxy. They stood with Orthodox ministers when faced with Unitarian and freethinking opposition to moral reform. At the same time, though some of the initial venom was gone, the western revivalists continued an internal campaign to modernize the church. "As freemen and as Christians," complained revival leader N. S. S. Beman, "we have breathed an air too liberal and elastic, to feel ourselves at home, and in our own element, when hemmed in by such confined narrow walls" as Orthodoxy maintained. "I am glad, for one," he continued, "that God, in his march of mercy through the world, is not confined to the modes and forms which men, in their arrogance, would prescribe for his operations." The challenge lay in creating new "modes and forms" of religious experience and organization, ones that would facilitate tasks as widely disparate and yet interconnected as encouraging conversions, mediating other forms of personal religious experience, promoting Christian behavior in society at large, and bringing on the millennial day.[9]

At first glance, the new "modes and forms" the Finneyites celebrated as their own might not seem all that new. Beman made much of the effectiveness of voluntary reform societies, such as those to promote temperance, yet they had existed for years with the blessing of the church. Some of Finney's vaunted "new measures" had been used informally and without much protest by other ministers in the newly settled regions of the West. Even the Plan of Union of 1801, that agreement between Congregationalists and Presbyterians to pool resources ecumenically in order to wage common battle against infidelity and ignorance, had the effect of blurring some sectarian lines long before Finneyites proclaimed their confinement by "narrow walls."

Yet there was something new about the Finney revival and the movement it inspired, something that had less to do with individual features than with a general attitude. In the past, breaks from tradition had been seen as pragmatic endeavors meant to adapt the old order to new conditions without challenging the legitimacy of that old order. Finney and his band, however, had declared war on the legitimacy of Orthodoxy itself. After the first explosions of 1825 and 1826, they dedicated themselves to a more orderly dismantling from within, fighting for power in local churches and presbyteries, as well as pushing for greater lay involvement in church councils.[10]

Weld's participation in the Finney crusade, whether ostensibly battling Orthodoxy or the more patently heretical members of society, illustrated just how varied and complex the implications of that movement might be. For example, in the five or six years after his conversion Theodore became known as one of the most powerful temperance lecturers in upstate New York. At the height of his fame in the Rochester revival of 1830, he swayed people by arguing that alcohol was responsible for "kill[ing] more bodies and damn[ing] more souls" than any other cause. Weld calculated that three-fourths of all paupers, four-fifths of all criminals, and half the insane incarcerated in various institutions owed their fate to drink. He gave the example of Johnson, an "infidel" printer from New York City. Johnson ordinarily did not drink, Weld claimed, but he did know of alcohol's effects. When he had decided to kill his wife but found that he could not carry through his plan sober, he took three glasses of spirit and promptly did away with her.[11]

Weld's temperance appeal would, on the surface, seem to be merely one element in the Finneyite and Orthodox quest to rid society of unchristian behavior. Yet it is also true that much of the momentum for the temperance campaigns originally came from those, including Lyman Beecher, who wished to stop what they thought to be embarrassing and injurious drunkenness among the clergy itself. Indeed, the Hampton Church's wish for a strong temperance minister may have been one of the reasons for Ludovicus Weld's being relieved of his duties. In short, the temperance campaign, while most obviously an attempt to put society at large in order, may also have functioned among Finneyites as one more strike against what they considered to be an older and more corrupt Orthodox generation.[12]

On a more philosophical level, the temperance argument as

set forth by Beecher, Weld, and others exemplified a new emphasis on the body and self-control as keys to social order. As opposed to Orthodoxy's faith in churchly and other established governing structures, temperance advocates like Weld argued implicitly and explicitly that order would have to come from the individual. Thus, though Weld maintained that most men were driven to drink by the "universal insecurity of life and property which quivered the land over," he refrained from calling for regulation of society. Instead, he argued, men must develop the will to stop drinking through faith and through an understanding of the physiological and social effects of alcohol.[13]

"My wretched cold heart hardly rejoices at all," responded Weld to Finney's reports of revival successes in the spring of 1828. "Oh for that joy *unspeakable,* that full-of-glory-joy, that would stir the sluggish spirit and trouble the dead water of my stagnant soul." Two years after conversion, fatigued by overwork and "billious fever," almost all he could see was failure. Pride stood in the way of his own spiritual advance. As for others, conditions were worse still. "The state of feeling in Oneida County is dreadfully low," he complained. "Christians have talked themselves to death." Even recent converts had rushed back to worldly pleasures: "Many of the most engaged have frequently danced till a late hour at parties this winter." Nor did Finney himself escape unscathed. Weld accused him of neglecting the "culture of personal holiness," and of running revivals as "a sort of trade, to be worked at so many hours every day and then laid aside." "The machinery all moves on, every wheel and spring and chord in its place; but is'nt [sic] the *main spring,*" he asked, "waxing weaker?"[14]

This despairing side of what normally appeared to be a self-confident, even boisterous revival movement, underlined an important but often obscured aspect of the Finneyite insurgency. That is, in attacking Orthodoxy and therefore undermining traditional understandings of human capacity in relation to God, revivalists had loosed themselves from the normal comforts due them under the old system. Arguably they felt communion with God more intensely without the checks of Orthodoxy; so too, however, did they feel ever more deeply the deathliness of a cold heart. For a movement that paraded man's ability to seek his own salvation before a more cautious tradition, failure of heart and mind was a damning indictment indeed.

Facing the everyday peaks and valleys of emotional and spiritual life armed only with a tradition weakened by disestablishment and demystification, many in the nominally Orthodox community sought new explanations of human behavior and new bases for order. In this quest, they expanded upon the implicit and explicit messages of the temperance argument and began to see the human body as a source of individual moral and physical order that might help collectively reshape society. Aside from temperance and broader in its application, the first chief expression of this fusion between Enlightenment physiology and Christian millennialism was the manual labor movement. Weld himself became its principal advocate in the late 1820s and early 1830s. Simply stated, manual laborites campaigned for the addition of physical labor programs to the traditional curricula of theological seminaries. Unexceptional on its face, this program of intellectual and physical balance in school led one enthusiast to dub it "a system of education that is to introduce the millennium"—and within ten to twenty years at that.[15]

It was, in fact, amidst the 1820s' sense of heightened struggle that some in the church turned to manual labor. No problem seemed more pressing than the staffing of a church militant with ministers ready and able to battle the Devil's forces. Yet at the very moment in cosmic history when requirements for an energetic clergy were higher than ever, seminaries were turning out weaklings hardly capable of hobbling away after graduation. Or so it seemed. The American Education Society, for instance, reported that many of its scholarship students had died of overstudying, and that others had been reduced to a feeble state by the seminary routine. The age of energy was devouring those who would be its redeemers.[16]

In this situation leaders at various schools became interested in European experiments that merged manual labor with normal courses of study. Fellenberg's "Hofwyl" school, in particular, seemed to display an ideal of balance wanting in the United States. By 1825, Maine Wesleyan Seminary had established an experimental program. Andover began an extensive workshop adjunct in 1826. These institutions hoped that the ravages documented by the American Education Society would soon cease as scholars integrated useful exercise with traditional study.[17]

As Weld's experience at Andover less than a decade earlier had shown, the fears of the Education Society had some basis in reality. At the time, Theodore had had no clear explanation of his own disorder except those of his doctors. Now, in manual labor's adaptation of physiology, he had found a way to link his own and others' disorders to history and to offer a cure:

> So rapidly and unceasingly [advances] the march of discovery, that one [has] to apply whip and spur to keep up with the times. Let any one attempt merely to take an inventory of modern discoveries and improvements, and he would find them multiplying upon him without number: and a man must have a smattering acquaintance with them all, to be qualified for anything but a schoolmaster of the last century. What a field of investigation then is thrown open to the modern student, and what numberless temptations to overwork the brain beset him on every side![18]

Overworking the brain led to use of energy meant for other parts of the body, and that led to severe physical disability. The exigencies of the age had maimed Theodore, but he was not alone. Beriah Green, who would later be instrumental in converting Weld to abolition, had worked himself to a frazzle as a student at Andover. He had dropped out, consulted a physician to no avail, and finally experienced a complete breakdown while serving with the Board of Foreign Missions. "I [had] 'run down' to the point of spitting blood," Green remembered. "Miserable enough—I now abandoned all efforts at public speaking; bade adieu to my books, which I had enjoyed some broken communion with, through the eyes of a friend, and gave up the labor of continuous, close thinking."[19] Others like John Frost, a leader of the Finney faction in the Oneida Presbytery, and Thomas S. Grimké, the South Carolina reformer, told much the same story.[20]

All these men had ameliorated their situations through systematic exercise. Weld indulged in a variety of physical activities; Beriah Green found salvation at the woodpile; Grimké once stated, "I doubt whether I could have gone through college without the system of constant exercise."[21] Particularly interesting to the modern observer of such testimonials is the way in which these men applied an almost purely physical solution to what might seem to us psychological problems. Beriah Green, for instance, always awoke "oppressed with fatigue," a condition he alleviated by chopping wood. "Whether in exercise or in study," Green wrote, "I felt continually hurried. Every nerve was strained."[22] For John Frost the case is less clear, but even he attributed ailments that today might be termed psychoneurotic to his leaving the farm to go to school: "I soon began to experience the injurious influence of study without sufficient bodily exercise. Indigestion, constipation of bowels, headache, depression of spirits, indistinct vision, clouded intellect, defective memory, and general debility, followed in rapid succession."[23] Green and Frost, like Weld, had felt driven and confused by the age and assaulted by the physical symptoms of overwork and disorientation. What they recommended was not mere exercise, but rather a *system* of exercise, one that would order their lives, forcibly limit the possibility of mental overload, and, at the same time, strengthen their bodies for the tasks ahead.

Indeed, soon after his meetings with Beecher in 1827, Theodore enrolled in the first class at the vanguard manual labor institution, the Oneida Institute. The Oneida program displayed once again the ways in which the Finney revival and its institutional offspring both shared in and radicalized Orthodoxy's responses to the age. At Andover and other more traditional institutions, manual labor was made available as an elective, leaving untouched traditional conceptions of ministerial training. At Oneida it was mandatory and at the core of the educational experience; and it encouraged a significantly new ministerial ideal.[24]

Oddly enough, the new school had been founded by Finney's old foil George W. Gale, who more recently had become a convert in the revival. Never a hardy soul, Gale nonetheless seemed to have become concerned about his health only after conversion. Perhaps he had come to see himself as the worst example of the listless, worn-out minister of the past; almost as if by way of repentance he started a manual labor experiment in 1826. He invited eight students to live and study with him; they did farm work as payment for room, board, and instruction. Eight months later, he judged the experiment a success. Gale presented a more elaborate plan to the Oneida Presbytery, which unanimously voted to establish Oneida Academy in Whitestown, near Utica. Part of the Presbytery's enthusiasm grew from the fact that Hamilton College, which had been the favored Presbyterian institution, had become largely unfriendly to the revival. Weld probably left on that account, and many pro-Finney philanthropists sought a new school to support. The Presbytery soon raised two thousand dollars, purchased a one hundred and fourteen-acre farm, and hired a set of congenial teachers. The first term commenced early in May, 1827.[25]

The Oneida boys were sparked by an élan born of participating in what they believed to be the building of a model, revolutionary institution. They literally built the school, for not much of a physical plant had been constructed before the fifty or so students began to arrive in Whitestown. They had come to work, however, and most were energetic veterans of the revival campaigns. Weld, already plainly a magnetic figure, became the effective leader among Oneida students.[26] He personified that new ideal combining extreme piety and physical brawn. The Christian pilgrim had merged with the nineteenth-century common man.

This amalgam of primitive-Christian and common-man style pervaded many facets of life at Oneida; it even dictated student dress. Charles Grandison Finney, who had broken ministerial precedent by preaching in a business suit, criticized the Oneidans for going too far on that account. "I fear a want of cleanliness and good breeding, an inattention to the decencies of life," the revivalist wrote to Weld, "will injure some of your young men if not the reputation of the School." Finney's language revealed the awkwardness of his position vis-à-vis these his most zealous followers:

> You know that I am recommending the stiffness of scholastic manners, from such buckram refinements the Lord delivers ministers. Nor am I in favor of those pretty dandy airs which are sometimes affected by clowns who set up for gentlemen. But when a man appears in good company let him see that his boots and clothing are clean so as not to create disgust by his inattention to *what they will insist upon discussing*.[27]

The Oneida boys did not stop at dress in their efforts to merge the image of student and laborer and to separate themselves from an embarrassing tradition of churchly hierarchies and deferential manners. They worked in the fields not only for health, but also to show neighboring farmers that students were of the common folk. One local yeoman, Weld remembered, "who did not think much of student's work, told me he would give us all the timber we would cut with our own hands, and what was more he would haul it to the canal. I went and organized the boys with axes, and we cut down the timber, made a raft, and built a large barn, with sheds."[28]

The routine at Oneida offered days full of labor and study. A horn sounded reveille at four in the morning, at which time Weld, who headed the cow-milking operations, made sure his product was ready to be shipped to Utica before breakfast. Meals were simple, consisting largely of breads, puddings, potatoes, and occasional rations of fish. A charged atmosphere surrounded activities, so much so that even while dining students read reports and notices. And of course there was time for classes and study. "I was delighted to see young men," marveled Lewis Tappan, "who a few hours previously were reaping, milking, etc come onto the platform before a large assembly and deliver their compositions in Latin and English—orations, poems, colloquys etc with ease and dignity."[29]

Whatever the details of daily life, the students aimed at one goal: to prepare for the millennial struggle. Into already crowded schedules they squeezed in the work of reform. Colonization, temperance, and missionary inquiry societies were soon founded, and the news of Christian undertakings far and wide became the grist of everyday conversation. The greater task ahead sometimes inspired students to question seemingly irrelevant curriculum. Charles Stuart Renshaw, an Oneidan who eventually became deeply involved in antislavery and missionary work, best summed up the mood. "The desideratum is *what course of studies to pursue*," he wrote Finney. "I cannot see what good it will be to study *Latin and Greek*—if I were the best linguist in the universe, it would not aid me in telling a heathen sinner the way to go to the saviour's feet . . . a man *must be* thoroughly furnished—but can he not be so without so much time spent. . . ."[30]

This was not an uncommon attitude, and it pointed toward a conception of the ministry somewhat removed from the learned scholarship of Presbyterian and Congregational tradition, and at odds with the concept of venerating only wisdom gleaned from old age. The ministerial ideal common at places like Oneida stressed youth, brawn, and practical education. It represented one more expression of contempt for tradition. In addition, it indicated by implication the apocalyptic sensibility of a young Christian cadre preparing for Armageddon, seeing no personal or future histories beyond the fast approaching end of days.[31]

Theodore himself had constantly to choose between the demands of reform and those of study. In general he opted for the life of action. Once he and a fellow student were mobbed at the Whitestown courthouse while attempting to organize a temperance society.[32] Weld caused another commotion when he invaded a supposedly public but frankly antisabbatarian gathering and held forth against Sunday mail delivery amidst insults, hoots, and hollers.[33] But perhaps the greatest drain on his study time was the constant round of lectures he gave to raise funds for Oneida Academy itself.[34]

His audacious style found other outlets while at Oneida. On one occasion, while visiting his parents in Fabius, Theodore got up to speak at church, and held forth *"all* through the intermission between the forenoon and afternoon services, and all the afternoon, too until the clergyman—who had gone up into his pulpit by the stairs opposite those where Weld was standing—arose as Weld took his seat, saying: 'We will close this afternoon's service with prayer.'"[35] Another time he spontaneously delivered a sermon when the congregation found out that the minister was ill.[36]

Such ventures must have given Weld an exhilarating sense of being loved and appreciated; even in cases of hostile responses, he could always turn to God for approval. However, he had not yet given up the ultimate goal of being a minister, and if his own guilt was not enough to get him to open a book, he could always count on letters from his parents and from Charles Stuart to push him in that direction. Stuart urged him not to forget the "main object" of his stay at Oneida, which was a "studious preparation for the Gospel ministry."[37] "We regret that your time is so much occupied with *much serving,*" wrote his mother; "it seems that you can have but little opportunity to attend to the ultimate object of a residence in the Oneida Academy. Try, try my dear son, to throw off some of your numerous avocations and attend to your studies."[38] Ludovicus was more direct: "I verily believe you have continued long enough at that infant institution where the laboring oar has been constantly in your hand, and where you enjoy comparatively imperfect advantages for study. I wish you were at Andover."[39]

But Theodore, in mind and spirit, was far from Andover. He had embraced the romance of millennial reform. The pious activist in an age of action, he felt more and more drawn to the stump and less to the studious preparation necessary to become a minister in the old style. It was while at Oneida that he met Lewis Tappan, the wealthy New York merchant who, with his pious brother Arthur, would fund many of the era's reform movements. Tappan had sent his two sons to Oneida on the recommendation of Finney.[40] He was a concerned parent, and after meeting Weld, he entrusted him with his sons' spiritual care; through Weld they both underwent conversion.[41] Tappan and Weld were two very different sorts of men, but they shared a common dream in the coming Millennium. The relationship was crucial to Theodore's continuing pull toward the reform community.

Meanwhile, George W. Gale had failed to provide the dramatic leadership necessary to hold the allegiance of his students. They became enraged when, perhaps out of jealousy, he slighted Weld's contribution to the school in Oneida's annual report.[42] By 1831 the boys had mounted a campaign to replace Gale with N. S. S. Beman, but that endeavor had failed.[43] Things were in a bad way at Oneida, and Weld looked for new challenges. He turned down offers of pulpits in New Orleans and New York City, feeling unqualified for a formal ministry.[44]

He did accept Tappan's offer of the post of general agent for the newly formed Society for the Promotion of Manual Labor in Literary Institutions. His job was twofold. First, he was to travel throughout the country compiling facts concerning the progress and future of the manual labor system. Second, he was to find a site for the proposed National Manual Labor Seminary, one that might become a model for all others. Theodore commenced his labors in late 1831, lecturing on manual labor, temperance, and female education (the latter two seen as related topics and ones likely to draw otherwise uninterested parties to a manual labor meeting), soliciting opinions about the system, and encouraging support for the planned national institution.[45]

In late 1832, after a long and arduous journey involving several hair-raising accidents and covering 4,575 miles, Theodore sat down to write his report. It illustrated the growing importance of physiology in Weld's view of society and its needs. Theodore began his report with a statement of faith: "God revealed his will to man upon the subject of education, and has furnished every human being with a copy of the revelation. It is written in the language of nature, and can be understood without a commentary."[46] The body became a physiological companion to the Bible, accessible to all and most easily understood through scientific observation.

The manual labor philosophy hoped to elucidate the natural order God proclaimed for the human body so that man could function morally and efficiently. But for Weld the system came to mean far more than merely a way to train healthy ministers. Manual labor, rooted as it was in the laws of nature, would have a salutary effect on every aspect of existence. Manual labor education thus became one solution to problems that had plagued the Puritan mind for years—the passions, disorder, divisiveness, and mistrust found in society. According to manual labor advocates, the solution to these problems lay in reuniting body and mind in healthful order. This internal order would effect a change in the strained relations among men. Continued education without manual labor, though, would "sunder what God [had] joined together, and impeach the wisdom which pronounced that union good." It would destroy the "symmetry of human proportion and make man a monster."[47]

Disorder in society, Weld seemed to say, was in large part a product of these physiological monsters; reinstituting order in the collective physiology might ameliorate the causes of immorality and social tensions. For instance, moral laxity among students was clearly the result of improper channeling of bodily energies.

In several ways manual labor would provide a remedy. First, exercise could fill free hours, which otherwise "practically legalize[d] those innumerable devices of mischief, indecency, and outrage, which abound in our literary institutions."[48] Second, useful exercise "would be a preventive of moral evils *by supplying that demand for vivid sensation so characteristic of youth,* whose clamors for indulgence drive multitudes to licentious indulgence or to ardent spirits, tobacco, and other unnatural stimulants. It would preserve the equilibrium of the system, moderate the inordinate demands of animal excitability, and quell the insurrection of appetite." Third, it would remove "those *causes* of irritability, jealousy, fickleness, and depression of spirits, which are found in an unhealthful state of the system."[49]

Manual labor, besides habituating the body to exertion, reconciled the mind to an acceptance of labor as honorable, and Weld saw this as essential to the success of America's republican experiment. Schools that did not practice manual labor fostered serious class distinctions: "Hence learning comes to be associated as a matter of course with inactivity, puts honor upon it, and buoys it upward; while ignorance becomes associated with labor, cleaves fast to it, sits upon it as an incubus, and crushes it into the dust."[50] Manual labor also strengthened the republic by enabling sons of the laboring classes to gain an education by giving them a means of earning while they learned. It would eliminate the caste system that threatened the future of the nation. The chasm between rich and poor, idle and laboring, Weld reminded his readers, "already yawns deep and broad; and if it be not speedily bridged, by bringing education within the reach of the poor, it will widen into an impassable gulf, and our free institutions, our national character, our bright visions of the future, our glory and our joy, will go down into it."[51] Even with all the money spent by governments on education, the fact remained that only the wealthy could afford it. "Thus," he continued, "our legislatures have in effect aided those who needed no assistance, and *tantalized the needy with a show of aid so far removed, that it can never avail them.* There is no benevolence in pointing a starving man to a leaf suspended in the air, *unless you give him wings to fly to it.*"[52]

Just as manual labor might allow those in need a boost upward, Weld thought it could also provide a ladder for the privileged downward so that they could better understand the common man. Theodore had worked out a number of strategies to lessen the gap between rich and poor and thus to avoid the disdain and jealousy that had plagued him since his youth. He came to invest a romantic notion of naturalness in the common

American. Having taken on his habits of dress, he now wished to come into closer contact with his feelings. "The middling and lower classes of society," wrote Weld, "which are not wrapped up in the innumerable folds of ceremony, nor entangled in the endless meshes of fashionable forms, furnish the best text book in the science of the heart."[53] If the student wished to study this text, he must "narrow down the distance between the learned and the laboring classes, and thus get sufficiently near the latter to see them as they are. He may mingle with them a lifetime, but if he cannot make them *feel at home with him,* he can never see that unobstructed flow of thought and feeling which constitutes nature."[54] He might bridge that gap by involving himself in labor, for

> The thousand repulsions arising from dissimilarity of habits which have so long operated to estrange [men] from each other, cease with the causes which produced them. Instead of being driven asunder by jealousies, and smothered animosities, they approach each other with looks of kindness, and form a compact, based upon republican equality, and the interchange of mutual offices of courtesy of kindness.[55]

Weld's argument, supported by his own experience and perennial concerns over a disordered society, left the defensive, institutionally oriented visions of Federalism and Orthodoxy behind. Science, by providing a clear picture of God's physical dictates for mankind, had made the human body a new focus for order. The pursuit of a Christian Truth to live by had become as much a matter of physiology as theology.

Weld's report was not written in a vacuum; it was part of a veritable explosion of interest in the body that began around 1829. Weld's sources included works such as Edward Hitchcock's *Dyspepsy Forestalled and Resisted* (1831), the *Journal of Health* (which began publication in 1830), and correspondence with the Reverend Sylvester Graham, who had already begun to lecture on health and would someday become the most controversial of major health reformers.[56] Traditional concerns for order and balance, for a unified community, and for a new nation operating by the principles of Christian morality, had found in physiology a new rational basis.

Weld's energetic involvement in the world of revivalism and reform marked not only a significant era in his social and theological development, but also a turning point in his relation to his father. For years the senior Weld's perceived contempt had stood between Theodore and a secure sense of self; indeed, it had made him feel unworthy of God's salvation. It is no wonder then that one of his most vivid memories of childhood was of Ludovicus branding him a heretic. As is sometimes the case with rebellious sons, however, Theodore had stood Ludovicus's condemnation on its head. Rather than meekly returning to the Orthodox fold, he sought and found union with God in Finneyite heresy. Still unable to attack his father, he raged at his father's church.

At the same time, Ludovicus began to reveal nagging self-doubts to his son (albeit in the third person). "He hopes, he trusts, a sovereign God has made him an instrument of some good," wrote father to son in 1830. "But he often fears that more will perish through his unfaithfulness, than will be pardoned and saved through his instrumentality."[57] Old age, failed expectations, physical infirmity—all had driven him into a period of intense self-questioning. He who had always appeared the righteous judge began to sketch for the judged a different, more human portrait.

We do not know how Theodore reacted. He must have seen in Ludovicus's doubts a justification for his own wayward course; in fact, soon after receiving this letter he left school again, this time on the manual labor speaking tour. Yet his father's admissions may also have bewildered Weld; it may have seemed as if Ludovicus were bowing out of his adversary role, leaving Theodore to spar with a shadow.

The passage of two years and a near fatal accident further reshaped the strain between father and son. Eight miles from Columbus, Ohio, in February 1832, Weld nearly perished in a stagecoach accident. The vehicle overturned while fording the flood-swollen Alum River. Weld was thrown out, nearly trampled by horses, and then swept away by the current. He reached shore suffering from overexposure to the cold water. Miraculously, some men who had heard his faint cries came to his rescue.[58]

Friends and family reacted to his ordeal in a variety of ways. Finney warned him to take care of himself, lest the Devil succeed in ridding the world of his influence. However, most intimates emphasized the rescue more than the accident, seeing it as a sign of God's special interest in Weld. The reform press printed detailed accounts of the drama.[59] Lewis Weld exclaimed, "Oh my brother, you have been on the very threshold of the eternal world and yet you are restored to your friends, to society, to the church."[60] Elizabeth Weld wrote of her "heart torn with conflicting passions—by night and day I saw you struggling in the water," and of her fears that he might perish. "The Evening before your letter arrived," she remembered, "your father cautiously said to me—'It would by no means be a *strange* thing, if we were to receive a letter from Cincinnati informing of Theodores Death.'" She thanked God for his rescue with an ultimate gesture: "Now my Son I desire to be grateful to God and if I have never done it in sincerity before, now to give you to him—feeling that you are his, and that I have no right to call you mine."[61]

Cornelia urged Ludovicus to add some lines to the family letter. "I cannot now" was his reply.[62] Theodore responded with bitter salvos. As many times before, he accused his father of ignoring him, of never writing "a letter, I mean a sheet, nor even a whole page." He attacked Ludovicus's pastoral efforts as "the mere shadow of revivals." He even charged that prayer in the Weld household had been "most awfully neglected." Yet in the end Theodore still asked for paternal advice; he was unwilling to give up Ludovicus as father and judge, though it had now become the son's turn to hurt the father with words of rebuke.[63]

The father responded by reminding Theodore that he had written him regularly while at Andover and on the mnemonics tour. Still, he admitted, he had not sent him "many letters." "I have ever found it easier to write a sermon than a letter," he explained, and hoped that those from Elizabeth and Cornelia had sufficed. "I hope you do not ascribe what you consider my *silence* to forgetfulness, or want of affection. I think of you every day, and with affectionate interest and concern." He reminded Theodore of the abysmal physical state that hampered his writing—that "almost perpetual, depressing headache," and generally low level of "animal spirits" that had plagued him for a decade. "I have preferred solitude to society," he admitted, "and felt like a stranger in a strange land."[64]

Ludovicus could not help but concede some of Theodore's charges about his Christian conduct. "I have often an overwhelming sense of deficiency and unfaithfulness," he confessed, "and fear very much—fear that precious souls have perished through my default." As for the specific barbs, the father tried to defend his integrity while admitting to shortcomings. He insisted revivals in his church had been "attended with as much divine power, with as deep feeling, and with as genuine marks of real conversion as any revivals [he had] seen or heard." Yet he admitted that he might have viewed them "through a false medium." As for neglect in family prayer, he both denied the charge and admitted to its "correctness."[65]

This growing sense of frustration and guilt about his own ministry and the Alum River incident had weakened Ludovicus's resolve about Theodore's future. "Your life and health and the business of your agency [manual labor] have appeared to me of late much more important than before," he wrote, "have appeared almost wholly in a new light." He urged his son to recognize that he was a divine instrument: "I think I have of late sensibly enjoyed the thought that you are in the hand, and entirely at the disposal of a sover[eign] God. To him I commend you and to the word of his grace." There appeared no mention of study for the ministry, and no advice more specific than the normal Christian injunctions for prayer, good conduct, and humility. Ludovicus had joined Elizabeth in consigning Theodore to God's care.[66]

Though freed from the conscious plans and judgments of his own father, Weld continued to battle the church of the Fathers. In fact, he and comrades from Oneida would soon confront their elders over the most explosive issue in American society—the abolition of slavery.

V

Lane Seminary I

Theodore's assignment for the Manual Labor Society included the task of finding the best location for a National Manual Labor Institution, one that would be the model school for training a millennial ministry. Though some in the manual labor camp favored Rochester, New York, voices from over the mountains turned Weld's attention toward Cincinnati. J. L. Tracy, a fellow Oneidan who now taught school in Kentucky, reminded Theodore that the Ohio Valley was "to be the great battlefield between the powers of light and darkness," and asked, "Why not train the soldiers of the Cross within sight of the enemies camp?"[1] At the same time, F. Y. Vail, a Cincinnati educator, offered his fledgling Lane Seminary as a site for the great experiment.[2]

Tracy's argument was particularly compelling to Weld, who had long stressed the importance of the West. As early as 1827 he had urged Finney to work in the hinterland rather than in eastern cities. "Kindle *back fires back fires back fires* far and wide," he had advised; "let them stretch over the interior then while you are engaged there the cities are preparing fast [;] when ripe—at the favorable nick of time—give the word—rally your forces and in the twinkling of an eye make a plunge—and they are a wreck."[3] By 1832, as Finney preached in New York City, Weld argued ever more urgently that the "battlefield of the

Lane Seminary (*Ohio Historical Society*)

world," "Satan's seat," could not be won "by working the lever in Boston, New York, or Philadelphia." Only in the West could Finney "electrify the whole mass."[4]

Weld's advice was well within one important tradition in Christian thought. As the scholar George H. Williams has argued, the wilderness, whether existing in the mind or in the world, symbolized to the Christian a "moral waste but a potential paradise," a ground upon which to fight one's personal battle for salvation or mankind's struggle for the Second Coming.[5] Thus to Theodore a physically describable land of hills, lakes, rivers, and forests had become a stage for the enactment of prophecy. For his ancestors, that wilderness had been New England; but he would take New England's mission to new ground. Nor was this an unusual move. The founders of Oberlin College had compared their choice of an Ohio site to that of the Pilgrims at Plymouth.[6] The parallel, while indicating a westward shift of millennial hopes, also raised a significant point about the relation of New Englanders to the West. Weld and others saw themselves as transplanting the mission, already compromised in the East, to new and fertile soil. "It is here," Catharine Beecher wrote to her Connecticut students from Cincinnati, "that in the *moral* as well as the natural world, the same amount of labour brings forth an hundred fold more than it could do in the fixed, steady unexcitable soil of New England."[7] However, New Englanders were needed to do the job. As one visitor to Ohio put it, "There is only one thing wanting to make this country prosperous. That is half a million yankey farmers."[8]

Weld's romance with the West also came out of his association of that region with the common man and his natural ways. In his manual labor report, Theodore wrote of having "experienced largely that hospitality and kindness which have always distinguished the *new world of the West*."[9] Nor was this new world merely a figment of Weld's imagination. One Connecticut traveler reported that "you cannot form any idea of difference in the young people here from those at the east [;] all that stiffness and formality is laid aside and they are all united male and female [;] there is no hard *feelings*, they all seem so interested in one another."[10] Language, so often an indicator of the quality of human interaction, was also less formal. Catharine Beecher wrote in somewhat shocked amusement about current expressions such as "despert bad fix" and (to express pain) "seems as if it would use us up bodyaciously" and "make one feel powerful weak."[11]

In the end, Weld chose Lane for the experiment and his backers concurred. Unable to lure Finney from his New York activities, the manual laborites turned to Lyman Beecher as their choice for president of Lane. The peppery minister had moved strongly toward the Finneyite camp in the years after the Oneida revival, and he gladly accepted this position of leadership in the Christian vanguard. "If we gain the West," he wrote to his daughter, "all is safe; if we lose it, all is lost."[12] Beecher told his Boston congregation that the decision to go to Lane was "of as great importance as was ever permitted a human mind to decide." It was his chance to make the decisive step, "to give a

Lyman Beecher (*Ohio Historical Society*)

complexion probably forever to the doctrine and revivals of that great world."[13] Later, in appealing for funds, Beecher warned of the consequences should Lane fail. ". . . our intelligence and virtue will falter and fall back into a dark minded, vicious populace—a poor, uneducated, reckless mass of infuriated animalism, to rush on resistless as the tornado, or to burn as if set on fire of hell."[14]

Lyman Beecher was the kind of man who felt that the world depended on him for ultimate salvation; his hyperbolic prose spilled over with notions of disaster if his own way were blocked. Beecher's defensive tone—protection of American destiny from ignorant Catholics and infidels—rarely admitted a note of self-questioning. He concentrated on the defense of institutions and the defeat of external enemies. His Truths were embodied in the church and its auxiliaries. Debates over what constituted the true Christian life mattered less than solidarity in the larger battle. Weld and those who followed him from Oneida to Lane held a somewhat different view. To them victory in the millennial cause depended upon discovering the Truth and then acting in accord with its dictates; such an attitude called for scrupulous self-cleansing by both individuals and institutions as the first order of business. Purging oneself of sin was a prerequisite to dealing with Satan's legions. Still, as the Beecher family, Weld and his Oneida boys, and a miscellany of new students and faculty marched toward Lane, implicit differences could be ignored for awhile in the glow of Christian mission.

The Queen City to which these soldiers of the Lord headed might have appeared to an unbiased contemporary observer more common than royal; like most nineteenth-century population centers, it suffered from poor roadways, bad sanitation, periodic famines, and epidemics due to uncontrollable natural conditions.

Cincinnati was, at least, set in a place of natural beauty, a point where the Ohio River passed between magnificent hills. Atop Walnut Hill was the site of Lane Seminary. The Lane brothers, two New Orleans merchants, had founded the school in the evangelical and manual labor spirit, hoping to enable "any enterprising individual [to] assist himself, and to bring forward that class of talented individuals, who through the depression of means, have been kept back from greater usefulness."[15] They believed in New School ecumenicism; nominally Presbyterian, Lane's first trustees looked to a fast approaching millennial day when God would give His children "a new name, even the name of christian." Thus as supporters cheered the construction of a new building's walls they sought a symbolic day when walls would be broken down, when "no party distinctions [would] be known, save that of the *righteous* and the *wicked*."[16]

It was the familiar millennial refrain, and though the Oneida boys who followed Weld to Lane were enthusiastic about the prospects, they harbored a vigorous skepticism about the motives and qualifications of those outside their group. Men like Henry B. Stanton, Sereno W. Streeter, Calvin Waterbury, and John Alvord had learned too much about human fallibility at Oneida to allow a more charitable view, especially when the Millennium was at stake. In that mood they bemoaned the mistakes of the past. "Oneida has lost the spirit which she once possessed," Streeter wrote to Weld in 1832; "her soul has gone."[17] He complained of "an injudicious admission of students, [those] who care[d] for little except the gratification of self."[18] Professors also came under fire. Streeter criticized a Mr. Grant, for instance, because he refused to be an example for the rest: "His influence was not a straw. He walked among the students like a speechless ghost. He gave no compositions nor declamations, lay abed late in the mor[ning], drank tea and coffee stoutly and his manual labor consisted in journeying from his room to the backhouse."[19]

Fearing repetition of such mistakes at Lane, the Oneidans promoted their own nominees for faculty and criticized others whose names had been suggested. They were desperately afraid that antimanual labor men would "crush us by their caresses when they find they can't ever shin us by their kicks."[20] More galling were the rumors that some trustees "were of the opinion that the Oneida boys had conspired to overthrow Lane Seminary."[21] In fact, the image that the Oneidans presented might have inspired such fear. They flaunted their power, referred to Lane as their "ship," and at least one of them nicknamed the group "Illuminati."[22] Camaraderie ran high. Months apart in the summer were sad and expectant, a time when a letter from a fellow Lane boy came "like a meteor throwing a blaze of light and love over the solitude and loneliness that darkens and blackens around."[23] As twenty-four of the forty who entered Lane's first theological class, the Oneidans managed to create a school of spirit within the school of classes and chores, what Charles Beecher called "a kind of *imperium in imperio.*"[24]

At the center was Weld. Beecher thought him a genius; he noted that the students considered him "a god."[25] All could admire his hardy but saintlike presence. One story told how most of the students could not decide on room assignments; arguments became heated, and finally a lottery was decided upon. Weld drew second choice, but in a grand gesture said he would wait until the end; the act shamed the rest and they came to an "amicable adjustment"—all except, that is, for finding quarters for a particularly "slovenly and unsavory" fellow. Weld promptly offered part of his own room to him.[26] According to another legend, a deep and dangerous well once had to be cleaned; only Theodore cheerfully volunteered and did the job all by himself.[27] His physical courage, studied selflessness, and willingness to take command made him a model, a leader, a father. J. L. Tracy once even apologized for being "a source of grief" to Theodore. "You are the only one who has ever been faithful to me," Tracy wrote. "I trust your kind admonitions will not be lost upon me."[28] Another student felt that only Weld could lead the school, since Beecher had had no experience with manual labor: "Now the ship may be *victualed* and manned for a voyage round the world, but she wont go round a promontory if she has no *pilot.*"[29]

Theodore played his most heroic role in matters of life and

death. Cincinnati experienced a cholera plague that swept the nation in 1832 and 1833. It finally came to Lane Seminary, the first case breaking in the room next to Weld's. For ten days Theodore ministered to the sick and dying. Writing to his brother Lewis, he described the agonies and joys of death. One student, upon realizing his fate, called to Weld: "Yes, he calls me—yes, I am beginning to live!" Another could only exclaim "with a look of transport, 'The face of the Lord! The face of the Lord!'" There was a tragic case, however, one which "made upon us all an impression which can never be effaced." Henry B. Stanton's brother George, despite attendance at numerous revivals and the influence of family and friends, had "still resisted the Spirit, caviled, criticised, and started skeptical queries," and finally had taken a "desperate rush into infidelity." He came down with cholera and after medical consultation it was decided that Theodore must tell him the worst and "urge on his soul *the great salvation* provided for the chief of sinners." "I endeavored with the utmost gentleness and tenderness," Weld recounted, "to press the subject at intervals for an hour and a half, but, the more affectionate the approach, the fiercer did he repel it, till at last he screamed to drown my voice." Stanton's brother Henry cried, "What shall I tell your poor mother, George?" He replied, "Let me alone." Yet at the very end of his struggle, George screamed, "Oh, for a light! for a light! Bring me a light—the light of my salvation! No, never, never, never!" "This word he repeated as many as twelve or fifteen times," wrote Theodore, "all the while tossing his body from side to side with an energy which nothing could inspire but the death-struggle. He stopped, and with a phrensied look of horror, died!" Thus did Theodore and the evangelicals view death.[30]

Weld took his role as "master-spirit" with full confidence. "I have a fine class," he boasted to his brother, "and have never been placed in circumstances by any means so *imposing*. When I came here matters were getting at loose ends."[31] Presumably matters had been tightened up. Nor was the administration unappreciative; though leader of the students, Weld seemed far more responsible than his fellows. Professor Biggs, later a particular target of the Oneidans' contempt, wrote to Vail on the occasion of Theodore's return to school in July 1833: "Weld is here and we are glad."[32] A year later he would change his mind.

As long as issues between students and administration were not clear, as long as tensions lay in the realm of personal suspicion and fear, of complaints about the lack of exemplary behavior on the part of either students or faculty—as long as the vying concepts of a millennial strategy had not squared off on some important issue—then Lane Seminary could proceed with its educational tasks and keep private resentments private. In fact, it was the strategy of men like Beecher to make sure that disputes between Christians did not obscure the larger shared task of defending against infidelity. Men like Weld, however, once sure of the moral worth and importance of a particular stance, could not help but enter it into the millennial equation and demand the loyalty of all good Christians. It was Lane's and Beecher's bad luck that the issue Weld chose was that of slavery. Slavery and the question of the rights of black freemen had vexed Americans of conscience for years. Yet for Theodore, who pressed the issue of slavery and the condition of free blacks on Lane and Cincinnati, the very intractability of the problem inspired forthrightness. It had to be dealt with if America was to be saved and the Millennium achieved. By introducing the issue, Weld supplied Lane's uneasy populace with a cause over which to battle, a topic around which each side could mold a position against the other. The end result was that faculty and administration, despite their professed admiration for the theological class, asserted a belief in their own absolute authority. The students, for their part, left Lane, renouncing their commitment to an institution in favor of commitment to a set of ideals. Easy compliments faded as one found out the truth about the other.

The story of the Lane rebellion really begins with the saga of Weld's own conversion to abolition. The process was a long and subtle one, far more complex than indicated by Weld's own simple explanation of 1850, when he claimed that on the mnemonics tour he had seen "slavery at home, and became a radical abolitionist."[33] The truth was that he became no instant abolitionist in the early 1820s—hardly an American in those years came close to such a position—but rather that a combination of experiences, coincidences, and personal traits slowly built a web of thought that in late 1832 led to Theodore's conversion to the cause. Early childhood experiences such as his mother's stories of Hagar, the Clark family slave, and Weld's own rebellious camaraderie with his black classmate Jerry, predisposed him to sympathy for blacks. On the mnemonics tour he saw something of slavery firsthand. Also informing his views may have been a Federalist's contempt of a Jeffersonian South proclaiming liberty for all while holding some in bondage.

Yet a commitment to abolition required a stronger predisposition than a Northerner's contempt for the slaveholder and some sympathy for the black man. Theodore's own New England society treated its free black population as inferiors and feared the prospect of freed slaves crossing the Mason-Dixon line and populating the North. Before 1831 the best solution Christians could offer was colonization: the shipping of slaves and free blacks back to Africa.

Colonizationists assumed that the black man was inferior and could not prosper alongside whites in America; he would of necessity sink to the bottom of society, creating problems of crime and saddling white America with an unproductive and undesirable population. In addition, many colonizationists feared retribution from these inferior beings, retribution for slavery and its excesses. If slaves remained enslaved, they would revolt; if freed on American soil, they would use their freedom for revenge. The logical solution was colonization, which would gradually remove the festering sore of black presence without causing undue tumult in white society.

Giving up colonization meant giving up these assumptions. In Weld's case the bases for rejection of black inferiority had been building in the 1820s. In the revival he found and embraced an egalitarian concept of men at odds with hierarchical structures and deferential attitudes. His advocacy of manual labor was, in part, a call for respect between classes and, in part, a romantic, personal urge to bring men of all walks of life together. In fact, Weld's emphasis on the physiological aspects of man focused on the human body all men shared rather than on the distinctions of class, color, or sex that divided them. Although Weld's emerging egalitarian vision did not yet include the black man it was compatible with basic assumptions of abolition thought.

If Weld had gone a long way toward preparing himself to reject the assumption of black inferiority, he nonetheless had to contend with the fear of black revenge. Theodore's upbringing and career, however, worked toward mitigating the common racial fears rampant in America. His eminent ancestry and hard Puritan self-confidence immunized him from fears of status loss that plagued many Americans who otherwise might be committed egalitarians. Moreover, the very nature of his avoidance of deep involvement with the day-to-day workings of society, his gadfly existence on the outer rim of everyday life, allowed him a freedom from fears of direct damage from blacks. He had no job to protect, no wife and daughter to save from rape, no house to defend from pillage. The fears Theodore had were cosmic ones, fears of godly retribution if men did not cease their inhumanity toward other men.

A third factor must be set forth, though its amorphous and unprovable nature will become readily apparent. Weld and others of his generation must have felt something of a kinship with the slave in the romantic but powerful sense that through conversion they themselves had been led from a spiritual slavery to the ever-growing psychological freedom of living in the light of Truth. The very concepts slavery and freedom, in other words, conjured up emotions Theodore himself had felt. Though largely unexpressed, such parallels occasionally found their way into causes related to the revival, as in Heman Humphrey's temperance pamphlet, A Parallel between Intemperance and the Slave Trade.[34]

Such influences can only be considered preparatory in Weld's changing consciousness, very important preconditions that sensitized him to the plight of the slave or the free black but that did not immediately suggest the doctrine of abolition. First of all, issues like manual labor and temperance and Theodore's own shaky plans for completing his theological education stood in the forefront of his mind. Second, no one had yet presented him with some concrete argument and plan that might replace colonization as the solution to slavery. As late as September 27, 1832, Weld could write to his new friend James G. Birney, "I am ripe in the conviction that if the Colonization Society does not dissipate the horror of darkness which overhangs the southern country, we are undone. Light breaks *in from no other quarter*."[35] A sentence before this qualified, almost desperate endorsement of colonization, Theodore revealed his own sense of paralysis. "When I look at the great slave question, trace its innumerable and illimitable bearings upon the weal of the world, every year augmenting its difficulties, its dangers, its woe and its guilt," he wrote, "my heart aches with hope deferred, mocks all prescriptions and refuses to be comforted."[36]

At the root of this foreboding discomfort were various "signs of the times" that not only cast doubt on millennial progress, but that seemed to threaten the very existence of American society. Natural crises such as the cholera epidemic and droughts that caused low food production hinted at judgment from Heaven.[37] In the political sphere, nullification threatened to break up the Union a mere fifty years after its inception.[38] So sensitive was this topic that when Lewis Weld visited Charleston to promote asylums for the deaf, a local minister suggested that he not "intentionally allude" to "*questions of local policy* and to other *agitating subjects*."[39]

Intimately tied to nullification was slavery. Charlestonians still shuddered at the thought of the abortive Denmark Vesey Conspiracy of 1822.[40] Nat Turner's bloody rampage of 1831 shocked the entire nation. These events and the rebellious proclamations of David Walker's *Appeal* of 1829 led slaveholders to repressive measures, colonizationists to redoubled efforts, and William Lloyd Garrison to his immediate emancipation position.[41] Colonizationist Benjamin Silliman expressed the nightmare fear best: "When the molten rock bursts forth in a torrent of burning lava, it will overwhelm those who may be in its way, whether they had expected the explosion or not." Nor did Silliman see the danger in some distant year; a new awareness of population statistics demonstrated to colonizationists and abolitionists alike that the showdown was near. Projections indicated that the number of blacks would treble in forty years, and with each year of hardship and increased numbers the chances for a "protracted" insurrection, "reared and sustained . . . in connexion with the negro sway, already established in the West Indies" increased greatly.[42]

The first major direct influence turning Theodore toward a new position on slavery probably was Charles Stuart, who had become extremely active in British antislavery and anticolonization efforts.[43] "Pray for me, my beloved Theodore," Stuart wrote from England in March 1831; "I am traversing the country, holding meetings wherever I can, and endeavoring to awaken the conscience of the Nation, that Negro Slavery may be put off."[44] He wrote again in June, "long[ing] to hear of [Theodore] being engaged in the Sacred cause of Negro emancipation"; Stuart enclosed ten copies of his latest pamphlet on the subject.[45] The following spring he sent more material.[46] At the same time, Tappan and his circle in New York began to take a more active interest in the slavery issue. Weld carried the influence of Stuart's probings and antislavery interest among his reform cohorts as he entered the South for manual labor and temperance lectures. In Huntsville, Alabama, he engaged in long discussions with James G. Birney, a slaveholder who had begun to consider taking on an agency with the American Colonization Society. Weld encouraged him in this course and hoped that he would find it in his heart to emancipate his own slaves.[47]

Theodore's increased interest in the slavery question presented a crucial dilemma. Stuart had argued for immediate emancipation without colonization, but, with no slaves on English soil, it was relatively easy for an Englishman to advocate such a position. For an American it was different. Slavery had seeped into every aspect of politics, economics, and social custom in the United States; fear of blacks had pervaded the white consciousness. It was a working assumption among the citizenry that emancipation on American soil would cause a race war unmatched in history. They had before them the examples of Santo Domingo, Nat Turner, and the images of their own irrepressible fantasies. And so it was that a troubled Theodore Weld could endorse Birney's work for colonization, sensing that "light breaks *in from no other quarter.*"[48]

Soon new light shone in the small college town of Hudson, Ohio, where three members of the Western Reserve community—Beriah Green, Elizur Wright, and Charles B. Storrs—were already spreading Garrisonian doctrine.[49] Weld had come to speak on manual labor and temperance; by the time he left he had been converted to immediate emancipation. What exactly transpired is not known, but it is clear from what followed that two key points were stressed upon Weld's agitated conscience. The Hudson Garrisonians must have demonstrated that even by their own standards the colonizationists were doomed to failure, that they could not remove enough free blacks and newly freed slaves to reduce the black population to the point of safety. More important, however, they must have shown Weld that colonization doctrine itself avoided the central moral question of the black man's humanity and that not recognizing his humanity was a sin. Slavery and race discrimination were no mere misfortunes but sinful acts, whether engaged in actively or passively countenanced.[50]

The wages of sin were revolts, they argued, bloody racial conflicts rightly to be feared if deprivation of basic spiritual and human rights continued; indeed, God had already begun to visit wrath in small warning doses. He would continue to do so until Americans recognized the humanity and rights of the black man, until a collective change of heart rescued the nation from sin. Thus colonization, which sought to avoid rather than foster a change of heart, lulled America into a sleep of self-satisfaction while God's wrath continued to mount. The only answer was to convert slaveholders to immediate recognition of their sin and then to immediate emancipation, and to bring all Americans to a full recognition of the black man as a man. Then there would be no reason to fear freedom for the slave, for the attitudes that might have fostered contempt and rage would have begun to encourage love.[51]

These doctrines cleared Theodore's mind on this most difficult of issues. By December, Elizur Wright was corresponding with Weld as an abolitionist comrade-in-arms. Arthur Tappan, informed of Theodore's conversion to the cause, promptly informed William Lloyd Garrison. Garrison invited Weld to an organizing session for the proposed American Anti-Slavery Society. Theodore declined because of "engagements quite indispensable," but affirmed to Garrison what he had learned at Hudson. Endorsing the "expressive name" of the New England Anti-Slavery Society, he wrote:

> From that I infer that the Society is based upon the great bottom law of human right, that *nothing but crime* can forfeit liberty. That no condition of birth, no shade of color, no mere misfortune of circumstances, can annul that birth-right charter, which God has bequeated to every being upon whom he has stamped his own image, by making him *a free moral agent*, and that he who robs his fellow man of this tramples upon right, subverts justice, outrages humanity, unsettles the foundations of human safety, and sacrilegiously assumes the prerogative of God.[52]

Thus Theodore conjoined antislavery with the egalitarian principles of the revival, of manual labor, and of the broadest interpretation of the Declaration of Independence, leaving behind the dictates of "expediency or necessity."[53] He had pledged himself to millennial purity even on the most explosive topic current in American society, no doubt agreeing with Elizur Wright "that the Colonization doctrines in regard to slavery have been the worst obstacle in the path of our missionary effort; and, whether speaking the truth faithfully will remove slavery or not, that we must honestly gird ourselves for the attempt, before we can expect any great success in our enterprise of converting the world."[54]

"I hardly know how to contain myself," Theodore exclaimed to Wright in January 1833. "If I was not positively pledged for two or three years to come, and if I had finished my education, I would devote myself to the holy work, come life or death."[55] Nonetheless antislavery work edged into his life. He engaged in "many pitched battles" over slavery, sometimes even debating colonization agents.[56] In his enthusiasm Weld saw the North being converted to abolition in two years. After all, if the cause was wedded to "changeless eternal right God [had] decreed its ultimate triumph, and if the signs of the times are not mockers, the victory shout will ring round the world before the generation that now is, goes to the dead."[57]

It was inevitable that Theodore should bring the cause to Lane, though his policy at first was to wait for just the right moment to strike. He could hardly do otherwise. "This Institution stands fiercely committed for Colonization and *against* Abolition," Weld wrote to Amos Phelps. "*Our Theological Professors* are exceedingly anxious to keep us from bringing up the subject for discussion."[58] One reason was geography. "The proximity of Cincinnati and the whole eastern line of Ohio to slaveholding states," explained Theodore, "has thus far muzzled men both in public and private upon the subject of slavery. A universal paralysis pervades—tongues, pens, and presses."[59] He promised Phelps, however, that "in due time you may expect to hear from this Institution—a more favorable Report."[60]

In fact, Theodore had already begun to make plans for open discussion of immediate emancipation and colonization. After meeting with faculty and fellow students of colonization persuasion, he agreed not to "push" a debate for the fall 1833 term so that each side might have time "to prepare for a thorough discussion." Still, he was sure that a public meeting in the winter term might quadruple the small number of abolition advocates at Lane. These original supporters were among "the very first fellows in the Seminary," and included Asa Mahan of the Trustees and Professor John Morgan on the faculty.[61] Other sympathetic hearts in the Cincinnati area included Weld's old Oneida friend, Horace Bushnell, then minister at a nearby town, and Thomas Cole, a Newport, Kentucky pastor.[62] All told, the numbers were paltry; only faith in "changeless eternal right" buoyed their spirits.

It was with this faith that Theodore and his abolitionist fellows planned what were to become known as the Lane Debates. They were scheduled for February 1834, but months earlier preparations commenced in the revival style. "We early began to inculcate our views," Weld remembered, "by conversation, upon our fellow-students. Those of us who sympathized together in our abhorrence of slavery selected each his man to instruct, convince, and enlist in the cause. Thus we carried one after another, and, before ever we came to public debate, knew pretty well where we stood."[63] In other words, the meetings were hardly debates at all. Asking two questions—"Ought the people of the Slaveholding States to abolish Slavery immediately?" and "Are the doctrines, tendencies, and measures of the American Colonization Society, and the influence of its principal supporters, such as render it worthy of the patronage of the Christian public?"—they were conceived of as conversion-oriented educational barrages.[64] Despite doubts about the wisdom of such public meetings, President Beecher agreed not to stand in the way.[65]

The debates lasted eighteen days, each question being discussed two and a half hours each of nine evenings. Weld held forth on the first two days; he introduced the topic of immediate emancipation through "facts . . . gathered from various authentic documents" and drew appropriate conclusions.[66] The most dramatic moments of the series came not from Weld, but rather from Southerners who gave firsthand testimony concerning the "peculiar institution." James Bradley, an ex-slave, countered notions that emancipation would be "unsafe to the community" and that "the condition of the emancipated negroes would be worse than it now is." Bradley himself had worked for five years to buy his freedom; having done so, he left Arkansas for a free state and finally enrolled at Lane for an education.[67]

White Southerners, however, made the greatest impact. The audience could witness the sin of slavery as it acted in men's consciences; they could watch the process by which heartfelt recognition of sin would, if allowed to be spread, sweep the South and emancipate both master and slave. None of their speeches was recorded, but James A. Thome, a southern Lane student converted during the debates, described his experience to the first anniversary meeting of the American Anti-Slavery Society in May 1834. As Thome recounted it, he had always harbored uneasy feelings about slavery, but that these sentiments had led him to colonization. Colonization's only effect, Thome now conceded, had been to "lessen [his] conviction of the evil of slavery, and to deepen and sanctify [his] prejudice against the colored race."[68]

The debates showed to him that the true evil of slavery lay in the denial of black men's God-given rights and in the cruelty that enforced that denial. He described the burning sense of sin this realization brought: "Sin revived and I died."[69] Thus the debates were something of a special form of revival. Slavery's sin "seize[d] the conscience with an authoritative grasp; it [ran] across every path of the guilty, haunt[ed] him, goad[ed] him, and [rang] in his ear the cry of blood. . . . It [wrote] 'thou art the man,' upon the forehead of every oppressor." But the conviction of sin also brought in the sinner "every susceptibility to compassionate outraged humanity" and found him "pledged to do its work."[70]

In short, there seemed to Southerners like Thome no easy continuum between colonization and abolition. Colonizationists argued the line of mere "expediency," while abolitionists recognized that blacks, as fellowmen, must be afforded the legal and spiritual freedom of whites. But there was also a romantic element that went beyond, or rather askew from, notions of equality. Abolition converts tended to invest blacks with messianic qualities reminiscent of those Weld saw in the common man. For instance, William T. Allan of Alabama declared that blacks must be the "Lord's chosen people to carry on the great reformation."[71]

Such conversions fired Theodore's optimism about antislavery. Being on the side of unerring Truth helped, but here were concrete examples of Southerners with personal attachments to slavery succumbing dramatically to that Truth. As Thome put it: "When once the great proposition that negroes are *human beings,* a proposition now scouted by many with contempt, is clearly demonstrated and drawn out on the Southern sky, and when underneath it is written the bloody corollary, the sufferings of the negro race, the seared conscience will again sting, and the stony heart will melt."[72] Nor did Thome object to Northerners bringing Truth to the South, however Southerners might misconstrue abolition as "recklessness, false estimate of right, fanaticism, Quixotism." He pointed out that a single issue of the *Anti-Slavery Reporter* had converted a young Southern slave heir. "It is as unquestionably the province of the North to labour in this cause, as it is the duty of the church to convert the world," Thome explained.[73] Henry B. Stanton drew the basic lesson of the debates: "It is that southern minds, trained and educated amidst all the prejudices of a slaveholding community, can, with the blessing of God, be reached and influenced by facts and arguments as easy as any other class of our citizens."[74]

With the debates at an end, Theodore took a prominent role in galvanizing excited feeling into an Anti-Slavery Society. Its constitution summarized the meaning of immediate emancipation doctrine—what it was and what it was not. The society's object? "Immediate emancipation of the whole colored race, within the United States"—slave from master and "free colored man from the oppression of public sentiment"—"and the elevation of both to an intellectual, moral, and political equality with the whites."[75] Why? Because the black man was created by God as "a moral agent, the keeper of his own happiness, the executive of his own powers, the accountable arbiter of his own choice." Slavery denied this basic principle, "stifle[d] the moral affections, repress[ed] the innate longings of the spirit, paralyze[d] conscience, turn[ed] hope to despair, and kill[ed] the soul." As a system, slavery destroyed the family, excited "desperation and revenge, provoke[d] insurrection, and peril[ed] public safety." Furthermore, it "cripple[d] the energies of the whole nation, entail[ed] poverty and decay upon the states which [upheld] it, foment[ed] division and alienation in our public councils, and put in jeopardy the existence of the union." Finally, it paralyzed "all missionary effort" and "expose[d] the nation to the judgment of God."[76]

In acting on such propositions, the society promised to abide by the "law of love." It ruled out instigating slave rebellion as well as forcible intervention by the free states—one meant murder and the other meant war. Nor would it seek congressional interference. Rather the Lane abolitionists hoped to "induce [the slaveholder] to forsake *this,* as every other sin, by speaking the truth in love." They would demonstrate the advantage of emancipation by showing its "pecuniary interest," its safety, and by encouraging religious and secular public sentiment against slavery.[77]

Moreover, the constitution of Lane's Anti-Slavery Society attempted to dispel the terror that the very phrase "immediate emancipation" seemed to provoke. It defined the term first by excluding the intention of "turn[ing] loose [slaves] upon the nation, to roam as vagabonds and aliens," denying that "they would be instantly invested with all political rights and privileges," but also refusing to allow "that they shall be expelled from their native land to foreign clime, as the price and condition of their freedom." In positive terms "immediate emancipation" meant that slaves would receive protection of the law instead of being at the mercy of unbridled passions, that they should be employed as free laborers, "fairly compensated and protected in their earnings," and that "they shall be placed under a benevolent and disinterested supervision, which shall secure them the right to obtain secular and religious knowledge, to worship God according to the dictates of their consciences, and to seek an intellectual and moral equality with the whites."[78] While none of the sentiments expressed at Lane was new—William Lloyd Garrison and his followers had been espousing them since 1831—those at Lane propounded them as if they had just invented them. Yet it was not so much the doctrines as the wondrous process of conversion that made the Lane Debates a momentous eighteen days.

Forming an Anti-Slavery Society was only one way of working out the millennial mission in relation to blacks. With a zeal typical of Oneida men, Weld, Huntington Lyman, Augustus Wattles, and others began to promote religious and secular schools in Cincinnati's black community. "We believe that faith without *works* is dead," Weld wrote to Lewis Tappan in March 1834. "We have formed a large and efficient organization for elevating the colored people in Cincinnati—have established a Lyceum among them, and lecture three or four evenings a week, on grammar, geography, arithmetic, natural philosophy, etc."[79] Other activities included an evening school for reading skills, a library and a new reading room, three Sabbath schools and a number of Bible classes, all run or participated in by Lane students. Weld also suggested a plan for a "SELECT FEMALE SCHOOL."[80] Two students, Augustus Wattles and Marius Robinson, became so committed to these projects that they dropped out of Lane to devote themselves full time to running a school for blacks.[81]

Weld's notion of the black man was complex, but in some ways it paralleled his image of the common man. On the one hand, blacks were underprivileged and in need of social and moral uplift. On the other hand, Weld never stopped marveling at their incredible zeal for improvement, and at their superior energy, virtue, and will. "Of the almost 3000 blacks in C[incinnati] more than three-fourths of the adults are emancipated slaves," he wrote Tappan, "who worked out their own freedom. . . . Besides these, multitudes are toiling to purchase their friends, who are now in slavery."[82] Theodore sensed in blacks a natural kinship to feeling. One story has it that Weld, on hearing his grammar class sing a closing hymn, exclaimed: "Poor fellows. Bless the Lord they can sing."[83] And much as he had adopted the clothes of the common man, he now immersed himself in the life of the black community. "While I was at Lane Seminary my intercourse was with the Colored people at Cincinnati, I think I may say *exclusively*," he later maintained. "If I ate in the City it was at *their* tables. If I slept in the City it was at their homes. If I attended parties, it was *theirs—weddings—Funerals—theirs—Religious meetings—theirs—*Sabbath schools—Bible classes—theirs. During the eighteen months that I spent at Lane Seminary I *did not attend Dr. Beecher's Church once.*"[84]

Theodore's enthusiasm over the Lane Debates and subsequent work in Cincinnati's "Little Africa" was further strengthened by the news of James G. Birney's conversion to abolition. Since Weld's meetings and correspondence with Birney in 1832, the troubled slaveholder had become a star in the colonization galaxy. An exemplary agent, he also had fired well-reasoned salvos at the upstart immediate emancipationists in various newspapers and finally in the Colonization Society's *African Repository*.[85] It must have come as something of a shock to Weld when he received a letter from Birney announcing his turn to abolition and promising an open letter that would explain his position in full.[86] Theodore assured him that the news would be "ringing in the public ears within a few days, from different papers on both sides of the Alleghany, but of course *only as something* REPORTED *not definitely known.*"[87]

Weld thought that Birney's announcement "must produce an *immense effect.*"[88] It was the most important of what seemed to be a flock of conversions to abolition, all of which fed Theodore's cosmic optimism. "I am persuaded that no moral enterprize in this country has ever made such progress beyond expectation, prayer and hope as this most glorious millenial enterprize," he rhapsodized to Birney. "Difficulties there will be, and opposition, and misconstruction of motives, and perhaps and probably temporary alienation of friends, and very likely the sea and the waves roaring, but Oh my brother, what will be the peace and righteousness, and joy in the Holy Ghost, which will permeate the whole when these tempestuous elements shall have foamed out their fury and a voice Almighty hushes down the wild tumult and spreads over all the image of heaven."[89]

A few weeks later Weld made more specific predictions of success. "The signs of the times" told him that American slavery would end in twenty years, within five years in Kentucky and Missouri, and that in two years "the free people of Color in all the free States and in some of the *now* slave States [would] be raised to an equality of rights and privileges with the whites."[90] Such sanguine predictions emanated from that mixture of millennial enthusiasm and worship of statistics that permeated the manual labor quest and the revival. He hypothesized that abolition would merely have to maintain "the ratio" of growth it had demonstrated in the prior twelve months in order to fulfill his hopes. His proof:

> *One year ago* there were but three newspapers in the United States which advocated the *immediate* emancipation of the slave and deprecated the doctrines and influence of the Am. Col. Soc. *Now* there are between thirty and thirty-five. A year since *all* the Editors advocating immediate Emancipation, circulated *less* than four thousand papers weekly. *Now* Em. circulates weekly about eight thousand. A year since there were not more than three or four Anti Slavery Societies in the Country. *Now* there are about *two hundred.*[91]

Behind such mathematics and its hopes lay a specific view of social change. Society was a field of operation for the Truth, one in which God's workers merely had to reveal Truth and banish fear to produce the desired results. Men were waiting for the message, hoping for some way to realize their inner moral goodness. For instance, Weld saw hidden "scores of clergymen in slaveholding states who are *really with us* and wait only for some one to *give the lead* and they will *rally to his standard.*"[92] Birney's slaveholding background made him the perfect standardbearer. "I have not a doubt," Theodore assured him, "that you will be able to accomplish more *far* more for the termination of the system of slavery and elevation of the free colored race than any other man in the Union." God had given Birney "the longest and strongest lever" to remove that sinful system which was "the great obstacle in the way of the millenium."[93]

Even as Weld welcomed Birney to abolitionism, however, the citizens of Cincinnati were beginning to show their displeasure with antislavery activities at Lane and with the entry of Lane students into the black quarter of town. The confrontation that resulted became a major turning point in the history of abolition in America.

VI

Lane Seminary II

Sometime in 1834 an anonymous Cincinnatian excoriated Lane's antislavery advocates by defining a new term, "Weldites," for *Buck's Theological Dictionary*:[1]

> This is the name of a most deluded sect, the leader of which was a fanatic by name Theodore D. Weld, who under the *show* of great discernment, unequalled powers of mind, and more than apostolic self-denial, was at heart, a most proud, arrogant, self-conceited, disorganizing man. . . . In the year 1834, by the aid of a few men of some note in the religious world, he excited a great tumult on the subject of abolishing slavery at once, amalgamating blacks and whites, overturning the order and peace of the country, for sake of giving liberty and equality to a set of men who were incapable of self-government. From one grade of folly or madness, he proceeded with rapid strides to another, until at length he was held to be a fit subject for a prison or madhouse. . . . The 19th century, has not before witnessed so strange a compound of folly, madness, vanity, ambition, self-complacency, and total contempt of law and public sentiment.[2]

One wonders at first what all the fuss was about. The efforts of these seminarians in the black community hardly threatened slavery or even the caste system in Cincinnati. The students never broke a law and specifically excluded illegal acts from their program; at no time did social disorder become a reality.

By the same token one might wonder why, after the Lane trustees limited political activity by passing regulations that seemed to the community to be no more than normal and proper, most students chose to leave the school rather than continue their studies under such rules. In leaving they upset their own career plans and gutted an institution they believed to be in the vanguard of millennial mission. What did each side find so threatening, so intolerable? What was at stake for the community at large and for the students? The answers to these questions are complex; they involve not only race and slavery but conflicts over the structure and moral bases of society. As in the revival, men fought over the nature and relative importance of Truth and Order and, ultimately, the meaning of freedom: How much freedom, for whom, and to what end?

Lane's troubles did not occur in a vacuum. From the first distribution of *The Liberator* in 1831, pockets of abolitionist sentiment had begun to develop. Boston and New York were centers of activity, but all across New England and western New York, in Pennsylvania and Ohio, converts warmed to Garrison's message. Punctuating this early period of growth were threats of violence and actual attacks by antiabolitionists. In October 1833 a crowd attempted to break up the inaugural meeting of the New York Anti-Slavery Society. In May 1834 a celebration of antislavery week set off a month of mob threats and in the end led to riots, one of which culminated in the razing of Lewis Tappan's home. The fall of 1834 saw citizens of Canterbury, Connecticut, physically dismantle Prudence Crandall's school for black girls. By 1835 William Lloyd Garrison himself had weathered an attempted lynching in the streets of Boston.[3]

Curiously, while violence greeted antislavery efforts in more Northern climes, the Lane controversy ran its course on the very border of thraldom without blood, burnings, or even a jostled body. No special moral can be drawn from this quirk of history; Cincinnati had experienced racial violence before 1834 and soon would be the scene of antiabolitionist mobbings. The very fact, however, that violent words rather than fists and clubs marked the Lane controversy meant that a body of statements and actions, charges and maneuvers would be left from which to elicit the deeper meaning of events.

If there was no direct violence in Cincinnati, threats of violence helped shape the Lane troubles. Just five years earlier, the city had tasted mob action when some of its "lowest canaille[s]" rampaged through "Little Africa," the black district. This so-called Riot of 1829 climaxed a three-year effort by the newly formed Colonization Society to reduce Cincinnati's burgeoning black population, which had grown from 2 percent to 10 percent of the city between 1820 and 1829. One editor feared that whites would be "overwhelmed by an emigration at once wretched in its character and destructive in its consequences." The Colonization Society called for enforcement of Ohio's black laws, which required proof of freedom and registration and which effectively threatened the right of blacks to remain in the city. This campaign of fear, whose ultimate goal was to remove a source of social disorder, had ironically legitimized rioting among unruly whites. It was a bitter lesson for the colonizationists. Having witnessed the danger of unleashing the pent-up anger of whites, they condemned the rioters, backed down on their demands for expulsion, and contented themselves with an uneasy peace.[4] Their contempt for lower-class whites was mixed with a grudging recognition that the sensibilities of these people must be taken into account in the running of community affairs.

The "Weldites," then, represented a peculiar challenge. They not only rejected accepted opinion on slavery and race but mocked the wisdom of the elders by calling colonization a fraud. Moreover, they threatened to stir up social disorders by offending unruly whites and raising aspirations among blacks. In almost every way the Weldites' very existence undermined social custom and order.

Trouble first surfaced when largely accurate rumors were spread that Lane students advocated social equality for blacks and whites and that they were living by their principles. One member of the Abolition Society, too tired to return to Lane after a hard day of teaching, stayed overnight in the city with a black family. Other students courted public infamy by escorting a "colored female" to Lane and returning with her to the city "in like manner."[5] Public reaction was immediate and sharp. On May 16, the *Cincinnati Journal* condemned theological students for overestimating their powers and acting on "nothing but unfledged inexperience." Eli Taylor, the *Journal's* editor and a friend of Weld's from Oneida Institute, recommended that students stick to their books. Those who did not might appear "more self-denying than the apostles," he chided, but they were in fact "novices, half-informed themselves, and of course illy fitted to lead others."[6] As for slavery, Taylor had made his position clear five months earlier. Applauding the work of gradual emancipation societies in Kentucky, he had closed with this caveat: "*There is now at work a kind, steady, and powerful moral influence which, if not interrupted and checked by blind zeal, will soon abolish hereditary slavery.*"[7]

In his assessment of both theological students and the course of the gradual emancipation movement, Taylor suggested a view of the church at odds with Weld's vision. The editor was prepared to follow a long and orderly road to the Millennium; he distrusted and resented as precipitous the pronouncements and actions of Lane's antislavery cadre. A church of peace and order largely subsumed within the values of ongoing society was preferable, in other words, to a false revival of the primitive church. That Taylor intended this construction can be seen in his caricature of the students as "more self-denying than the apostles"; indeed, the author of Weldites mocked Weld's efforts as "under the *show* of great discernment, unequalled powers of mind, and more than apostolic self-denial." In the end, he urged that the community pray for those "young men who are in training for the ministry of reconciliation."[8]

Taylor's reaction was in part just commonsensical, an accurate reflection of the diminished role of the church in the republic. There might also have been, however, a strain of guilt turned outward. What Christian would not feel at least a bit uncomfortable when confronted with young pietists who sought a prophetic role, especially in light of widespread millennial hope? The Weldites may have seemed all too holy, their actions all too fraught with danger, yet there may have been something in men like Taylor that wished to respond positively but could not, and that turned on the source of discomfort with accusations of immaturity or false prophecy.

Taylor's piece was a gentle rap on the knuckles compared to the bludgeoning of James Hall's "Education and Slavery," which appeared in the May 1834 *Western Monthly Magazine*.[9] Hall dealt briefly with the slavery issue, calling Negro bondage a "national misfortune" and recommending the "splendid conception" of colonization as an antidote; he clearly feared immediate emancipation and compared it to a spring thaw that would "inundate the land, and spread devastation and distress over the whole country."[10] Yet Hall, like Taylor, directed most of his argument to the issue of student involvement in volatile public controversy. Hall, too, feared disorder, yet the object of that fear was the implicit disorder of student agitation of the slavery issue rather than actual riot and rebellion in the streets.

That a handful of students could come to personify disorder must be seen in the light of Hall's view of American society. Like many, he had grave misgivings about the implications of Jacksonian democracy; Hall made an almost aesthetic judgment on political noise in America and yearned for pockets of silence. All important were the lines of social structure that separated zones of battle from zones of peace. "Rancor of party" and "injudicious zeal of controversy" too often spilled over "proper barriers" into areas reserved for quiet and reflection.[11] Hall did not deny that this spillage was inevitable in America, nor did he wish to end the experiment in free government. Rather, he was sure that if rancor was a tendency of human nature under a system of freedom, legitimate countermeasures could be taken by insuring "some spot hallowed from the contamination of the malignant passions, where the mind might be imbued with the lessons of truth, and peace, and honor, unalloyed, with prejudice." That spot was school.[12]

One way to reinforce the school as a zone of peace was to emphasize the subordination of student to teacher. Students became objects of social parental benevolence, protected from the strife of Jacksonian America but also expected to submit to the basic values of their elders. Hall wished to make so clear the division between pupil and adult worlds that he refused to present his argument to the students themselves; rather, he chose to address those who "control[led] the institution."[13] Such paternalistic contempt lent an air of ridicule to Hall's tone:

> We have seen boys at school wearing paper caps, flourishing wooden swords, and fancying themselves, for the moment, endued with the prowess of Hector and Achilles—we have seen them declaiming the harangues of Cicero and Demosthenes, until they caught the fire of eloquence, and imagined themselves the orators they mimicked; but this is the first instance, that we have ever known, of a set of young gentlemen at school, dreaming themselves into full-grown patriots, and setting seriously to work, to organize a wide-spread political revolution; to alter the constitution of their country; to upset the internal policy of a dozen independent states; and to elevate a whole race of human beings to the scale of moral dignity.[14]

That violation of implicit boundaries elicited such highly emotive rhetoric should not be surprising. Especially in times of perceived unrest and transition, men well integrated into society's mainstream often make an incredible emotional investment in the protection of class and status lines, not to mention those of race and religion. Crossing these lines is an act of symbolic or real putrefaction of society, and is normally accompanied by the deep emotional reactions often associated with issues of purity and pollution. Hall saw questions of purity and pollution, in fact, at the heart of his argument. He justified writing "Education and Slavery" on grounds that the "purity of our public schools" was a matter of highest importance. "If our other institutions shall be polluted by the schemes of ambition," he argued, "let us keep the *fountains* of public sentiment pure, and not suffer the poison to be poured into the springs at which our children must drink, and our young men imbibe intellectual vigor."[15]

And therein lay the point. If students had acted as pranksters, as children, no issue of structure would have been joined, though more actual disorder might have occurred. Lane's students chose to address the world as men and on men's issues, choosing to be defiant on the most emotionally volatile issue facing the nation. The fountains might be polluted not only by the suggestion that slaves should be free, but also by actions that promoted the notion that students should be treated as men.

But the Weldites were not merely bad boys. They also challenged, as did all abolitionists, the pervasive assumption in Jacksonian culture that "public sentiment" was the measure of all things. Hall made no allowance for a normative framework by which to judge society beyond society's own democratically accepted practice. "Public confidence" and the "public mind" were the arbiters of behavior; retributive justice came not from God, but from the "decided and prompt rebuke of public sentiment."[16] When dealing with the issue of slavery, for instance, Hall's anguish concerned the claims of white society, not of Heaven. Bondage was a "national misfortune," not a sin, and a battle over its abolition might convulse and tear "asunder the whole of the newly-erected political fabric."[17]

He rejected, then, the validity of private Christian judgment when it challenged well-established social customs and stability. The very fact that Weld and his fellows exercised private judgment, that they pontificated upon a slave system "with which the patriots of the revolution dared not to interfere," made Hall furious. No doubt he would have grouped together the same set of adjectives and judgments used by the author of Weldites to describe Theodore: "He was at heart, a most proud, arrogant, self-conceited, disorganizing man . . . , a compound of folly, madness, vanity, ambition, self-complacency, and total contempt of law and public sentiment."[18] Hall and many of those who most bitterly fought Weld and his comrades feared the challenge of private judgment on society and made it a vice before the standards of public sentiment and order.

Soon after "Education and Slavery" appeared in print, Theodore called upon Hall at the *Monthly* office to see if he would modify his stance or correct his mistakes. He refused and charged Weld with purposeful deception and with seeking public notoriety. Theodore reminded him that such accusations were ungentlemanly and unchristian. At this Hall became deeply upset and insisted that Weld leave his office. Apparently the visceral, almost allergic tone of Hall's article genuinely reflected the depth and quality of his disdain. "Some who know him have told me since that he is exceedingly nervous and hypochondriacal," Weld wrote Birney a few days later, "and that protracted dyspepsia has rendered him greatly irritable. If so great allowances should be made for him."[19]

The appearance of Weld's rebuttal in the *Journal* for May 30 made it clear that Theodore's empathy did not extend beyond that of a fellow dyspeptic. His was a burning retort, one which Eli Taylor agreed to publish only on principle and in friendship and only then when prefaced by an editorial disclaimer.[20] Writing in the form of an open letter, Weld accused Hall of trying to "mislead the public mind," of resorting to "vague, vituperous harangue," of "making coarse appeals to the cruder elements, that reek on the surface, or *thicken at the bottom*," of presenting "false glosses and perversions of fact,"—in short, of stirring up the rancor and disorder that he claimed to abhor.[21]

Weld was disturbed not so much by Hall's brief remarks about slavery, but by those passages that attacked both the manhood of Weld and his fellows and the instrument of that manhood, moral freedom. Herein lay the significance of the Hall-Weld exchange; it highlighted the implicit juncture of Weld's concern for the slave's freedom and his own inner sense of freedom. It was no accident that when Theodore wrote to William Lloyd Garrison early in 1833 he stressed slavery's annulment of "that birth-right charter, which God has bequeathed on every being upon whom he has stamped his own image, by making him a *free moral agent.*"[22] He focused upon this element of slavery rather than its physical cruelty because it was the issue that resonated with his own struggle. For years Weld had worked to realize his own moral freedom, to liberate it from satanic pride, from physical malfunctions that limited effectiveness and clear thought, and from constraints individuals and institutions would place upon it. To the degree that Weld felt stymied he felt enslaved, and Negro slavery became the ultimate outer symbol of his own moral paralysis. In moral freedom lay hope for salvation and for the Millennium, for himself and for the slaves. In its exercise lay manhood.

Hall's attack must have echoed within Theodore past confrontations with authority and restimulated all the emotions attendant to them. His conflict with Ludovicus was archetypical of the tensions he felt in handling more institutionalized forms of patriarchy, whether within the church or at various educational institutions. Theodore never felt very comfortable with any authority but God. The clash of father and son, ranging from the personal to the institutional, was the keynote of Theodore's generation of young pietists. It was a major source of explosiveness in the Finney revival, where converts cursed their elders while church fathers invoked age and wisdom as sure signs of legitimacy. In heightened conflict, the old rallied around the structure that was theirs and the young around the energy of rebellion and faith.

Fortunately for Theodore it was easier to make a case against Hall than against one's father or one's church. He countered the editor's infantilization of the Lane students by noting that thirty of them were over twenty-six years of age; that fourteen were over twenty-eight; that nine were between thirty and thirty-five. Many had already pursued careers, he pointed out, and some had previously attended college: "So much for the babyhood of the theological students."[23] As a corollary, Weld defended the educational value and Christian decorum of the Lane Debates and refuted the implicit charge that the antislavery society was working for a violent upheaval of society.[24]

He saved his most telling remarks to refute Hall's denial of the place of God's moral authority in human actions. It was not that Weld had been left untouched by the Jacksonian faith in common men. His tract on manual labor testified to the contrary. Yet Theodore's romanticizing about the common man depended on his projection of unadulterated Christian feeling and moral sensibility on the simple folk; commonality was not itself evidence of moral right or authority.

In fact, Weld's language displayed an almost Federalist distrust of collective popular judgment. Ridiculing Hall for his argument that a seminary's concern with issues like slavery would decrease its public patronage, Weld asked: "What! are our theological seminaries to be awed into silence upon the great questions of human duty? Are they to be bribed over to the interests of an unholy public sentiment, by promises of patronage or by threats of its withdrawal? Shall they be tutored into passivity, and thrown to float like dead matter in the wake of the popular will, the satellite and the slave of its shifting vagaries?"[25] One is struck by the words "slave" and "vagaries." To be limited by public sentiment meant slavery to vagary. Here again we have a concern with order. If Hall felt threatened by the disorder of vague structural boundaries, Theodore felt enslaved by being trapped within a structure devoid of clear and high moral goals. He was particularly galled by Hall's assumption that apprentice members of the clergy should mold their consciences to the whims of the mass. "The only questions becoming theological students," cried Weld, "are which side of the question is popular: which will be huzza'd and hosanna'd? Which will tickle the multitude, and soak a sop for the Cerberus of popular favor."[26] Here surely was a moral wilderness, one that needed a counterforce, and Weld found his counterforce in the same place Hall did, in the schools and particularly in the seminaries.

Both men, then, found the schools of central importance to society's future, and their curriculum crucial to the maintenance of order. However, to Weld the task at hand was not the reinforcement of social structure, but rather the comprehension of moral dilemmas in society, and it was in this mission that he found the purpose of education. In doing so, he reasserted a major theme of the Finney revival. "Why," he asked, ". . . should not students examine into the subject of slavery? Is it not the business of theological seminaries to educate the *heart*, as well as the head? to mellow the sympathies, and deepen the emotions, as well as to provide the means of knowledge? If *not*, then give Lucifer a professorship. He is a prodigy of intellect, and an encyclopedia of learning."[27] Free speech, free moral agency to act as Christians on great issues—both were inextricably tied to the purpose of education. Only men with broadened intellect and sensibilities could properly order the world.[28]

How did Weld and his comrades find the strength to uphold his concept of education when clearly most of American society either didn't care or actively opposed them, and when they had little material power within the existing social order? Part of the explanation lies in the fact that they defined themselves as men in rebellion against the moral weakness or vagary of their fathers, or of society and its institutions. Earthly rewards meant little to them within the context of sociey as it was. But the negative component was not enough. From the time of the revival onward, men like Weld had ordered their lives increasingly around one idea that admitted of no compromise and that could not be altered by human authority. That is, they believed in the Millennium, to be made by men and made quickly, as the widest and most profound expression of the inncr freedom they sought. When all else was going badly, they could place their faith in eventual triumph as prophesied in the Bible and as heralded by signs of the times. One needed only to keep working at it.

The contrast between Weld's millennial activism and Hall's concern for institutional structure is highlighted in their differing uses of the body analogy. Hall envisioned society as basically a healthy organism to be protected from pollution. Its health was reflected by stasis. Weld, in arguing for discussion of controversial issues, saw society as sick. In this case referring to the duty of ministers, he spoke of the young clergyman as a doctor:

"If he would bless the church *now,* he must *know her now;* where she is, and what her moral latitude [is]—must scrutinize her condition—inspect her symptoms—ascertain the mode of previous treatment, and compare it with the prescriptions contained in God's book of directions, where the case is described. He must inquire diligently how obstructions are to be removed, the circulation quickened, the solids braced, the humors thrown off, and the sources of vitality replenished."[29] By God's book of directions the student needed to find out not what would preserve society's status quo, but rather what would "quicken the church, turn the nations from their idols, pioneer into being the glories of the millenium, and cause earth to bloom with the hues of heaven."[30]

That Weld believed in the ultimate triumph of his cause did not mean that he remained unaffected by opposition. In fact, the split between fear and confidence produced an excited prose style that sought to reconcile cause with risk, and risk with the surety of triumph. On the one hand, Hall's sentiments were a threat to all liberty: "Is research to be hoodwinked, and debate struck dumb, and scrutiny embargoed, and freedom of speech measured by the gag-law, and vision darkened, and sympathy made contraband, and vigilance drugged into slumber, and conscience death-struck in the act of resurrection, and moral combination against damning wrong to be forestalled by invocations of popular fury?"[31] On the other hand, the future of abolitionism was assured since it was the "cause of God."[32] God was with the Weldites, and with that knowledge they could dismiss the "council of worldly policy, time-serving expediency, suggestions of personal safety, popularity, ease, or earthly honor."[33] Doubters had mistaken "the cause, the age, and the men." Weld predicted that that would be made clear within five years.[34]

His letter, a cacophony of fear and faith, reached its resolution in a final, defiant flourish:

> What! think to put down discussion in eighteen hundred thirty-four! and that, too, by the dictum of self-clothed authority! Go, stop the stars in the courses, and puff out the sun with an infant's

breath. . . . Slavery, with its robbery of body and soul from birth to death, its exactions of toil unrecompensed, its sunderings of kindred, its frantic orgies of lust, its intellect levelled with the dust, its baptisms of blood, and its legacy of damning horrors to the eternity of the spirit—Slavery, in this land of liberty, and light, and revivals of millenial glory—its days are numbered and well-nigh finished. . . . The nation is shaking off its slumbers to sleep no more.[35]

It is a gripping passage, an angry assertion of manhood in the face of shackles. The indictment of slavery echoed in fury Weld's portrayal of the threat to free discussion—it was fury directed against the dual slaveries of black and student. Thus Theodore forged a bond of victimhood between abolitionist and slave that joined their fates. In this total sense did the issue of student action on slavery become a phenomenon far outreaching one of mere political or strategic interest. At stake were the souls of slaves, the manhood of abolitionists, and the coming of the millennial day. Where was there room for compromise?

If Hall thought student action a question upon which turned the survival of society and Weld saw it as a crucial element in the millennial struggle, there were those who concentrated on its effects on Lane Seminary proper. The trustees and faculty were confronted with both community and student fears and, since they had decision-making authority, pressure narrowed upon them. It was a poignant position.

At first there seemed to be a unity of approach; the administration asked for student caution but stopped short of disciplinary action. In answer to a student invitation to the planned debates, for instance, the faculty declared themselves in favor of "thorough investigation, free inquiry, and animated discussion," yet as guardians of the seminary and the students, they asked that discussion be postponed because of "excited feeling in our country." Discussion might cause divisions among the students and give Lane a reputation calculated to "repel the accession of the western students to the seminary." There was also the question of financial support. "[Lane Seminary] is in its infancy," they argued, "and has a character yet to form, confidences to earn, and funds for its complete endowment to collect; its patrons, past and to come, are deeply committed on both sides of this question." The faculty thus sought private and informal discussion of the race and slave issues, rather than public debate.[36]

Philosophically akin to Hall's argument, the faculty position nonetheless attempted to make some reasonable accommodation with student wishes and closed with a statement indicative of the fact that the faculty felt uncomfortable limiting the inquiries of its pupils. "We are confident that the movement of public sentiment, on this subject," the faculty assured them, "under the influences of causes which the Abolition Society did not originate, will not much accelerate, and, we hope, will not hinder, is fast approaching a crisis, which may render discussion in the seminary now injurious, either superfluous or safe."[37] They did not oppose such debates in principle, in other words, but only because the climate of feelings rendered them impolitic in terms of the survival of the seminary. The students politely ignored these sentiments and when they sent a note expressing their wish to hold the discussions, the faculty replied that it would not stand in their way.[38]

After the debates and with the spread of race-mixing rumors, community pressure demanded that the school control its students. The faculty assembled the Weldites and asked if they might not carry on their educational program for blacks without putting "the doctrine of intercourse into practical effect," as public reaction to such efforts might injure the seminary.[39] Members of the faculty specifically requested Theodore to use his influence to prevent boarding and other forms of mixing "which would offend the community and injure the seminary," but Weld replied that he could not. First, he pointed out that boarding with black families was indispensable to gaining their trust and confidence. Second, Theodore advised that "any reference to color, in social intercourse, was an odious and sinful prejudice," and that in order to erase such sin one had to refrain from practicing it, even if that were in advance of public sentiment.[40]

For many of the faculty and trustees, such requests were a matter of short-term expediency—to save the seminary was the simple goal. For Lyman Beecher the situation was more complicated. He greatly admired the students and none more than Weld, but fear tempered admiration, fear that zeal would undo the promise of their talents. Beecher counted on that talent to help win the millennial day, but his goals and strategies were different from those of the seminarians. Three great principles ordered Beecher's vision. First, he viewed the organized, visible church and its satellites as the key to God's victory, before whose interests theoretical claims of individual conscience remained subordinate. Second, he stressed the need for internal unity among Christians and acceptance in the democratic, secular community. Third, and as important as the other two, was Beecher's innate sense that only he could be the final arbiter of strategy—that he knew best.[41]

As applied to antislavery, Beecher's principles dictated a slow and diplomatic course. Indeed, Beecher had argued the point some years before with William Lloyd Garrison. "Well, then," Garrison insisted, according to the story, "in accordance with your doctrine of immediate repentance is it not the duty of this nation to repent immediately of the sin of slavery and emancipate the slaves?" "Oh, Garrison, you can't reason that way!" retorted Beecher. "Great economic and political questions can't be solved so simply. You must take into account what is expedient as well as what is right."[42]

At Lane, Beecher's task was not quite so simple as telling off an adamant abolitionist. He wanted both public support and the loyalty of his students. He walked a tightrope. Thus, when Weld came to Beecher with his letter to Hall, the President "had no fault to find with it."[43] At the same time he attempted to advise Weld on tactics, sometimes crassly. "When they founded colored schools," he remembered, "I conversed with Weld repeatedly, and pointed out these things [the effects of public opposition]. Said I, you are taking just the course to defeat your own object, and prevent yourself from doing good. If you want to teach colored schools, I can fill your pockets with money; but if you will visit in colored families, and walk with them in the streets, you will be overwhelmed."[44]

In public Beecher's aim was to soothe both sides of the controversy and argue that there existed no real cause for controversy or ill will. Most notable in this regard were his remarks before the Cincinnati Colonization Society delivered on June 4.[45] He began by defending Lane Seminary against some of the more extreme charges leveled against it, then turned to a broader analysis of the slavery question.[46] He asserted that slavery would vanish from America by the close of the nineteenth century and that abolitionists and colonizationists would be instrumental in its demise.[47]

The signs of the times that predicted ultimate victory thus taught Beecher a different lesson from the one gleaned by Weld. With the demise of slavery assured, he saw no point in making it a bone of contention among professing Christians. The complexity of the issue, he argued, eliminated the possibility that either side had an altogether workable solution; the proper stance was to eschew controversy and get on with the job in mutual respect. Abolitionist attacks on colonization were not only unfair and beside the point—they could be downright destructive. Beecher placed such antagonism in a historical framework, implicitly comparing it to the "vexations" Luther and other reformers faced from minds imbued with "indiscreet zeal"; to the dishonorable tarring and feathering indulged in by "patriot tory hunters" during and after the American Revolution; and to extremes perpetrated during religious revivals.[48]

Besides, Beecher argued, no conflict existed between the Colonization Society, whose main work rested in Africa, and societies committed to abolition, whose work centered upon uplift and emancipation in America. However, he made it clear that compared to the "providential" work to be done in Africa, "all the good accomplished in this country [was] merely incidental, and as a drop of the bucket in the ocean."[49] Though Beecher admitted that the condition of free blacks and slaves deserved attention, he did not want the problem to be taken on in a spirit of contention. What Hall feared for society as a whole Beecher feared for the Christian community. Abolitionist-Colonizationist controversy might

> separate very friends, now harmonious in the great enterprises of the day, and send discord and dismay through the sacramental host. . . . There would be great danger, that the collision would degenerate into party spirit, depreciating each other's success, and amplifying and rejoicing in each other's mistakes . . . and bring a deep reproach, over which angels must weep, upon our common Christianity. . . . It would be an anomaly in the history of our benevolent institutions; a root of bitterness, unknown in our churches before; a baleful comet athwart our heavens, shaking pestilence and war from its fiery train.[50]

This, of course, was a misreading of church history. Controversy was hardly an anomaly, as Beecher well knew from his clash with Finney in the mid-1820s. Yet the dream of Christian unity acted as catalyst and excuse to transform the moral problem raised by the black presence in America to a projected, externalized solution in Africa. There was, of course, a certain grandness in choosing an African mission, encompassing the geography and population of an entire continent, instead of limiting oneself to a few million blacks in the United States. Nor did this prevent Beecher from admitting the past sins of colonizationists or their lack of sympathy for the egalitarian notions of the Lane students. He admitted colonization advocates had "spoken in terms of unadvised depreciation of the free people of color."[51] Yet even these sentiments he turned into ammunition for the emigration cause. Beecher argued that American society would not allow blacks to develop themselves as human beings; given this pessimistic assumption, what more realistic alternative was there but colonization in Africa or in the far West of America: "We trust our colored brethren will take more comprehensive views in respect to their nation than those which would compel them to rise against the greatest possible obstacles, to a doubtful mediocrity, while the great body of the people continue literally servants, though nominally free!"[52]

This is an argument that has had adherents then and since, among both blacks and whites. Yet one can sense why colonization, even in as enlightened a form as Beecher's, never ignited the moral sensibilities of many Americans. Colonization preached quiet removal rather than real confrontation with sin. Unlike abolition, it never offered a challenge to the heart, never beckoned men to repent, never offered the intensity of the conversion experience. Beecher could end his address: "If I forget thee, O Africa, let my right hand forget her cunning. If I do not plead thy cause, let my tongue cleave to the roof of my mouth."[53] Who could disagree? But who could identify his own life with such a mission, or feel that his own sense of freedom and well-being depended upon it. Those who could often became African missionaries. But those like the Weldites who stayed at home saw colonization as a hypocritical evasion of the real issue. To them it was one more example of the church's compromise with sin in the name of social order, one more denial of the millennial necessity to act on the basis of inner purification and a changed heart. "I have heard with pain of Dr. Beecher's Colonization proceedings, and can only regard the fact as one of those hallucinations to which the greatest minds are sometimes liable," wrote Charles Stuart to Weld. "He seems either to overlook the whole history of Colonization, or to have abandoned his christianity entirely and to have put on the very spirit of the world in contemplating it."[54]

Beecher's strategy of avoiding the issues of race and slavery, his reluctance to recognize legitimate issues between parties, had its counterpart in his basic approach to the Lane crisis itself. *"If we and* our friends do not amplify the evil by too much alarm, impatience, and attempt at regulation," he wrote later in June, "the evil will subside and pass away."[55] Accordingly, at the close of spring term Beecher left for the East, there to stir up sentiment against the Pope and to promote support for Lane; he hoped that summer vacation would provide a time for healing reflection. This was wishful thinking.[56]

Beecher's plea for peace and Christian unity on the issue of slavery, with its implications for student compromise, had little effect. On June 16, a committee of the abolition society responded to the faculty request for limiting social intercourse with blacks with a firm no. Treating blacks as social equals was demanded by reason, by religion, by the very example of Jesus Christ; in all that had been done, the committee could "see nothing which duty to God, and love to man, did not require."[57]

Meanwhile Theodore and Huntington Lyman stayed in Cincinnati during the summer to direct abolitionist operations. They found "a little retreat within the hum of the city but so high and airy and withal so embosomed in shade as to make it one of the most pleasant spots of the earth."[58] From this Edenic garret they watched the forces of antiabolition gather like storm-clouds, kept in touch with far-flung Weldites, and continued the struggle. In early July the Abolition Society raised one hundred dollars to publish one thousand copies of Birney's letter on colonization for distribution by vacationing Lane students.[59] Those not personally distributed were posted. So it was that informants of the trustees, according to Lyman, detected "twenty grim Abolitionists . . . practicing their rites in the B[oard] Hall . . . , their sleeves rolled up surrounded by the paraphernalia of paper paste and preparing for the mail some thousands of Birney's incendiary letter!!"[60] In addition, various Weldites had fanned out in Ohio to awaken interest in abolition and to begin new black schools.[61]

Opposition was stiffening, however. Horace Bushnell, an ex-Oneida man and preacher at a nearby church, was attacked by a Lane trustee for advocating "niggerism" and berated "as a liar a scoundrel an agitator a traitor to Christ and his country."[62] Weld feared that antiabolitionists were tampering with the mails, since letters from Birney in Kentucky often took longer to get to Cincinnati than those from New York.[63] And when Birney requested a salary from the Tappans, Weld explained to him that there might be a delay since "(*inter nos*) the most untiring and systematic efforts are made by the *million* to cramp the leading abolitionists in their *business engagements*. This can be done you know *out of sight*."[64] Already Lewis Tappan had detailed the New York antiaboltion riot to Weld and had pleaded, "If we fall here at our posts don't desert the Anti Slavery cause."[65] Even

Birney was pessimistic; he wrote to Weld in despair that his own children thought abolition to be "chimerical and visionary." He wondered how long he could stay in Kentucky. More generally, Birney brooded on the possibility of converting slaveholders. "If I mistake not, the slaveholders South of Ky. will have to be as it were constrained to *give up*," he wrote. "An enlightened public opinion in the Free states must as it were *compel* them."[66]

Yet there was a counterspirit of fraternity and faith working in abolitionist ranks. "Our hearts are wonderfully knit together," Elizur Wright reported from New York. "And there is a determination henceforth to stick to our holy principles and our glorious leader more closely than ever."[67] Weld, adding his message to a letter from Huntington Lyman to James A. Thome, stated simply, "The Lord is our refuge and our strength." It was no mere platitude. "I believe and realize the truth of the sentiment," Lyman added. "No man can be conversant with the biblical denunciations of God's wrath against wrong and oppression, and then look at the great feeling now existing and extending in this country upon the subject without being persuaded that God will never let this work go back till all Israel has come up out of Egypt."[68]

Lyman voiced these sentiments on August 17, less than a week before the trustees finally cracked down on student activities. Since the student statement of June 16, public clamor had increased and ominous letters threatening withdrawal of monetary contributions began to appear.[69] On July 23, Professor Thomas Biggs, an implacable foe of student abolitionism, complained to F. Y. Vail that Lane had become "a reproach and a loathing in the land."[70] On August 10, in response to a joint letter from Beecher and Vail counseling patience, Biggs reiterated his view. "Unless my optics entirely deceive me," he wrote, "I see now in the Seminary the elements of its own destruction."[71] Biggs called for "decisive measures" before the next term commenced. Lane must settle the question: "Who shall govern? Students? or faculty in concurrence with trustees?"[72]

On August 20, the Executive Committee of the Trustees recommended that all student societies except those dealing directly with education be banned; that students obtain prior approval before making public announcements at meals; and that faculty and trustees exercise discretionary power to expel offenders. They warned that continued political activity in the seminary would only "pour into the controversies of Community a heated torrent of unextinguishable rancor." Nor did they ignore the effects on the students themselves. Party spirit mixed with education produced "a constitutional disease of the mind, extremely difficult of cure." Three days later the Executive Committee recommended dismissal of Professor John Morgan, the Weldites' only real ally on the faculty.[73] All proposals were printed in the *Gazette* of August 30 to mollify public opinion, though they would not be official until approved by the full Board.[74]

The Executive Committee's actions angered Beecher, who was still in the East. He wrote to ask for modifications and time, but his letter did not arrive until after publication of the resolutions.[75] He was even angrier at the students for creating the situation upon which the trustees acted. While at the Tappans' store in New York, he complained to Lewis Tappan of the students' flouting of public opinion on race, and insisted that there would have been no problem and no resolutions had there been no defiance in the first place. Tappan remained unconvinced and wrote to Weld of Beecher's tirade. "He then spoke of you," Tappan related, "—that they had wished that you would have been a semi-member of the faculty—but you would go on in your own way—would carry out your own system—could not be touched with a ten foot pole etc." Beecher was obviously agitated. He promised Tappan that all would be straightened out when he and Vail returned to Cincinnati. Tappan left Beecher with a parting blast: "If you, doctor, were a thorough Anti-Slavery man, how easy it w[ould] be for you and Mr. Weld to go on harmoniously." Beecher replied that he *was* an abolitionist, that he "wished to have the colored people raised here, only he would not say they *shall* be elevated here." Tappan closed to Weld with a warning: "Let me counsel you to be wise as serpents and harmless as doves—to do what we all shall vindicate and approve—that there be no falling out among true hearted abolitionists."[76]

Tappan should have expected no less. Even before the full Board voted on the measure, plans had been made to meet that eventuality. By early September it seemed a certainty that the theological class, almost to a man, would seek dismissal if the resolutions passed in October.[77] By October 4, Huntington Lyman could write to Thome that passage was a certainty and relate to him a plan for an alternative school. Lyman did not mail this letter immediately, and added a description of the actual process of passage some days later:

> Truly madness rules the hour. The laws are at this moment in process of passing in full. At the opening of the convention it was proposed to pass the laws without discussion for said one "we have come here with our minds made up and we will never alter them. . . . They have already enacted that either the *ExCom* or the faculty shall have the right to expel any student!! without assigning any reason!!?!

"Who that has an opinion and a soul will enter L. Seminary now?" Lyman asked. "Who *can* do it—without degrading himself?"[78]

All this occurred in Beecher's absence, but his presence would not have altered matters. He could not face the fact that, like it or not, there would be a showdown. By staying in the East he may have been attempting to avoid personal involvement in the crisis or hoping that his absence would delay matters until cooler heads prevailed, but all that really happened was that he lost whatever control he had of the situation and ended up having to choose sides. His choice was inevitable. Though on October 8 he wrote to Weld that the Lane students were "a set of glorious fellows, whom I would not at a venture exchange for any others," nine days later he signed his name to a statement that made certain their dismissal.[79] In a "Declaration of the Faculty of Lane Seminary," he joined with Biggs and Calvin Stowe, another moderate, in fully endorsing the new laws as proper. An accompanying statement expressed the faculty's dismay and sense of betrayal and singled out "an influential member of the Abolition Society," no doubt Weld; they accused him of acting "with the express design of making the institution subservient to the cause of abolition." They could not deny his talents, but lamented a "want of early guidance and subordination." "We regard it as an eminent instance of monomania," the declaration went on, "which not unfrequently is the result of the concentration of a powerful intellect and burning zeal upon any one momentous subject to the exclusion of others."[80]

"The Russian Auto-crat might say to his subjects, You are the freest people on earth," wrote John Morgan to his ex-students on October 30, "for I can grant you all the privileges you want and am disposed to do it. This is the sum total of the exposition of the Faculty."[81]

Disappointed in their elders' lack of commitment to free speech and antislavery, Lane's students decided to leave. *A Statement of the Reasons which Induced the Students of Lane Seminary to Dissolve Their Connection with That Institution,* published anonymously but written by Weld, demonstrated the students' own anger and disenchantment. They had come to Lane to lead a millennial struggle, they said, and to follow "a course of holy living and self-denying action, as our successors might with safety imitate."[82]

Their first principle had been *"that free discussion, with correspondent effort, is a DUTY, of course a RIGHT."* This led Lane students to mission, temperance, Sunday school, and moral reform work. In the same spirit they broached the question of slavery. When "free discussion and correspondent action" were prohibited by regulation, they seceded. "Sustaining relations to the church of Christ now rendered somewhat peculiar," the *Statement* continued, "duty to His cause demands from us an explicit statement of the grounds of our secession."[83]

Weld and his fellows believed the school to be the institutional embodiment of the search for immutable truth rather than just another strut to support ongoing society. Since the single object for learning truth was to know how to act, they had to act on what truth dictated. Such a duty to truth and action existed for all men and could not be altered upon entering a seminary. For a theological seminary such as Lane to deny this inalienable right and duty was sacrilege. "If institutions cannot stand upon this broad footing, let them fall," Weld exclaimed. "Better, infinitely better, that the mob demolish every building or the incendiary wrap them in flames; and the young men be sent home to ask their fathers 'what is truth'—to question nature's million voices—her forests and her hoary mountains 'what is truth?' than that our theological seminaries should become Bastilles, our theological students, thinkers by *permission,* and the right of free discussion tamed down into a soulless thing of gracious, condescending sufferance."[84]

It was up to the faculty to inform their students of this right of inquiry and action, and to direct the search for truth. That such a search might be dangerous Weld readily conceded— "Heaven was abused by devils and Paradise was prostituted by Adam"—but inhibiting free discussion on these grounds was "*ruin,* not *remedy.*" As for Lane, "the point of utter difference" between students and faculty revolved around the fact that trustees and professors used public opinion as a standard by which to judge moral duty or abuse of freedom. This was what endangered every moral cause. At any point "a perverted public sentiment" could command: " 'Hitherto shalt thou come and no farther.' "[85]

If there were some ages in which men could afford to be stopped in their search for truth, the millennial promise and devilish opposition made free speech in 1834 indispensable:

Is this a time to destroy our society, when truth is fallen in the streets, and judgment turned away backward? When the pulpit is overawed, the press panders to power, conscience surrenders to expediency, discussion to proscription, and law to anarchy? When the heart of the slave is breaking with the anguish of hope deferred, and our free colored brethren are persecuted even unto strange cities?[86]

The answer was clear:

> No! God forbid that we should abandon a cause that strikes its
> roots so deep into the soil of human interests, and human rights,
> and throws its branches upward and abroad, so high and wide
> into the sunlight of human hopes, and human well-being.[87]

The slave's cause was the student's; for both, the object was
freedom. As slaves were not to be treated as things, students
were not to be treated as children. Weld concluded the *Statement* with a challenge to those at Lane. "Finally, we would re-
spectfully remind the trustees," he wrote, "that men, though as
students of a theological seminary, should be treated as men."[88]
In leaving Lane Seminary, Theodore and his comrades reaffirmed
a manhood that could not thrive within its walls.

VII

Abolitionist Orator

Theodore resolved one major question when he left Lane Seminary. Since early youth he had ostensibly been following a path to the ministry. No matter what the detours—a breakdown at Andover, the mnemonics tour, conversion by Finney, revival and temperance work, and finally the manual labor agency—he had returned to seminary. Yet upon leaving Lane, he gave up school and a career within the church forever. Instead he chose the life of an antislavery orator. Others among the Lane rebels, his closest comrades, had decided to continue their educations. They first set up a school of their own in Cumminsville, Ohio, and later flocked to Oberlin when Finney himself became head of its theological department.[1] In June 1834, however, Weld made his own commitments clear in a letter declining a professorship at Oberlin. "The Providence of God has for some time made it plain to me," he wrote, "that the Abolition of Slavery and the elevation of the free colored race have intrinsic demands upon me superior to every other cause."[2]

Theodore accepted an antislavery agency for Ohio and by late fall was in action. Hearing of Weld's decision, James G. Birney wrote in his diary, "I give him one year to abolitionize Ohio."[3] Lewis Tappan made the same prediction.[4] In the year and eight months that followed, Weld would become an antislavery legend. Theodore began his campaign at Ripley, an Ohio River town across the water from Kentucky. There he lectured eleven times and formed an antislavery society with little fuss.[5] He then moved on to West Union, "one of the most hopeless places for anti-slavery effort," where he thought he had done some good.[6] For the balance of December, he canvassed Hillsborough and Greenfield, and in January penetrated the Ross County towns of Concord and Frankfort.[7] In February and March, Weld concentrated on the Circleville and Bloomingsberg areas. In April he led the planning of the Ohio State Antislavery Society's first meeting, which took place at Putnam on April 22–24.[8] After this convention he continued his tour, moving south to Marietta and on to Pittsburgh, Pennsylvania, for the Presbyterian Church's General Assembly, then back to Ohio and into the Western Reserve—to Cleveland, Ravenna, Elyria, and Oberlin. Late in the year Weld moved back into Pennsylvania; by then the American Antislavery Society had persuaded him to break new ground in New York State.[9]

In preaching the antislavery cause Theodore followed a routine reminiscent of his prior agencies and illustrative of his ambivalence about authority. As in the past, he chose to work in the West, far from what in his mind were those oppressive centers of authority, the cities of the East. Some years earlier, he had assured Lewis Tappan that God had marked out for him a "diocese" in "the highways and hedges of the West."[10] He dressed simply, in what he termed a "John the Baptist attire," emphasizing again his direct responsibility to God rather than to some earthly church or organization.[11] Normally Weld stayed with a local minister or other sympathetic townsman, sought a hall or church, and then lectured on antislavery anywhere from six to twenty-five times.[12] He then left town, expecting that local supporters would build upon the interest in abolition he had sparked.

To be sure, Theodore corresponded regularly with the leaders of the antislavery society in New York. He recognized their authority and they valued him as an advisor on policy and as a leader in his own right. Yet Tappan could say truthfully that "a man like Weld thinks the center of the world is where he acts."[13] The roots of such an attitude lay partially in the compelling nature of the cause and in the deep religious commitment Theodore felt. But one also must consider the way in which the apostolic, itinerant style allowed Weld to deal with his fear of authority and social institutions. It gave him firm control over his own life, and enabled him to choose the ground upon which to engage or challenge others. He traveled alone much of the time, when little could press in upon his freedom except for the vicissitudes of public transit. Even when he entered a town to speak on abolition, it was as a visitor, untouched by local webs of duty and authority. He exposed himself to criticism and censure on the chosen ground of antislavery, where his talent usually meant eventual success.

Opposition varied from town to town. Sometimes, as at West Union, Weld's enemies displayed no more than "a good deal of squirming and some noise and blustering threats, etc."[14] Other towns, like Circleville, were not quite so hospitable. Mobs pelted him with stones through the open windows; one missile struck Weld on the head and stunned him for a few minutes. In typically heroic fashion, however, he finished the lecture.[15] Theodore remembered another incident when a mob tramped four abreast into the courtroom where he was speaking and pushed his audience out into the night. The meeting reconvened at a schoolhouse, but the mob soon returned, this time bringing sleigh bells, tin pans, tin trumpets, and a dog. As Weld commenced, horns tooted, pans rattled, bells rang, and one man pulled the dog's ears to make it bark.[16]

Despite the mobs, Weld was optimistic. In February 1836, after almost a year and a half of lecturing, he predicted to Tappan that within five years half a million slaves would be free, one million and a half within the decade.[17] Such a view necessitated an extraordinary reading of abolitionist power and public reactions. In all, the world view and strategy of Weld and his comrades require close examination, for they were beliefs that allowed these men and women to struggle against seemingly impossible odds.

Theirs was first of all a religious vision, one based upon the evangelical notion of converting the world to bring on the Millennium. Weld, in fact, described his antislavery efforts in terms reminiscent of a classic revival meeting. First he met "coldness, suspicion, opposition, and threats of personal violence and *thin* attendance."[18] Gradually, interest and "anxious inquiry" increased. Finally, victory came—conversions, contributions, and perhaps a local antislavery society.[19] "In each place the opposition has been strong, in two instances rising to absolute ferocity," Weld reported in February 1835, "but the Lord enabled me to move deliberately onward until the truth triumphed gloriously."[20] A year later he reported the same pattern of triumph from Utica, New York: "I lectured for the eleventh time in the Bleecker Street Church tonight—great crowd. The Lord is with us—truth *tells*. Mob dead, buried, and rotten."[21]

But why were there mobs in the first place? Violent opposition meant only that "the probe [had] touched the quick," that the doctrine of slavery as sin had barbed the conscience of complicitous Northerners and had aroused the forces of Satan.[22] "The Devil will not give up his hold with[out] a death struggle," Weld wrote to Birney. "It must come sooner or later, and the sooner it begins the sooner it will be over."[23] Thus antislavery's enemies became specimens of that resistance to conversion that Weld and others had felt within themselves in that penultimate hour before conversion; they became signs of impending success rather than of failure.

A troubling fact not lost on contemporaries was that the abolitionists staged their holy drama in the slaveless North rather than in the South. "The great objection you know in Free States is this," Weld lamented to Birney, "—it will never do good to discuss slavery here. Why don't you go to *slave* states."[24] One answer was simply that by and large the Southern states would not allow antislavery agitation.[25] But that still left the question of what good agitation did in the North, and here Weld had an answer. It centered around the power of public sentiment, the very force against which Weld fought so diligently at Lane. In this case he meant aroused and just public sentiment. Writing to Birney, Theodore asked for confirmation of a statement from a Southern minister moved North, who set forth "the conviction which he always entertained while in a slave state and since coming to a free state—that is that the public sentiment of the Free states could if embodied speedily do away *slavery*."[26]

Public sentiment, of course, was as amorphous as it was powerful, and so an important aspect of abolitionist strategy lay in the location of the wellsprings of public opinion and an attack on these sources in each town or city. Largely because of the religious background of the abolitionists and their millennial expectations, the church and its ministry came to be viewed as the "hinges of the community," and voluntary associations (in this case antislavery societies) as "centres of light, and means of future access to people."[27] One enemy within the church posed far more of a threat to the cause than a multitude of the unchurched. Implicit in this concern with self-cleansing was the faith that with purity would come a resurgence of power for Christianity within the community and an ever-quickening move toward the establishment of a Christian republic as a harbinger of the Millennium.[28]

Such an understanding of abolitionist strategy makes clear on a practical level the importance that abolitionists placed on discrediting the American Colonization Society. As long as colonization remained the favored stance of established religion on slavery, public sentiment would continue to be poisoned at the wellspring. Colonization had to be neutralized before abolitionism could flow unimpeded into public consciousness. Weld summed up his position and that of abolitionists in general as early as June 1834:

> . . . the *"Colonization Society"* with its *score* of Legislatures, its hundreds of Presbyteries and Synods, its conferences, conventions, associations and *long long* lists of great names—itself I repeat *itself constitutes* public sentiment—*itself keeps in existence*

and renders more and more these very disabilities, outrages and wrongs from which it purposes to relieve the colored man *only by throwing him out of their reach* when it is perfectly in the *power* of society to change public sentiment and thus remove the necessity of colonizing which it has always alleged.[29]

Birney put it even more directly as he attempted to rouse Gerrit Smith from his colonization position: "Truly it does seem to me, that Colonization has done more to rock the conscience of the Slaveholder into Slumber, and to make this slumber soft and peaceful than all other causes united."[30]

It was no wonder that Weld placed so much significance on his work at the General Assembly of the Presbyterian Church in June 1835. In 1834, he noted, only two commissioners of the church leaned toward abolition. After two weeks of his own work at the Assembly in 1835, forty-eight commissioners, including six from slave states, had been converted. He concluded that colonization had become "in the main vitally extinct, except in a few of the cities and larger towns of the free states, where, by a sort of hot-bed process it keeps up a forced existence under artificial stimulation." It displayed, however, "irregular pulses and spasmodic action which indicate speedy dissolution."[31]

Some colonizationists unwittingly corroborated Weld's diagnosis. "It is to me the source of extreme moritification," wrote one colonization agent from Licking County, Ohio, in March 1836, "that there are more than Three Hundred Abolition Publications come to this Post Office, and although this County is only the fourth or fifth County in the great state of Ohio, I do not know that there is another individual in the County who contributes to the A.C.S. or one indeed who takes a single periodical devoted to that object."[32] Other colonizationists brooded over abolitionist gains, but few could admit that their cause had become moribund.[33]

Thus abolition, with its daring commitment to freedom and coexistence with blacks, engendered ardent support in a way colonization never could with its easily supported doctrine of expatriation. Abolitionism did not appeal to many people, but those most attracted to it were young men and women with the explosive, rebellious energy to get things done. Abolitionists tapped the same vein of discontent that sparked earlier and contemporaneous revivals of religion. Indeed, one colonizationist surmised with dismay, "I find that where New Measures flourish there Abolition (and kindred fanaticisms), flourishes."[34] Colonizationists asked men to contribute time or money to solve what they considered an unfortunate moral, political, and economic problem, one open to solution without a basic change of heart on the part of the white man. Such a lukewarm appeal could only inspire a lukewarm response. But abolition asked men, dared men to confront the sins of slavery and racism as their own and demanded a regenerative commitment to the cause. Such an appeal was bound to infuriate most and inspire zealous devotion in a chosen few.

The conversion aspect of commitment to abolition had a direct effect on oratorical style. Weld, reflecting on his own methods, put it perfectly: "If it is not *FELT* in the very *vital tissues of the spirit,* all the reasoning in the world is a feather thrown against the wind."[35] Yet it is not enough to say that Weld was effective because people felt what he said, for it was not only his impressive style but also what he said that mattered. Something about the call for immediate emancipation moved people, something about the times allowed them to feel Weld's particular message. First, abolitionists felt the "signs of the times" pointing toward cosmic upheaval and millennial judgment quite as strongly as colonizationists such as Lyman Beecher and Benjamin Silliman. Colonization attempted to insure social order through existing institutions in the face of godly judgment by purifying the country of a dangerous black population.[36] Abolitionists, intolerant of a social order that tolerated slavery and race prejudice, saw the only solution in a change of heart on the part of white America.[37] In turn, colonizationists charged abolitionists with devilish fanaticism in that the very advocacy of immediate emancipation, whether right or wrong in the abstract, threatened the social order to the extent that it caused social and sectional strife. It was, after all, the time of the Nullification Controversy and Nat Turner's Rebellion, and to the extent that one invested hope for the future in social stability, to that extent one feared abolitionist agitation.[38]

Race war constituted the ultimate fear and horror, one which justified repression in the South and sympathy with that repression in the North. Colonizationists used the fear of race war as a compelling argument for their program of removal. Yet fear of a racial bloodbath also inspired the abolitionists, for to them slave rebellion became the wages of sin, Nat Turner's Rebellion the harbinger of a crueler fate to be meted out to an unrepentant populace.[39]

We do not know how important a theme race war became in Weld's oratory, but one vivid letter has been preserved that may suggest the manner in which Theodore could bring this fear to consciousness.[40] A Mrs. Sturges of Putnam, Ohio, wrote to Weld of a dream she had immediately after attending one of his lectures.[41] Deeply agitated by his words, she returned home, threw herself into a chair, and slipped into deep reverie. She was suddenly transported to a remote part of the universe from where she could view the world at a distance. Her eyes passed over the continents and noted their wonders and evils. Finally she saw America, with its riches and its freedom, where the humblest claimed equal rights with the best. She gazed in admiration and said, "It is my country."

At that moment a mysterious figure tapped her on the shoulder and begged that she look again. At first Mrs. Sturges saw nothing but a happy, industrious people and a land filled with schools, stores, and churches. The stranger then pointed to the South, where she saw few signs of civilization. The white population seemed "thinly scattered and enervated," while

> multitudes of sable figures, bending beneath a scorching sun—their backs lacerated by the whip—scourged, maimed loaded with irons—subject to every insult—and exposed to every gust of unbridled passions—condemned to incessant toil—without remuneration—without motive of any kind to excite their industry, they gleaned a scanty harvest from the luxuriant soil, and impoverished rather than enriched their oppressors. . . .

She wept and remembered that slavery was sanctified by the laws of her beloved country; all the while "groaning mingled with piteous cries of mournful lamentations" filled her ears. And she heard from Heaven: "Vengeance is mine I will repay saith the Lord."

Meanwhile the stranger pointed out the abolitionists, weaponless save their arguments and Bible, who asked only for a hearing before the public. She watched as her countrymen "stormed and raved, and threatened, and vilified the men, who dared to plead in behalf of an oppressed and downtrodden people." She saw Christians joining with the infidel: "It was, as if a viper stung me,—and covering my face with both my hands, and laying my mouth in the dust,—I cried, 'Unclean unclean! O Church of the living God! come out of thine abominations, and wash thy hands of this sin.'"

She then looked toward Heaven and saw that God had removed the chain that restrained men from violence:

> Spreading like wild fire from plantation to plantation; from cane-brake to cane-brake, a mighty army of blacks, goaded to madness by inhuman taskmasters, and unheard of wrongs, . . . arose upon their oppressors . . . the land was . . . deluged with blood, and as the yell of the assassins, and the shrieks of his expiring victims, pierced my ear—my imagination started from her reverie, exclaiming, "Is this fancy or is it fact."

Mrs. Sturges feared the worst. Blacks were increasing in numbers and the West Indian emancipation would cause unrest among slaves in the United States. It came down to a simple choice—whites must either grant blacks freedom or find "a horde of barbarians on our border—sending their troops of bandits, to make predatory incursions on all our villages."

Weld's lecture had clearly evoked a multiplicity of feelings. On one level was the theme of America's millennial promise doomed by inaction on the sin of slavery. Mrs. Sturges asserted the positive values of progress, industry, and nationalism; she visualized an American landscape dotted with schools, churches, and "emporiums of commerce." Yet slavery in the South and indifference to the plight of the black in the North threatened America's progressive march to the millennial day; slavery and prejudice, in fact, promised cataclysmic race war that would leave the country in waste. In this sense, Mrs. Sturges dreamed the dream of a Christian patriot, warning her country of disaster before it was too late.

On another level, she dreamed the dream of a slave. The paean to America seemed tepid alongside her engagement with the miseries of the Negro. Mrs. Sturges may have feared slave rebellion, but it was fear filled with a certain excitement and satisfaction over the villain receiving his just deserts. Indeed, one cannot help but feel that identification with the slave ran deep, that women like Mrs. Sturges allowed themselves to feel the anger and frustration of their own sense of enslavement through the Negro's passion. A violent dream allowed the enactment of personal vengeance in a guise acceptable to a pious Christian woman.

Though Weld's masterful oratory elicited such responses from both sexes, it is understandable why he might wield peculiar power over women. Here was a man, after all, the symbol of authority, of a "masculine, Roman, nature," speaking the language of emotion and liberation.[42] By combining an authoritative bearing and a deep empathy with the problem of unjust authority, he could bring to consciousness and legitimize angry feelings of rebellion. Though apparently the enormous pull some women felt toward Weld never found direct sexual consummation, the language some used to describe his presence left little doubt as to his powerful appeal. Sarah Carpenter, wife of an antislavery editor with whom Weld stayed while in Cleveland, experienced an emotional awakening. "I have slept since you left us, but not in peace. . . . I am moved like the quivering touch of a lacerated limb," she wrote, "the convulsive throb of a crushed bosom, the sinking ebb of life's last tide, and the bursting throe of revivification."[43] She recommended that he speak more to women, that they would "feel when they under[stood]," and that he help them form a women's antislavery society. Three days later, after putting the letter aside, she closed by quoting a French expression to the effect that there was not a man who would not be mortified, if he knew all that a woman thought of him, and then commenced to tell Theodore exactly how she felt:

> I have seen a *form* pass by unearthly in aspect, and, as he moved, the brow of justice softens to a smile, an untouched chord is strung, and, deliverance for the slave, breathes through the symphonies of heaven, the holy vibrations circle us round, our hearts are not dead to the touch—Forgive me this folly—I dread to bid you good bye. . . .[44]

We can be fairly certain that Mrs. Carpenter had no conscious sexual designs on Theodore, and that he did not consciously court explicit sexual response. He would have been horrified and guilt-stricken. Ironically, the clarity of moral boundaries among pious Christians allowed for such freely emotional, if nervous, responses to the opposite sex. Mrs. Carpenter's own language testified to her view of him as a religious more than a sexual being in her life; he was "unearthly in aspect," capable of unloosing the "bursting throe of revivification" that lay at the core of evangelical Protestantism. Besides, men as well as women allowed themselves to surrender under Theodore's spell, and perhaps for some of the same reasons. They may have been men who felt the oppression of distant fathers and unjust authority as well as the strict demands of Christianity, and found through Weld and antislavery a morally sound and socially engaging release. For men as well as women, antislavery functioned not only as a way to right society's wrongs for the greater glory of God, but also as a cause around which, through feeling and action, they could build their own inner sense of freedom.

It is not surprising that a man of Weld's background, who had fought long and hard inside against a perceived paternal and institutional oppression, could communicate the struggle of the slave against absolute domination in a way magnetically attractive to those similarly sensitized. It is also not surprising that Weld's argument against slavery revolved around the central issue of absolute authority, that the problem with slavery was simply that it made men unfree. No matter how seemingly tauto-logical, the point is an important one, since contemporary critics and a number of historians have criticized the abolitionists for overemphasizing and exaggerating the deprivations and physical cruelties endemic to slavery in the South.[45]

The recitation of cruelty stories did play a dramatic role in the antislavery argument. Theodore kept a notebook of facts and anecdotes; he actively sought new material illustrative of slav-ery's barbarity. In October 1834, for instance, he recounted to Birney six separate stories of whippings, burnings, and the sale of children from their mothers.[46] "Mr. Reuben Blakey, Hemico Co. Va had a slave," went one of the accounts, "who frequently used to work for the father of Mr. Poe. One morning he came into the field with his back completely cut up from his head to his heels, and so stiff and sore that he could scarcely move. This same Blakey knocked down and struck out the eye of one of his negro men with a mall. The eyes of several of his negroes were injured by similar violence—some of them nearly put it out."[47] By the same token, to some extent stories of sexual violence may have appealed to the repressed desires of Northern readers; in this case, however, it is quite possible that such stories reflected the fantasized fears of domination rather than the desire to dominate.

In spite of this, it would be a mistake to place such horror stories at the center of the antislavery argument. Weld stated his own point of view on such material, its uses and limitations, in a letter to the New York Young Men's Anti-Slavery Society. "*In-stances of cruelty*," he wrote, could not carry the day because they would be criticized as unbelievable or exceptional and, more important, because "treatment, however bad, [was] but an appendage of slavery."[48] Slavery itself, with or without the lash, destroyed the humanity of the slave and on that point alone it stood condemned: "The inflictions of slavery on mind—its pros-tration of conscience—its reduction of accountability to a chattel —its destruction of personality—its death-stab into the soul of the slave—should constitute the main prominence before the public mind."[49]

For Weld, at least, material illustrative of abuse helped create an emotional dimension to what could have been a dry study of human nature. In this sense he followed the highest of evangelical traditions in an attempt to fuse head and heart. "I have aimed to produce an abiding, inwrought, thoroughly intelligent feeling, based on principle," Theodore wrote, "and acting out with the energy and high intensity of passion, but with none of its irregularity and impulsiveness."[50] But the focus always remained on what Weld believed to be irrefutable laws of human behavior: "That men are indifferent to the *interests* of others in proportion as they disesteem and despise the *persons* . . . that the greatest abuses of power are when men exercise it over their own species . . . these and a variety of other principles in human nature, and facts in human history, constitute a mass of testimony utterly unimpeachable, and establish the position far more satisfactorily to thinking minds, than millions of instances of cruelty."[51]

An extant account of one of Weld's antislavery addresses illustrates the point.[52] Not whippings, not cruelty, but the "longings of the slave for liberty" was his focus.[53] He recounted his visit to the house of a kindly master in Alabama, where even the well-treated house servants wished to be free.[54] He then read a poem written, or rather dictated, by a North Carolina slave. By way of preface, Weld observed that the slave had "said nothing of positive inflictions as the cause of his wretchedness, nothing but that he was treated with the utmost kindness." The poem began:

> Come, melting pity, from afar,
> And break this vast enormous bar
> Between an wretch and thee;
> Purchase a few short days of time,
> And bid a vassal soar sublime,
> On wings of Liberty.[55]

He saved one of his most successful stories for the finale.[56] A boat carrying the wives and children of some planters was sinking offshore near St. Kitts and Nevis. The husbands and fathers, gathering helplessly on the beach, appealed to and then whipped their slaves in an attempt to get them to man rescue boats, without success. Then came the dramatic moment:

> At last one of the planters mounted a stump, and swinging his hat, cried out, *"Liberty! Liberty!"* At the sound of that word, every slave started. He then proclaimed liberty for life to every slave who would man the boats.[57]

Three boats were quickly launched. Two of them soon sank, but the third effected the rescue. Weld drew his lesson. "When called upon to encounter the awful peril, they were perfectly dead to every other motive," he said; "—neither flattery, threatening, bribes nor the lash moved them. But the sound of that word, Liberty, struck a cord, which vibrated to the very centre of their souls, and wrought them up to desperation in a moment."[58]

Nor did Weld rely only on incidents from slavery to illustrate the issue of freedom. Threats to abolitionists and attempts to deny them freedom of speech brought home the issue of liberty even to those not immediately drawn to the slave.[59] Early, Theodore noticed that heavy opposition could do more for the cause than anything he said. "I have encountered two mobs both of which mobbed *up* the cause," he reported from the Western Reserve in September 1835, "vastly more than I could have *lectured it up*."[60] At Painesville, Ohio, when trustees of the town attempted to stop him, Theodore pointed out to his audience that seven men wished to stop a meeting that two hundred had chosen to attend. At the next meeting General Paine, grandson of the founder of Painesville, burst in to demand that the lecture cease. According to Huntington Lyman, Weld responded with his own demand:

> The issue is fairly made. I must not lecture any more and you must not come to hear me. Friends when I came here I came to lecture among a FREE PEOPLE. I assumed that I was speaking to the FREE *people* of Painesville. Is the assumption made by the Gentleman who has intruded himself upon our meeting warranted by facts as they exist here? is that, my friends, your master? Ladies are you the wives of slaves!? This question goes immediately into chancery.[61]

Weld then asked the townspeople to come back the next day as a "No" vote to General Paine's lordship over them. The usual number did return, and soon after fifty men and women pledged themselves to form an antislavery society. Fifty more joined after Weld left.[62]

The abolitionists, however, could not claim complete dominion over the civil liberties issue. Many of their opponents, sensitive as Jacksonians were to the power of vested interests, saw antislavery activists as dangerous agents of an Eastern cabal of church and money interests. Calvin Colton, one of the harshest critics of moral reform, argued that abolitionism represented the most radical wing of a quasi-Jesuitical force in American Protestantism that hoped, he argued, to reinstate the power of the disestablished churches.[63] Weld himself engendered bitter opposition on this count. In the Western Reserve of Ohio, the *Elyria Republican* and the anticlerical *Ohio Watchman* led the attack; the *Watchman* urged its readers to ignore Weld as the best way to combat the "scheme of the clergy, to raise a party in our country, with themselves at its head, thus to increase their importance and power, regardless of the influence of their mad course on the people of the slaveholding states, and the Union."[64] It was also the era of the bank controversy, and, with logic that must have seemed fantastic to Theodore, the *Watchman* accounted for the lack of opposition to Weld by connecting him with the banking interests: "This *Theodore Dwight* Weld was but the echo of the Dwights of New York, by whom a majority of the stock of both banks in Cleveland was held, and by whose influence they were controlled. That no man that was beholden to either of the banks for accommodations, dare speak against the abolition project."[65] For the *Watchman* this power to "apply the screws to the purses of the people, and wring a submission to their unhallowed desires" explained, if it did not justify, the use of mob violence: "Although we cannot approve, we do not wonder at the frequent resort to what is termed Lynches Law."[66]

Yet citizens of Elyria thronged to hear Weld, and the *Republican* stood mortified that "instead of shunning him as a viper," men and women chose to "pass away a dull hour or gratify a morbid curiosity" by attending the lectures.[67] Unable to argue that the banking interests had forced anyone to hear Weld, the editor conjured up images of the results of antislavery agitation highly reminiscent in spirit to Mrs. Sturges's dream: "Why, what would be said by a congregation sitting upon a powder magazine, should a mad man approach, torch in hand, to ignite the mine which could scatter them in atoms to the four winds of heaven?"[68] Thus antislavery men, who imitated primitive Christians, became in the eyes of the opposition "desperadoes" and "incendiaries."[69]

Even if one were sympathetic to the plight of the slave, how one viewed the abolitionists—as saints or criminals, prophets or dangerous if well-meaning fools—depended in large part on one's ability to deal with fears of race war and sectional conflict through an act of faith. For the abolitionists that act of faith was embedded in their central argument and strategy: "Insist principally on the SIN OF SLAVERY, because our main hope is in the consciences of men, and it requires little logic to prove that it is always safe to do right. To question this, is to impeach the superintending Providence of God."[70] They recognized, however, the nagging fears of race war in themselves and others and the consequent need to prove beyond mere faith the safety of emancipation. Weld made this point to Birney in 1834, sending him "Clarkson's Thoughts" to aid the new abolitionist in arguing the point of safety.[71] Emancipation in the West Indies provided the abolitionists with further evidence of the possibility of a peaceful transition.[72]

The problem of safety highlighted a general dilemma of strategy facing antislavery forces: the question of proffering a detailed plan for freedom. The American Antislavery Society decided to avoid such discussion as best it could and concentrate on slavery as a sin. "Do not allow yourself to be drawn away from the main object," advised the society to its agents, "to exhibit a detailed PLAN of abolition."[73] Arguments about the merits of a particular plan might lead listeners away from confronting the central issue of sin. As for the legal state of would-be freed slaves, the society stated simply:

> The people of color ought at once to be emancipated and recognized as citizens, and their rights secured as such, equal in all respects to others, according to the cardinal principle laid down in the American Declaration of Independence. Of course we have nothing to do with any *equal* laws which the states may make, to prevent or punish vagrancy, idleness, and crime, either in whites or blacks.[74]

Yet even on this basic point abolitionists differed to some degree. "I further stated that we did not claim for the slave the right of voting, immediately, or eligibility to office," James Thome wrote to Weld in 1836 concerning one of his speeches. "Also that we did not wish them *turned loose,* having the possession of unlicensed liberty; nor even to be governed by the same *code* of Laws which are *adapted* to intelligent citizens. That on the contrary we believed that it would be necessary to form a *special code* of Laws restricting them in their freedom, upon the same general principles that apply to foreigners, minors, etc."[75] Lydia Maria Child wrote in much the same spirit in *The Oasis,* an early antislavery compendium that served as one of the key sources for the first generation of antislavery orators and propagandists. "No judicious person would wish to see the right of suffrage bestowed upon the emancipated slaves," she assured her audience, "while they were in a state of ignorance and degradation; and all would acknowledge the wisdom of strict police regulations to prevent idleness and crime."[76]

We can only speculate on Weld's feelings concerning the freedman's status. Thome did not ask him to accept his views, which may have indicated that Theodore at least tolerated them. But Weld's propensities to deny the distinctions of class and his yearning to destroy whatever distinctions men erected, as well as his willingness to act on these beliefs, no doubt made him gravitate closer to the absolute stand of the society. He might have winced at Child's claim that abolitionists had "not the slightest wish to do violence to the distinctions of society, by forcing the rude and illiterate into the presence of the learned and refined."[77] Nor did he bear the burden of Thome's aristocratic upbringing and a Southerner's heightened fear of revenge. Whatever tensions Weld may have felt on this count were quite well compensated for by his romantically pietistic attachment to and imitation of the Christian common man.

Attitudes toward class distinction, in any case, only predisposed men and women one way or the other toward a much more troubling issue, that of their own attitude toward blacks themselves. The inevitable uneasiness with which nearly all white Americans of the age viewed blacks undercut and perhaps, ironically, necessitated the leap of faith that allowed advocacy of immediate emancipation. Abolitionists could, through assigning blacks a forgiving role if whites owned up to their sins, deal with the guilt-ridden fear of whites toward blacks. But what of the well-inculcated revulsions ingrained in whites against blacks, what of the beliefs in black inferiority? To some extent, focusing on the inner-directed question of slavery's sin obviated the necessity of dealing with one's own feelings about the object of antislavery benevolence. Yet racial attitudes were so strongly imbued in most Americans' minds that even the strongest advocates of immediate emancipation sometimes faltered in relating to blacks as human beings and as equals.[78]

In Weld's own circle questions and antagonism sometimes arose over this issue. Charles Stuart, the man who had first opened Theodore's eyes to antislavery, asked him his opinion of the "general intelligence (not learning) of the slaves," as well as the "general consciousness of Liberty being their natural right."[79] In the same year Phebe Mathews, a woman with whom Weld had worked in Cincinnati, complained about the conduct of some of her comrades. "I said to Br. Wattles the other evening I shall be glad when Mr. Mahan, Mrs. Gridley, Misses Dewey, Fletcher, etc., etc. are gone," she wrote to Theodore, "for none of them are more than half-hearted abolitionists and I cannot endure to be shackled as they wish me to be." "I love these sisters," she explained, "but they do wish us to stoop so often to prejudice, to shake hands and say how do you do to it. And they feel so bad if perchance we lay our hands on a curly head, or kiss a coloured face. It distresses me to be in the society of the coloured people with them."[80]

We do not know how Weld responded to Phebe Mathews and Charles Stuart, but he probably expressed a high opinion of the slave's intelligence and consciousness and warm empathy for Miss Mathews's anger. Theodore acted upon the principle of racial equality as part of his scrupulously monitored pietistic contract with God. Among other things, this meant that in Cincinnati and later in New York City he elected to live and worship among blacks. Whatever fears and prejudices he may have had were suppressed by this passion to do right.[81]

However one wishes to explain Weld's plunge into black community life, the experience itself gave him a certain sanity about race that appears to have eluded other abolitionists. He came to balance his initial view of blacks as objects of benevolence and noble carriers of natural religious feeling with a more intimate appreciation of them as human beings with day-to-day concerns. This sensitivity came out most strikingly in an exchange with Lewis Tappan over the participation of blacks at the first meeting in Putnam. Tappan accused him of excluding blacks from the meeting. An infuriated Weld defended himself first by reasserting his belief in the principle that " 'persons are to be treated according to their intrinsic worth *irrespective of Color, shape, condition* or what not,' " neatly adding that he acted on the additional principle: "Take *more pains* to treat with attention, courtesy, and cordiality a colored person than a white, from the *fact* that he *is* colored."[82]

As for the convention, Weld's account indicated both his own common sense and the extremely trying situations antislavery agitation sometimes produced for blacks. Before the meeting, Weld had invited blacks from all over the state. When he arrived in Zanesville he found that the town had been closed against him; Weld moved across the river to Putnam to make preliminary lectures before the convention, but was mobbed.

Worse still, the opposition directed its vengeance against the local black population. "Large numbers of poor Colored people were turned out of employ," Weld explained to Tappan, "men were prosecuted under the vandal laws of Ohio for employing them, and the four hundred Colored people in Zanesville and Putnam were greatly oppressed in continued apprehension and panic."[83] Black leaders then decided among themselves to stay away from the antislavery proceedings entirely since, as Theodore explained: "1. If *they* attended, it would keep away that very class of persons which they wished to go—the *prejudiced* ones. 2. If they attended, it would expose them not only to insult and outrage while there, but it would be seized as ground for the pretence of mobbing them, tearing down their houses, etc."[84] The one black to attend the remaining preliminary lectures was assaulted on his way home, and the only black to attend the convention agreed not to stay after being apprised of the local situation.[85]

Theodore also recalled his Lane years in arguing common sense on racial equality to Tappan. He would not have walked arm-in-arm with a black woman down Main Street in Cincinnati, for instance, not out of fear or prejudice, but simply because it would have brought down "a storm of vengeance upon the defenceless people of Color."[86] Such *"blustering bravado defiance"* also might have obscured the main point, that being the righting of social, political, and economic wrongs to the black community.[87] Theodore capped his argument by asserting that every black person with whom he had talked about the matter agreed with him "in toto."[88]

The exchange between Weld and Tappan highlighted an interesting though often ignored element of antislavery—the relationship between abolitionists and free blacks. Not only were there great variations in personal attitudes, but also in ideas about policy.[89] Many abolitionists seemed content to berate the South without making a serious effort to better conditions for blacks at home. However, to Theodore the elevation of free blacks in the North was an essential part of the antislavery cause.

In February 1836, he listed for Tappan the advantages of such work beyond the good it did the blacks themselves. It would convince slaveholders that abolitionists were truly benevolent, and not motivated by "politics, sectional feeling, *party*ism, filthy lucre or any other filthy thing."[90] Elevated blacks in the North would also display, by contrast, the costs of slavery to white and black, and "ought easily be such as to burn slavery out by the roots."[91] "It would show both to South and North that blacks are *men*," he continued, "and in every respect equal to whites. At least ⅗ths of the northerners *now* believe the blacks are an *inferior* race."[92]

Weld also argued that abolitionists themselves would benefit from such a campaign. Aiding blacks in their own cities and villages would enliven them—"Thus Abolitionism will be living abolitionism, all its fluids kept in brisk circulation." In addition, abolitionists might refute the central charge of colonizationists that the black population could not be elevated within the United States. Finally, abolitionist activity among Northern blacks would act as a trumpet call to self-help.[93]

Toward these ends Theodore suggested that the Antislavery Society launch a far-reaching uplift campaign. Gathering pertinent information on the condition of Northern blacks, deciding on locations for new schools, encouraging public sentiment for school integration, cheering the black community, and searching for talented young blacks to be sent to schools such as Oneida and Oberlin—these were the first tasks of a new effort. Weld suggested that Augustus Wattles, his comrade from Lane and one of the most talented workers in Cincinnati, head the project.[94]

Controversy over race and the elevation of Northern blacks, while important, should not obscure what remained an essentially optimistic view of the cause and general sense of unity among abolitionists in the years 1835–36.[95] Local societies grew in numbers and flourished; public interest ran high; antislavery newspapers and pamphlets flooded the North. Not for another two years did differences among abolitionists explode into schismatic rancor.[96]

Theodore shared the optimism and good feelings, at least into the first half of 1836. Yet for a pietist such as Weld the demands of an organization posed problems, and even a most benevolent one, the American Antislavery Society, was no exception. There always existed a tension—sometimes imperceptible, sometimes annoying, and other times exasperating—between Theodore Weld the Christian working out his personal salvation and Weld the antislavery society agent. Weld the humble pietist, for instance, almost vainly concerned with pride, balked at the publication of accounts of his heroic exploits. In the spring of 1835 Elizur Wright published Weld's private letter-account of his lectures at Circleville. Theodore agonized over the fact that publicizing his victory over the mob smacked of "egotism" and "vanity."[97] Wright responded by stressing the needs of the cause against Weld's personal concerns. "To square accounts about the Circleville letter," he began, "let me say, you *must* send us *something* to *publish*. Remember we are asking of the abolition public *money*. They say to us, what are you doing with money? We print a little. Very well, so far; is that all? Suppose now our agents write us not a word but under the seal of secrecy; what shall we answer?" Wright then posed the key question: "Has an agent a right to be more 'egotistical' to one of us than to the public?"[98] Yet to Theodore one did have more of a right to describe God's victories to brethren who would understand them as such than to parade publicly successes under the name Theodore Dwight Weld.

Such qualms were symptomatic of a more general standoffish relationship to the antislavery organizational structure, for even in this holiest of causes Theodore kept his habitual distance from human authority. Garrison might be ensconced in the offices of the *Liberator;* Wright and Tappan in the organizational thicket of New York; but Weld was his own man, on the stump, free to send praise or barbs and receive the same by mail, but relatively untouched by the day-to-day demands of others. Weld preferred the physically peripheral role.

Despite the distance and tension, optimism and success allowed Weld to coexist with the antislavery East. But by 1836, as some signs of the times pointed to trouble as well as accomplishment, Theodore began to define his own role against the abolitionist establishment, producing both a pietist's critique of the movement and an ever more explicit statement of his own persona. A major shift in Weld's mood came with the great fire in New York in December 1835, which wiped out much of downtown Manhattan, including the Tappan brothers' store and warehouse.[99] "The terrors of God!" he exclaimed to Tappan upon hearing the news. "The faintest gleam of them smites men with trembling or maddens with frenzy. Oh then whose heart can endure, whose hands be strong when the breath of God set the Universe on fire and a million worlds burn down at once! My brother I cant resist the conviction that this terrible rebuke is but a single herald sent in advance to announce the coming of a host."[100] Only repentance and work to free the slave, to feed the hungry, and to save souls could rescue the nation from an awful fate.

Theodore meant it when he said "work" and made a model of his own relentless efforts. He took Tappan to task for inviting him to the Antislavery Anniversary meeting in the spring of 1836, condemning such gatherings as wasteful pomp. "It seems so like ostentatious display," he wrote, "a mere make believe and mouthing, a sham and show off." He feared that antislavery agents would get used to "*gadding*, attending anniversaries, sailing round in Cleopatras barge" and might forget that "the great desideratum in our Cause is *work, work*, boneing down to it."[101] After the anniversary, Weld again insisted that the "only thing needed now is *work* by *piece meal*—taking up the country—and turning up the sod acre by acre."[102]

Nor was this Theodore's only complaint. He chided Tappan for the society's inaction concerning Northern blacks, arguing that abolitionists thereby played into the hands of colonizationist doctrines that slaves could not be elevated in America. "Our theory is right on this subject but what has been *done*," he asked. "Ans. Great cry and little wool."[103] Weld also pointed out that he was the only agent for New York State, though New England's smaller population was tended by a multitude of anti-slavery activists.[104]

Weld's charges were for the most part unanswerable. One could always do more; one could always demand more. Elizur Wright, ever trying to reason with him on such matters, defended the anniversaries. Wright argued that at these meetings "leading minds catch the spirit of our cause" and that if he came, Weld might inspire "a thousand little scruples, and objections, and sophisms, and fears, and *prudences*, [to] fly off in vapor."[105] In addition, he thought Theodore could be of great help in mapping out strategies for the coming year. They needed his wisdom.[106]

Wright's was certainly a reasonable response to Weld's objections to the anniversary, but it could not deal with one important element of his position. Along with Weld's call for work came a self-definition in imagery that separated him from the people, places, and culture of the East where the anniversaries were held. "I am a Backwoodsman—can grub up stumps and roll logs and burn brush heaps and break green sward," he stated flatly to Lewis Tappan. "Let me keep about my *own* business and stay in my *own* place."[107] A few days before, Weld had harped more playfully on the same theme, praising himself with a faint damn. Anne Warren Weston had invited Theodore to address the Boston Female Anti-Slavery Society and to labor in the area for a few months.[108] He refused the offer, stating that his commitment to New York State would not allow the trip. He claimed that he was a *"Backwoodsman untamed*—my bearish proportions have never been licked into *City Shape*—and are quite too uncombed and shaggy for 'Boston notions.'" Eschewing the "Artificialities of *City Life*," he only felt comfortable in the back country: "A *stump* is my throne my parish my home—My element the *everydayisms* of plain common life."[109] And when in June the society requested him to appear before the Rhode Island Legislature, he added to the self-caricature: "I was made to stand [?] about among the yeomanry. . . . As to the taste . . . aristocracy and *double* refined upper crustery of the land—I never *did* more than a *hair*—It isn't in me—my *rough and tumbleism repels* them."[110]

During 1835 and early 1836 Weld found little reason to question this bold and narrow conception of himself. Success had followed success in Ohio and upstate New York. In February 1836, Theodore had brought between six and seven hundred new members into the Utica Antislavery Society. Twelve hundred persons, mostly men of voting age, had signed antislavery petitions after the Utica lectures. In March he had moved on to Rochester, in this case recruiting more than eight hundred new members to the local society.[111] What further proof did Weld need that he was among his own, that he understood Westerners and that God was on his side? It seemed as if he had found his niche: "Whoever knows me knows that I am a Lecturer on Abolition. It is my *trade*."[112]

All this sufficed when things turned out well, when converts were made and good triumphed over evil. But at Troy in May and June, Theodore met his match. Expecting not much more than the usual opposition, Weld encountered "an entire upcarting from the bottom."[113] Crowds forced the trustees of N. S. S. Beman's old church to cancel the lecture series even as Weld and Beman stood in the pulpit waiting to begin. Ousted from the church, they were followed by a hostile mob, one which ringed Weld's lodgings until late in the evening.[114]

Meanwhile Elizur Wright and Simeon Jocelyn had requested Theodore to speak before the Rhode Island Legislature.[115] Ten days later, on May 29, the Rhode Island Antislavery Society urged him to quit Troy for Providence, indicating that strong forces in the legislature were out to "*convict us of attempting to excite the slaves to INSURRECTION*."[116] Though he had qualms about being the right man—Henry B. Stanton, agent for Rhode Island, seemed a more logical choice—Theodore indicated that he would come if events in Troy came to a successful resolution.[117] By June 11, however, the situation worsened to the point that Weld felt he could not give up the fight. The Mayor of

Troy encouraged the mob and at least one city officer was among those who attacked the beleaguered abolitionist. Finally Theodore found a new church, but twice his foes rushed up the aisle in attempts to drag him from the pulpit. "Stones, pieces of bricks, eggs, cents, sticks, etc.," he reported, "were thrown at me while speaking."[118] Nor was that all. At every point along the way between the church and his lodgings crowds hurled stones and twice wounded him. Only the protection of friends enabled him to survive. As for the right of free speech: "Suffice it to say the Mayor and Common Council declare that they cannot keep the peace of the City, that they cannot protect the Citizens in the exercise of their Constitutional rights!!" To the Mayor's position Weld retorted publicly that he would advertise lectures till the law was enforced or he himself was killed.[119]

Here was the ultimate test of commitment to his work. He closed his letter declining the Rhode Island invitation with a heroic flourish:

> Let every abolitionist debate the matter once for all, and settle it with himself whether he is an abolitionist from *impulse* or principle—whether he can lie upon the rack—and clasp the faggot—and tread with steady step the scaffold—whether he can stand at the post of duty and having done all and suffered all, stand—and if cloven down, fall and die a martyr "not accepting deliverance." O what revelations of character have already been made by this question, *and yet these are but the shadow of those to come.* . . . Blessed are they who die in the harness and are buried on the field or bleach there.[120]

Not everyone thought the stakes to be so high at Troy. William Lloyd Garrison hoped that Weld could be persuaded to come to Rhode Island and, at least for the moment, give up the fight in Troy. Garrison could not find fault with Theodore's bravery; he admired it. Still he felt that the importance of the Rhode Island engagement was "sufficient excuse" for him to leave and in any case, "What is Troy compared to the nation? and it is a *national* effect at which we must aim before your legislative committee [he was writing to a member of the Rhode

Island society]."[121] At any rate, Garrison thought, the way to achieve victory at Troy was not to continue a losing battle, but rather to disengage temporarily and allow "the leaven of sympathy, of humanity, of truth" to work among the multitude. He admitted his advice might be different if Weld were actually in the clutches of a mob or in prison. "No! in such a case, it would be his duty to go to the gibbet or the stake," Garrison insisted, "rather than to comply with such an impious requisition. But he is neither in the hands of ruffians, nor in prison, nor has any such test been required of his fidelity."[122]

Strategically sound, Garrison's comments did not speak to Weld's inner condition; if Theodore's enemies did not literally have him by the throat, a much deeper sense of inner mission and conviction did. He was putting to the test not only his courage, but his own self-image. These people of Troy were his people, not the aristocrats of the East. He saw the situation in Troy as similar to others in Ohio and upstate New York. If only he fought hard enough and long enough, would not the Lord allow all opposition to be overcome and things to turn out right? Facing the mob was to Weld the essence of abolition, for it was in fact facing the Devil and his forces and defeating them.

But this time there would be no victory, and when the Mayor of Troy finally told Weld to leave or be forcefully transported out of the city, when he finally did leave without a triumph, it was no ordinary defeat. It was an event that helped set in motion a process of reevaluation that touched his most inner self and his relation to antislavery.

VIII

Reevaluation and Departures

However cruelly the defeat at Troy violated Weld's image of self, his reputation in the antislavery community seemed only to grow. More important, strategies he advocated were beginning to find favor with the leadership. Elizur Wright, from his desk in Manhattan, echoed Theodore's oft-repeated nostrum on the importance of rural victories: "Let us take hold of the country— the yeomanry of the *country towns,* leaving the cities to them-. selves for the present, and we shall soon carry the question."[1] The Anti-Slavery Society finally answered Weld's plea for more agents by giving him the authority to reorganize the entire agency system. As Moses had chosen seventy elders with whom to confront the Lord, as Jesus had selected seventy new helpers to aid the twelve apostles, so Weld imagined choosing an anti-slavery "seventy" to fill the land with oratory.[2]

In July 1836, at meetings with Tappan and others, Theodore's mission took shape. He would scour the countryside in search of new agents; he would give only the best orators a place in the "seventy," but he promised to leave no possible talent unexamined. He left Manhattan in late July on a relentless, four-month tour through New York State, Ohio, and New England. To get his men he used all the powers of persuasion at his disposal, including those of the pious bully. He boasted to Anne Warren

Weston that he went after those whom "everybody says 'you can't get,'" and then threatened them with God's judgment unless they accepted an agency.[3]

Theodore's search gave many New England abolitionists a chance to meet the young legend from Ohio and near-martyr at Troy. John Greenleaf Whittier's sister Elizabeth, for instance, had heard all about the "thunderer of the West" and meeting him was no disappointment. "His appearance is just what I anticipated," she wrote at the time, "giving evidence of a God like and expanded soul. . . . He has been haunting me like a glorious vision of benevolence ever since he left us."[4] Anne Warren Weston encountered Weld while she was sick in bed at the home of Dr. Amos Farnsworth, a Boston abolitionist. She heard Farnsworth greet someone, but supposed the visitor to be "some Masonic crony." When the doctor's wife rushed in exclaiming "Theodore Weld has come," Weston bolted down the stairs to meet him. She was so entranced that she totally forgot the pain of the blister that had immobilized her.[5]

By November, Weld had recruited about fifty talented agents to open up new areas or take over the territories of ineffective propagandists who had previously plagued the ranks. He had gathered his "seventy" at an opportune moment, since distribution of pamphlets—the other major strategic thrust in antislavery—had been shown to be not nearly so effective as good oratory. By 1836, printing of pamphlets had dropped from a peak of ninety thousand per month to twenty-eight thousand.[6] These new men, chosen from Weld's own acquaintances and through recommendations, would be doing double duty in troubled times.

The price of Weld's triumph was the loss of a modicum of anonymity. Elizur Wright insisted that he not only assemble a new cast of agents but also bring them together "for the purpose of kindling, warming, 'combustionizing' and in short getting the whole mass to a *welding* heat."[7] Theodore balked, but by November he had agreed to be chairman of an agents' convention.[8]

Thirty to forty of the new recruits attended the meeting, which took place in New York from November 15 to December

2, 1836. Also there were Garrison, Birney, and many of the New York abolitionists, as well as the Grimké sisters of South Carolina, converts to the cause who had begun to make a stir in antislavery circles. A number of people addressed the meeting, but according to Garrison all revolved around Weld.[9] Drawing upon his own experience, he suggested the most effective answers to questions asked routinely by audiences: What was slavery? What about immediate emancipation? Why didn't the abolitionists campaign in the South? What about the threat of vengeful ex-slaves? Would emancipation ruin the South? Didn't the ancient Hebrews hold slaves? Should slaveholders be compensated? Why not support colonization? Simple, powerful answers, he argued, might win independent Northern minds for the cause.[10]

It was an intense time for all. Day after day delegates met from nine to one, from three to five, and finally from seven to nine in the evening. Theodore tested himself to the limit. Despite a severe cold and failing voice, he spoke often and at length, and kept long hours—sometimes until two or three in the morning—preparing material for presentation. By the final day of the convention, Weld, the master orator training those who would follow, could not speak above a whisper.[11]

Ironically for Weld, the very acceptance and adoption of a strategy for which he had so long fought marked an end to his own participation. The agents' convention was his swan song as an orator. After his final whispered phrases at New York, he rarely ascended the speaker's platform for the fifty-seven remaining years of his life. Just as striking was the geographical reorientation that had occurred after 1836. Once the great champion of the West, Weld would never again live beyond an easy commute to New York or Boston. Finally, though the ascendancy of oratory and the agency system represented a victory for revivalist tactics, Weld himself had begun to move away from revival-centered efforts toward an almost completely noninstitutional, body-based personal piety.

Imagine Weld with but a whisper of a voice. His ability to move crowds had been central to Theodore's sense of himself and his calling. But was Weld's severe throat irritation simply a physical condition? The traditional version has it that Weld's near drowning in Alum Creek six years earlier severely impaired his health and eventually caused his voice to fail.[12] Such a theory does not explain why Weld did not lose his normal speaking voice; nor does it take into account that he lived another sixty years in good health. More important, the Alum Creek story ignores the rich psychological possibilities inherent in his loss of voice. One recent account does offer a psychological interpretation: Weld unconsciously brought about his own voice loss because the glories reaped as a charismatic orator conflicted with his pietistic view of life.[13] This explanation is consonant with one theme in Theodore's complex psyche, but others are as plausible. Weld may have lost his voice in protest against God's abandoning him at Troy. At the same time, Weld the orator may have chosen to withdraw physically because, at least in his own mind's eye, Troy had proved his unworthiness. Indeed, all these unconscious scenarios may have been played out at once.

Perhaps the problem can be understood best as one more chapter in a history of Theodore's physical disorders, one that inevitably followed the pattern of great exertion and collapse. In some cases, as in Theodore's contraction of blindness at Andover, the ailment might locate in a single organ; in others, as when he literally exhausted himself while working for Finney, the physical symptoms were more general. In the period 1836–37, Weld not only lost his voice but suffered from depression and debilitating fatigue.

One might ask, then, not why Weld lost his voice, but why he chose to break the cycle of overexertion and collapse at this point in his life. Earlier in his career, he had turned to various remedies—rest, vegetable diet, and manual labor—in order to fit out his body for ever more strenuous tasks in the service of God. As late as the antislavery tour, friends cautioned him about overwork as Weld continued to exhaust himself.[14] What kept him going on this course was an unswerving belief in the cause and in his own more personal self-image as backwoodsman orator of the West. He defined his life and fate within that cause and image. When both began to crumble, a major reevaluation was bound to occur.

At least since the Finney revival, Weld had thoroughly identified himself with the "new world of the West" as opposed to New York City and his native New England. By 1836 he professed not only a Western identity but also profound ignorance of the region in which he had spent the first twenty years of his life. Indeed, one of Theodore's arguments against leaving Troy to testify in Rhode Island was that he was "one who never opened his mouth in Rhode Island, and never *in any part of New England* except to say A.B.C. and other small matters when a child at school there."[15]

The defeat at Troy shattered this romantic self-image. Westerners, after all, had let him down. Weld made no direct attack on the region, but there are indications of rejection and a shift eastward. Soon after Troy, for example, Weld answered his parent's request for information on the town of Manlius, a possible choice for Ludovicus's planned relocation, with a "philippic" his father termed *"rather* too severe."[16] Theodore may have been attacking one specific town, but he also may have been using Manlius to express more general bitterness toward the West. In any case, he had decided to transfer his antislavery efforts to the East. In September 1836, before resolving to give up oratory, Weld indicated that after choosing the "seventy" he would become agent for Connecticut.[17] Thus, in a matter of months after claiming ignorance of New England, he chose to become the agent for his native state, the very seat of Yankeedom.

The inner geography of Weld's life was also shifting, and this shift inevitably concerned his search for consonance between holiness and the visible church. His experiences as an abolitionist strengthened antisectarian attitudes originally fostered by the revival. He recognized that support came from members of many denominations, and that often the most resistant were fellow Presbyterians. At Circleville, for instance, the Presbyterian minister had marked Weld as an insolent rebel and closed the church to him; the Episcopal minister, however, had offered him his church.[18] Later in 1835 Theodore advised Birney against using a Presbyterian newspaper as a forum; he argued that it would cut him off from two-thirds of the Ohio abolitionists who were not Presbyterians.[19] "Those who still adhere and are *most active* in the support of colonization," Weld observed, "generally constitute the aristocracy and fashionable worldliness of the church."[20] Or, as Lewis Tappan recorded in his diary: "Mr. Weld and myself had a good deal of talk on the prospect before us. . . . He thinks there is but little religion in the churches."[21]

In the past, Theodore had been able to feel at one in spirit at least with the Finneyite community, that group of revival adherents who intuitively sensed a common mission. But beginning in late 1835 and continuing through 1836, disturbing signs appeared that the commitment of Finney himself to abolition was equivocal. Lewis Tappan was the first to recognize Finney's uncertainty, and accused the evangelist of cowardice and "sinning against conviction." To such charges Weld offered a spirited defense. "That Finney is a coward I cannot believe," he wrote, "and for this simple reason: I have seen him in more frequent and more striking exhibitions of courage physical and moral than in any other man living." Theodore voiced solidarity with Tappan on the primacy of abolition, but he reminded him that perhaps abolitionists had not worried enough about Finney's main concern, the saving of souls.[22] In any case, Weld proposed a pluralist solution: "God has called *some* prophets, *some apostles,* some *teachers.* All the members of the body of Christ have not the same office. Let Delavan drive Temperance, McDowell moral Reform, Finney Revivals, Tappan antislavery, etc."[23]

Yet Theodore felt uncomfortable enough with this solution to repeat ever more strongly his own position, especially his view that Finney "misconceive[d]" the situation. To Weld the sin of slavery overshadowed all others; it so polluted society that millennial reform must falter until the church forthrightly rejected bondage, "until the Temple [was] cleansed." To the extent that Finney ignored this fact, so he inadvertently allied himself with "the thieves, the man stealers, the whore mongers. . . ."[24]

Weld's defense of Finney seems on its face peculiarly rational. As Weld pointed out, Tappan did have the "habit of coming to unfavorable conclusions about men on *slight grounds*."[25] Yet, as Tappan charged, Weld's argument did smack of "ancient prejudice for brother Finney"; Theodore had trouble facing the fact of his spiritual father's reticence about slavery.[26] At one and the same time, he "grieved" at Finney's refusal to pray for the slave in public and characterized his actions as "thoroughly honest and conscientious."[27] There was something odd in this mixture of disappointment and relativism when the Millennium was at stake.

The abolition issue did finally weaken Weld's tie to Finney, and in doing so it ended the marvelous community of feeling that had existed among Weld and his band of "Illuminati" from Oneida and Lane. While Finney wanted those of the group who continued at Oberlin to become evangelists, Weld wished them to become abolitionist orators.

Finney broached the issue in general terms to Weld in July 1836. He sensed division among revivalist Christians over slavery and feared that unless abolitionists toned down their appeal they would lead America to civil war. Finney then proposed that abolition be made an "appendage of a general revival of religion," just as temperance had been during the prior decade.[28] To this conciliatory proposal he added an attack on abolitionists for their recklessness and denunciatory tone and singled out Henry B. Stanton for displaying the "spirit and the language of a slave driver."[29]

About the same time, Sereno W. Streeter warned Weld: "Mr. Finney is making a strong effort to have us Evangelize instead of abolitionizing."[30] In early August the issue came to a head. In a pained letter, Streeter, William Allan, J. W. Alvord, and James A. Thome—all comrades at Lane—presented their dilemma: "Thus we are situated—You and Stanton groaning on one side and Finney on the other."[31] Allan wrote first. He had no trouble in choosing abolition as his course, but he was deeply troubled by a sense that the group was fragmenting and that Weld, the leader, was too distant. Streeter, his resolve shaken by Finney, admitted that he was "with respect to this subject in mists and clouds." Alvord stood by Finney.[32]

James A. Thome, ever a solid abolitionist, wanted to cry as he read the notes by Streeter and Alvord. "It looks so much like desertion in the hour of darkest trial," he complained, "—desertion from the *van* of the army, and by its *best friends*." He pleaded for advice and hoped that Theodore would not judge too harshly those who had chosen Finney's side. Meanwhile, Streeter added a postscript that must have spoken for all concerned: "Dear Brother you know not how my heart is PAINED at the thought that our little ranks will be broken. May God direct us."[33]

In the aftermath of 1836, the members of the Illuminati retained a variety of connections with each other. Finney's relation to Weld grew more distant. Something had been lost, that naive assumption of spiritual unity that informed both the revival and antislavery movements in general, and clusters of comrades on another, more intimate level. With that loss Theodore experienced one more painful blow to his sense of relation to the world. No wonder that Weld the orator, who once knew his place and mission, might now have doubts about reappearing after temporary illness.

No wonder, too, that roads to personal piety, always attractive to Weld, might appear all the more compelling as other certainties fell by the wayside. Unlike his brother Charles, who became enamored of Perfectionist doctrines, Theodore did not seem very concerned in the 1830s with working out the details of a narrowly theological order.[34] Rather, he intensified his abiding interest in the body to comprehend the world. Grahamism and, to a lesser extent, Phrenology gave to Weld visions of godly order that did not revolve around the actions of some fallible, human churchly institution and that seemed to conform in every detail with his personal experience. Each contributed to the systemization of a "natural theology" of daily piety.[35]

Theodore's interest in Sylvester Graham's system of diet and daily habit was in many ways an expansion of his prior interests in manual labor and temperance. Graham set forth a comprehensive theory of daily life that encompassed many prior, partial reforms and added new ones as well. His regimen formed around a vegetarian diet (which had as one of its staples the famous Graham Cracker), but Graham also included advice to sleep on a hard mattress, to provide better ventilation in rooms, to wear looser-fitting clothing, to exercise, and to moderate one's sexual life.[36] He molded his mixture of commonsense wisdom, scientific research, and Puritan moralism with the sureness of a prophet. "I *feel* that I know the mind of God," he once wrote to Gerrit Smith, and in an evangelical age feeling counted as much as knowing.[37]

Ridiculed by many, Graham and his doctrines nonetheless found ready acceptance among reformers. Weld, Garrison, Finney, Smith, Horace Greeley, and others swore by the system. It appealed to their need for explanation and cure of physical symptoms and for a structured life regimen. Grahamism was different from other systems, however, since in addition to being more comprehensive it was also more central in one's life vision. In the 1820s physiological reform functioned as an adjunct to more purely moral and theological reform. For instance, manual labor would provide a stronger ministry to battle at Armageddon. Issues of piety usually did not revolve around the body. By the 1830s, bodily health had become an end as well as a means, the body a shrine of God to be cared for or desecrated. In advising the Grimké sisters on health, Weld admitted to his own abuse of the body as if it were a heinous crime.

> . . . my own sins in this respect rise up before me in crimsoned crowds and shriek them in the ears of others till they tingle. I have sinned with a high hand and I trust God has granted me *repentance* unto *life* even in this world (for I feel new health every day). And now my daily prayer is touching this matter, "deliver me from *blood guiltiness* oh God, thou God of *my* salvation."[38]

Grahamism put into an everyday routine the means by which Theodore might concentrate on realizing bodily salvation.

Though less essential to his well-being, Theodore also found Phrenology fascinating. Like Grahamism, this popular science of the day lent itself to easy ridicule. Imagine the Phrenologist poring over an unwitting client's skull to measure capacities for thirty-seven traits from Amativeness to Alimentiveness.[39] The usually skeptical Weld found amusing confirmation of the system's accuracy when he finally allowed his head to be read in 1836. His examiner noticed a hollow near the eyebrow and guessed that he was color-blind. Theodore immediately remembered that his mother had stopped sending him for skeins of silk since he never brought the right color. Meanwhile others in the Phrenology parlor noticed that Theodore's pantaloon leggings were different shades of green.[40] Still not entirely convinced, Weld visited one of the famous Fowler brothers for a reading a year later. He disguised himself as a common omnibus driver, but the Phrenologist still attributed extraordinary characteristics to his skull.[41]

Underlying Phrenology's parlor theatrics was a philosophy bound to appeal to those looking for new light on human motivation and an explanation for churchly failures. Orson Squires Fowler's American adaptation of the research of Gall and Spurzheim attempted to make "those connexions and relations which exist between *the conditions and developments of the BRAIN, and the manifestations of the MIND*," discovering each from observation of the other.[42] The phrenologist inspected and measured thirty-seven brain areas, each of which controlled the strength of various personality traits. He then charted a literal personality profile of supposedly scientific objectivity.[43]

As applied to religion, Phrenology shifted the relation of the individual to church, piety, and God. It incorporated a theoretical basis for the already apparent cravings of men like Weld for a life based more on scrutiny of the individual than allegiance to the form of a visible church. Phrenology's American spokesmen based their systems on the values of piety but made the proof-text the human skull. Some in the church shouted heresy, and one could not blame them. Fowler did not hedge on the theological implications of his system. He saw himself responding to the malaise of the age, that "men now hardly know *what to* believe." Phrenology provided the "starting point," the "base line," "fixed and settled *first principles,*" and was therefore "the NATURAL THEOLOGY." "*Modern* Christianity, the religion *of the day,* the *isms,* the Church and creed piety, the *hollow, worldly-minded, money-seeking, animal* Christianity of the *nineteenth century,*" pronounced Fowler, "deserves severe rebuke, and will receive merited castigation." He compared modern Christianity to heathenism, mocked the churches for being Sunday and not weekday institutions, and condemned the entry of fashion into religion: "How long, Oh, how long, ye daughters of Zion, will ye *profane* the sanctuary with your bran [sic] images, your corsets, and your cotton bosoms!"[44]

Behind the bombast was an explanation of the religious state. The faculty of Veneration both proved the existence of God and urged men toward worship. But other faculties interacted with Veneration to produce different doctrines and churches. "One sect, has one set of organs," Fowler analogized, "and looks through glasses of one color, and another sect has on glasses of another color, and both are looking at the same object [God] and quarreling about its *color.*" Fowler endorsed the Quaker principle of "letting every one do up his *own* thinking, provided he but *live* aright." Church organizations, he continued, were doing great mischief, and would soon "be supplanted by *private piety.*"[45]

Private piety. Through Grahamism and Phrenology, Weld and others were able to piece together and find grounding for the personal religious life when all authority but the Bible seemed in question. And this was especially important to Theodore as 1836 turned into 1837, as some of the most important relationships in his life and his own self-image were undergoing significant change, and as these changes found reflection in his deteriorating health. At age thirty-three an era in his life and feelings was ending; at the beginning of 1837, his voice destroyed and his sureties threatened, Theodore could see only the glimmers of a new beginning.

After the December meetings Theodore remained in New York to work on agencies and publications at the Antislavery Office. He chose to live in a small attic room and took meals with some fellow abolitionists in a dark hovel with boards for a table and newspapers pasted over the cracks in its bare walls. To poverty he added his own brand of piety by rising punctually at six and retiring at eleven and providing for regular exercise and a Graham diet.[46] His days were filled with work and companionship at the office; abolition, no longer the source of romantic adventure, at least acted as a daily organizing principle in his life.

New York did not live up to the fantasies of the pious country boy who once had imagined even Christians "whirling in [its] hustle and bustle and chaffering and purchasing, confused and perplexed with the details and statistics of filthy lucre."[47] Most of all it was a lonely place. Theodore enjoyed a reasonable social life, but it touched the mere "barren *suburbs* of the soul." Missing were those electric connections, those "*deep* communings of spirit and answerings of *soul* to *soul*," to which he had been accustomed with the likes of Charles Stuart and the Illuminati.[48] On the surface busily working on this or that problem or text, inside he had become a "hermit here in the midst of throngs."[49] Indeed, he would sometimes hide from those around him.[50]

It was a curious, disturbing time of introspection for Theodore, one of mourning and reevaluation. Occasionally signs of this process appeared, as when Anne Warren Weston requested Weld's appearance at the upcoming Anti-Slavery Convention of American Women. He refused, as usual, but his reason was no longer that his rough-hewn Western style would be out of place or that he could not spare time from oratory. Given his condition in New York, these would have been hollow excuses. Rather, Theodore explained his reluctance as the product of some secret consideration which to others might seem "a mere whim—or at best a puerility to be set down among the instincts of babyhood." Without revealing the nature of this trait, he only volunteered that "instead of leaving it behind among the rattle boxes and—leading strings of the nursery—it has grown into my manhood and holds a life lease of me."[51] He played the same game of mystifying his fears so that he might remain distant; this time the content was more ironic and also perhaps more germane, for he had begun to locate the wellsprings of his personality in the distant past of his own life rather than in his surroundings.

Some of these unresolved inner questions revealed themselves in passing as Weld began to change from orator to writer by setting down the Bible argument against slavery that had served him so well in the field. As early as July 1835, the Antislavery Society had requested a written version of the argument, but not until April 1837 did it find its way into print.[52]

The Bible Against Slavery attempted to counteract the pro-slavery position that since the moral law of the Bible was unchangeable, and since the Bible did not condemn slavery among the ancient Hebrews, it followed that the Bible and Christian religion endorsed slavery in America. Weld argued that Biblical slavery and Southern slavery were not the same thing. The Hebrews, he noted, afforded their slaves far more choice and contractual guarantees in day-to-day life than did slaveholders in America. He built his case around a basic definition of enslavement: "THE REDUCTION OF PERSONS TO THINGS!"[53] Since Weld's argument rested on proof that this totalistic state existed in the South and that textual exegesis showed that this was not the case among the Hebrews, it became almost entirely an essay in translation and semantics.

Most abolitionists applauded the tract. However, one sympathetic critic, the Reverend William C. Wisner, pointed out that Weld had greatly overstated and made absolute the case against interpreting Hebrew slavery as slavery, and in doing so had grossly misunderstood several key Biblical passages.[54] Nor was such an extreme position necessary. The fact that slavery existed among the Hebrews, noted Wisner, could certainly not be used as evidence that God had endorsed that system or that even had He tolerated slavery then, He should or would tolerate Southern slavery.[55]

The ground separating Weld and Wisner may have been sim-

ply that separating a Biblical literalist from one with a more his-
torical-developmental theological view. But Weld's need to ab-
solve Hebrew slavery and to isolate Southern slavery can also
be viewed as a sweeping solution to his own inner conflicts
about authority. Though his rebellion against church and father
clearly helped draw him to antislavery, it is just as clear that
Theodore felt deep guilt about his course. He could compensate
by validating and even idealizing those paternalistic relationships which by nature resembled slavery, thus paying public
homage to ways of life his own rebellion had questioned. Minors
were not to be considered slaves, Weld argued, simply because
they could not vote. Women were not slaves because they could
not hold public office. Apprenticeship, with its limited commitments, could not be considered slavery. Weld was right in the
sense that none of these statuses corresponded with the total reduction of persons to things. But in differentiating these relationships from slavery in its pure form, he avoided facing that
one might better understand them by investigating characteristics they shared with total bondage.[56]

Even more striking are Weld's comments on familial and social obligations. First he defended "Filial Subordination and Parental Claims"; his words provide us with the ideal by which he
judged his own rebellion and give us one clue to the wellsprings
of his guilt:

> [Filial Subordination and Parental Claims] are nature's dictates,
> and intrinsic elements of the social state; the natural affections
> which blend parent and child in one, excite each to discharge
> those offices incidental to the relation, and are a shield for mutual
> protection. The parent's legal claim to the child's services, is a
> slight return for the care and toil of his rearing, exclusively of
> outlays for support and education. This provision is, with a mass
> of mankind, indispensable to the preservation of the family state.
> The child, in helping his parents, helps himself—increases a com-
> mon stock, in which he has a share; while his most faithful ser-
> vices do but acknowledge a debt that money cannot conceal.[57]

As for society in general, he noted that "subjects owe[d] just
governments allegiance and support," since the obligations and

benefits were reciprocal. In addition, Theodore argued, some very important restraints upon freedom were in fact essential aids to the preservation of society. Parents restrained children, teachers restrained pupils, and physicians controlled patients. "Restraints are the web of civilized society," Weld concluded, "warp and woof. Are they slavery? then a government of LAW, is the climax of slavery!"[58] All this came from the pen of Theodore Weld—rebellious son, upstart at Lane Seminary, and abolitionist challenger of one of his society's most deeply entrenched institutions. Restraint and freedom, they were the unreconciled poles of Theodore's inner struggle.

Weld's defense of traditional institutional obligations might not have been so important if others in the movement had taken the same course. But just about the time Theodore was writing *The Bible Against Slavery,* Garrison and other notable abolitionists had begun explicitly to reject government and the church as oppressors and barriers in the road to a Christian life. Rather than isolating Southern slavery, "no government" adherents chose to see it as the paradigm of all coercive tendencies in human society. The issues involved helped define a more general schism in antislavery ranks soon to come.[59] And that split in the ranks would figure importantly not only in Weld's future public life, but in his private one as well.

IX

The Grief of Joy

Long, long I've known the joy of grief,
but now I know the grief of joy, and I sink
before it.

Weld to Angelina Grimké, 1838.

One winter evening in 1837, Theodore enforced upon himself an awkward silence as he walked Angelina Grimké to an antislavery meeting. He had been cajoled into taking her arm, but no one could force him to talk. It was not as if they were strangers. He and the renegade South Carolina abolitionist had met at the agents' convention in December, and had developed a warm friendship amidst the dreary New York winter. Yet always there had been others in their company, usually at least Angelina's sister Sarah. Now they were alone, and Weld felt cramped and anxious. Later he would reveal that for a moment he was driven to admit his love for her. Immediately this impulse was overwhelmed by a sense that he was a "vile groveling selfish wretch" for entertaining passionate feelings for Angelina; besides, he thought, he hardly deserved such a woman. So he maintained a stiff silence and even managed to avoid escorting her home after the meeting. Nonetheless in a little more than a year they were husband and wife.[1]

That Theodore could fall in love and marry hardly conformed to his own prior views and expectations. At age thirty-three, he had never before surrendered his adult self to a woman. Only three years earlier, he had ended a friendship at Lane when he concluded that his comrade's marriage plans would interfere with his political effectiveness.[2] More generally, courtship had always seemed to him too "artificial and facetious," "repellant" to both his principles and "instincts"; in short, "a misshapen compound of sentimentality, abnormality, caprices of mere taste and fancy . . . vapid admirations of the *person* merely . . . the form . . . the complexion . . . the glance . . . the gait and carriage. . . ."[3]

Beneath these sure pronouncements of the pietistic Weld lay a long, guilt-ridden struggle for love and against desire. He had experienced the awesome power and, as we have seen in the events surrounding Cornelia's birth, the dangers of his mother's love. Worshipping the piety of Elizabeth Weld yet distancing himself from her agonized caring, he had established his most affectionate familial relationship with his sister. He was her constant protector during childhood, and in their youth she exhibited toward him a spunky affection quite untinctured by formality. Witness the loving playfulness of thirteen-year-old Cornelia's letter to her already wandering brother:

> I have conversed with you by way of pen ink and paper for some time, and fear shall some time longer, if you don't hasten home. I am quite impatient to see you. I hope you have not forgotten that you have friends in the world, who love and wish to see you. In case you have forgotten I will tell you that in Hampton, Connecticut, you have friends, who still remember and love and long to see you. "I *beg* and *beseech* and *conjure*" you to come home before another month expires. . . .[4]

There even developed something of a holy triangle between Theodore, his sister, and Charles Stuart; Stuart eventually proposed marriage to a hesitant Cornelia, and it took him years to admit that she would never agree.[5] In any case, she alone cut through Weld's airs of pious mission; Cornelia teased him, cajoled him, and loved him as no other woman had, all in the safety of a sisterly relation.

It was, in fact, through a combination of the satisfactions of this sisterly love and the veneration of his mother that Weld filtered his desires. He had relationships with "many precious and noble women," and they all conformed to a simple formula. Whether in the revival, in the antislavery cause, or in simple friendship, he would act as guide and adviser, one who would press home to women the need for piety and social action. Whatever ideas he set off in his advisees, the magnetic young Weld couched his own involvement in the language and action of a brotherly, holy intimacy.

A touching example of such a relationship was revealed by John Morgan, Weld's old teacher at Lane. Theodore had urged Morgan to look up a woman named Kate while he was in Hartford, and Morgan promptly fell under her spell. But all Kate could talk about was her affection for Weld. Morgan learned of the "searching talks" she and Weld had had and the good he had done for her soul. "She loves you so much that it formed a cord of attraction between us," he wrote, "—at least a good theme for chat. . . . She told me you promised to write her, which I hope you will do forthwith, or you are a false friend and a false knight."[6] There is no record that Weld ever did pursue the relation.

Besides thwarting the desires of those who fell in love with him, Theodore's self-enforced sexual distance from women created and fed a vibrant chord of self-hate. He came to think of thoughts other men considered more or less natural as signs of his own sinful nature. His secret life reeked of *"stains* and *shame"* and delighted in images "earthly-sensual and devilish, grovellers in the dust and loving to grovel." But for God's guidance, he would have "rushed to sin headlong" early on.[7]

He had been guided by God to pursue what he considered to be the higher goal of a calling, and to surrender to a woman seemed to him a perilous distraction. Besides, most of all he needed the love and example of a father, and he spent his twenties and early thirties in that quest. "My dearest friends were all among my own sex and most of them much older than myself," Weld recalled, "some of them by twenty-five or thirty years. No female had ever *taken hold* of my soul." So he pursued intimacy with the likes of Erastus Clark, Charles Finney, Lewis Tappan, and, more than any other, Charles Stuart. And he pursued manhood and a sense of self through the rebellious calling of abolitionist oratory.[8]

As long as success greeted him on the antislavery circuit, Weld could continue to allow his mythic quest as an itinerant orator to substitute for more intimate satisfactions. The debacle at Troy, however, unhinged his faith in destiny and as a result made him more appreciative of and more vulnerable to his emotional needs. The first sign of such a change could be seen in July 1836, when Cornelia expressed cheerful shock that Theodore had just given his blessing to the marriage of one of the "sisters" involved in black uplift work in Cincinnati.[9]

The failure at Troy, however, filled him as much with a spirit of self-deprecation as it did with emotional need. "Since my early boyhood disappointment, frustration of plans, crushing of hopes, sudden revolutions in the whole scope of my life and in the violent disruption of cherished aims," he would confess, "have been the course of God's providence toward me." His father and older brothers were men; he was still a wandering boy. Failure had become the "settled habitude" of his inner life. What woman worthy of his attention would find him worthy of hers?[10]

Still in all, Theodore's vulnerability should not be exaggerated. It defined only a new and small possibility, and the woman who could fulfill his definition of worthiness would have to display the moral courage of his male comrades, the piety of his mother, and the waspish but frank affections of Cornelia. However, in Angelina Grimké he had met his match. If we are to believe a lover's memory, Weld's heart had been won years before they had made each other's personal acquaintance. In 1835 he had read a letter in the *Liberator* from a South Carolinian, the daughter of a slaveholder, which denounced slavery and championed abolition as a "cause worth dying for." "Your letter to Wm. Lloyd Garrison formed an era in my feelings," he later wrote, "and a crisis in my history that drew my spirit toward yours by irrepressible affinities. I read it over and over and over, and in the deep consciousness that I should find in the spirit that dictated that letter the searchless power of *congenial communings*—which I had always been pining for and of which I had never found but one (C. Stuart)—I forgot utterly that you were not of my own sex!"[11]

Had Theodore roamed as far south as Charleston, South Carolina on his mnemonics tour; had he by chance run across the young Angelina, outwardly whirling through the dances and house parties of young Charleston society, he might not have found the spirit of "congenial communings" and certainly could not have mistaken her sex. Yet at the core of this "gay, fashionable girl" lay a bright, forceful, but deeply troubled mind.[12] Born in 1805, the youngest of Judge John and Mary Grimké's fourteen children, Angelina seemed endowed with a special strength and sensitivity. Part of her could play the slave-pampered child and gay Charlestonian, but another part felt guilt-ridden and suffocated by the world in which she lived. This anxiety first surfaced in her resistance to Episcopal confirmation and soon after in her heartfelt conversion to Presbyterianism.[13]

It was under the guidance of sister Sarah, thirteen years her senior and so compelling a figure that Angelina called her "mother," that her religious yearnings and doubts found direction. Angelina followed Sarah to Philadelphia, and under her tutelage embraced Quakerism. For a while, she was at peace. But unlike Sarah, whose dour and bitter personality found a home in Quaker garb, Angelina had a bright and assertive streak in her nature that proved too explosive for quietism. As her soul began to comprehend the horror of slavery from the immediacy of childhood memory and the distance of Philadelphia, that powerful woman who could charm a Charleston gala now hoped to turned her countrymen against slavery.[14]

Sometime in 1836 Angelina's heart, too, was drawn to a letter in the *Liberator*, this one by Theodore, or so she later claimed.

Sarah M. Grimké (*The Bettman Archive, Inc.*)

Angelina E. Grimké (*The Bettmann Archive, Inc.*)

It was not until the agents' convention that they met. Theodore fell in love. Angelina revealed her interest to Jane Smith, an intimate in Philadelphia. Never had she heard such eloquence as Weld's, never "so grand and beautiful an exposition of the dignity and nobility of men." Upon seeing him for the first time, she wrote, there was "nothing remarkable to me in his appearance and I wondered whether he really was as great as I had heard, but as soon as his countenance became animated by speaking I found it was one which portrayed the noblest quality of the heart and head."[15]

Weld and the inseparable sisters soon became good friends. He took on the familiar part of adviser and guide. The Grimkés were Southerners in New York, women playing roles usually reserved for men, strong but vulnerable individuals who needed the support of friends and comrades. Weld was always there. He encouraged them to hold meetings and, according to Angelina, "grieved over that factitious state of society which bound up the energy of women instead of allowing her to exercise them to the glory of God and the good of her fellow creatures." After making her first appearance before a large audience, Angelina recovered over tea at the Tappans. She and Theodore shared a laugh about Henry Ludlow, host of the Grimkés and monitor at the meeting, who asked the one man in attendance to leave because he thought it improper that a woman speak before a "promiscuous" audience. "We smiled and said we did not know how it seemed to others," she wrote her close friend Jane Smith, "but it looked very strange in our eyes."[16]

Meanwhile, he touched Angelina with the story of his defense of the small black boy in his Connecticut common school. She was so taken by this anecdote that she related it in its entirety to Jane Smith.[17] Theodore and Angelina exchanged such stories and discussed antislavery through the winter. And, of course, Theodore advised. Angelina struck a new note, however, by being forthright enough to return advice of her own. For instance, when Theodore read aloud to her from his forthcoming *The Bible Against Slavery*, she apparently told him what she thought.

To Jane Smith she reported: "I do not admire the style, so don't expect too much from it, but the plan and arguments are admirable and conclusive."[18]

Weld felt relaxed enough in the sisters' parlor to reveal something of himself besides self-congratulatory tales from childhood. He talked about his family and especially Cornelia, so much so that Angelina would soon write of the Welds in intimate terms.[19] Each was falling in love, though without much suspicion of the other's feelings. Some friends saw what was happening. "Brother Ludlow used often to tease me about the *welding* warmth of your love for me," Angelina later revealed, "and tell me how he should like to marry us."[20]

Neither was ready for such vows in the winter and spring of 1837, but it was not for lack of interest. For instance, at the moment Weld was torturing himself with guilt while walking Angelina to the antislavery meeting, she was feeling "wounded" in her own way. "When we left our lodgings you seemed determined not to take my arm," she later recounted, "—you were actually forced by brother Wright—then the silent walk and you not walking home with me, all seemed to say *I dont care about you*, I pay you the attention I do, *only* because I love the cause of the slave and you are laboring for his redemption."[21] Despite such frustrations, the relationship continued. Theodore retreated to the role of adviser, and Angelina began to develop a lovingly jocular style. Responding, for instance, to Weld's unwillingness to participate in a local women's antislavery convention, Angelina relayed a message from one of the leaders: "Tell Mr. Weld said she, that when the women got together, they found they had *minds* of their own, and could transact their business without his directions."[22]

In the same letter Angelina teased him again in what sister Sarah called a "saucy" message: "Tell brother Weld I am much obliged to him for his hypocritical offer to serve us and then taking care to go so far that we cannot get him to do anything."[23] The letter was addressed to Hartford, and Angelina knew that Theodore had gone there for good reasons. He was close to another breakdown. Weld's throat still had not recovered since the convention, but his raspy voice symbolized a more general malaise. Theodore needed to get away from New York; instead of going to Manlius, as his family urged, he chose to revisit the land of his boyhood. While there he took care of some antislavery business and rested at his brother Lewis's home long enough to sense that his health was "pretty good."[24] But at the heart of his trip was a return to the scene of his earliest communings, the Connecticut countryside. "I have been taking a week's ramble over my native hills in Hampton," Weld wrote to James G. Birney. "Dear old hills and rocks and deep ravines, wild woods, and waterfalls. My young heart grew to them, and tho' fifteen years have gone since they blessed my vision they were all as dear, and dearer than ever and I laughed and wept amidst their solitudes till my brain dizzied and my heart ached with the crowd of thronging memories that rushed up from my childhood and poured over them."[25] A refreshed Theodore returned in June to the grueling New York summer and the planning of a new petition campaign to flood Congress with proof of antislavery sentiment.[26]

Just before Theodore left for Hartford and Hampton, he had accompanied the Grimkés to the Philadelphia steamboat. They were off on a short visit to friends, after which they would return to New York briefly and then move to Boston for new antislavery assignments. "It was an agonizing parting to me," Angelina wrote later, "—your whole manner seemed to say, I care not for you. . . . O! how my pride was wounded, how my heart died within me, but I believe I betrayed *no* emotion even to my sister." It was the last time they saw each other that year. When the sisters came back to New York, Theodore had already departed for Hartford. Angelina was crushed; her life became, at least for a little while, "days of weariness."[27]

Theodore had probably avoided Angelina to ease the pain of his own hopeless love. But it was just the beginning of the pain, for soon Angelina was entranced with the vigor of reform life in

Boston and less dependent on Weld. She became friendly with leading abolitionists—Garrison, Henry C. Wright, Lydia Maria Child, Maria Chapman and Anne Weston, among others—and lectured to excited audiences around Boston. There were protests, for it seemed odd to some that a woman should speak to mixed audiences, and to others that she should agitate public issues at all. Especially incensed were Orthodox ministers, who finally issued a joint "pastoral letter" condemning the agitation of antislavery in the pulpits of New England by nonministers and protesting the participation of women as destructive of "Female Character."[28]

Fellow abolitionists generally supported the right of the Grimkés to speak, though more than a few felt twinges of discomfort.[29] However, they split over whether the sisters should explicitly answer their critics' arguments or merely continue to agitate antislavery without reference to the controversy their appearances provoked. The issue involved two related questions. First, was the women's rights issue by itself important enough to sap energy from abolition work? Second, would raising the women's rights issue, which potentially struck at the heart of every Northern household, alienate support from antislavery?

The specific issue of women explicitly defending their rights was the most palpable of a number of issues that began to define a rift in antislavery ranks. Garrison, Henry C. Wright, and a number of other Boston-based abolitionists wished to widen the scope of reform concerns to include such controversial subjects as pacifism and perfectionist theology, and, in general, to take a comprehensive view of social and individual regeneration. Tappan, Birney, and Amos Anson Phelps, among others, opposed the comprehensive reformers and generally took a hostile stance toward any activity by antislavery societies not narrowly focused on slavery or race.[30]

Weld, as always, carved out his own path. He was linked by friendship and activity to the New York abolitionists and certainly felt with them that the central concern for reform should be antislavery. Yet Weld's own consciousness, steeped as it was in hostility to authority and striving toward individual piety and perfection, in some ways made him a spiritual if not practical ally of the Garrison faction. However, a combination of common sense and fear of destroying authority per se held him back from directly espousing no government, perfectionist doctrine.

Besides, such issues had compounded his private tortures over Angelina, and this too was likely to have put him in a defensive posture. The first serious signs of trouble appeared in June, when Sarah wrote from Boston that she had found the doctrines of John Humphrey Noyes as elucidated in his *Perfectionist* "in many respects a transcript of my heart."[31] This revelation must have been especially galling to Theodore because of his brother Charles's once close but now bitterly ruptured intimacy with Noyes.[32] However, in the same letter, Angelina sent playful messages chiding Weld for the disrespect he showed her by writing in pencil rather than pen; the sisters also chided him for not taking care of his own health as well as he did the cause of the slave.[33]

By mid-July the controversy over the Grimkés' speaking to "promiscuous" audiences had become hot, and Angelina asked Weld how he felt about it and what official position the antislavery society might take. Theodore indicated that since the sisters were not officially agents of the society, but only in "a sort of *cooperative* relation," the Executive Committee had no right or wish to take a position. He himself heartily endorsed their actions, stating that if men wished to hear them it was "downright *slaveholding* to shut them out." He added:

> Why! folks talk about women's preaching as tho' it was next to highway robbery—eyes astare and mouth agape. Pity women were not born with a split stick on their tongues! Ghostly dictums have fairly beaten it into the heads of the whole world save a fraction, that *mind* is *sexed*, and *Human rights* are *sexed, moral obligation sex'd*. . . .[34]

Having pontificated, Theodore could be playful. He protested Angelina's scolding for using pencil, screaming "Quarter! quarter! quarter!" and pledging that he would use pen and ink. He slyly complimented her charge of "hypocritical pretence" as being pretty good for a beginner at "hard language."[35] Theodore then turned to such language himself, giving Angelina a searching critique of her letters to Catharine Beecher in answer to Beecher's public condemnation of the Grimké speaking tour.[36] "So you see I am at my old tricks of fault finding with you," he admitted, though he had a justification. "Be patient, in this hollow world where even *most* of those who call themselves *friends* show it only by flattery, you will escape criticism *pretty much.*"[37]

After the "pastoral letter" was issued, Angelina wanted more than just support for her antislavery activities. Too many other abolitionists were hedging. Amos Anson Phelps urged the sisters to stop speaking in front of mixed audiences, though in private he conceded the idiocy of the ministers' position.[38] The sisters refused to stop and indeed insisted on their "free agency" to agitate and clarify women's rights as an adjunct to the antislavery position. Angelina admitted to Phelps that she herself had been wary and even timid about challenging the taboo of mixed audiences, but that the opposition convinced her that she must stand for the principle that "rights and duties depend *not* on *sex* but on our *relations* in life." And she asked, "Has not the attempt to draw a line of demarkation between the duties of men and women always failed[?]"[39] It was time to defend these principles in public.

Garrison, Henry Wright, and other Bostonians warmly supported Angelina's position. However, two good friends in New York, Weld and John Greenleaf Whittier, were disturbed to find the Grimkés taking time out from antislavery work to answer their critics explicitly. Whittier, poet and good friend of Weld at the antislavery office, who had written a poem satirizing the "pastoral letter," nonetheless advised the Grimkés not to agitate women's rights. He criticized the Bostonians for widening the antislavery platform and the sisters for contributing to that effort. Whittier characterized the women's rights issues involved as "some trifling oppression," "some paltry grievance," and urged them to return to the great cause of antislavery.[40]

Weld wrote the next day. Once again he made sure to establish his credentials as an advocate of women's rights, this time tracing adherence to the cause from the time he debated the issue in Hampton's field school. He even argued egalitarian notions of courtship, believing that women had as much right to propose marriage as men. Perhaps Weld hoped secretly that Angelina would act on his permissions, though in the letter he predicted she would cry out " 'oh shocking!!' " instead. In any case, he asked that they concentrate on antislavery, especially since as Southerners the sisters made a unique contribution to abolition. Theodore, for all his talk of women's rights, could not help but categorize it as "lesser work," though not with Whittier's contempt. It was a question of priorities:

> Let us all *first* wake up the nation to lift millions of slaves of both sexes from the dust, and turn them into MEN and then when we all have our hand in, it will be an easy matter to take millions of females from their knees and set them on their feet, or in other words transform them from *babies* into *women*.[41]

It was a curious argument, one that at once defined most women as "babies" and urged Angelina to practice rather than preach her equal rights as if they were self-evident. It was a convenient argument, too, for it enabled Weld to view Angelina as an exception, a woman untouched by the normal though regrettable weaknesses of her sex. Such a view allowed him to avoid facing her self-doubt and, perhaps, his own.

Angelina was stung by Theodore's letter, so much so that she replied in a message addressed jointly to Whittier and Weld. She had wanted empathetic understanding of her vulnerability to attack and her need to declare her rights as much for herself as for others. Indeed, a few days before answering Weld, Angelina had written to Amos Phelps explaining her inner sense of the issue; she compared the sisters' plight with that of free colored people, since they both had internalized feelings of inferiority. Though her principles were all for equality, inside, she admitted, "*I feel that I am inferior* in as much as I have not had the advantages of a liberal education."[42]

Writing to Weld and Whittier, she chided her friends for not remembering the similar quandary abolitionists once faced, and even alluded to Weld's actions at Lane Seminary:

> Now my dear brothers this *invasion of our rights* was just such an attack upon *us,* as that made upon Abolitionists generally when they were told a few years ago that *they had no right* to discuss the subject of Slavery. Did *you* take no notice of this assertion? Why no! With one heart and one voice you said, *We* will settle *this right before* we go one step further. *The time* to assert a right is *the* time when *that* right is denied.[43]

Angelina also feared that many came to see the sisters out of curiosity, and that once the novelty wore off churches and halls might be closed to them if their rights were not cemented in principle.[44]

In addition, Angelina endorsed the Garrisonian approach to reform. Different moral reform efforts, she argued, were bound together and "blend[ed] with each other like the colors of the rain bow." Since the ministry rejected this notion, she demanded that "the whole Church Government must come down," perhaps even before slavery was removed. She even suggested that there be female ministers. "Is brother Weld frightened at *my ultraism?*" she taunted. As for Theodore's jibe about marriage, Angelina claimed not to be shocked at all. Women, she agreed, should be able to propose marriage. "But I am *too proud* ever to exercise the right," she added. "The fact is we are living in such an artificial state of society that there are some things about which we dare not speak out, or act out the most natural and best feelings of our hearts." She once again made the distinction Weld refused to make, between what should be and what was.[45] Then, as if to atone for her fire, Angelina assured her two friends that in fact she and Sarah devoted very little time to women's rights anyway.[46]

Angelina's letter, dated August 20, only reached Weld in the first week of September, along with an even more tardy one dated August 12. This earlier note, an answer to Weld's lovingly critical letter of July 22, revealed the depth of Angelina's personal hurt in the women's right controversy. The Reverend Hubbard Winslow's sermon concerning the limitations divinely placed on women, she reported, had insulted her womanhood and outraged her moral feelings. She urged Theodore to read Sarah's article on woman's place in the *New England Spectator*. She also revealed that vulnerable and doubting part of herself that did not wish Weld to be present at her lectures, her intense pride and fear of failure. The presence of his empathy was best: "At times when I feel so miserable and little and incompetent I remember what thou told us about thy feelings before speaking and am really strengthened by thy experience." Perhaps if Weld had received this letter on time, his own reaction to Angelina's plight might have been more sensitive.[47]

As it was, it arrived on September 6. In the meantime Theodore's anxieties about Angelina had increased. Letters were no substitute for personal contact, and her turn toward comprehensive reform threatened Weld's sense of communion. Angelina's growing friendship with Henry C. Wright did not help matters. He had read Wright's "Domestic Scene" and other columns in which Wright reported the doings of the "Misses Grimke" for the *Liberator,* and Weld no doubt wondered if he was being replaced in their lives.[48]

Angelina's letter of August 27 could only have increased Theodore's fears. She asked again about the sisters' status in relation to the Antislavery Society, and complained of "all this unsettlement and complaint among the *friends* of the cause." And she indirectly implicated Weld in charges of "*worldly policy*" and "smothering the truth," closing with a demand to "Abandon the law of expediency NOW."[49]

Though always glad to get a letter from Angelina, Weld called this one an "ear boxing." He even compared it to the corporal punishment of his youth, though he added: "But I utterly forgot!! You dont believe in 'physical force' as I learn by H. C. W[right]s 'Domestic Scene,' so this illustration is lost upon you." He told the sisters that they were helpers but not official antislavery agents. He might have stopped there, but Theodore felt compelled to make a comparison with his own role as agent as a way of criticizing the sisters' agitation of the women's rights issue. He, after all, was an agent though he had no official appointment. "Why? Because I spend all my time in laboring in the antislavery cause," he taunted, "in doing here at the centre a hundred things which cant be named exactly nor defined, but enough to keep me busy as I ever was night and day in promoting the cause."[50]

Weld finally received the early August letter from Groton; he thought it was now time to deal at length (eight foolscap pages crammed with almost illegible script) with the differences separating him from the Grimkés. Theodore took offense at the sisters' need to argue the rudiments of women's rights as if he did not agree with them. He disputed their pessimism in relation to the church and their insistence that "the Clergy and the whole Church government must come down" before slavery could be defeated. In Weld's view, however, they disagreed on only one *major* point: "The question at issue between us *is* whether *you* SM and AE Grimke should engage in the public discussion of the rights of women as a distinct topic—Here you affirm and I deny." And he paraded before them variations of all the major themes in his case for their agitating antislavery exclusively.[51]

Angered again by the need to reiterate these points, Theodore turned his explanation into an attack. He criticized Angelina's "obstinacy"; her tendency "every moment to turn short from the main point" in order to deal with "some little one side annoyance"; and her pride "so closely curtained as to be almost searchless to her self." These were harsh words, and coupled with Weld's relentless and cocksure logic in the rest of the letter they produced an impenetrable screen for his unspoken affections. He was angry and jealous, and even lost control in a side comment on Henry C. Wright's "Domestic Scene," charging that the Grimkés were "made to figure conspicuously among the conquests of the victor—as rare spoils gracing the triumphal car. . . ." If Wright had begun to replace Weld as chief adviser, he would argue the sisters back into submission.[52]

So great was Weld's anguish that he soon wrote another lengthy defense of his views on women. Imagining other men to be as liberal as he was, Theodore was sure that women had merely to demonstrate to men and ministers that they were not *"inferior beings,"* that they were not "silly," and barriers would crumble. Yet again he emphasized the wisdom of pursuing the main goal of antislavery, leaving collateral issues such as women's rights for later.[53]

Sarah took on the task of answering Weld (she said her sister was too "wrathy" to do so). In the very first sentence the older sister called Theodore's letters good and Angelina crossed out the adjective and wrote in bad. Sarah, acting as an appreciative friend, answered a number of points, hinted that Theodore's mind might have been "beclouded by the fears which seem to have seized some of the brotherhood least [sic] we should usurp dominion over our lords and masters" (a notion she finally rejected but which had a grain of truth), and chided Weld for not treating Henry Wright's motives with the law of love.[54]

Angelina could not resist striking with her own "venemous serpent" of a pen. "What is the matter with thee?" she scolded. "One would really suppose that we had actually abandoned the A. Sl'y cause." And why should *she* be criticized because Sarah wrote letters about women's rights? "Indeed, I should like to know what *I have done* yet," she protested. Then she let loose her most potent weapon. Henry C. Wright, it seems, had been transferred to Pennsylvania by the agency committee in New York. Angelina complained that she and Sarah missed Wright "very much," and that the agent sent to replace him opposed their lecturing. This created a problem since Wright had supervised their lecture tour. Later in the letter she reemphasized: "I cant have as many meetings this week as I want because I have not brother *Wright to appoint them.*"[55]

In a separate letter to Weld, she accused the Executive Committee of deceiving her about Wright's transfer. In fact, she was sure that those in New York had *"parted company* with Garrison, H. C. Wright, and the Grimkés.[56] Weld replied with a new sense of strain and yearning. Oh, that they could hold their debate face to face! "This arms length way of getting at truth or even of letting another know *what you mean*," he complained, "is so loose jointed that it can hardly be called a *medium* of communication, especially where habits of thought and modes of investigation are entirely dissimilar." Theodore felt misunderstood on almost every point and conceded that the two sisters might feel quite the same. It was a problem, he said, of different assumptions, different angles of vision, and different modes of argument.[57]

Such recognition did not prevent him from taking the offensive. Admitting that he had misunderstood some matters, Theodore fixed the blame for such misconstructions on the sisters themselves. They had presented him contradictory information, and in order to "teach Angelina a practical lesson" he felt almost "half ass enough to copy off" some of these contradictions and send them along. In any case, it seemed to Weld that even the latest information from and about the Grimkés indicated that he should fear their apostasy. For instance, Angelina had mentioned that she had come close to thinking of women's rights and not antislavery as the taproot of human rights reform. He also had heard from reliable sources that she was preparing a lecture series on women's rights. Should he not be afraid that she was abandoning the slave?[58]

But Theodore moved quickly to the topic that dominated his long letter—Henry C. Wright. He apologized for any intemperate comments, but apology only made way for a heartier blast:

> His benevolence, frankness, generosity, sympathy, deep social affections, self denial, and conscience I greatly honor and love. To this I must add that owing to a peculiar and perhaps most unfortunate structure, exhibitions of personal vanity, ostentatious display, self complacency, an overweening restlessness to show oneself and to be conspicuous and attract attention, have from childhood so excited my disgust and loathing that language cannot express the repulsion they excite in my soul. Now I do not say that brother Wright has *any such feeling*, but I *do* say that I have rarely seen one who *seems* to have such an itching to be *known*.[59]

Vanity, pure and simple, was Wright's crime; perhaps Theodore could not help but wonder whether Angelina found attractive in Wright what he so abhorred in himself.

Once caught in jealous obsession with Wright, nothing could control him. He relived his fury over the *"conquest"* of the sisters in the "Domestic Scene," even overstating Wright's own estimate of agreement with the Grimkés on major issues. To Weld, however, Wright had reached into the intimate realm of the sisters' world, and that was a conquest that threatened his own position in their lives. He predicted more incursions: "Strange that the next paper did not contain a special bulletin from brother Wright officially announcing to the world the exact measurement of his own hatbrim and your *cap* brims, with other items equally indispensable for the public to know and *appreciate*." Was this sort of behavior on Wright's part, he asked, "ACCORDING TO YOUR TASTE?"[60]

As for Angelina's charges about Wright's transfer, Theodore countered by accusing her of bad faith. "Low and groveling and dull to upward lures as *I* know *my* heart to be," he moaned, "could I have believed *you* or *Sarah* guilty of such baseness as you charge upon the Ex. Com., and that too when the only data was *vague circumstances* which could never [have] been made to excite suspicion but by the torturing rack of uncharitable construction." He promised a full explanation later, and meanwhile remarked, "To *explain* and state facts and show reasons to clear them from accusations of the very meanest hypocrisy almost makes me feel as tho' I was myself guilty of a meanness in doing it."[61] Whether Weld had any hand in the transfer from behind the scenes, he must have been secretly happy about it and felt guilty when pressed with accusations.

Six days later he felt settled enough to explain Wright's transfer in detail. Weld examined general committee policy, cited other transfers, and accounted for the case in point by the fact that Massachusetts had too many agents and Pennsylvania too few. Wright was transferred because his faults made him the most expendable agent. Though disavowing any responsibility in the action, Weld affirmed the judgment of the agency committee.[62]

Meanwhile, Theodore's anger rose and burst through his sober explanation as he realized the time he had spent explaining routine actions. Why could not the Grimkés have accepted the hasty but honest account of Henry B. Stanton: "A mighty easy thing it is for you my dear sister to sit down in your retired room and con and scan with your quizzing glass, a letter of his written in such circumstances [the commotion of the antislavery office], and then gather inferences of dishonesty, deception, hypocrisy, double dealing. SO DID NOT CHRIST."[63]

The blasts continued. "ALL MOONSHINE" was his response to Angelina's charge that the committee wished to silence Wright. He termed "ludicrous" Angelina's idea that the Society wished to disown them, attributing it to *"Miss Construction!"* Weld predicted that Angelina might find the letter "censorious and harsh if not *ill tempered,*" but so be it if it opened the gates to self-knowledge: "Whether or not as the old Greeks said 'Know Thyself' came down from heaven, it IS the gate at the entrance of the ONLY road that leads there. Oh Angelina! enter in! enter in!"[64]

After the storm came quiet. He and the sisters agreed that little would be gained by further correspondence about Wright or women's rights, so they called a truce. Still, Weld's last letter had hurt Angelina deeply. Though he indicated that that pained him, it also caused him to *"rejoice."* Perhaps he had in mind the drama of conversion. Humbling Angelina would help her along the road to conviction of sin; he would regain his honored role as mentor. The secret lover in him also rejoiced, for though he felt Angelina's hurt he also felt reassured by his power to wound. With that security, he allowed an ever stronger empathy to enter his letters, as when he spoke of his own resistance to self-knowledge in the past and the realization of how much more remained to be done for his own soul.[65]

Meanwhile, it was a dreary winter for both Theodore and Angelina. Angelina, exhausted by incessant work and the tension surrounding her public life, took ill. Theodore, though work continued to dominate his days, felt ever more needful of deep communing. The uneasy truce between them held for a while; they corresponded as concerned friends rather than as engaged souls. Theodore advised the sisters on health; the Grimkés reminded him to practice what he preached.[66]

Beneath the calm, Weld was developing new ways of expressing his affections, as in his reply when Angelina wrote in disappointment that he was not a "Peace Man."[67] While stating his basic disagreement with "no government" theories, he refused to engage in another free-for-all. He had no heart for more misunderstandings, and told her so. Apology for not being in the debating mood led to whimsy: "What a world of enigmas, anomalies, solecisms, and contradictory whims is that mysterious riddle, the human mind." Whimsy led to love, the evocation of his love for Charles Stuart, whose friendship had taught him that men might commune without agreeing on every point. Indeed, he remarked, they had led an almost *"indivisible existence"* though they were poles apart on most important issues. He was lonely for such "refreshment of *deep* communings of spirit and the answerings of *soul* to *soul,* the congeniality and incorporation of spirit with spirit in dissoluble identity. . . ."[68] The very revelation of his yearning, though ostensibly directed toward Charles Stuart, opened his heart to Angelina.

In this spirit, Theodore probed a more personal problem with caring honesty. The sisters had always been perturbed by their familial link with the slave system. Both of them had adored their late brother, Thomas S. Grimké, a reformer with whom Weld had had contact years before in the manual labor campaign. Now Angelina expressed grief because her brother had not seen the light on slavery before his death. She also agonized over her mother's slaveholding principles. She revealed to Weld deep and awful feelings within her soul. Theodore responded by supporting her steadfastness in judging all men by the word of God, no matter the pain. But he also felt her agony: "My dear sisters my heart bleeds for you. Exiles from your homes, your friends, and all your kindred according to the flesh, in the midst of strangers. . . ." As his heart opened to them, Theodore added a note in which the approaching explosion of his soul colored his view of the world: "The uproar on the Canada border, the Seminoles, Mexicans, the Western and Northwestern Indians, the conflicts in congress, all foreshow a storm blast with God in the midst. I feel in perfect peace. I rejoice and leap for joy." In the whirlwind of apocalypse he felt at one with himself.[69]

Angelina as well took more risks with her emotions. She admitted her disappointment in Quakerism and pondered: "I *feel* as if my little bark had been again cut loose from its mooring and was tossing on the dark and troubled waves of doubt and perplexity." Her only consolation was that in the search for truth, and in every change, she had advanced in the way of faith.[70]

Meanwhile Angelina received and answered Weld's letter about Charles Stuart. She wrote of friendship, the deep friendship that was love. Angelina had mentioned the name Jane Smith to Theodore; now she revealed that she was to her what Charles Stuart was to him. In fact, only three people were really her friends—Jane, sister Sarah, and Theodore. "And now let me tell you how often I have thanked God for such a friend as you have proved to me," she wrote, "one who *will* tell me my faults. . . . You dear brother have, I must acknowledge, dived deeper into the *hidden* sins of my heart than any one ever did before, and you can therefore do me more good." She wrote of the pain of his friendship, his relentless criticism, and especially the whipping she felt from *"that letter never to be forgotten"* of October 16. It had so angered and hurt her that she could not bear to look at it again, though she admitted it might now seem less cruel. "You know too, whilst the wound rankles we feel but little inclination to examine critically the weapon which dealt the blow," she added, "even tho' we may love the hand which dealt the blow and above all *bless God* for the chastisement." And in the admission of love she drew back, "enough of self," and remembered the pain again. Perhaps they could talk it over, she continued, but by writing "WE CAN NOT UNDERSTAND EACH OTHER, and I have unintentionally said too much perhaps."[71]

Sarah wrote the same day, and Weld received both letters about the same time. He responded to both on February 9. To Sarah he dashed off a short note, concentrating on a topic of common interest, health and health reform. He assured her that he was taking care of himself and promised a lecture on the subject when next they met.[72]

To Angelina he revealed his heart. "A paragraph in your last letter, Angelina," he wrote, "went *to my soul.*" He had been deeply pained by her doubts about the spirit of his love and her foreboding that they could not understand each other; but most of all he felt guilt ridden over the "ABIDING PAIN" that seemed to have been inflicted by his October letter. "Oh, surely the probe that finds the core," he wrote, "need not be tipped with *fire,* nor lodge a rankling poison in the wound." His criticism had exceeded usefulness, "thrust through and through with a rude and lacerating violence." He did not mean to be so cruel, Weld explained, but an explanation of his higher motives could wait until he revealed a secret kept long inside, a secret he had intended to keep until death.[73]

"I know it will surprise and even amaze you, Angelina," wrote Weld, "when I say to you as I now do, that for a long time, *you have had my whole heart.*"[74]

Not his whole heart, of course, for Weld loved God more than Angelina or himself; it was his love for God, however, which gave his affection for her its special quality.[75]

Theodore recounted how long he had pined for her and how he strove against his feelings because he felt the cause was hopeless. So much to say and explain, but he would rest for the moment by reiterating, "I took up my pen for a *single* purpose, *—to tell you without reserve all that is in my heart toward you.*" He could not close without allowing for the fact that he had no expectation of reciprocal feelings from Angelina; Theodore half suspected that his sudden disclosure would "shock and repel" her. If she did not love him, he declared, she should not pause to say the whole truth. At the end of the letter there was no "your brother" or other phrase, just Theodore D. Weld.[76]

It took but three days for Angelina to get Theodore's avowal. She responded immediately. His letter had surprised her, "yet it was no surprise at all," for even before his revelation her heart had cleaved to something in his. But not even the "private" written at the top of the sheet made her guess its content—she thought he had prepared another chastisement. In fact, the "abiding pain" caused by his earlier letter had come from a feeling that with such a view of her character he could not love her, "save as a poor unworthy sinner, the love which we bear in *pity* to one who is sunk in moral pollution." His letter came as a healing balm.[77]

Angelina revealed the growth of her love for him, one that, like his, had begun with the reading of a letter to the *Liberator* and that grew after their first meeting. She was shocked that Weld might have kept until death the secret of his love, and she scolded him for it. "The customs of Society gave *you* privileges, *rights* which it denied to me, and I was too proud to break the fetters which had been fastened upon," she wrote. "I resolved to *suffer in silence*." Now that he had declared his love, she could do the same: "I *feel* my Theodore that we are the two halves of one whole, a twain one, two bodies animated by one soul and that the Lord has given us each other."[78]

"My heart is full!!" exclaimed Theodore, "THAT LETTER found me *four* days ago! I tried to answer it *immediately* but could not, and again the next day but could not write a word! and again yesterday but in vain." His heart ached for "*utterance* but oh *not* the utterance of words!"—but words streamed forth. He had felt "like a blind giant stifling by violence all the intensities of [his] nature." But when her letter allowed him to unleash his feelings—"it was as the life touch to one *dead;* all the pent up tides of my being so long shut out from light and air, broke forth at once and spurned control." He had been more prepared for rejection than for this. "Long, long I've known the *joy of grief,* but *now* I know the grief of joy, and I sink before it."[79]

And of course he was not worthy of her. It was no mere lover's rhapsody. He had reasoned it through; she had not seen him for the man he was. She would know all the imperfections right down to the last. But these must await the next letter; he had already used up his paper. There was space for a note acknowledging Sarah's endorsement of their love, and a fateful commitment. Theodore vowed that Sarah's connection to Angelina was too important to sunder, so she would become part of their life together.[80]

Two days later Weld wrote again, this time to reassure Angelina that his inner joys were not interfering with his work. "Now not a soul here has detected the least difference in my appearance," he wrote, "nor has the last suspicion that, within a week, all the fountains of my being have been unsealed." Not even his roommate suspected a thing. "A quivering mass of intensities kept in subjection only by the *rod of iron*," was the way he described himself. Inside, however, he felt sublime in his feeling for her, effortless and natural and beyond description: "What mockers of the heart are *words* WORDS!! They have no *room* in them." Not even Charles Stuart evoked such bliss. "Many a time I have wept on his neck from *very love to him*," Weld remembered, "and yet at those very times I have felt in my inmost soul that there remained other intense necessities of my compound *human* nature untouched by the ministrations of his love and communion and panting for congenial affiliation. Those necessities you alone have reached and filled—I say no more."[81]

They naturally wished to be with each other; the sisters wanted Weld to come to Boston. But at that very moment Angelina was preparing for her most important speaking engagement to date, an appearance before the Massachusetts Legislature on behalf of the slave. She was the first woman ever to appear before a legislative body in America, and thus the usual opposition to abolitionism was compounded by the fear and ridicule provoked by a woman taking on such public responsibility. Theodore thought it best to stay away for awhile, both because Angelina could not afford the emotional distraction and because he felt the need to master his own inner turmoil.[82]

Angelina thanked Weld for not coming; she would have "utterly sunk" under the emotion. But she worried about his holding in his feelings for her. Angelina was not impressed with the fact that no one could detect a change, and was sure that it would lead to a decline in his health. "Cant you trust brother Stanton or any one of your friends," she asked, "rather than struggle as you are assuredly doing against the laws of your being? *Why* not betray your feelings?" As for his feelings of unworthiness, she was amazed at how similar they were to hers. "I wish I had a complete phrenological character to send you," she wrote, "for I *dont want* you to be deceived." Whatever both their faults, however, such love was clearly the Lord's doing, and Angelina suffered as did Theodore from its "indescribable, *grievous, joyous weight.*"[83]

The next day Angelina wrote with satisfaction of her second meeting before the legislature, and then balked lest she seem too prideful. As for Theodore, the very unburdening of her feelings toward him brought momentary calm, though it still amazed her that she and not the pure Charles Stuart could satisfy his soul: "I want to know why those of our own sex *cannot* fill the void in human hearts."[84] That same day Angelina told Jane Smith of her love for Theodore.[85]

Meanwhile Weld decided not to write for awhile, fearing that his letters might upset Angelina's work routine. He informed Sarah of his decision. Two days later, Angelina complained bitterly. "Indeed my heart is so foolish that it beats with vague expectation whenever I hear the house door open," she admitted, "though you have twice told me that you *cannot*, you *must* not, you *dare* not see me et [sic]." Four days later, on March 2, she added a note to the same letter, which she had not mailed, no doubt in the expectation of hearing from him. But still no letter, and Angelina chided him for his *"cruel* kindness," since she had read Theodore's explanation to Sarah.[86] Indeed, on February 27, she had reproached him for hiding his feelings. She told him that his letters had called forth a deeper love than she had known earlier, one that was as "hidden water in a deep well, which rose and overflowed as soon as the mountain torrent with which they had been secretly connected broke the icy bands which had bound it." And she declared her rights in love:

> You *seem* to be a *little* surprised at my so *freely* expressing my feelings towards you—I should once have thot it *unladylike,* but as a *woman* I feel you have a right to know them, and I have a right to express them, and no reason to be ashamed of them.[87]

In the same letter Sarah urged that they come together after the legislative meetings were over, but Angelina added: "Don't come with fetters on your soul—I *cannot* see you until we can meet *just as we are.*"[88]

Theodore responded by breaking his silence with a torrent of words, most of which set forth a "sickening catalogue" of defects that proved his contention of unworthiness. He was selfish, Weld assured her, and proud, impatient of contradiction, self-indulgent, prone to "deal in sarcasm and contemptuous irony" when in debate, and possessed of "a stupid and mulish prefference for [his] own notions and [his] own way." And these were just the beginning. Could he in good conscience ask for her heart and offer such, "the cheapest and most worthless wares," in return? His revelations were fraught with contradiction, for he could make them only once he was sure of Angelina's love.[89]

Theodore then revealed his fear that he would never marry, that God had ordained him to travel the world alone. Besides, he had never met a woman before who seemed to be so free of the common views of courtship, views that "so utterly sickened [his] soul that the thought of marrying a woman with the taint of this almost universal plague spot upon her would have filled [him] with revulsions." And he did not have to add, a woman with high enough notions could not possibly have been interested in his soiled mind.[90] Theodore hoped that by now the severity of some of his earlier letters might seem explicable. "I knew that every moment I was in great danger of betraying in some way my feelings toward you," he admitted, "and struggling to guard against that, I doubtless lost my balance often and plunged to an opposite extreme."[91]

Theodore tried to shed some light on attraction between the sexes, though he admitted ignorance from the outset. Still, he launched a minor essay that concluded that those of the same sex could not experience the deepest love because that depended on combining mutually exclusive characteristics. As for unburdening his soul, he had written to Charles Stuart about Angelina but otherwise remained silent with his friends. He still chose to battle against "the tide and headwinds of a long violated nature," and when that battle was done he would consent to see his beloved.[92]

Angelina shuddered at the exposé of his faults. "Yes I am afraid, I am almost terror stricken—I *fear* you will break my heart." His tales of severity filled her with "the gloomiest of forebodings," and reminded her again of the letters he had written before their avowals, those letters that seemed to be "an *extinguisher* or the *last ray* of hope" for his love. But then she remembered her own faults—her temper, her pride, all those unpleasantnesses that she knew would make Weld "despise and abhor" her. "Let us know each other *fully*," she agreed, "that we may help each other faithfully."[93]

Angelina felt at one with Weld on courtship. Her soul loathed it; her womanhood was outraged by it. It seemed almost invariable that the baser passions took control of nobler sentiments, rather than the reverse. "Well I am convinced that men in general, the vast majority," she complained, "believe most seriously that women were made to gratify their animal appetites, *expressly* to minister to *their* pleasure—yea christian men too."[94]

Even as Angelina spent her rage on the common practices of men courting, Theodore was training his sights on the common ruses of women, especially those who withheld true affections except to "dole out the sustenance to the famishing man in the minutest grains." To let herself tell of her feelings "*to* him round whom they cluster as the glad child bounds unto its father and lays its head on its mothers bosom—Oh shocking—horrible! What indelicacy!"[95]

But Angelina was no ordinary woman. She had expressed herself freely, and it was that *"free spirit* that *took hold"* of him. "The strong and artless outburst of your heart," he explained, and "the tide of the heart—and soul dashing thus the antiquated wicker work and venerated dust" of "usage," this had made the difference. Her spirit had shown itself to be "in *its nature irrepressible.*"[96]

Meanwhile he must see her. Theodore, with a lover's sense of self-importance, deeply feared that there would be much publicity if his travel plans and intentions became known. He wanted to slip into Boston secretly. He imagined encountering "all the hollow chat—and nods and winks and things and half speeches and light jesting and empty insipid nonsense and rallying about courtship and lovers and marriage and all that." Rather would Weld "encounter a *giggler* at [his] mothers funeral" than be "annoyed by the calls and gapings and speculations and musing of a prying Yankee curiosity."[97]

Angelina did her best to make their meeting at the home of Samuel Philbrick a clandestine one, but she could not help but be a little irked by his apparent shame in seeing her. Calling him the *"New York runaway,"* she gave him explicit instructions as to rail and coach lines, all the while chiding him for the secrecy, which eventually, she noted, must be forsaken. In this same letter Angelina revealed another fact about herself—that she had once loved another man. They had never been engaged; indeed, he had taken ill and died early in their courtship. The Lord had given her perfect resignation through this trial, when "all [her] pleasant pictures were spoiled," and only as she blossomed into her public career could she see the fatefulness of his death. In any case, her love for him did not approach what she felt for Theodore. In Weld she had found the other half of her self.[98]

Theodore, while having no old loves to reveal, had not yet finished his confessions. He had mixed feelings about the catalogue of shames and even saw his last letter as "nothing but a mean base *self-gratification.*" Besides, he suspected these outbursts of both love and self-deprecation. "The alternative with me is either *total abstinence* or *intoxication,*" he wrote, "much like other *drunkards*." Intoxicated and bent on gratification, however, he continued his list of faults with added zeal. After all, if he did not tell her, nobody would; men "stupidly idolized" him and were blind to his weaknesses. He forgot things, for instance: names, faces, ages, dates, seasons, hats, coats. "Half the time I forget to wind my watch when I go to bed," he recounted, "and down its runs. I pare an apple and throw the apple into the street or the fire and hold fast to the *parings*."[99]

He was reckless. As a boy and as an adult, "jumping, wrestling, leaping fences and chasms, standing on my head, jumping and diving into deep water from the limbs of over-hanging trees or from rocks high above the tide—such things have always been my delight and are now." Oh the worry, the *"anxiety"* he would cause her, with this unquenchable thirst to *"cut all sorts of boyish capers."* As for his personal appearance:

> I have always been slovenly and careless in my appearance, a slouching gait, a listless air, shoes slip shod, not blacked once a month, coat not brushed as *often* as that, beard generally as long as a hermits, never yet had any fixed time for shaving, no particular times in the week nor in the day, wear my beard till it gets so long that its chafing against my collar obliges me from pain to shave in self-defence, or till some of my friends *beg* of me to do it.

His hair stuck out like the quills of a porcupine; indeed, Weld's mother called his head her "oven broom."[100]

Sloppiness aside, he would credit himself with one virtue. He was clean. "I have a mortal instinctive shrinking from *all dirt*," he wrote, happy to find a positive instinct in the morass of vice. "If I were to pass a single [day] winter or summer without washing myself all over in water, I dont know but I should lose absolutely all self respect and self toleration."[101]

But back to his faults. "I often swing like a pendulum in a dreamy totally abstracted revery, dont hear questions that are asked me, and sometimes I am told that I go on making a sort of inarticulate nasal um, um, um, um," he admitted, "as a sort of unconscious mechanical assent to some one talking to me and keep this up for five minutes perhaps without knowing or even hearing a single word he has said." In a number of other ways, when with others, he found himself particularly unaware of their needs. And of course there was his loathing of all the "artificial and factitious life" of the middle classes, a view he would defend but not to the excess of his own practice. Theodore also revealed his frustrated career as a scholar, finding that the total of his education about equaled that of a "learned pig."[102]

Done with his list of faults, Theodore admitted that he could not have faced Angelina in peace without making these disclosures. Knowing what she now knew, had she rejected him it would have broken his heart; but, he said, "I *cannot* and God helping me I WILL NOT marry you Angelina with a curtain round my heart or a false gloss on my character or a false light hung out on my history." As for Angelina's hint that if she thought it would do him good she would give him up: *"I'll marry you in spite of earth or hell."*[103]

On Wednesday, Angelina sent Theodore final instructions to Worcester for their Saturday meeting at the Philbricks. Philbrick would meet Theodore at five o'clock at the train station. Meanwhile the rest of the Philbrick family and Sarah would attend a lecture by Sylvester Graham, leaving the house to Theodore and Angelina. They would meet *"alone"* in the parlor. Until then she would carry the lock of his hair he had sent at her bosom.[104]

Finally Saturday came. Meeting with overburdened hearts, day by day they came to feel in the flesh all that they had written to each other, so that Angelina could truly say, "I felt our *parting* to be *more joyous than our meeting.*" Theodore described it more deliriously, not knowing whether their rendezvous was "an actual reality or an Eden dream."[105] Amidst the bliss they made concrete plans. They would be married, of course, but the couple decided that they wished the presence of neither minister nor magistrate; their union would be blessed only by God and witnessing friends. This was possible under the laws of Pennsylvania, so Angelina wrote to her sister, Anna Frost, who lived in Philadelphia, to see if they could hold the wedding at her home. Meanwhile, Theodore set off for New Jersey to find a suitable home across from New York but with the seclusion of the countryside. Angelina began to collect things for the household.[106]

The first act of their private drama having ended, they began the process of making their intentions public. First, the families were informed. Angelina feared her mother's reaction to her marrying an abolitionist. Actually, her mother was more concerned with Angelina's unfeminine behavior in the public sphere, and she welcomed the coming marriage. "After you are married I hope you will feel that *retirement* is best suited to your station," wrote Mary Grimké, "and that you will desire to *retire* from the busy scenes of *publicity* and enjoy that happiness which I hope your *home* will yield you."[107] Angelina must have gained little satisfaction from such a direct message, but she worried too about the polite assent of Anna Frost to the use of her house. She was sure Anna felt deep regret "at the very anticipation of such a motley assembly of white and black," which would assemble for the service.[108]

As for Theodore's family, they both feared that Angelina's political activities and Quaker persuasion might cause disapproval. It had been no issue in Theodore's mind; he had vowed long ago that if he ever did marry "it might be some one of a different religious persuasion from [him]self, that we might both give a testimony to the world that in Christ Jesus there is neither Jew nor Greek."[109]

As it turned out, the family was more receptive than he expected; Theodore's marriage plans were an occasion for new family understandings. His first surprise came when he told Lewis in Hartford. After midnight, when Lewis's wife Mary had retired, the two brothers talked. Theodore told him everything in his heart, and Lewis burst into tears, threw his arms around him, and thanked God for blessing his younger brother with love. As for Angelina's Quaker views, Lewis explained that for some time God had been weakening his prejudices and helping him rethink his "aristocratic feeling" toward other denominations and toward the role of women.[110] Most of all, however, as Lewis revealed in a letter to Angelina, he was happy that Theodore might finally be *"settled in life."* "We have formed plans almost innumerable for his regulation in various courses of life which *we* have marked out," he admitted to his sister-to-be, "and we have seen them frustrated, one after another, until I believe, we have all long since given him up to the guidance of that all-wise and merciful Providence which has so remarkably preserved and sustained him, and made him an instrument of so much good in His service."[111]

Still, Theodore feared Ludovicus's reaction. He knew his father viewed Quakerism "with a sort of horror," and feared that he would say, "My son my conscience forbids me to give you my blessing." Instead, Ludovicus rejoiced. Not that he had become a convert to the Friends or an advocate of females speaking in public assembly; he had come to believe, however, that these were not essential differences. He too had given up hope that Theodore would ever marry, so their plans were something of a surprise. Yet it was clear to the father that "the hand of God [was] visible and very conspicuous in the whole affair." Elizabeth, for her part, warmly welcomed Angelina into the family.[112]

Abolitionist friends and acquaintances displayed a variety of responses. Charles Stuart was overjoyed.[113] Maria Chapman approved, stating that it was rare for a wise man to marry a wise woman rather than one whom he could lead without resistance.[114] Some male reformers were threatened by the likes of Angelina. For instance William Ladd, leader of the American Peace Society, had always thought that she would marry "a strapping negro."[115] Even Lewis Tappan joked nervously about Theodore's great moral courage in taking as his wife so strong a woman.[116]

Others expressed doubts about the wisdom of Angelina's choice. One woman comrade saw it as too commonplace an act to comport well with Angelina's past.[117] William Lloyd Garrison, who had written to one friend that the match was "a splendid alliance of mind!," nonetheless reported to his wife:

I frankly told Angelina my feelings, and expressed my fear that bro. Weld's sectarianism would bring her into bondage, unless she could succeed in emancipating *him*. She heard my remarks very pleasantly, and trusted "the experiment," as she termed it, would prove mutually serviceable.[118]

Whatever the minor quibbles and backbitings, Theodore could honestly report to Angelina that he had not seen one of his abolitionist friends "who [did] not really seem to be *overjoyed* at [their] union." With the exception of Henry C. Wright. "Brother Wright too *says* he is rejoiced and he really thinks so doubtless," Weld wrote, "but dear me! he *looks* as tho' his heart was broke when he speaks of it." Later, when Angelina invited Wright to the ceremony, Theodore took exception. "Dearest," he wrote, "I was very sorry that you said in your letter inviting H.C. Wright to our marriage, 'We know you will feel for us and be *helpers of our joy* in the Lord,' for I *cannot* say such a thing. I do believe he feels for us in *one* sense, that is, the thought that you should marry *me* is to him like *poison*." Even in victory Weld's jealousy had not died.[119]

Theodore and Angelina were married on May 14, 1838, in the home of Anna Frost. Thirty-one guests signed the wedding certificate, including William Lloyd Garrison, Henry B. Stanton, Abby Kelley, Lewis Weld, Jane Smith, Anne Warren Weston, Maria Weston Chapman, Gerrit Smith, Lewis Tappan, and a number of Weld's comrades from Oneida and Lane. John Greenleaf Whittier also attended, but because of his orthodox Quaker allegiance absented himself from the service.[120]

The ceremony was as unusual as the guest list. Theodore and Angelina, without aid of attending magistrate or clergy, stood before their friends and took each other's right hand. Theodore spoke first: "Angelina, I take you to be my lawful, wedded wife, and promise to love, honor and cherish and in all things to recognize your equality with me." He testified against the unrighteous power given to a husband over the person and property of his wife by the laws of the United States; then, in Sarah's words, he "abjured all authority, all government, save the influence which love would give to them over each other as moral and immortal beings."[121]

Angelina promised to honor, prefer, and love him. At this point all present knelt, while Theodore prayed fervently for God's blessing in marriage and for antislavery. Angelina followed with a prayer of her own, after which two ministers, a black Presbyterian followed by a white one, prayed. Finally, Sarah poured out words of joy and praise. The service concluded, William Lloyd Garrison read the certificate of marriage and invited those who had witnessed the ceremony to sign it. In the evening Theodore and Angelina presided over a reception at which several blacks were present, including two former slaves once owned by John Faucheraud Grimké but liberated by Anna Frost when she inherited them.[122]

The next day James Thome wrote the Welds to apologize for his absence from the service and went on to characterize the event in terms even the newlyweds must have felt were accurate. This, according to Thome, was the most singular of matches:

> Who but Angelina E. Grimke could have arrested the solitary eagle in his sun-high aims and brought him arrow-pierced and fluttering down to Hymen's altar, owning that "marriage *is* honorable"? And who but Theodore D. Weld could ever have satisfied the aspiring champion of women's rights (forgive my pleasantry, sister) that *after all* "the husband is the head of the wife"?[123]

X

A Reforming Marriage

One Sunday in the summer of 1852, two reformers, Henry Black-well and Samuel Dorrance, came to visit the Welds at their Belle-ville, New Jersey residence.[1] As they approached the tree-shaded piazza, they were greeted by Angelina and Sarah, both sporting that latest of reform costumes, the Bloomer. The sisters were sur-rounded by a dozen children busily reading and chatting the sabbath away. Nine of the children were students at Theodore's small residential school, three of them—two boys and a girl—were the Welds' own. The visitors found Weld himself working in the garden, a slightly balding man of forty-eight who other-wise displayed in his visage the fire that had once made him famous. The guests stayed for dinner, and after the meal retired with the trio to a parlor built into the spreading branches of a pine tree. There they talked about the world of reform.

Blackwell finally asked the inevitable question: Why had the Welds retired from active service in reform movements? It was a puzzle to many, but by 1844 these once zealous public figures had withdrawn from the battlefield. Theodore answered for him-self, but in some ways he spoke for Angelina and Sarah as well.

It all began with the loss of his voice in 1836, which had occa-sioned a period of deep self-questioning. Weld had found that he was "all wrong," that he had made the mistake of fighting evil with evil, and that this was not the best way to rid the world of error. "All his old opinions and principles began to loosen and scale off," went Blackwell's version of Weld's answer. "He threw aside books, newspapers, everything, and for ten years found there was nothing on earth for him to do but to dig ditches and work upon his farm."[2]

Blackwell argued against this position, but Weld replied with almost kind condescension. " 'There is a fighting era in everyone's life. While you feel it so, fight on; it is your duty, and the best thing you can possibly do. But when your work in that line is done, you will reach another and a higher view.' " He claimed that he had reached this "higher sphere of experience," that within it he lived a manly life of warm piety. The visitor thought this strange and insisted that one should fight error until it had been annihilated.

Nonetheless Blackwell did want to scotch one commonly held view of the Welds' retirement. "I don't think it was marriage which is to blame for their withdrawal from public life, as so many suppose," he wrote to his future wife Lucy Stone, "but that it arose from a combination of physical, intellectual and moral causes quite independent of it."[3]

In his last judgment, Blackwell was both right and wrong. He saw correctly Weld's sense of a higher existence as one of myriad causes and manifestations. But he dismissed too easily the role of marriage in Weld's transformation. Theodore's surrender to romantic passion marked as vivid and profound a watershed as his religious conversion of 1826. The similarity was great in style as well as significance. Weld's guilt-ridden resistance to desire; his conviction of sin over hurting Angelina; the joyful waves of love's confession; and the sense of new worlds of feeling and rapture—all marked rough parallels with the conversion experience. Similar too was the way he forged passion into Christian duty. It was in the transforming power of love and surrender that his "higher sphere of experience" had its roots, and it was in the consciousness that he was soon to be married that the first signs of a new path appeared. At the time, he could not know how long and torturous a path it would be.

"I feel gathering in and settling down upon me an inexpressibly solemn sense of myriad responsibilities never distinctly contemplated before." So wrote Theodore to Angelina a month before their wedding. He wished to "search out all the *relations* of our responsibilties and *know thoroughly ALL* of them, *what* they [were] from the *least* to the *greatest,* and every minute particular of duty to which they summon us." Confident that they would agree down to the last point, Weld set forth his ideal of the pietist's marriage. Point one commanded that those to be married should "STUDY EACH OTHER PROFOUNDLY" and should especially concentrate on informing the other of "defects in principles, habits, tastes, temper, talents, judgment, prudence, moral feeling, sympathy, etc. so all *weaknesses,* prejudices, predilections, impulses, passions, and especially easily besettings."[4]

They should also freely converse on all aspects of marital responsibility, especially those relating to the raising of children to be "vessels of usefulness and honor to God and man." In addition, they must create rules of order in the household relating to dress, furniture, diet, exercise, hours of rising and sleeping, and every other detail of the domestic environment. Finally, they should establish rules for proper relations with others—neighbors, visitors, local communities, churches, civil governments, and objects of charity.[5]

Theodore knew that carrying through this program with love and honesty would be a difficult task, since marriage had been warped by a "horrible and almost universal perversion and degeneracy of mind and heart"; it made even clear thinking about this most important of Divine institutions well-nigh impossible. Therein lay the challenge, for Weld now saw marriage as the most important and responsible human relationship, "touching as it d[id] and giving character to all others." Every element of society "gravitate[d] toward it with centripetal force and receive[d] from it abiding impress." They, as reformers in a new age of reformation, in the "crisis age of the world," must redeem marriage from its perversions—"and who knoweth but God has brought us into this state for such a time as this?" Indeed, Weld saw his new mission potentially as important as antislavery, since of all the horrors in the world that needed reforming, marriages as they were might be "the most horrible perversions of all."[6]

Having already placed a significant portion of the world's weight on the impending marriage, Theodore added more to Angelina's particular load. He lamented that nine-tenths of the community considered her "spoiled for domestic life," and that these doubters included many reformers. A "friend" once confided to Weld that he thought it *"impossible* for a man of high and pure feeling ever to *marry* [her]," and that Angelina's case should be a warning to young women contemplating public careers. As Theodore wrote, his anger welled in contempt at such views and their pervasiveness: "I know that the devil of dominion over woman will be *one* of the last that will be cast out of [men]; and when finally it is effected by some word of power or fiery ministration or bloody baptism, they will rave like legion among the tombs and wallow foaming." But more to the main point:

> I think I was speaking of the peculiar responsibility resting on *you,* Beloved, on account of your *doctrine* and *practice* touching the sphere of woman. I will only add that you are the FIRST woman everywhere known to be on this ground, to whom in the Providence of God the *practical test* of married life will be applied.

Thousands would wait with "Satanic eagerness" for her to fail.[7]

Theodore saw his own test in more personal terms. He had never faced the challenge of living closely with another, of compromising with or surrendering to the will of someone else. Others had always yielded or deferred to him. Though he had always "loathed and spurned" positions of leadership, somehow he managed to "control and give shape to a thousand things with which [he] *seemed* to have nothing to do." This had happened because others had "unlimited" though unwarranted confidence in his talent, opinions, wisdom, judgment, farsightedness, integrity, conscience, fearlessness, and "freedom from unworthy motives."[8] Weld's confessional letters could have left no doubt in

Angelina's mind of his flawed nature; he longed to see what effect life with a woman who knew the truth about him would have, "what developments would be brought about in [his] character by a *counteraction* of [his] wishes or by others not adopting [his] views and plans and by their not being willing to do as *I think best.*"[9]

His account of the past, while both self-serving and inaccurate, did reveal a serious inner concern. For Weld the life of leadership had been a lonely one; he had felt compelled to maintain his saintly image, never to reveal his full humanity to those around him. With Angelina he had managed to show the vulnerable side of himself, and it was important for him to make more permanent its revelation in marriage. Ironically, the very tone of Weld's discourse on the meaning of marriage, final in its judgment and sure of Angelina's complete agreement, indicated just how far he was from that openness to the will of another and just how much of an inner battle had yet to be waged.

Still, a sense of playfulness began to appear side by side with the grave pronouncements of marital mission. Nowhere was this more evident than in Theodore's search for a proper home. An itinerant for almost twenty years, a sort of prodigal son, he relished the thought of finally living within emotional and physical dimensions larger than his New York hovel. And those dimensions more than faintly resembled the Hampton farm of his boyhood. Thus, though he planned to work in Manhattan, he looked across the Hudson to New Jersey for a spread with land to till, wilds to walk, streams to leap, and trees to climb. As Weld investigated possibilities, boyhood memories of farming crossed his mind. Theodore wrote to Angelina about one piece of property that caught his fancy, and suggested ways in which they could get around the fact that it was too large and too expensive. They might share the house with the Birneys to help fill space and pay the rent; more important, Weld could raise vegetables enough for all and "ten times more to speculate upon and thus play the *yankee.*"[10] Five days later, still ruminating over the large house, Weld argued that, being so close to a city market, he could raise the entire rent working three hours a day. "For you must know that you are going to marry a *farmer*. When but fourteen years old I had the entire charge of a farm of near one hundred acres—but enough of this."[11] Enough indeed. Weld the Yankee farmer struggled with Weld the pietist. They could not take the house—it was too showy. Besides, he could not bear to live with the Birneys, "For you and dear Sarah and I are a strange trio, different from all the world beside I do believe."[12]

Theodore finally found a smaller house with land enough to till; the trio visited the Welds in Manlius after the wedding, and settled down at Fort Lee, New Jersey in mid-July. The trappings of home life were simple. The Welds eschewed stylized furniture, all "*gew gawed* and gilded and tipt off with variegated colors," and chose plain cherrywood instead.[13] Soon they mounted a large picture entitled "Kneeling Slave" over the mantelpiece. "It is just such a speaking monument of suffering as we want in our parlor," Angelina wrote to the friend who had given it to them. "We want those who come into our house to see at a glance that we are on the side of the oppressed and the poor."[14]

Within this plain but pointed setting the Welds ran their household according to the scientific piety of various popular advisers. They kept a Graham table, which excluded meat, condiments, and stimulants such as alcohol, tea, and coffee. Still the Welds were thrilled with the taste and variety of foods allowed— potatoes, rice, asparagus, mush, Indian bread, stewed fruit, milk, beans, and, of course, the famous "Graham" wholewheat crackers and bread. Sarah and Angelina went beyond mere dietary reform in adopting the time-saving features recommended by William Andrus Alcott's *Young Housekeeper*.[15] Alcott considered housekeeping to be one of the most important callings, indeed too crucial to be practiced without the aid of scientific analysis. Comparing the housekeeper to the legislator, Alcott declared: "Let me have the control of the nursery—let me direct the sweeping, the washing, the fire-building, the cooking, the conversation, etc., of the infant and the child—and I care little whether the laws are made by one man, by a few men, or by many men."[16]

The Alcott system emphasized that efficient management of time could free the young wife for study and moral elevation. Alcott suggested that time spent in the kitchen might be cut by as much as three-fourths. He advocated adherence to a schedule as the sure way to allow a balanced and productive day. Simplicity was the essence, and it was on grounds of easy preparation as well as well-being that Alcott recommended a vegetable diet. "We believe it is the most conducive to health," wrote Sarah of the Graham diet and the Alcott system, "and, besides, it is such an emancipation of woman from the toils of the kitchen, and saves so much precious time for purposes of more importance than eating and drinking. . . . This week I am cook, and am writing this while my beans are boiling and pears stewing for dinner." They had even become efficient enough to do all the cooking for a week on one day.[17]

Angelina entered the world of domesticity with enthusiasm and not without some humor. "Indeed I think our enemies would rejoice," she wrote Anne Warren Weston, "could they only look in upon us from day to day and see us toiling in domestic life instead of lecturing to *promiscuous* audiences."[18] Yet she insisted that the sisters were *"thus* doing *as much"* for women's rights as in their lecturing. They must show that when the appropriate time came they were "as anxious to make good bread as [they] ever were to deliver a good lecture."[19] It was a struggle, since she had been served by slaves as a child and had lived as a guest for most of her adult life. But Theodore hired a friend to instruct her in the art of Graham cooking, and she looked forward to the day when she might feel confident enough to invite friends for meals.[20] Theodore's own mood helped Angelina immeasurably in the adjustment to domestic life. His "contented and cheerful mind" comforted her through the frustrations of occasional bad meals; she speculated that labor in the garden gave him such an appetite that "everything [was] sweet to him . . . though some might think [it] not fit to eat."[21]

Life in general tasted sweet to Weld. From a life unrooted and driven, one capped by physical debility and depression, he had emerged into a world of some security and emotional release. Never forgetting the cause of the slave or the Lord, he could nevertheless find simple happiness in his garden, contemplate nature all around him, and surrender to Angelina's tenderness. The romance of courtship lingered long at Fort Lee and thrived in a setting of pious Grahamism and antislavery work. A letter written by Angelina to Sarah while the older sister was visiting Philadelphia gives us a window through which to view day-to-day life with the Welds. Writing just before she and Theodore took a "moonlight ramble on the river bank," Angelina recounted daily events since Sarah's departure. After Theodore and Sarah had left for the steamer, Angelina cleared the kitchen and began to sweep the house; she reached the kitchen just in time for the evening meal, which she relished despite being alone—"constant exercise gives a good appetite thou knowest."[22] She then continued her housework, all the while expecting to hear the pistons of the steamboat *Echo* announce Theodore's return. "Soon I heard it, and blew my whistle which was *not* responded to, and I began to fear my Thoda was not on board, but I blew it again and the glad sound came merrily over the water and I tho't I saw him." They walked along the river and discussed the events of the day.[23]

The following morning they decided to suspend Bible study until Sarah returned. Angelina spent the day "meeting and writing," while Weld worked on a revision of *Bible Against Slavery*. In the evening Angelina walked a mile and a half down the river and back, farther than she had ever been. The next day, when the sun finally emerged from a cloudy morning, Angelina and Theodore ran up the palisades and sunned themselves on a rock. Some days later, they gathered beans and apples; in the evening they shelled and pared them, all the while reviewing Weld's Bible argument. Angelina also decided to stew some apples in the fire so as to save time; she only managed to burn them. Theodore ate them anyway: "They were just as nice to our dear Thoda, who *never* complains of any thing."[24]

A Reforming Marriage

One evening, instead of walking along the river banks, they hiked to the palisades and surveyed the scene:

> The moon shone most beautifully and threw her mantle of light all abroad over the blue arch of heaven, the gentle flowing river and the woods and vales around us. We stood for some time admiring the scene before me and could not help thinking if earth was so lovely and bright, what must be the glories of that upper temple which needeth not the light of the sun or of the moon, for the Lord God and the Lamb are the light thereof. . . . We returned to our dear little home and went to bed by the lamp of heaven for we needed no other so brightly did she shine thro' our windows.[25]

There is a certain marvel in the way Angelina and Theodore, in their middle thirties, could recapture the innocence and wonder of youthful love and integrate it into the committed life they led. Conscious of their regained youth, these two serious people could playfully assign the role of mother to Sarah. "Our dearest A. has told you how we have been, what we have done, and what good children we have been since you left us," Theodore added to Angelina's letter. "She should have told you however that Thoda 'has been as usual, tum naughty.'" Apparently even marriage had not cured Theodore of occasional dyspepsia.[26]

At times Theodore was left alone, as when the sisters traveled to Philadelphia in June 1839. Weld gazed after them at the dock, watched the steamboat round the bend, and whatever feelings of anxiety he felt were lost in a "quiet thankful and joyous spirit"; he knew that God had ordered all things, and that He would "make this little separation a blessing to us a seasonable and *needed discipline.*" In that spirit he went to the antislavery office, there to find in his mail box "a letter direct to Theodore D. Grimke (Womens rights!)." It turned out to be the postmaster's mistake or joke, the letter being a bill for a Mr. Grimké of Charleston.[27]

While the sisters were away, Theodore took an exhausted Henry B. Stanton home to Fort Lee, there "bachellor-hall-ing" with him for the weekend. Weld lavished upon his guest a spread of Graham bread and rice, fruits, jams, radishes, milk,

Cheese and Graham wafers, Graham cake, raisins and almonds—
"(Variety variety!)." Stanton thought him the "handiest *house
maid*" and the delicious fare disappeared into their hungry
mouths "by platoons." Weld took joy not only in cooking, but
also in cleaning and arranging everything as his "Nina" would
have; at night he dreamed about her.[28]

In these first years of marriage—times of moonlit walks and
Grahamite feasts—the Welds' contribution to reform did not
diminish, but rather changed in nature. Theodore continued as
editor of the *Antislavery Almanac* and other nonperiodical publications. In May 1839 he asked that his salary be reduced; motivated in part by his understanding of the society's fiscal crisis,
this action may also have reflected the fact that he worked fewer
hours at the antislavery office and spent more time at home.[29]
He also refused two new jobs—those of Corresponding Secretary
and member of the Executive Committee.[30] Sarah's and Angelina's
lives changed more drastically. Two days after her marriage,
Angelina gave her last public address for many years. At Fort
Lee she and Sarah engaged in local petition campaigns, but the
ruling emotion in their lives was perhaps best expressed by
Angelina in a letter to Elizabeth Pease: "I cannot tell thee how
I love this private life—how I have thanked my heavenly Father
for this respite from public labor." She left open the possibility
of a return to more active public service, but for the moment she
would concentrate on solving "this mystery of housewifery."[31]

Oddly enough, it was during this period of retrenchment that
the trio produced their most tangible and lasting contribution to
the antislavery cause, *American Slavery As It Is: Testimony of a
Thousand Witnesses;* almost instantly it became antislavery's
most influential and widely circulated pamphlet. Sometime in
1838, Theodore began to formulate the idea that the slaveholder
might be hanged by his own words, that Southern newspapers
and the testimony of those who had viewed slavery personally
might provide the most telling case against bondage. Beginning
late in 1838, working six hours a day and for six months, the sis-

ters searched through more than twenty thousand copies of Southern newspapers, marking and clipping proofs of slavery's depravity. Meanwhile, Weld had prepared a form letter requesting testimony from those who had visited or were then living in the South. This mosaic of clippings and firsthand accounts, tied together by trenchant analyses by Weld himself, became *American Slavery As It Is*.[32]

Two of the thousand witnesses were Sarah and Angelina; each contributed lengthy descriptions of slavery as they had known it in Charleston, emphasizing both the moral bankruptcy and physical cruelties endemic to the institution. Their essays were remarkably searing and almost confessional in tone. Angelina recalled awful scenes from her childhood. Particularly vivid were her memories of the treadmill Charlestonians had created to punish "incorrigibles." She told of a prominent woman, one of the city's elite and a Christian, who regularly had slaves transported to the mill:

> One poor girl, whom she sent there to be flogged, and who was accordingly stripped *naked* and whipped, showed me the deep gashes on her back—I might have laid my whole finger in them— *large pieces of flesh had actually been cut out by the torturing lash.*[33]

She also described a slave boy, a servant at her school, whose head had been shaved to disgrace him and who had been whipped so badly that he could hardly walk. "So horrible was the impression produced upon my mind by his heart-broken countenance and crippled person that I fainted away."[34] These were but two of Angelina's memories as recorded in *American Slavery As It Is;* her full statement comprised but five of over two hundred double-columned, tightly printed pages. Her experiences were neither atypical nor the most horrific.

American Slavery As It Is marked a major change in Weld's antislavery strategy. Only three years earlier, his speeches had stressed the glory of freedom for the slave as much as the horrors of bondage, and he rarely described the latter in vivid detail. This balanced approach functioned within a moral suasion argument—the hope was that through the ameliorative spirit of Christian love the South as well as the North would be converted to antislavery. By 1838 it was clear to most abolitionists that the South could not be convinced by such tactics; many wondered about the effectiveness of moral suasion in the North.[35] This change in view brought an increased severity of tone and content in antislavery propaganda.

The very first words of Weld's introduction to *Slavery As It Is* caught this new mood. The benevolent Christian had become a prosecuting attorney:

> Reader, you are empannelled as a juror to try a plain case and bring in an honest verdict. The question at issue is not one of law, but of fact—"What is the actual condition of the slaves in the United States?" A plainer case never went to a jury. . . . The case of Human Rights against Slavery has been adjudicated in the court of conscience times innumerable. The same verdict has always been rendered—"Guilty"; the same sentence has always been pronounced, "Let it be accursed."[36]

Weld argued his case as a rebuttal to the master's claim that slavery was a benign institution. He posed simple tests of sincerity: "Try him; clank the chains in his ears, and tell him they are for *him*. Give him an hour to prepare his wife and children for a life of slavery . . . , then look at his pale lips and trembling knees, and you have *nature's* testimony against slavery." Was robbing men of their freedom for no reason "right, just, benevolent"? Could the masters who robbed the slave of his body and freedom be at the same time kind and "quite too tenderhearted ever to cuff or kick" him? Yet this was what slaveholders wished Northerners to believe. "The only marvel is, that men of sense can be gulled by such professions. Despots always insist that they are merciful," scoffed Weld. "The greatest tyrants that ever dripped with blood have assumed the titles of 'most gracious,' 'most clement,' 'most merciful,' etc., and have ordered their crouching vassals to accost them thus."[37]

In earlier appeals Weld had relied on the capability of his audience to understand the psychology of tyranny; this time he demonstrated with material facts that slaves in the United States were treated "with barbarous inhumanity." He summarized at the outset what his evidence would prove:

> They are overworked, underfed, wretchedly clad and lodged, and have insufficient sleep; that they are often made to wear round their necks iron collars armed with prongs, to drag heavy chains and weights at their feet while working in the field, and to wear yokes, and bells, and iron horns; that they are often kept confined in the stocks day and night for weeks together, made to wear gags in their mouths for hours or days, have some of their front teeth torn out or broken off, that they may be easily detected when they run away; that they are frequently flogged with terrible severity, have red pepper rubbed into their lacerated flesh, and hot brine, spirits of turpentine, etc., poured over the gashes to increase the torture; that they are often stripped naked, their backs and limbs cut with knives, bruised and mangled by scores and hundreds of blows with the paddle, and terribly torn by the claws of cats, drawn over them by their tormentors . . . that their ears are often cut off, their eyes knocked out, their bones broken, their flesh branded with red hot irons; that they are maimed, mutilated and burned to death over slow fires. All these things, and more, and worse, we shall *prove*.[38]

The proof followed, in endless columns of fine print, from travelers, former residents in the South, slaveholders, and advertisements in Southern newspapers. One by one, Weld demolished the most common defenses of slavery.

American Slavery As It Is met with mixed but predictable response. Abolitionist papers lauded it, some evincing shock over the cruelties documented; after all, most abolitionists were innocents when it came to the details of slave existence. The popular press ignored the tract. Nevertheless it sold over one hundred thousand copies in its first year and continued to gain circulation and sales as its reputation spread.[39]

There is an apparent irony in the fact that Weld conceived and produced this grim, almost ghoulish, account of slavery at the most exciting and fulfilling point in his own personal life. Perhaps it was mere coincidence; the demands of the antislavery cause at that time may have been enough to account for the tract. However, the deepening of Weld's sensibilities through romance and marriage may also have helped him to feel the horror of slavery more intensely. His first ideas about bondage had been forged when he was a rebellious seeker of freedom; he had stressed in his speeches the drama of the passage from slavery to freedom. Now he was a married man, reveling in the first glow of familial and sexual intimacy, ever more sensitive to aspects of life that the slave system twisted or denied to blacks. In addition, he had passionately surrendered to a woman tortured by the guilt of a slaveholding past. Her horrors had become his, and for him this meant that the slave issue could no longer be treated in the naive and loving terms of moral suasion.

The intensity with which Weld and the sisters plunged into their new existence could not help but cause strain in relations with the outside world. In Theodore's case, it appeared to old friends that in abandoning bachelorhood he was also saying goodbye to the comradeship of the past. John Greenleaf Whittier transformed his anxieties on this count into a sly wedding poem which began:

> Alack and Alas! that a brother of mine,
> A bachelor sworn on celibacy's altar,
> Should leave me alone at the desolate shrine
> And stoop his own neck to the enemy's halter![40]

James A. Thome, whose awe and love for Theodore had remained constant since their meeting at Lane, felt a mixture of abandonment and anger at news of the marriage. Weld, after all, had called Thome a "Jack ass" for considering marriage himself. Thome's anger prevented him from attending the wedding; later he hoped that he had not injured their friendship. Angelina consoled Thome on this point; she insisted that now Theodore knew a bit more about love. Writing to the Welds, Thome tried to understand:

> I am *tempted* to believe [Angelina] is more than half correct in her notions of Theodore, notwithstanding he treated me so scurvily in my days of love. It is true I can hardly forgive him for

that; but I shall lay it to the charge of his total inexperience in love affairs. I know he would not treat one so now. He has learned somewhat of the delicacy of those chords which the finger of love has strung, *too much* to torture them by the touch of rudeness.[41]

Yet for Weld these early years of marriage, and especially soliciting evidence for *Slavery As It Is,* were sometimes the occasion for renewal of lost or neglected relationships. For example, he added a personal note to the form letter sent to ex-Lane boy Sereno W. Streeter. "I thank you a thousand times for your kind remembrance of an old but unworthy friend," replied Streeter. "I was apprehensive that my name had ere this been erased from the *heart* if not from the memory. I can truly say that the language of my own soul is—Weld is *still Weld.*"[42]

Old associates treated Sarah and Angelina less lovingly. The Quakers excommunicated them for participating in the non-Quaker ceremony that united the Welds.[43] Their Southern relatives criticized them mercilessly for their contributions to *American Slavery As It Is.* Whatever distress this caused the sisters was compounded by the death of their mother, Mary Grimké, just after the publication of the tract. Implying that Angelina had directed her narrative against her mother, sister Anna taunted: "Now that she slumbers sweetly in her saviors Bosom, your unmeasured shafts will be pointed at her in vain."[44]

Angelina responded with firm conviction. She was attacking an institution, not individuals and certainly not her mother. "It cost us more *agony of soul* to write those testimonies than any thing we ever did," she confessed; "but the Lord required it and gave us strength to do it, leaving *all* the consequences in HIS holy hands."[45]

The sisters fared little better with women friends in the antislavery movement. Angelina and Sarah were valued as effective and somewhat exotic allies among Garrisonians and budding feminists, and their "retirement" to Fort Lee appeared to be a betrayal of duty. Few thought of the sisters' personal happiness, nor did they consider the production of *American Slavery As It*

Is a substitute for the public speaking that had made the Grimkés famous. For instance, five months after marriage Lydia Maria Child replied to Angelina's first letter since the wedding with a quip: "I began to think it was with you as with a girl, who being met by a person with whom she had formerly lived at service, was asked, 'Where do you live now, Nancy?' 'Please, ma'am, I dont live anywhere now; I'm married.'"[46] Child was relieved that this did not seem to be the case. By May 1839, however, even as the Grimkés finished their arduous labors on *Slavery As It Is*, rumors circulated of their apostasy. It was rumored that they had written Samuel Philbrick expressing revised views on the peace issue, and Deborah Weston promptly called the letters "vile beyond description."[47] Lucia Weston dubbed them "the most ludicrous stuff" and expressed particular shock that Angelina had not found time to read the *Liberator*, though she was able to work on "Theodore's book" [*American Slavery As It Is*] and even to seed the flower beds.[48] "The Grimkes," chided Deborah Weston, "I think are extinct."[49]

From a distance the disappointed ones could carp, but those who took a closer look at the happenings in Fort Lee came away with a different impression. Abby Kelley, a fervent Garrisonian, visited the Welds in May 1839. She found Angelina, instead of happily ignoring the *Liberator* and planting her garden, enfeebled by overwork on *American Slavery As It Is* and enervated by the first stages of pregnancy. Kelley engaged Theodore in an "unsparingly severe" debate on the peace issue: "[He] says all that Garrison, M. W. Chapman, and all others who have adopted the will o wisp delusions of non-resistance can possibly do for the emancipation of the slave will be undermined and counteracted by their idle notions on this subject—Yet not *idle, pernicious* is even too soft a name. . . . Indeed it seems to me that he looks upon the whole matter with deep contempt mingled with pity."[50] Notwithstanding such fierce combat, Kelley left remarkably refreshed. "I think I never passed a week more profitably," she wrote, "—It was a school which called into exercise almost every better principle and feeling of the heart."[51]

The nonresistance issue with which Abby Kelley and Weld wrestled was but part of a broader battle of factions within antislavery, a battle that had begun to drive abolitionism into schism and eventually left permanent scars on the participants and on the movement as a whole. Garrison's introduction of nonresistance, women's rights, and anticlerical propaganda into the columns of the *Liberator* provided the specific source of upheaval. Conservative abolitionists such as Lewis Tappan and Amos Anson Phelps opposed the mixing of other causes with antislavery for two reasons. First, they genuinely opposed these doctrines. Second, they feared that such radical advocacy would limit antislavery's appeal to the general public. The first open battle occurred at the annual meeting of the Massachusetts Antislavery Society in January 1839. Anti-Garrison forces led by Henry B. Stanton presented resolutions that favored voting for antislavery candidates and the founding of a new antislavery newspaper to counteract the *Liberator*. The Garrisonians carried the day, however, at which point the opposition formed a new society and newspaper.[52] The New York-based Executive Committee of the American Antislavery Society, largely sympathetic to the defeated faction, prepared to do battle with the Garrisonians. The showdown finally came in May 1840, when at the annual meeting Garrisonians gained control of the national society. Tappan and his allies promptly seceded and founded the American and Foreign Antislavery Society, which among other things explicitly denied women the right to vote in society elections or on policy issues.[53]

The split put Weld in an awkward position. Most of his friends in the movement, men such as Tappan and Stanton, were in the New York conservative camp. Yet on the key issue of women's rights, he stood closer to the Garrisonians and in fact could not accept the exclusionary policies of the American and Foreign Antislavery Society. In part because of this anomalous position, he remained neutral. Yet Weld's neutrality was less dependent on issues and personal loyalties than on the distinct perspective from which he viewed the movement. His measures for success were those of the pietist—how diligently did an individual or organization work for the cause at hand, and how closely did those involved hew to the highest standards of Christian conduct? On those counts, he had criticisms of the movement and antislavery men and women that honored no lines of faction. Astounded by the lack of response to his appeals for help in compiling information for *American Slavery As It Is,* he reiterated an old complaint: "The great body of Abolitionists seem to be mere *passengers* on a pleasure sail . . . they are willing to take the helm, or handle the speaking trumpet or *go up aloft* to see and *be seen,* but to bone down to *ship work* as a common sailor, especially in the *hold,* is a sort of business that cometh not with observation, and they are off."[54]

Weld was even more horrified by the ever increasing battlings of abolitionists among themselves, and the animosity and posturing that accompanied these disputes. "Oh when, when will the wrath and malice and most unChristlike conflicts in Massachusetts cease!" he exclaimed to Gerrit Smith in September 1839. "Come Lord Jesus, Come quickly."[55] A month later, he was more dismayed than ever:

> Their calling each other *dishonest hypocritical* double tongued false witnesses, etc. is probably what each *really believes* of the others, and *believing* it, let them say it; but the manifest *state of mind* toward each other in which it is all said, Oh how it crucifies the Savior afresh. I instinctively recoil from its fiery contact and charge my soul "come not thou into their secret." The spirit of Scott and Johnson is the spirit of slaveholders *undiluted;* that of Garrison, St. Clair, Wise, Mrs. Chapman, Phelps and Torrey, though less personally rancorous, is hardly less at war with the spirit of Jesus.[56]

Thus Weld was bothered less by the issues than by the inability of the combatants to honor each other as they fought. Why could they not joust as he did with Abby Kelley, yet come away elevated and refreshed? If approached in a Christian spirit, differences among comrades might even become the supreme test of manhood. He expressed this opinion in correspondence to

Amos Anson Phelps, with whom he disagreed on women's rights. Despite the fact that Theodore abhorred Phelps's antifeminist position, he loved and respected him all the more for cleaving to his convictions: "To go against enemies is easy enough—indeed *not* to go against them is a sublime conquest of human nature—but to go against *friends* is the only real test of genuine *independence.*"[57] As it turned out, Weld's own route to "genuine *independence*" came through standing aloof from the battle and playing the movement's critic from within. But if the antislavery movement was proving to be less and less conducive to Christian conduct, Weld felt he had found more fertile ground for piety at home.

XI

"I have ceased to know myself"

Weld's first year of marriage had been something of an extended honeymoon, one that encompassed few responsibilities beyond survival, mutual self-discovery, and feverish antislavery work. It was Christian bliss. With the birth of Charles Stuart Faucheraud Weld on December 13, 1839, however, life became increasingly more complex and trying. Parenthood brought Theodore and Angelina face to face with tasks, feelings, and conflicts unimagined in the first year of marriage. The years that followed brought much pain and even tragedy; but they also brought a deepened sense of human love and intimacy that radically changed Theodore's conception of the public life and his own place in the world of reform.

Angelina's pregnancy was uneventful, as was the delivery. Theodore responded in joyful awe punctuated with tearful gushes. Sarah, who would never be a natural mother, loved the infant as her own. "Oh, the ecstacy and the gratitude!" she wrote. "How I opened the little blanket and peeped in to gaze, with swimming eyes, at my treasure, and looked upon that face forever so dear!"[1]

As for Angelina, the first joys of birth were darkened by her inability to nurse little Charley. "I can't tell thee how I felt as I pressed him to an *empty* breast on one side and a *stony* breast on the other," she lamented to Jane Smith. Angelina wanted to cry, but instead forced upon herself a hollow resignation.[2] The Welds looked to Andrew Combe's *Physiology of Digestion* for a practical solution to feeding the child. Combe recommended the daily consumption of "a few teaspoonfuls of fresh cow's milk diluted with water," a course they followed till an emaciated Charley had practically wasted away.[3] Sarah stepped in while Theodore and Angelina were away on a brief trip; she fed the infant until he was sated. Charley quickly recovered and all learned a lesson about advice books.[4]

Meanwhile Theodore faced a new problem and challenge, the earning of an income sufficient to care for his family. He had mixed feelings about money; it was all so much "filthy lucre" to him. He joked uneasily about his New England background in this regard because of that region's legendary pecuniary preoccupations. When Weld was alone he had always lived on the margin, accepting minimal remuneration from the antislavery society and borrowing whatever else he needed from friends and family. Marriage had actually solved some economic problems, since both sisters had modest inheritances; but the arrival of Charley forced upon him the need to make more money and to settle down.

Actually Weld may have secretly welcomed this new responsibility, for he had joked about a hidden desire to *"play the yankee."*[5] It permitted him to concentrate even more on farming, to imitate the yeomen of Hampton. He could finally have a farm of his own. In March 1840, Theodore scraped together $5,750 to purchase at a sheriff's sale a rundown, fifty-acre spread on the Passaic River near Belleville, New Jersey. As Angelina put it to Jane Smith, the property was "sadly out of order."[6] Almost every structure—house, fences, corn crib, barn, and stable—needed some repair. Still it had rich possibilities. The farm included seven hundred feet of river frontage, a pretty yard, a gate framed by lilac trees and weeping willows, grounds dotted with Gilead-pine and hemlock, and a rosebush-lined forty-eight-foot piazza. To the south of the house lay a garden with grapevines, raspberry, currant, and gooseberry bushes, as well as numerous fruit trees. The house itself was basically of stone, with two rooms on the first floor and three on the second. A wooden addition increased the number of rooms to ten—space enough for a growing family and guests.[7]

At first all was bliss again as the Welds moved to Belleville in early summer of 1840. Angelina now called the once starving Charley "*Sunny face.*"[8] The garden flourished in sweet corn, summer beans, new potatoes, beets, and onions. "Thoda's" fields yielded oats, corn, potatoes, beans, squash, and pumpkins— enough for market and for home.[9]

As summer turned to fall, however, complications strained the household. Weld, who had boldly set out to play the Yankee, felt himself done in. One R. L. Pomeroy had sold Theodore land incorporated into the Belleville property at seventy-five dollars per acre rather than at the market price of fifty, and in addition forced him to buy property he did not want. There was nothing illegal in any of these matters, but Theodore burned with indignation that business could not be conducted more scrupulously. In the end, he asked Lewis Tappan to intercede for him. One might as well let businessmen deal with businessmen.[10]

Pecuniary problems such as those with Pomeroy paled before more serious matters. In early September, Weld set out to rebuild the fallen walls that had shielded the property from river flooding and to drain parts of the property that had already been swamped. Sarah had come down with a severe fever, and all feared that Angelina and Charley would be next if these water-logged breeding grounds for mosquitoes were not dried up. Theodore and four hired men labored ten to twelve hours a day to clean up the mess.[11]

Other responsibilities piled up. The Welds had taken on the burden of caring for Stephen, an ex-slave of the Grimkés who had come North at the invitation of the sisters. In addition, Angelina was pregnant again. With the burden of pregnancy, the Welds decided to indulge in the luxury of domestic help.[12] Life had become so hectic that Angelina looked forward to her confinement if only "as a time of *rest, rest,* for I sometimes feel as if I could lie down for days and *enjoy* doing *nothing—nothing* if I only had a good excuse for such laziness."[13] By October, with Angelina in her seventh month, Theodore and Sarah had entirely taken over care of Charley except for bottle feeding him and putting him to bed.[14]

Angelina gave birth to Theodore Grimké Weld on January 3, 1841; this time she had no problem nursing. "Often when he is drinking down the full stream of milk which flows from my bosom," she confided to Jane Smith, "do I remember with mingled feelings of anguish and gratitude that breast of stone and that fountain of pollution and death which was all I had for my poor little Charles." Still, with all her present happiness, she did not think she would ever love Theodore Grimké Weld with the same intensity as she did her firstborn.[15]

Amidst all this activity, the Welds welcomed a steady stream of houseguests, and a number of them reported an atmosphere at Belleville unchanged in excitement and candor from the time Abby Kelley visited. The English abolitionist Joseph Sturge arrived to find Weld driving his wagon and oxen with a load of rails. Soon after he arrived, two or three ex-Lane rebels came by. They all discussed the issues of the day. Sturge found the experience exhilarating. "Differences of opinions on [antislavery matters] did not, for a moment, interrupt the pleasure of our intercourse," he wrote; "and I could not but wish, that those, of whatever party, who are accustomed to judge harshly of all who cannot pronounce their 'shibboleth,' might be instructed by the candid, charitable, and peace-loving deportment of THEODORE WELD."[16] James G. Birney, who by this time had taken a course of antislavery action very different from Theodore's, went even further in his praise. "Weld," noted Birney during a Belleville visit, "I believe is the most perfect man, intellectually and morally, that I know."[17]

This visitor's view of Weld was only part of the picture. Those closer to him noticed disturbing signs in his behavior. Lewis Tappan even made some ill-guarded observations about him, which mushroomed into rumors questioning Theodore's sanity.[18] Sarah accused him of being inconsiderate and impatient with those around him, and of habitually neglecting the little duties of life while claiming that "great trains of thought" occupied his mind.[19] Weld's own assessment of his behavior from 1839 through 1841, written in answer to Sarah's complaints, was striking:

> All the pride and impatience which you lay to my account, yea, *more far more,* IS MINE. The pride I have always been aware of; the impatience is a monstrous growth of the last two years. Like a tropical plant in a hotbed, it has sprung up into a fearful strength, and oh how deep it has struck it[s] roots! . . . For more than two years I have ceased to know myself. Terrific visions have risen before me and haunted me everywhere and forever. . . .[20]

Years later he still remembered this frightening period. Sending a picture of himself made in 1841 to the sons of William Lloyd Garrison for their father's biography, Weld sized himself up at thirty-eight as "a contemplative milk sop, half a sleep, squinting into space but *seeing* nothing."[21]

It would seem, then, that the bliss of Fort Lee did not survive at Belleville. The move coincided with ever deepening troubles in the antislavery movement, and there can be no question that the abolitionists' internecine warfare took its toll on Weld's hopes for both human nature and reform. More important, however, the harsh realities of two infants and a complicated household began to affect Weld's own fantasy of domestic mission. Theodore Weld the lover was also Theodore Weld the recluse and lone orator; the man who had longed for intimacy and had found it with Angelina was also the child who had spent long hours in the fields and woods, who finally escaped the smothering atmosphere of home as an itinerant orator. Despite the best of intentions, Theodore was peculiarly ill-prepared for the pressures that beset him at Belleville.

He responded to the situation in typical ways. Of course, Weld the pietist could not admit, perhaps even to himself, that the realities of child-rearing and domesticity rubbed raw against part of his own nature. Instead he held in his frustrations and turned them upon his body—he was plagued, for instance, by a return of dyspepsia.[22] In addition, he sought escape by the usual means. He retired to his study for long hours. When the river walls of the property collapsed, Weld took that opportunity to devote himself full-time for four months, twelve hours a day to "ploughing, hoeing, felling trees, splitting rails, digging post holes, making fence, digging and hauling rocks, etc., etc."[23] Certainly the farm needed to be maintained, but Theodore's zeal smacked as much of escape as of pure necessity.

Meanwhile, seemingly miraculously, Weld's speaking voice returned. It improved so much by June 1841 that he agreed to speak at the Newark Antislavery Society's July 4th meeting; he expressed the hope to Gerrit Smith that henceforth he would be able to lecture once a week.[24] He thus recovered one more ticket to freedom. His reentry into antislavery oratory caused more tensions in the household, where no doubt it raised unspoken feelings of jealousy among the sisters. Weld himself became more careless than ever about his household duties and courtesies, and Sarah minced no words in describing his dereliction: "As for instance, thou are going to antislavery meeting thy mind is absorbed with the subject, the arguments, fact etc thou goest to prepare (in haste almost always) thy wardrobe is tumbled one thing is thrown here, and another there and thou art perfectly unconscious of course unmindful, that the time of someone must be consumed in setting them in order. . . ."[25] Such tensions surfaced only occasionally, of course, since the proper response was joy at Weld's return to the rostrum.

Though he was ready to reassert himself in antislavery battle, the channels for such a move were not at all clear in the summer of 1841. Lewis Tappan and Beriah Green, among others, congratulated him on his return, but neither man could offer Theodore an acceptable role in an acceptable organization. He would have nothing to do with the American and Foreign Antislavery Society because of its stance on women, and he continued to keep his distance from the Garrisonians. Weld was an orator with no itinerary, an activist with no clear course of action—and he was aching to get out of the house.[26]

His chance came in December 1841. Joshua Leavitt, editor of the *Emancipator* and now involved in the antislavery lobby in Washington, asked Weld to help a number of antislavery Congressmen prepare a case against the recently passed gag rule, which automatically tabled petitions against slavery and the slave trade. Leavitt hoped that agitation of the gag rule issue on civil libertarian grounds might pave the way for direct consideration of the slavery issue itself. The proposition excited Theodore; it gave him a chance to influence the political process directly, without resorting to the suspect mechanism of a third party. "On the whole the more I look at the subject," he wrote Lewis Tappan, "the more I feel as though I *dare* not assume the responsibility of refusing to comply with such a request."[27]

Only Weld's responsibility to Angelina, Sarah, the children, and the farm stood in the way. Just before receiving Leavitt's letter, he had reduced his hired help to a single domestic servant; he had decided to do all the work on the farm, since money for wages was in short supply. If he were to go to Washington, he would have to ask Tappan for enough money to keep up the farm (the lobbyists had agreed to pay his expenses for travel and maintenance in Washington). He found it hard, however, to ask for charity. Theodore finally wrote Tappan for the money, though not without almost throwing the letter into the fire. "So much for pride—for I am pretty sure it is nothing else," he wrote in a postscript, "and therefore [I] WILL send it."[28] Tappan quickly pledged his support.

Theodore arrived in Washington in late December. He found comfortable lodgings at Mrs. Sprigg's boardinghouse, across from the Capitol, where Leavitt and other abolitionists also stayed. Into these unfamiliar surroundings he injected reminders of home. He arranged for a Graham regimen and made sure to exercise for an hour every morning in the park fronting the Capitol. Soon Weld was hard at work in the Library of Congress. He spent weekdays from nine to five researching legal and historical points for the lobby; in the evenings he and Joshua Leavitt discussed the day's work and goings-on in Congress.[29] At other times Weld simply observed the Washington whirl, attending House and Senate debates and gawking at the general rush of parties, ceremony, and hoopla. "The Worlds splendor which blazes around me," he wrote Angelina, "the pride and fashion, prodigality, ostentatious display and vanity, the desperate strugglings and vaultings of ambition, the envyings and fierce encounters of rivals for office and popular sway, are lessons to my soul that are to be learned nowhere in this country as they are to be learned here."[30]

Weld's own vanity was not a problem, for in Washington he worked without public credit or exposure. He played a significant behind-the-scenes role in the gag rule debates, and positively gloried in watching rather than doing. Particularly poignant was his relationship to John Quincy Adams, for whom he did much research. Theodore wrote Angelina spirited accounts of Adams's speeches, which left no doubt that he adored the shrewd, energetic ex-President who now sat in the House. Weld even allowed himself the indulgence of identifying with the Congressman, since Adams and Ludovicus Weld had known each other at Harvard, and Ezra Weld, Theodore's grandfather, had baptized him.[31] Adams, for his part, noted that his family and the Grimkés were blood relations through the Smiths of the Carolinas; Weld, relating this to Angelina, noted that Ludovicus and John Quincy Adams were second cousins: "Now I confess this scrap of genealogy is the only one that ever gave me any real pleasure, and in this I *do* take a great interest, for it proves *you me* to be actually 'blood relations.' . . . So YOU AND I MUST BE ABOUT SIXTH COUSINS!!"[32]

As it turned out, they were not cousins.[33] Adams had made a mistake. But the "real pleasure" Weld experienced in the thought was extraordinary in itself, since he was a man more prone to duty than pleasure. It was just one indication that his trip to Washington was producing salubrious effects. Another was that since arriving in Washington he had experienced no dyspepsia.[34] Indeed, his physical recovery accompanied what Weld recognized as a spiritual renewal. Reassuring Angelina that his unseemly behavior of the past two years was at an end, he wrote, "[But] though the baptism has been with coals of fire, blessed be God, a sweet hope begins to dawn upon me, that it is to be a baptism unto life and not unto death."[35]

Ironically, Theodore found renewal in escape from the tension-filled life at Belleville—that domestic scene he had idealized at the time of his marriage. Yet Weld did not really want to escape the marriage; it remained his foremost commitment in life. What Theodore and Angelina needed was distance; consciously or unconsciously, purposefully or not, they gained that distance with Weld's trip. It forced them to write to each other, to engage in the style of communication that had allowed these two proud but fragile people to fall in love in the first place. They thus initiated a second courtship, one that concentrated on renewal of trust between husband and wife and the sharpening of Weld's sense of the particulars in that Christian mission of marriage and child-rearing that so dominated his thoughts in the first flush of wedlock.

Despite the obvious costs of having Theodore away from Belleville—the sense of abandonment and lack of help and companionship—Angelina benefited from the correspondence as well. Apparently what Weld feared most had come to pass in the first years of marriage; his opinions held sway on most matters without effective challenge. Angelina admitted as much during Theodore's second trip to Washington: "You ask in one of your letters why I cannot talk before you—only because I have always felt since I knew you such a crushing sense of my own inferiority that it has seemed impossible to rise above it."[36] Their correspondence between Belleville and Washington, though it too was dominated by Angelina's questions and Theodore's answers, still left more room for Angelina to express her own opinions and demands.

The dialogue between the two often took curious turns. On

the surface, Angelina reacted quite favorably to Theodore's endless anecdotes and assessments of the progress of the antislavery
cause. This was to be expected from one so closely identified
with abolition. But what of the frustrated, activist side of Angelina, now home barely coping with two infant sons and totally
hamstrung in her relation with the world of reform? That side of
her became obsessed with the end of the world. It was in late
1841 that she first showed interest in the prophecies of William
Miller, who had constructed a detailed, Biblically based mathe-
matical calculation that predicted the destruction of the world
sometime in 1843.[37] Millerism appealed to Angelina for at least
two reasons. For one thing, an apocalyptic end to earthly existence may have answered secret prayers of escape from her ever
more exhausting role in the household. Even if the prophecy
were to fail, the theological issues raised gave Angelina exercise
for a powerful intellect fast falling into disuse. She longed for
discovery, controversy, and intricate reasoning; she found all of
these in the consideration of Millerism.[38]

It is also clear that Angelina used her fascination with Millerite prophecy as a clandestine weapon against Theodore, whose
work in Washington seemed to provoke a good deal of jealousy.
Millerism explicitly rejected the very foundation of reform work—
the conversion of the world by men to make possible the Millennium—and Angelina faced that issue squarely:

> I feel entirely prepared to give up the old idea of a Millennium
> and to embrace the opinion that the destruction of the world will
> *precede* it, and it certainly is very extraordinary that Daniels date
> should appear to terminate in '43, if there is no truth in these cal-
> culations—There are some things in the Bible which have always
> been inexplicable to me if the old ideas of the conversions of the
> whole world were true, but the new ideas of the Millennium con-
> flict with none so far as I have examined the subject.[39]

If she were right, Weld's work in Washington meant nothing.

Theodore dismissed her musings: "The history of the church
shows that with few if any exceptions, great zeal for the study of
the prophecies and little *practical spirituality* have gone to-

gether." He did not rule out the study of all prophecy, but rather emphasized that "*God* is *first* to be studied, and so studied and communed with as to have the soul taken into captivity, moulded, filled with him."[40] Angelina, first physically abandoned and now almost mocked, fell deeper into despair.

One manifestation of her agitated mind was her fear that Theodore might be assassinated. Washington was a slaveholding city, after all, and abolitionists were hardly popular. When she voiced her apprehension, Weld answered that he had weighed the possibility and trusted in God.[41]

Balancing the tension, however, was a common concern for the proper rearing of Charley and little Thoda. Angelina, whatever her unconscious misgivings, came more and more to believe that "God established families in this state of probation, that they might be *nurseries for heaven*"; she realized that she "never had any thing to do in [her] life of half the importance, as tending [her] babes."[42] Theodore agreed. He especially wished to avoid what he saw as the "misconception" and "misdirection" of his own rearing. Exactly what he meant by this is not clear, for he had mixed feelings about his childhood. Sometimes he regretted his being too much the cut-up; sometimes he felt too harshly punished. In raising his own children, he strived for a sensitive mean between discipline and self-expression.[43]

The foremost problem they faced was two-year-old Charley's temper, ferocious in its own right and quite disturbing when directed at little Theodore. At first Angelina tried locking him in the closet, but gave this up in favor of disapproving of his behavior "in a very firm authoritative tone." If he began to scream again, she repeated the reprimand. Once, after a second berating, Charley leaned toward his mother and pleaded, "Ma kiss Ma kiss—naughty boy, naughty boy—done—done—Ma kiss—Ma kiss."[44] "Now is the time [to subdue his temper]," she wrote, "or it will sweep like a whirlwind over our little family, destroying our peace and *his soul*."[45]

Weld endorsed such actions and warned against "a weak, vacillating, *irresolute, undecided* course" which might ruin Charley forever. A firm, uniform, and prompt response to his tantrums, "mingled with kindness" and free from passion or impatience, seemed best.[46] But as he thought about it longer, Theodore felt that it was not enough to be reactive; one must model and cultivate the proper balance of affections. He displayed the pietist's concern with every detail:

> Effectually to soften and subdue those *impulses* must be the work of every hour and moment, by the cultivation of gentle forbearing, benevolent affections, and by exhibiting them in our example, thus filling the soil with springing wheat which, in its sure growth, will root out the tares. In *connection* with this work of every hour and moment, of every word and look and tone on our part, a firm, steady, prompt and strong expression of disapprobation whenever he exhibits passion, and depriving him of some pleasure or of what he wants when he gets angry about it, will, with Gods blessing, not fail of effect.[47]

Cultivation of Charley's better instincts took three specific forms. First, his parents encouraged him to share and be of help to his younger brother.[48] Second, they made him aware of the plight of the slave. For instance, Angelina showed him the famous picture of a slave ship in Clarkson's slave trade tract and "told him how poor and naked and miserable the slaves were." The next morning Charley asked to see the " 'poor slaves pack up in ship.' " Angelina questioned him as to their condition; he looked at the picture and answered, "no shoes, no sock, no bed, poor slave pack up in ship."[49] Third, Theodore emphasized the good effects of early religious training. "A feeling of reverence for God and his service," Weld wrote, "can be implanted in a child long before the CLEAR IDEA of a God takes distinct forms."[50] A child understands *acts* and *looks* long before he understands words, he argued, and "the *act of worship* witnessed is natures appropriate stimulus to excite the element." "I have no doubt that a child can feel the stirring of that element, when wisely operated upon by the appropriate means," he concluded, "long before the *idea* of a God can be conveyed to its understanding by means of words."[51]

Despite Theodore's emphasis on careful indoctrination, he did fear excessive demands being placed upon a child's intellect. He warned against three common errors: "1st. Not to confuse and repel their minds by *complexity*, 2. Not to *exhaust* the mind by intense effort, and 3. Not to weary it by monotony and long continuance of the same *kind* of effort." He noted that a healthy child's mind should be a swarm of ideas untrammeled by demands for order, and that complex ideas and thoughts were for mature minds. "Thousands of minds have been dwarfed in childhood by having their minds crammed with stuff from which their *elemental* powers could digest no *nutriment*."[52] In the end, the ideal was to coax and mold without cramping the imagination and unique abilities of the child.

The intellectual sources of Weld's child-rearing views are not clear, though his vocabulary and his sense of the child as a multifaceted, unique being to be prodded and trained comes close to the viewpoint of Phrenology and other popular health philosophies that preached a careful, ameliorative control of a child's upbringing. Balance, moderation, firmness—all were values to be found in the work of men such as William Alcott and Sylvester Graham.[53] The emotional sources of Weld's interest are easier to locate, the most obvious being the wonder and passion of a parent. But Weld's compulsion to reform and adjust, to state clearly and methodically the "way," suggests the degree to which he felt damaged by and did not wish to repeat the "misconception" and "misdirection" that he felt had characterized his own upbringing.[54]

Still, there was the problem of distance. Weld pontificated on the raising and educating of children from Mrs. Sprigg's boardinghouse, in the middle of adult Washington, miles away from Charley and Thoda. Was he not simply playing Ludovicus to his own Elizabeth, with different sermons but with the same reserve? For his sons, was not Washington as inaccessible as the parson's study? It would be easy to mock Weld's concern. More accurately, one might say that Theodore's mind and heart were moving faster than his feet, that even while he waged the mil-

lennial war in Washington, his own understanding and relationship to the world were shrinking in scale from the cosmic to the
familial.

Even as Weld deepened his personal stake and involvement in
affairs at home, he began to formulate a political vision so fateful that personal participation seemed almost beside the point.
The future he sketched was in marked contrast to the old evangelical vision of a world converted by the individual efforts of
Christians. Writing to James G. Birney in January, 1842, Weld
fleshed out the specifics of his view:

> Whoever has not seen, even since so long ago as Jacksons veto of
> the U.S. Bank, that, from every quarter, the elements of conflict,
> the last conflict between liberty and slavery, were rushing head-
> long into the central focus—has been asleep. Nothing short of
> miracles, constant miracles, and such as the world has never seen
> can keep at bay the two great antagonist forces, which since the
> first blow on the currency started from their moorings and drove
> against each other. They must drive against each till *one* of them
> goes to the bottom. Events, the master of men, have for years
> been silently but without a moments pause, settling the basis of
> two great parties, the nucleus of one slavery, of the other free-
> dom. This has been the real practical issue for twenty years with
> the south, but the north has, by incessant shifts of position, (all
> *false*) succeeded in staving off the only true and irrevocable one.
> Now they begin to see what thoughtful Abolitionists discovered
> years ago, that where half of a government live by their own
> work and pay as they go and the other half, by others' work and
> by the longest possible credit, and where these halves are made
> by Climate—a mighty pecuniary convulsion *must*, if of long con-
> tinuance, hurl these two systems of labor and living into mortal
> conflict, and *that must* demolish the basis of all existing parties,
> and recast them in the mould of necessity upon the all controlling
> principle, and under the omnipotent affinities of *self preservation*.
> This *will, must*, make the other *one* party. The great cause now
> at work producing this, may, in its progress, encounter obstacles,
> (the third party I think is one) but it cannot be *arrested. The
> end must come*.[55]

Events indeed had become the master of men. And what was
the abolitionist to do? He might become only an adjunct helper

of one of the great political parties, a dismal fate considering he had once been in the van of God's legions at Armageddon. In fact, Weld was not yet ready to accept this implication of his own acute and compelling vision. Writing to Angelina a few weeks later, he returned to less political, more generally religious conceptions of the struggle. He warned her that though the slaveholders felt the foundations shaking, they would resist "with energy and desperation and fury such as only fiends can summon when they know their hour has come." "Satan," he lamented, "never retreats without a death struggle." In this final hour God would demand of abolitionists vigilance, zeal, fortitude, daring, patience, and labors of love in ever greater quantity.[56]

In the end, however, Weld wondered whether the "Infinite abolitionist" in Heaven could count on his flock. "It has for some time impressed me with more than usual power," he wrote, "that mighty delivering providences marshalled by God, wait and are striving for the start, delaying only for the watch word of faith and prayer. 'For this I will be *inquired* of by the house of Israel to do it for them. He did not many mighty works there because of their unbelief.' "[57]

Weld's thoughts on the future of reform continued to take shape as he returned home in March. He planned to return to Washington in the fall and meantime resumed antislavery lecturing in the Belleville area. He continued to resist calls from Tappan's American and Foreign Anti-Slavery Society and remained convinced, despite Birney's best arguments, that the Liberty Party was an ill-conceived project. Indeed, he had begun to formulate a general critique of reform groups, the drift being that individual prayer and testimony, combined with God's providences, were "the *truly effectual organizations.*"[58] In May 1842 Weld revealed to Birney the thoughts on his troubled mind:

> That the tendencies of the times to sink the individual and exalt the *social* are so strong as to have become utterly morbid—that the body even of good men has rejected truth as the grand author of actual progress in the soul and instituted for it appeals to fear,

love of popularity—the pride of caste, etc.—that *association* is employed mainly not as a reflection to gather and flood abroad
truth, but as a condenser to consolidate public sentiment and to
use it as *the* quickener of the soul—the omnipresent and omni-
potent motive to action—that mankind are a *great herd* tied together by the horns and fated to stand still, unless they all lift
their hoofs together and in the same direction. . . .[59]

These topics and more he hoped to investigate, but the crush of
farm and family responsibilities and mountains of unanswered
correspondence stood in the way.[60]

Theodore returned to Washington and Mrs. Sprigg's boardinghouse in late December 1842. He dutifully carried on as re-
searcher, writer, and adviser to the antislavery Whigs. However,
his heart was in Belleville. For one thing, the children were no
longer babbling infants; Weld took ever greater joy in participating in their upbringing. Upon arriving in Washington, he almost immediately purchased "two mammoth sheets of 'pics' "
for them, one entitled "New World" and the other "Brother Jonathan"; unable to inspect "New World," he asked Angelina to
censor violent and other inappropriate material. Theodore sent
along kisses for the children now, lumpy clouds at the bottom of
letters to Angelina; each child could press his lips to "Thoda's
kiss" or "Charley's kiss."[61] The child in Theodore came beaming
through one letter as he told them about the fun they would
have upon his return:

> If Heavenly father please fa will be at home pretty soon and play
> by toop and ceep, and blind mans bluff and ride shuffle and hop
> and hipitee hop. and draw his little boys up into the woods and
> down to the bath house and see the high ships and down to the
> village and on to the bridge and down to Aunt Annas and up to
> run on the top of the house—and oh what fine times we shall
> have if Heavenly father please to let fa come home.[62]

The children were already having fine times with their absent
father. "It would amuse you to see the boys personating fa in almost every thing they do," Sarah wrote, "—fa puts on his big
coat and rides away to Washy, fa burns in the water [either a

reference to Weld's famous stagecoach accident or else to his use of the water cure], climbs the trees etc etc etc." Sometimes Thoda would play his father to Charley's John Quincy Adams.[63] "They talk about you continually," Angelina assured him, "and always take fa's kisses off the letters when they come."[64]

The boys were not always a source of joy. Weld worried that neither of them had a naturally *"benevolent* disposition." In other words, they fought with each other rather than sharing; Theodore meant to correct this by "set[ting] them about the doing of things to make each other *Happy.*" At the same time, he hoped that they were learning "self reliance and independence," the cardinal values of American culture.[65]

Weld became particularly disturbed, however, by little Charley's indulgences in masturbation, "that filthy and most dangerous habit of *handling* himself to which he was getting much addicted." Seth Gates, an antislavery congressman, had just shown Theodore a book on "self-pollution"; it told of one case where a child began by handling his "privy parts" and died of consumption at five years of age. Weld felt that Charley, just three in December, "must be most *closely watched.*"[66] Sarah reported that the child's habit seemed partially broken, but that the sisters were working on a more permanent solution—sewing up his drawers. "I thot nothing else would be effectual," Angelina confided, "for I dreaded his refraining in our presence for fear of punishment. this would have driven him to do it secretly and the habit would then become inveterate."[67]

Even as she struggled with Charley's "vice," Angelina herself fell deeper and deeper into hysterical exhaustion. Pregnant again and silently angry at Theodore for leaving, exhausted by periodic weak spells and "internal soreness," she found it increasingly difficult to bear up under the stress of daily tasks and the "incessant chattering" of the children. Finally, sometime in the middle of January, Angelina had a miscarriage.[68]

Though they promised frankness in their letters to Theodore, the sisters wrote cryptically of Angelina's "indisposition." No doubt they felt under great obligation not to disturb Theodore's antislavery work; a full description of her condition might well have caused him to return home. They quite accurately wrote to Theodore about Angelina's undue "mental excitement," which led him to believe that her interest in Millerism was to blame: "Understand me dearest: it is not reading nor even much reading and thought that seems to me injurious to you, but that *kind* of reading and thought which excites intense feeling, an *absorbing* interest, and an *abiding* one."[69] Absorbing and abiding indeed. According to Miller, the world would end within four months.

Angelina's obsession with the end of the world did not so much cause her "mental excitement" as make sense of and promise relief from it. As she had the winter before, she used her Millerite beliefs as unconscious weapons in her correspondence with Theodore. This time, rather than using Millerism to proclaim her independence, she made it the vehicle for expressing hurt over his leaving and for creating a situation that would force an early return to Belleville—all the while insisting that he stay in Washington for the good of the cause.

On January 22, Theodore announced that he was willing to return home to take care of her.[70] Angelina insisted that he not leave. At the same time, she grew angry about his unwillingness to investigate Millerism.[71] A few days later, she told him of her reluctance to send along a good book on Millerite doctrine, since she felt he was not ready "to know the truth for the *truth's sake*."[72] This must have affected Theodore less than Angelina's assertion that she no longer worried much about the farm, for (as she said) "really I find my mind is becoming so much more convinced of the truth of Millers views, that it appears perfectly useless to lay any plans for the future."[73] She had apparently fallen into a hysterical, fatalistic calm. Even new predictions that the world would end on February 15, a week before Theodore's expected arrival, failed to ruffle her.[74] Theodore decided that he must leave Washington. He arrived in Belleville on February 11.[75]

Weld's comrades in Washington missed him sorely. Joshua

Leavitt, perhaps privy to Angelina's condition, wrote to thank her for having given up Theodore for two winters and to assure her that his work had been of the "deepest importance." "He has been doing foundation work," wrote Leavitt, "and we all feel that our future labors will be the more available for the services of a wise master-builder."[76] Joshua Giddings, who found in Weld a teacher and counselor, added his own regrets at Weld's loss to the antislavery lobby.[77]

For Weld, Washington had been a transitional experience. He had worked dutifully and effectively for Adams and the other antislavery congressmen, but discovered that the emotional commitments and theological understandings that had propelled him in the past were open to question. Though in some sense he had fled the pressures of home life, Theodore found that his heart was really in Belleville with wife and children. In addition, he now questioned the ability of reform organizations to transform the world. Men seemed less and less able to effect change; they had become players in an inexorable, providential drama. At the same time, it seemed clearer than ever to him that man's task had become the cultivation of personal holiness in the more controllable world of self, family, and community.

He began to work out an extreme form of individualistic Christianity as early as January 1842, and occasionally revealed his views in letters. "I fear brother Dorrance is smiting his soul with barrenness," he wrote about one friend, "by thinking and discussing and poring over the mere *intellectual theories* of religion. He is beginning at the wrong end. The simple *practicals* of religion, *these, these* are the Alpha and Omega." Or: "He can fully comprehend this—that it is the *perfection* of *reason* to *be like* God, to enter into sympathy with his holy nature, to commune with him without a cloud between, to feel his abiding presence and to be transformed by it into his image."[78]

That was in January 1842. By May, Weld was complaining to Birney that he had been "so kept on the jump the live long day and night too" that he had no time to consider the implications of such feelings. He knew that what passed for truth in churches was not in the Bible, and that indeed worldly aspirations had exposed religion to the "utterly morbid" tendency to "sink the *individual* and exalt the *social*."[79] By the following January he had begun to express tentative formulations of his individualistic Christianity to Charles Stuart, with whom he had already crossed swords on the woman question. "Thy letter pains and refreshes me, my Theodore," wrote Stuart; "refreshes me by its fulness of love; pains me by the evidence which it gives of the wide difference between our views of christian character, as well as the national societies which labour for the peaceful abolition of Slavery by lawful means."[80]

But it was not until Weld was home in February 1843, that he could act upon his views. First of all, he and Angelina became reconciled on religious as well as personal issues. She now understood Millerite prophecies "spiritually"; no longer did she believe that the destruction of the material world was at hand, but rather that "the Lord has been for some years preparing his way in the hearts of the people and that a great and mighty revolution is at hand."[81] This comported well with Theodore's notion of an irrepressible, Heaven-ordained final struggle between the forces of slavery and freedom. Second, the family began to practice home religion to the virtual exclusion of churchgoing, following the belief that church organization would be "superseded by the power of religion and the simplicity of the teaching of Jesus and his apostles." "Dear Theodore with the simplicity of a child talks to us," wrote Angelina to Jane Smith, "and if any difficulty arises in any mind we freely express it." These meetings were not at all formal, she noted, but rather in the manner that " 'they that loved the Lord spake often one to another,' and whoever feels that he can go to God in prayer does so."[82]

Criticisms of the visible church and reliance on personal religious experience, of course, were nothing new. They had been the keystone of the revival and had continually informed Weld's religious thinking since his conversion in 1826. Formerly, however, Weld saw the answer to unholy church structures and ministers as holy ones. New ministers, new seminaries, new churches—

all were cures for what ailed the world.[83] The spirit that had generated Finneyite opposition within established church bodies and new institutions such as Oberlin and Lane were but a part of the total reform vision of a manmade Millennium, a world converted. Now Weld had moved closer to the belief that all church structures stood between the individual and God. He discussed this "personal religion" with Lewis Tappan. According to Tappan, Theodore thought less of his past reform efforts than he once did, and argued that in tending to home and family, and contemplating religious matters, he was now "doing more than he ever did."[84]

Weld's views could only have hardened with the disclosure of two scandals within the reform community. One involved Horace Campbell Taylor, ex-antislavery agent and official at Oberlin College. The news broke that for years he had stolen mail and pilfered funds from the *Evangelist,* Oberlin's newspaper; worst of all, he had seduced an innocent woman, forced her to abort their child at great risk to the mother, and then married another woman.[85] These facts were shocking enough, but Weld found most appalling Oberlin's own "timid, irresolute counsels, and tardy action," a sign that reformers found it easier to reform others than themselves or their colleagues.[86]

Closer to home and even more hurtful were the revelations surrounding Weld's friend Russell Judd, minister of the free church in Brooklyn. A mutual friend informed Theodore that Judd had confessed "in substance that he had handled in a vile manner a little girl living in his family and exposed his nudities to her. Also that he had similarly handled two or three other small girls."[87] Two months later, in February 1844, Tappan confirmed this story and added that Judd had molested ten girls: "He did it, he says, to produce in him the same affect as if he had had illicit commerce with a woman!"[88] The news stunned Weld: "From your letter it is plain that J's vile lusts instead of having broken loose for a moment, have really been, and it would seem *habitually,* his *permanent masters,* leading him captive at their will. *It is one of the most monstrous and humiliating developments of this age of horrible revelations.*"[89]

Such news drove Theodore deeper into a quest for personal holiness. "To turn all minds from doctrines to *living* is the great pressure on my spirit," he wrote.[90] He continued to participate in local antislavery affairs, but for the most part his vision of the public life grew progressively dimmer.[91] On February 14, 1844, at the Newark Lyceum, Weld delivered a bitter valedictory to his public career. He entitled the speech "Truth's Hindrances," and its conclusion was that Truth had no place in American public life.[92]

"Truth's Hindrances" can be understood on various levels. It reaffirmed the value of "Truth" as opposed to popular or public sentiment, and located the main source of both truth and its hindrances within the individual. Seemingly outward hindrances were in fact "so many permanent forms of bad mind; so many different modes in which bad mind stamps itself upon things without, their *producer*, not their product." It was a case of the chicken and the egg, however, since most men grew up in a society that terrified its inhabitants into conformity. Whatever the problems, Weld argued, men must confront that inner voice that spoke Truth, no matter how faint, and follow its dictates. He challenged his audience with language reminiscent of years past: "Dare thou openly espouse a hated cause and make thyself one of a meagre despised minority . . . [?]" Yet this challenge promoted no specific reform, and what followed seemed to speak directly to Weld himself as well as to his audience:

> Dare thou for the truth's sake withdraw from thy sect and abjure opinions which thou hast zealously propagated . . . ? Disavow measures, modes of action and systems of policy with which thou hast long been publicly identified. repudiate thy party with its tactics and machinery and the subtle and potent witchery of its *esprit de corps?* Dare thou sunder thyself from cooperation with men and associations, affiliated to thee by kindred sympathies and whom mutual toils, perils, sacrifices, defeats and triumphs, have made dear to thee as the apple of thine eye . . . ?[93]

The public world (including that of reform), which systematically excluded the consideration of Truth, worked in more subtle fashion than mob violence or torture. Tyranny of thought in 1844 was more ingrained and therefore harder to remove: "On the brow of our own age, on the face of our own people, vainly boast ourselves as we may, despotism has [omitted words?] lineaments and written out its autograph. Not in those old characters of fire and blood—blood can be washed off and burns healed over—not traced upon the features, but incorporate with and constituting them." Public sentiment and conformity

> plies its victims with studied neglect . . . refuses to exchange civilities and disdainfully passes without recognition; whispers suspicions, withholds employment, withdraws patronage, stigmatizes with odious epithets . . . , scents rank heresy in every breath of those who fail to articulate its shibboleth with due emphasis and euphony. . . . It refuses to apply the proper name, designation or title, and brands with nicknames. It calls clergymen, priests; all reformers, fanatics, dissenters from a popular creed, heretics; rejecters of the commandments of men, schismatics, disorganizers and infidels. It calls Irishmen, paddies; Frenchmen, frog eaters; Dutchmen, sour Kraut; New Englanders, yankees; Farmers, clod-hoppers; Merchants, counter hoppers; Physicians, pill pedlars; Temperance societies, church and state party; abolitionists, incendiaries; and people of color, no matter how light the color, niggers.[94]

In such an atmosphere of distortion and defamation, the exercise of free moral agency became well-nigh impossible. What chance did individual conscience have against the power of public sentiment: "Like the insect amid devouring flames, it perishes before the breath of its nostrils, or is whelmed under the mountains with which it strews its pathway." Americans, claiming to be a free people, were in fact "the self made fools and slaves and the self doomed victims of a tyranny more absolute and inexorable than ever, from the throne of the Caesars."

In the face of such power, Weld concluded with an injunction too heroic for the age: "The most fatal delusion that ever besotted a nation, and the commonest one too, is that a nation may be free without first being true; and the most prodigal waste of power since time began, has been made in the ceaseless paroxysms of the struggle prompted by that delusion:

"I have ceased to know myself"

"He is a freeman whom the truth makes free
And all are slaves beside,"[95]

In following the argument of "Truth's Hindrances," one is struck by the similarity of its critique to that found in de Tocqueville's *Democracy in America,* which had just recently appeared in an English translation. Weld's views as applied to reform organizations also closely parallel those of Ralph Waldo Emerson in his perceptive "New England Reformers," an essay that called for men to see the limitations of surface changes in society and instead to seek "the man within man."[96] Yet it is doubtful that Theodore had read either work. He had come by his insights the hard way. It was thus with deep conviction that on May 2, 1844, Weld made a definitive farewell to public reform. Answering Lewis Tappan's plea for active antislavery work, he said simply: "God does not call me to such a position." The problems of the age, he explained, demanded different remedial agents than the ones Tappan proposed. Organized reform might rustle leaves, but it left "branches, trunk, and deep shot roots, to propagate anew with a vigor of production vastly increased by the pruning."[97]

Even as Theodore was moving to close his public career as a reformer, events in his private life were moving toward important endings. Angelina became pregnant again in the summer of 1843, this time with the Welds' last child. In August, Theodore moved his aged, weary parents from Manlius to Belleville so that they might live out their days in his care. In March 1844, Angelina gave birth to a bubbly Sarah Grimké Weld. In April 1844, just a week or two before Theodore wrote to Lewis Tappan concerning reform, a friend came to visit and described the scene at the farm: "Theodore has changed greatly. He is a real Lady Guion christian—has learned what 'introversion of soul' is. I wish you could see what a child he is. It would make you weary of the 'outward.' Sarah and Angelina are led much in the same way. Dear old Mr. Weld is very feeble—will probably not live long—He is full of joy and peace."[98] Ludovicus died the following year.

All within a year of his forty-first birthday, Theodore had watched his father die, had seen his last child born, and had ended his long commitment to public reform. As he looked ahead, little seemed clear except an unquenchable urge to clarify life, to quest for inner Truth and self.

XII

New Theology,
New Career

In the spring of 1847, John Greenleaf Whittier asked Lewis Tappan if he knew the whereabouts of their mutual friend Weld. "He is in a ditch opposite his house," Tappan replied crustily, "doing the work any Irishman could do for 75 cents a day. His wife is 'suckling fools and chronicling small beer.'"[1] One might have expected such bitterness from a man who had been Theodore's patron in reform for over fifteen years, but Tappan's description hardly caught the essence of life at the Belleville farm. As Theodore repaired his neglected land, stake by stake and furrow by furrow, in his mind he took stock of dead dreams and visions and slowly but surely plotted out the course for a new life. In an age and country of self-made men, Weld was orchestrating a self-made rite of passage. It was one born of despair.

Weld's style dictated that he hide the depth of that despair. He played father or brother to those in crisis more easily than he admitted his own needs: only before God, Angelina, and perhaps Charles Stuart had he ever revealed deep fear. However, how could not some part of him recognize that an era in his life and expectations was dead? His marriage, once the focus of sublime hope and passion, stood numbed by undercurrents of envy and anger. More tragically, three births, a miscarriage, and household chores had rendered Angelina a cripple, in almost constant pain from a prolapsed uterus and a hernia.[2]

It is clear from later events that Theodore and Angelina regained a caring understanding of each other. As for Angelina's physical injuries, they had an effect on Theodore impossible to chart yet important all the same. No doubt his opportunities for a sexual life were drastically reduced or completely eliminated for fear of further injury or a new pregnancy. More important, Theodore must have taken upon himself much responsibility for Angelina's fate—*he* had impregnated her, and she had wounded her body giving birth to and caring for *his* children. He was that kind of man. No direct evidence confirms such speculation, though we do know that Angelina never had another child and that Theodore never again wandered far from home, save for a few months during the Civil War.[3]

As for his life in reform, a life he had pursued for twenty years, he left it in exhaustion and disillusionment. His leaving can be explained only partially by external events. It is true that the antislavery cause had experienced major setbacks, and belief in a quick end to the institution through moral suasion had long since vanished. Yet others fought on and new converts entered the field every year. Besides, in the past Theodore had faced setbacks squarely and had gone on to fight harder. This time, however, he was listening to an inner voice that conceded that the cosmic vision that had made him a reformer was in error; it is only by seeing his retirement from reform as the death knell of an old world view and the harbinger of a new one that we can grasp its full significance.

The evangelical vision had dominated Weld's life since his conversion under Finney twenty years prior. In that tumultuous episode, his senses of identity and calling became fused with the Finneyite mission—reform and conversion of the world to bring on the millennial age—and that fusion unleased an almost mythic power in this energetic man. Failure and division in the antislavery movement, his own humbling at Troy, and a halting recognition of deep emotional starvation—all had allowed Weld the chance slowly to separate his self from evangelical mission. His trips to Washington provided a final test for the old calling, and in the end he did not hear the call. Rather he felt inexorably drawn home to his family and to a more intimate sense of Christian duty.

Weld's quiet and largely unexplained withdrawal troubled reformers around him; in particular Lewis Tappan and Charles Stuart, those whom one might call his fathers in reform, pressed him to justify his decision. Finally, Stuart, in November 1845, expressed the fear that Weld was "declining from that noble walk of glorious usefulness, into which God had led [him] so graciously," and called upon him to present in detail and with scriptural defenses his new religious and reform views. What emerged was a triangular exchange—Weld wrote letters to Stuart, which Tappan later read—in which Theodore made clear his rejection of the evangelical view of Christian man and set forth a more autonomous notion of Christian piety, one in which man sought Truth within himself, untrammeled by doctrine or creed.[4]

Weld specifically expressed his disenchantment with organized churches and reform movements. His correspondents could not deny that there was some basis for this feeling. Stuart agreed that reformers could not regenerate souls, but he insisted that they could remove institutions and habits that blocked the road to holiness. For his part, Tappan admitted that Christianity as practiced in the churches was largely a sham; still, he felt that there were enough true Christians in the world to effect change, and that Weld's desire for solitude was wrong. "Do not hide the light under a bushel," he chided.[5]

But the issue between Weld and his mentors transcended questions of action or even of doctrine. "Your letter, full of solemn and tender feeling as it is," moaned Stuart, "throws a dense cloud around you, impenetrable to me." At the center of that cloud lay the question of ultimate authority. Stuart and Tappan had entered into correspondence with Weld assuming a certain agreement as to accepted authority, in particular a view of the Bible as the revealed word of God. Yet the Bible and its literal inspiration had come to be less important to Weld. We do not know how clearly Theodore expressed his apostasy in the letters of 1845 and 1846, but by 1848 he could report to Birney a simple fact: "Creeds have lost all hold upon me, and in the state of mind that exalts them I search in vain for the elements of healthful growth. How speculative notions have usurped the functions of spiritual vitality!" The standards of Christian manhood had become not so much a question of doctrines as one of "healthful growth" and "spiritual vitality," and the doctrines and proof-texts that had once anchored Weld's feeling of oneness with God in the cosmos now only kept the heart from its true course. He made this point again three years later, this time altering and simplifying his own struggle with theology in order to press home his point:

> As to changes in mere speculative views, they have long been to me matters of such indifference that I take no note of them. Once I labored after speculative truth—now I see that even theoretic truth cannot *truly* exist, unless *practical, preexist.* . . . If the grand aim of life is to *be* the truth, out of that true *being,* true thoughts of truth will grow—and in *no other soil*—and all false thoughts of truth will thus and thus only be forestalled.[6]

And what was this "true being"? In one sense, it resembled the converted soul, infused with grace, so familiar to Weld at twenty-three as he basked in the first light of salvation. Yet at forty-two the chords of this inner harmony, this *being* the truth, did not resound with youthful thunder. Rather Weld the adult, the father, sought an intimate faith built upon worldly experience and resignation. Weld's truth in 1845 was that of a battered man, one whose great expectations had been seen to be so much folly.

Weld's transformation illustrated a general trend in reform circles toward more autonomous and personally ameliorative forms of religious life. Transcendentalism, Perfectionism, Swedenborgianism, Spiritualism—these were some of the world views through which a generation caught up in an overexacting vision of sin and mission sought escape. Though the new faiths differed on some points and attracted a widely varying clientele, they held in common a rejection of the millennial drama of world conversion and even the personal conversion experience of surrender to God. Men were not in need of saving, if they only knew it; they had the capacity to feel within themselves harmony with God and the Universe. Even death posed no difficulty for man's transcendent spirit; it would move to different and higher spheres of existence after passing from the earth.

These new views, of course, were not simply a response to a burdensome and frustrating world view; each developed from particular intellectual and social traditions and settings. Weld's version had its roots in two basic influences. First, Theodore had kept in touch with Perfectionist doctrine through his brother Charles, who continued to develop and communicate his views on personal holiness. Second, Weld's proximity to New York afforded him contact with George Bush, America's leading disseminator of Swedenborgian ideas. No evidence exists by which to calculate the precise influence of each of these men. Suffice it to say, however, that Weld's developing views reflected both a Perfectionist and a Swedenborgian influence.[7]

While no one label can possibly cover the varieties of religious belief present in the Weld household after 1845, they can best be explored through the thought of Andrew Jackson Davis, the "Poughkeepsie Seer," a leading and pioneering American Spiritualist with whom Theodore and the sisters found personal as well as theological communion. Davis first came to public notice in 1845 when, as an uneducated youth of nineteen, he gave a series of more than one hundred and fifty lectures in New York City in trance state, lectures that plotted out the Universe and its laws of creation and progression. Specifically, Davis described in detail a multisphered spirit world through which departed souls passed, sphere by sphere, until they reached the highest stage of perfection. He explained the operation of this Universe in terms of Natural Law and an ultimate force, the Divine Positive Mind, both of which worked toward promoting total Harmony in the Spheres. Davis reduced the Bible to a mythological text, Jesus to a great human reformer, and divine revelation (aside from his own) to a nullity.

He claimed his inspiration to be spirit communications with Galen and Swedenborg. Nonetheless he scandalized Bush and other New York Swedenborgians by presenting views at wide variance with those of the philosopher. The most important divergence involved the connection between virtue and otherworldly rewards. Swedenborg saw men's actions on earth as determining the Heaven or Hell to which they would be assigned, and he accepted the traditional categorical fates of eternal happiness or unhappiness. By contrast, Davis described a progression of higher and higher Harmony, which any soul would follow as it left earth and experienced each sphere in turn. Thus Davis promised ultimate happiness for all, and did so within a system of belief expressed in a vocabulary consonant in form with the laws of science and progress.[8]

Weld and the sisters must have been aware of Davis's lectures and possibly attended some of them; perhaps they had perused the eight-hundred-page printed version of his talks, *Principles of Nature, Her Divine Revelations, and a Voice to Mankind*. However, Davis and his views did not have significant impact on the Welds until Angelina encountered the "Poughkeepsie Seer" in 1849, while both were in residence at the nearby South Orange Water-Cure.[9]

We do not know what particular ailment prompted Angelina to seek treatment, or which hosings, soaks, or spongings she utilized. If she sought a cure for her prolapsed uterus, she might have followed this popular regimen: a daily tepid dripping-sheet bath, followed by a hip bath, a foot bath in the evening, and two or three injections of cold water into the vagina.[10] But Angelina may have come simply for a rest from a wearying routine. She could have found no better place, for, as its founder boasted, Orange Mountain was "planned particularly with a view to the comfort and convenience of the patient." Each person had a private room with attached private bath. The grounds, sixteen acres on the side of a mountain, featured woods, meadows, streams, marvelous views of New Jersey and New York, and a number of outdoor wave, plunge, and douche baths. Orange Mountain even sported a bowling alley, one which Angelina used because Theodore suggested that the exercise would strengthen her weak lungs.[11]

Relaxation, then, as much as hydrotherapy per se, lay at the heart of the water-cure experience. Leisurely meals, polite mingling of guests, and special social and cultural events diverted one from the cares of life. For example, Angelina wrote home about a particularly pleasing "Soirée Musicale." She also noted that a "Soirée Phrenologicale" had been planned; none other than Andrew Jackson Davis, at Orange Mountain accompanying his ailing wife Silona, would be the phrenologist. "You would be amused to see how afraid some are to put their heads under Davis' fingers," she wrote to Sarah, "little knowing that he reads character *without* manipulation."[12]

Angelina met Davis quite by accident at mealtime and was almost immediately entranced. The reasons are not hard to understand. Davis was in general a sympathetic and (so he thought) literally magnetic soul, one who cared especially about the troubles of women. He also ministered to one of Angelina's peculiar hungers—for new and detailed explanations of the Universe. One can imagine that, after Weld's cavalier rejection of her Millerite speculations, Davis's eager evocations of his latest theories must have made Angelina's spirits soar. She was especially taken with his "*great, great* production," the "Progressive History and Approaching Destiny of the Human Race," which outlined the evolution of mankind through the ages. Davis ranked man's social states progressively, from Savagism to Republicanism. Racial groups he placed in order of development and achievement: Negro, Aborig-American, Malay-Mongolian, Caucasian, Anglo-American. In all, sixteen categories of parallel development in art, science, government, philosophy, theology, and language filled out his scheme of ongoing movement toward Harmony and Perfection. Thus Davis added a detailed conception of order on Earth to his already famous guide to the Spiritual Heavens, and linked these worlds through Spirit communication.[13]

Behind this vision lay an old faith, albeit one now expressed in new terms. Angelina found its quintessential expression in what she called Andrew Jackson Davis's "creed," and felt moved to quote it to Theodore:

A. J. Davis believes and teaches that the time will come when mankind can say, Each is as the whole, and the whole are as one. Whose temple is the experience and wisdom of every age and nation—Whose book is nature, whose master is Reason, whose language is all forms and kingdoms, whose creed is love to man—Whose religion is Justice, and whose light is Truth; whose oneness is Association—whose path is Progression; whose works are Development; whose motto is Excelsior, whose home is Heaven, whose Heaven is Harmony, and whose God is the Universal Father.[14]

Angelina and other reformers found Davis's reformulation of the world attractive for a number of reasons. Most centrally, it retained a version of the millennial dream—"the time will come when mankind can say, Each is as the whole, and the whole are as one"—and yet did not place upon mankind the responsibility for making that Millennium. Davis argued that cosmic, mechanistic forces drove the Universe toward higher states of being. In embracing Spiritualism, then, the reformer might reduce the heavy load of guilt emanating from failed expectations. In addition, the "Poughkeepsie Seer" supplied a system whose complexities reflected the more mature, sobered sense of the world possessed by men and women who were no longer youthful rebels. As wives and husbands, fathers and mothers, or simply as seasoned veterans of adult life, they could not ignore the fact that a workable view of the world required more than simple conversion of deeply felt longings and communions into equally simple missions.

Spiritualism also helped men face new realities by giving radically new answers to the old questions of death and salvation—answers so radical that they wished out of existence the questions themselves. To musings concerning the meaning of death, the Spiritualist responded, "There is no death." To the question which lay at the heart of the revival, "What shall I do to be saved?" the answer came back: It makes no difference, for all men are saved. At least, all men journey progressively higher from earth and through the spheres.[15]

By undercutting the drama of salvation, Davis robbed men of one explanation and cure for their innermost anxieties and religious yearnings. In its place, he suggested that men bring their inner lives and intimate relationships into harmony with the perfect Universe he described. An individual could widen his consciousness through trance states, dreams, and simple reflection, and work toward "self-development and self-harmonization." "In this way," Davis assured his readers, "he bec[ame] acquainted with the divine within him, and the divine within others."[16] Thus the true spiritual reformer remained a pietist; however, he practiced a piety centered in self more than in God, using as yardsticks of growth perceptions of "character" more than signs of holiness.

While Angelina found herself most attracted to the systematic nature of Davis's doctrines, and Sarah drew most satisfaction from communications with the spirit-world, it was this new formulation of piety that appealed most to Theodore. Davis had built an entire cosmology around a sense of commitment to personal character growth which comported well with Weld's own most recent discoveries. Having had to face the disapproval of close companions such as Tappan and Stuart, it must have been reassuring to find others in the world who saw the meaning of existence in a new light.

Still, enough of the old Theodore, the one committed to some sort of usefulness in the community, struggled with the new Theodore who seemed content with personal piety. He might proclaim inner peace as his lot, but those who knew him best read a different message in his face. Angelina told him as much in 1849:

My heart has felt sad ever since you were here on Sunday, because *you* seemed so sad—you seemed oppressed and depressed—

and I felt the weight on your spirit and gladly would I bear it with you. Why is it that we are not happy when duty, interest and almost all the circumstances around us, call for cheerfulness and contentment. I know *no* family so blessed. None with so much to make them happy. And yet the fear often comes over me like a dark cloud, that we are not doing the will of God. We are not fulfilling our destiny and yet I cannot see anything definite—don't see any particular thing, to do. Believe I would gladly do any thing and see you or sister do any thing—no matter what, if I only knew *that* to be the Lord's will concerning us—It seems to me dearest One—the days of *your* preparation must be over—the time must have come for you to give up your drudgery. *Don't you feel it is?*[17]

She continued: Should he not give up new projects on the farm, and stop his worries about every detail of life? "You *greatly mistake me* if you think it pleases me to see *you* working as you do on the farm—in such a state of mind," she wrote, "because you feel constantly that you are *not* in your right place, you are not *now* doing the Lord's will, but your own—and it seems to me this is the thing that is eating at the root of your peace." She recommended that he let go of his petty cares, throw himself upon the will of God, and say, "Here I am send me."[18]

Angelina's appraisal may not have been entirely accurate, since she had her own reasons for portraying Theodore's situation in such a dismal light. The man she married had been a great crusader, and her words no doubt expressed disappointment with him. In addition, she may have felt responsible for his early return from Washington and his subsequent retirement, and so felt the need to encourage a return to *any* mission. Yet the main thrust of her observation must have been accurate; a man like Weld, used to acting so forcefully in the world for so many years, could not have helped but feel deeply ambivalent about his new course. It was one thing to adopt a new philosophy, it was another to deny his very nature.

Fortunately, an "answer" had already begun to appear before Angelina's plea, one that had developed from a serious question: "Where to educate Charley and Thoda?" As Weld later confided to Birney, he would not expose their children to the "havoc" of the local schools. "1st—We knew of none whose *moral contact* was not corrupting," he explained. "2nd—We knew of none whose processes of training, development, and instruction were such as we desired for our children." So the Welds decided to educate their own children and, considering the time and effort involved, felt that they might as well open their own small academy.[19] In doing so, Theodore found a second calling in his life—that of teacher. Originally it seemed a rather routine undertaking, but after the passage of some years Weld grew into the role and in doing so became one of the most beloved and innovative of educators in the reform community.

The "Weld Institute," as it was called at first, began classes on the Belleville farm in October 1848. Angelina and Sarah aided Theodore as teachers and caretakers, and under the guidance of the trio the school soon attracted a group of about twenty students. The Gerrit Smiths, Birneys, and Stantons, among others, eagerly sent their children to sit at Theodore's feet. As Henry B. Stanton wrote: "I sincerely rejoice that you have, after much groping, at last found the niche for which I have always told you, nature designed you. I learned more from you, during the years we were together, than from all other men and all books. . . ."[20]

The Welds' specific offerings included composition, history, mathematics, drawing, and French. Transcending any specific class, however, was Weld's concern for fostering character, that *"inward unity"* he had just begun to redefine in his own life. Angelina saw this mission as impressing on students that they had "character[s] to form for future manhood, and that life [was] not given merely to make fun for [one]self and others." Sarah trembled—"it makes me quail and shrink and almost paralyzes my powers"—at the responsibility of training those who would "mark the age" and influence the fate of the human race.[21] Aside from lecturing about and modeling good character, Weld spent hours writing detailed letters to parents appraising the moral health of their children and recommending proper corrective action in the case of deficiencies. Often he was blunt, as with Gerrit Smith concerning his son Greenie: "Your permission for him to go to NY and be there *by himself* was disastrous—It quite unsettled and put him back in this process of forming right habits. Besides I am satisfied that his relatives in New York are most injudicious in their methods with him. He always comes back drunk with flattery—His *smartness* amuses them."[22]

This attention to every detail of environment and every action, so reminiscent of Weld's pietistic tendencies throughout his life, also typified a growing concern among reformers and religious leaders for the proper setting and process for moral education. For instance, William Andrus Alcott began in the 1830s to set forth a comprehensive vision of the schoolroom as both physical and moral environment with the goal of producing in students a sense of moral rectitude. Horace Bushnell, in his famous treatise on *Christian Nurture* (1847), argued that revivalistic conversion did not suffice to make a true Christian; rather, close and careful cultivation of Christian ideas and behavior from the cradle on was necessary to produce the desired effect. Similar, though secularized, concerns inspired educational innovators such as Horace Mann and Henry Barnard, who saw in the public schools the only chance to inculcate proper values of democratic citizenship in a potentially unruly and ignorant populace.[23] All were responding to two related developments in American culture. First, the fading of theological structures which bore some relation to social structure and expected behavior meant that those who wished to preserve quasi-Christian values felt the need to teach such lessons early and have children internalize them into "character." Second, an overwhelming sense of social disorder, loss of control, in American society in these years made the breeding of character and responsibility not only a personal concern, but a social one as well. Only men of character might lead the nation to safe ground.[24]

Such concerns led Weld to highly protective measures for his own children, one of which was a special education removed from the "havoc" present in other schools. Nor was this protection from contaminants limited to such major questions as education. In 1846 Theodore and Angelina agreed that they should not entertain two children from the West Indies. "The contact of children brought up in slavery," wrote Weld, "is, almost of necessity, *pollution*."[25] Nor did the Welds perceive any possible hint of racism in their action. After all, one might fight slavery without sacrificially exposing one's family to its deleterious effects. In fact, Weld followed the same course in the field of education. In 1847 he became the local Superintendent of Schools, all the while tending to his own very exclusive academy.[26]

Despite the air of protectiveness and grim mission, Weld's students adored their mentor and his school. They had the run of the house and studied on the roof, along the piazza, and in the woods. Theodore combined warm fathering with a challenging curriculum. "Mr. Weld gives me the greatest lot of lessons and the hardest," wrote one student. "A great history lesson that I cannot understand one word of. . . ."[27] In addition, the Weld Institute was coeducational, which marked an important innovation in boarding schools of the time. Theodore thought the segregation of sexes to be unnatural; it tended to distort the natural affections. And innocent natural affections did flourish at Belleville. Ellie Wright, for instance, confided to a friend at home: "You don't know how I'm smit with Fitzhugh Birney. He's a splendour."[28] The boys seemed less interested in the opposite sex; they cavorted in the woods, hunting reptiles for pets. "The rage here is for turtles," Ellie reported; "Mr. Weld took one of Willie's and let it go. Willie almost cried. The boys have had snakes!!!!"[29] Though in this case Weld felt impelled to teach Willie respect for tiny creatures, his students' adventures in nature must have allowed him to recapture a very lively sense of his own boyhood romps in the woods of Hampton, Connecticut. Indeed, it might be said that in running a virtual family of a school, Theodore had found a means to grow up again through his students. Only this time he would correct the mistakes of his parents.

In one sense this quest proved to be cruelly ironic, for in tending to his flock of students Weld neglected his own children—even as Ludovicus had once neglected him. He became a distant authority, leaving the nurturing to Angelina and Sarah. Little Sarah seemed unaffected by this situation; it may be that Theodore allowed himself a loving posture toward his daughter. As for Charley and Thoda, they found their father expropriated and their house overrun by strangers. For the most part the historical record stands mute on the crucial years of early puberty when the Weld children found themselves sharing both parents and home. However, we do know that in later years Weld would harvest letters of love from ex-students and much misery from his two sons.

XIII

Eagleswood

Despite Weld's promising beginnings as an educator, life at Belleville was still marked by frustration. Even with income from both school and crops, the household managed only to break even. That left little margin to face unexpected setbacks, and certainly ruled out the possibility of an expanded curriculum or a larger student body. Theodore, Angelina, and Sarah were weary from overwork and periodic illness, and by the end of 1852 the future of the school was in doubt.

Then, in almost storybook fashion, an opportunity arose. Marcus Spring, a wealthy reformer, invited Weld to run a school at his new Raritan Bay Union, a projected utopian community in Perth Amboy, New Jersey. Spring had been a member of the Fourierist North American Phalanx, but disputes within the community over finances inspired him to lead a group of thirty to forty discontented compatriots in the formation of the new Raritan Bay colony. They offered Weld the luxury of a newly constructed school building and complete freedom to teach as he wished.[1] The Welds embraced the idea and in 1854 purchased three thousand dollars worth of shares in Raritan Bay's joint-stock company. Not only did it give them the opportunity to put the school on a more secure financial foundation; the community also offered them the chance to participate in yet another reform alternative to participation in the wider political scene—that of creating an ideal society in miniature. The Welds could only applaud the aims of the Union as expressed in its constitution:

> To establish branches of agriculture and mechanics whereby in-dustry, education and social life may in principle and practice be arranged in conformity to the Christian religion and where all ties conjugal, parental, filial, fraternal and communal which are sanctified by the will of God, the laws of nature and the highest experience of mankind, may be purified and perfected; where the advantages of co-operation may be secured and the evils of com-petition avoided by such methods of joint stock association as shall commend themselves to enlightened conscience and com-mon sense.[2]

Though the move to Perth Amboy was of clearest benefit to Theodore, the sisters expressed excitement as well. To Angelina, Raritan Bay promised "a new life" of financial security and in-fluence.[3] Sarah's feelings pervaded her description of their new home:

> Our location here is enchanting far far superior to our Belleville home. We have a fine expanse of water in front, have a view of the Never sink hills and away up the bay towards the So. East the landscape is also beautiful and the setting of the sun glori-ous. . . . I cannot tell you how I luxuriate in the light of the sun which [shines] in clear and bright, unobstructed by those heavy evergreens which surrounded us at Belleville.[4]

On just about every count, however—financial advantage, com-munitarian endeavor, and physical comfort—Raritan Bay Union proved to be a crushing disappointment. The Welds' stock never yielded a dividend; members of the community bickered as fero-ciously as they had at the North American Phalanx and finally disbanded the Union in 1856; and it took Marcus Spring a num-ber of years to make good his promise of first-rate facilities for living and teaching.[5] Indeed, insufficient heat during the first winter helped keep Theodore under constant attack from fever and made the rest of the family very uncomfortable. By the

Eagleswood

Raritan Bay Union (Eagleswood) (*From map of Perth Amboy, Staten Island, and South Amboy. By Thomas A. Hurley. 1858. Courtesy of the New York Public Library.*)

spring of 1855, they were ready to leave. About the only positive legacy of the school's first year was Theodore's new snowy-white beard, which he grew at one point because he was too sick to shave.[6] It would become a symbol of wisdom among his students and later among the citizens of the town in which he spent his last years.

Somehow Spring persuaded Theodore to stay on, and when the Union failed, Eagleswood School remained to become the central institution of this now uncommunal community of reformers. This was just as well, for Weld had far more faith and interest in education than he had in communal experiments.[7] Meanwhile, Spring finally made the necessary improvements in physical plant at Eagleswood; he even provided a fully equipped gymnasium.[8]

Within this ever-improving setting, Theodore forged an educational philosophy and curriculum that brought together long-standing reform concerns and his somewhat newer sense of the importance of the family. "We institute our educational processes," proclaimed the Eagleswood brochure, "upon the basis of God's model school, the family." Indeed, he wished to "combine the advantages of home nurture, in physical, mental and moral training, with instruction in Literature, Science, and Art."[9] At Eagleswood, Weld articulated the idea of nurturance and development as the basic mission of education, the idea that implicitly underlay his first attempts as a teacher at Belleville. Thus he made central the coeducational character of Eagleswood:

> There is in the constitution of the sexes a law of reciprocal action, vital to the highest weal of both. To restrict each sex to schools exclusive of the other, is to set at naught this law, subvert the Divine Order, and rob development of a ministration essential to its highest results. In reverent recognition of this truth, we . . . receive as pupils, youth of both sexes.
>
> The education of the sexes together, under a wise supervision, gives symmetry to mental and moral development, excites attention to personal habits, quickens the perception of those nameless proprieties which adorn mutual relations, adds refinement to feelings, gentleness, grace and courtesy to manners, simplicity, modesty, purity, and general elevation and equilibrium to character.[10]

To protect this process of breeding "character," the Welds placed a restriction upon admission of students similar to the one used to screen guests at home. No child of "vicious habits" was allowed at the family-school; he or she might pollute more innocent students. Nor were profanity or intoxicants tolerated, or even fancy dress: "Neatness, good taste, and simplicity in dress, the natural expressions of good sense . . . befit schooldays; while ambitious attempts to fashionable display, the paroxysms of a mind weak, ill-balanced, and essentially vulgar, disturb educational processes, depress scholarship, and render young life turbid at its fountain-head."[11]

As for the curriculum, it reflected Weld's forty-year concern with the delicate balance of mind and body. Academic subjects included reading, writing, arithmetic, "the Sciences of Nature, Material and Intellectual," ancient and modern languages, history, drawing, painting, and music. Daily gymnastic and calisthenic drills, for both sexes, balanced academic pursuits. In addition, students were encouraged to engage in rowing, swimming, diving, and other sports.[12]

The responsibilities of such a program clearly created too heavy a burden for Theodore, Angelina, and Sarah to bear alone. In choosing a faculty, therefore, Weld made sure to find sympathetic minds and talents. Margaret Corliss and William Henry Channing, who had helped out at Belleville, became regular faculty at Eagleswood. Weld also enticed Elizabeth Peabody to come; Peabody was an important educational innovator in her own right, having collaborated with Bronson Alcott at his "Temple" school in Boston.[13] Meanwhile, Angelina taught history and acted as school nurse. Sarah taught French and was a counselor for the boarders.

If in some ways the Eagleswood philosophy and curriculum marked a mature integration of themes in Weld's long reform career, it also allowed the reintegration into his personal life of many significant figures. Within his immediate family, brother Charles and sister Cornelia came to live out their lives at the school. James G. Birney, with whom Weld had had only intermittent contact since Birney's entry into Liberty Party politics, also chose to spend his last years at Eagleswood. And, of course, there were the children of old friends such as Henry B. Stanton, Gerrit Smith, and Lane rebel Augustus Wattles, children who provided a focus for friendship even when political philosophies differed.[14]

Ties were strained or broken with two important figures, however—the two men who had fathered Weld in evangelical reform. Weld and Lewis Tappan, stymied over the question of participation in reform, fell into estranged silence in the late 1840s. Charles Stuart, hoping against hope that he was reading the signs wrongly, continued to question Weld closely on his religious eclipse and carped at the *"Bible-less"* nature of Eagleswood education. Stuart conceded the moral rectitude of his friend's motives, but nonetheless could see only disaster ahead for children raised without full schooling in the Bible. "The result of your plan to your pupils, as far as Sovereign Grace, do not thwart it," he moaned, "must be various phases of infidelity, leading to practices more or less ungodly."[15]

So offended was Stuart that he could continue to love Weld only by making a distinction between the general social effects of blasphemous doctrine and the relatively insignificant effects of speculative thinking upon the minds of a few individuals (including Weld) whose hearts were "pure." Still, in an extraordinary letter to Birney, Stuart confessed the turbulent mixture of dread and love that defined his relation to Theodore and his new role. He was sure that giving up the Bible left

> fallen man, without a law or a standard of any valid authority, each with equal claim to right, to worship himself, or his Maker; to choose for his Master, Satan, or Jehovah. Supposing the Bible to be an imposition; and leaving out the Eternity of infinite happiness or misery, according to Character, which it foretells, let all men be Theodores, and the world would be a happy world for a time—But, oh, what for Eternity!! and how could we surely have any hope for a world full of Theodores, the sole supreme law of which was individual conscience—I love him—I could almost wish myself accursed from Christ, for him—But I tremble for him, and for you, and for all who agree with him. . . .[16]

In part the words of a disappointed old man, Stuart's jeremiad nonetheless touched upon a central problem of the reform community in the 1850s. It had become a bit too comfortable and self-indulgent for its own good. This was especially true of recent arrivals to the reform cause. Usually of good social standing and economically comfortable, these new reformers had struggled less than those of Weld's generation, and were more inclined to see themselves as an exclusive and elite group in society. It was not the lack of Bible Christianity per se, as Stuart thought, but a certain lack of self-scrutiny that many of Weld's new acquaintances displayed.

To some of these persons, sending one's child to Eagleswood became less an educational commitment and more a confirmation of exclusivity. Take the observations of Martha Coffin

Wright, mother of the irrepressible Ellie Wright. "In looking round at the school," she wrote her husband, "I was struck with the superiority of the heads, over those in ordinary schools, and it would naturally be so, inasmuch as the bigoted and narrow choose other schools for their children, and few, if any send to Theodore D. Weld who have not by earnest thought, emancipated themselves from the prejudices of education and circumstance."[17] Such phrenologically informed snobbery typified a creeping narrowness that in some leaped to a level of smug racism.

Not that such attitudes did not exist when the Bible was present as mediator; Weld and his generation had rebelled against similar narrowness in their Bible-preaching fathers. However, the new scripture of Science, whether expressed in Davis's Spiritualism, Fowler's Phrenology, or other rational accounts of the nature of man and the universe, seemed impervious to question or to rebellion. Science, unlike Protestantism, provided little space for that individual communion that might challenge all that had been held to be Truth.[18]

Connection is not the same as complicity, and it is clear that Weld never accepted the racist implications of the new sciences. It is also clear that if he did raise his voice against the snobberies and ethnocentric extremes of his compatriots, his remonstrances have not been preserved. We should not be surprised by the silence. Weld's passionate commitment to egalitarianism had been nurtured by his rebellion against all visible signs that he was a New England Weld, apart from others; this youthful, "backwoodsman" Weld had remade himself into just another American. The mature Weld, however, seemed intent on recapturing his roots, even if that meant tolerating snobbery. The need to deny differences, to merge, to lose one's self, receded before the ever-growing need to come to terms with one's past. That he could reclaim his New England roots without unduly proclaiming their superiority speaks, however, for the quiet staying power of lessons learned in youth.

Weld brought to the Eagleswood curriculum another legacy

from the past—the conscious search for selfhood, without which molding of "character" might become a hollow exercise. The touchstone of autonomy was no longer an agonizing conversion experience, fraught with guilt-ridden self-scrutiny. Instead, Weld now celebrated liberation from inner agony through self-discovery and self-expression. In some sense he had finally come to terms with that "vanity" that had plagued his sense of self.

He built his new approach to the achievement of autonomy upon the works of Shakespeare and the process of drama. In fact, Shakespeare became for him a new father or, in the language of Spiritualism, a control; one whose sensibilities were at once extraordinary and human, one whose presence excited rather than judged. Weld would expound upon the virtues of the bard for the rest of his life. At Eagleswood, Weld had his students both study and perform Shakespeare. As an object of study, he felt that students would find in his plays the best model of idiomatic English as well as the most rewarding subject for analyzing language as an instrument of thought. Shakespeare's "transcendent imagery" stimulated the imagination while expressing profound truths, and thus provided an ideal of "terse, vivid, strong and graceful style." Finally, according to Weld, "Shakespeare being the most original and profound of mental analysts, his works [were] beyond all other's revelations of human nature and priceless lessons in it."[19]

Performing Shakespeare helped students get outside themselves, a process Weld deemed especially important for girls. "Multitudes of these writhe thro' their school days," he wrote, "the impaled victims of a morbid self consciousness making every moment and expression artificial and distorted, a stifling constraint half paralyzing thought, utterance and action; intensifying self-friction, distrust and mortification, and thus perpetuating a misery self-inflicted and intolerable. Such cases demand a special process to call out *self-assertion*."[20] Thus dramatic performance, foreshadowing some modern psychological therapies, replaced the conversion drama as a method of purging debilitating self-consciousness.

Performance, in fact, became one of the most memorable aspects of an Eagleswood education; Saturday night student shows were highlights of community life. Typical was the first annual show of the Gamma Sigma Society, July 21, 1857. Part One included an oration by Charles Stuart Weld, a Poem read by Lottie Pope, and an Ode composed and read by Lucy McKim. Part Two featured a performance of *Pyramus and Thisbe*, featuring such notables as Charley playing Demetrius, Ellie Wright as Hermia, Lucy McKim as Bottom, Fitzhugh Birney as Starveling, and Thody as Snug. Another cast, this from the 1860 production of *The Rival Queens*, read like a reform directory: Spring, Weld, Wattles, Bellows, McKim.[21]

Weld's ideal of intellectual challenge and unselfconscious being found expression in events other than drama. Weekends routinely combined Saturday evening dances with Sunday lectures. The entire community attended the dances, and Weld himself enjoyed taking his turn on the floor. At the end of the evening, Theodore kissed each student and the students themselves exchanged kisses before retiring.[22] On Sunday, they would be treated to lectures by the likes of Ralph Waldo Emerson, Bronson Alcott, William Cullen Bryant, Horace Greeley, and sometimes Weld himself.[23] These so-called free meetings did not always attract the most interesting guests and often were dominated by locals who, in Sarah's words, "love[d] to hear themselves talk." But at least they encouraged a spirit of self-expression before the community and thus a possible escape from inner isolation. The communal sense at weekends and during other parts of the Eagleswood routine may have even bordered on the coercive. At least that is what one guest, the inveterate hermit Henry David Thoreau, suggested: "This Saturday evening dance is a regular thing, and it is thought something strange if you don't attend. They take it for granted that you want society!"[24] But to Weld, Thoreau's comment was really beside the point. He had had enough of the isolation so prized by the author of *Walden*, an isolation that for him had been marked by self-recrimination and pain. In an innocent dance, in a ritual of kisses goodnight, and in the firm but kind wisdom suggested by his flowing white beard—one could see that Eagleswood and its way of life represented not only a boon to its students, but also a sign that this once grim and driven Theodore had placed the simple joys of intimacy somewhat near the center of his being.

Angelina and Sarah were not quite as successful as Theodore in finding their proper niche in the world. Each had assigned roles at the school, but neither found deep satisfaction in either teaching or counseling. Occasionally they would admit as much to confidantes; more commonly, they professed their devotion to Eagleswood while at the same time expressing displeasure in strained relationships with students.[25] However, both Angelina and Sarah did attempt to face the demands of their unfulfilled selves.

First they found it necessary to confront each other. It must be remembered that from the time of Angelina's birth Sarah had pledged to be her sister's guide and mother, and it was as nearly inseparable mother and daughter that the two sisters found the strength to rebel against the world of their family.[26] Though each had thought about independent existences, not even Angelina's marriage to Theodore could separate them. Marriage and motherhood for the younger sister, however, had drastically changed the nature of their relationship. Sarah, though sometimes of great help around the household, nonetheless acted to keep her subtle and traditional dominion over Angelina. Sarah's aid and guidance, whether with the children or with finances, too often carried with it a confirmation that Angelina was either too unskilled or too helpless in such matters. The younger sister suffered so from this shadow war that she admitted it had almost turned her into a "Maniac"; in 1853, after fifteen years, the sisters could no longer ignore the tension.[27]

The crisis began over money. Angelina, fed up with Sarah's use of her contributions to family finances as a weapon to belittle Theodore and Angelina's own financial wisdom, suggested the sisters separate the pecuniary aspect of their lives. Sarah took the suggestion as a total rejection, and retaliated by threatening to abandon the Welds entirely. She would leave and begin life on her own. But rather than recanting, Angelina seconded this proposal. Sarah did leave—for about a year—at which time the Grimkés confronted each other in the frankest of terms. And being apart, each could not avoid a long, hard look within.[28]

For Angelina, the shock helped goad her out of her languor and back into active interest in reform. She felt particularly drawn to feminist calls for dress reform; indeed, visitors to Eagleswood nearly always commented on the prevalence of the revolutionary "Bloomer" costume. Angelina promoted the bloomer as a utilitarian alternative to unhealthy and frivolous dress norms for women. She later rejected the bloomer, but she did not give up the search for some better answer to the demands of fashion.[29]

In addition, she attempted to reintegrate herself into the company of old antislavery friends, taking time for visits to Boston and reunions with friends such as the Philbricks. Unfortunately, she found that issues and resentments from the past were very much alive. At one point, she felt obligated to refuse Gerrit Smith's invitation for her to appear at an antislavery function with Lewis Tappan and others of his faction, largely because they continued to hold antifeminist positions. Yet even such an action did not guarantee a warm welcome among her former feminist comrades. Meeting the waspish Maria Weston Chapman at an antislavery fair in Boston, Angelina became apologetic about leaving reform. She tried to show how loyal she had been and cited her refusal to join with Lewis Tappan as proof. "You ought to have felt that eighteen years ago," replied Chapman; ". . . you had the same call of duty we all had—that every soul on earth has who sees a conflict between right and wrong. What I find fault with you for is that on a certain occasion you had vouchsafed to you a vision of the moral sublime; and you were not able to appreciate it." These could have been the words of Angelina's own troubled conscience. Characteristically, she thanked Chapman for her candor.[30]

Such problems, however, paled before those faced by Sarah. The older sister, too, felt the need to reengage herself in reform; when she heard of the actions of others she would be stricken with guilt: "Sometimes I feel as if I could not be still, but must utter myself."[31] Still, she faced a more profound problem. Sarah felt that her life had been a waste. "At 60," she confided to Harriot Hunt, "I look back on a life of deep disappointment, of withered hopes, of unlooked for suffering, of severe discipline." She had tasted joy, it was true, "in the innocence and earnest love of Theodore's children."[32] But now she had to face two facts. First, the children were in reality Angelina's and not Sarah's. Second, the routines of housekeeping and schoolmarming bored and frustrated her. For sixty years Sarah had been denied or had denied herself the opportunities to develop her mind and useful skills. Now she could only complain: "There is plenty of work to be done, but I see nothing in the wide world that I can do."[33] For some dismal months in 1852 and 1853, Sarah felt at once close to death and with no reason to live.

She defended herself against such despair in a number of ways. First, she continued to explore what might lie beyond death by engaging in philosophical dialogues with the spirit world, either in dreams or at séances. She gained assurance that a loving God guaranteed immortality to all. At the same time, from the depths of her personal understanding she began to formulate ideas about the history and condition of women, beginning but never completing manuscripts on marriage, divorce, and the future of her sex. Sarah even found the energy to research and expose discrimination against women in the laws of the various states; the project took her to both New England and the District of Columbia. She also became interested in the legal status of children and hoped to become their advocate before the law. Yet this marvelous burst of energy came to naught. Women could not become lawyers, and Sarah's deathly inner sense that she had begun too late qualified her verve.[34] In the end, she accepted Angelina's invitation to rejoin the family. She returned to those "darling children, who [had] brightened a few years of [her] lonely and sorrowful life."[35]

Even as such dramas played themselves out within the Weld family circle, events outside the idyllic confines of Eagleswood were gathering a fateful momentum. The sectional conflict, once seemingly settled by the Compromise of 1850, was reborn in the debate over and passage of the Kansas-Nebraska Act. "So, Mr. Chairman," Congressman Gerrit Smith bellowed in the House, "the slavery question is up again!—up again, even in Congress!! It will not keep down."[36] Indeed, it would not. Yet Theodore still resisted entering the battle, though he encouraged the efforts of his friends. He would no longer pass judgment on whole movements, taking instead the position that each person must find his proper mode of action. When Smith, for instance, urged Weld to endorse the Liberty Party, he refused on personal grounds:

> As a declaration of *sentiments*—it is mine from *my* inmost, to *its* uttermost. As a programme of *operations* with the machinery involved it is *not mine,* and I cannot make it so. Saul's *armor* was just the thing for *Saul,* but when the little shepherd put it on, though he had found a king, as now he had *lost* himself!

At the same time, he thrilled at Smith's own activities—"My heart leaps at your great shout as it comes to me from the heights of the field"—and even encouraged him to reconsider his decision to retire from Congress before the end of the first term. "You are the slaves *tongue* and have the nations *ear,*" Weld reminded Smith. "This is true of no other man in this generation."[37]

Not that Weld shuttered Eagleswood from the crisis. On the contrary, awareness of the political situation and constant preaching against slavery and racism were core elements of the curriculum. Weld often took the podium at Sunday morning meetings and, while students busied themselves with knitting and crocheting articles for the poor, he would hold forth in the cause of the black man until his voice screeched. Despite the rasp, he seemed as compelling as he had been twenty years earlier. "Mr. Weld has been telling us stories about how black people are slighted," Ellie Wright wrote in her diary; "—It's scandalous! Its a shame! I wish something would happen that I might defend a black person. I'd do so gladly."[38]

This almost innocent reenactment of abolitionism's first strategy, moral suasion, stood in marked contrast to the realities of antislavery struggle in the 1850s. In "Bleeding Kansas," battles were fought with guns and knives rather than with words. In the wake of past frustrations and the realities of violence in Kansas, abolitionists with the most fervent belief in nonresistance began to change their minds about use of force. Even Sarah Grimké, once the most adamant of nonresistance advocates, moved to a more neutral position. She had an extraordinary opportunity to test new beliefs vicariously in correspondence with Augustus and Sarah Wattles, who had left their daughter at Eagleswood and settled in Kansas to run an antislavery newspaper. Sarah had adopted Theodore's position that anything heightening the conflict might be good, since it would bring on the inevitable confrontation more swiftly. Thus she admitted to Wattles that she hoped Kansas would be admitted as a slave state; this might push the North to disunion, an action Sarah envisioned as the sections "quietly separating."[39]

She only hoped for a peaceful settlement; she did not demand it. As to the immediate question of violence in Kansas, she assured Augustus Wattles that she would not condemn or disown him if he bore arms. And who knew how she herself would act?

> Indeed dear Augustus I hardly dare say I have a standard for if I were in a condition, if I had the power to save the lives of my dearly loved ones by taking the life of the murderer I dare not say I should quietly see my darlings butchered; then comes the question are we not bound to do for others the same that we should do for ourselves and our own. I puzzled years over this query and finally have come to the conclusion that God did not make my heart to embrace in its holiest, strongest, tenderest affections the world—that to pretend to such philanthropy was overstepping the boundary of duty—But this is all theory God only knows how I should be in the hour of trial and temptation.[40]

As the 1850s wore on, fewer and fewer abolitionists remained firmly committed to nonviolence. Indeed, a small group of them were willing to finance and help plan John Brown's raid on

Harper's Ferry in 1859. As it happened, Marcus Spring's wife knew Brown. No sooner did the attack fail than she left Raritan Bay to visit the raiders in prison. She promised two of them that after their execution (which was taken for granted even before the trial), she would bury them in Northern soil, at Raritan Bay. Meanwhile, she brought Mrs. Brown to the community. Annie McKim, daughter of abolitionist James Miller McKim, described the scene in a letter to Ellie Wright:

> I suppose you would like to know what Mrs. Brown looks like from an "eye-witness"—large; good head, plain yet pleasant-looking—and as the paper states just such a woman as you would imagine John Browns wife would be. She spoke but little having just received per. Father a letter from her husband which overcame her considerably she requested Mr. S[pring] to read it aloud—Oh! it was so beautiful. and there shone from it, such great, good, nobleness of heart, is he not a man to be proud of? may we not feel that such worth will find its way to the heart of everyone.[41]

Soon after, Brown was executed. Two of his comrades were buried at the Eagleswood Cemetery, but an angry mob at Perth Amboy forced their caskets to be landed in secret at nearby Rahway.[42]

As John Brown's raid closed out an era in American life, the year 1859 witnessed a much quieter ending in Weld's personal life—a final parting with Charles Stuart. Stuart visited Eagleswood in the spring. To this friend of thirty-five years, to this man who had continually declared his love and loyalty, Theodore gave a rather brusque brush-off, claiming that he had "more important duties" to attend to at the school. Stuart later complained about their "hasty conversation" but continued to press Weld on his supposed apostasy. This theological cross-examination represented a last, slender thread of connection between the two.

In all, Stuart posed eleven questions of faith, each of which revolved around either acceptance of the Bible's divine authority, belief in the Trinity, belief in divine revelation as the key to human wisdom, or acceptance of evangelical notions of sin, repentance, rebirth, and divine judgment of sin. He then recounted to Weld the story of his own coming to Christ, and the joy of discovering peace in the Bible. But enough about himself. He wanted to know about his beloved Theodore: "My soul yet longs after you," he wrote, "—I long to know *you*, as exactly as possible as *you are.* not in enmity but in love; yet in love more devoted to God and His truth, than to you; for my heart's voice, in the best measure of its feeble faith, is with the apostle. . . ."[43]

Theodore's reply only reaffirmed Stuart's fear that he had lost all sense of the divine, that he had foolishly attributed to fallen man the ability to know eternal truths. Stuart felt compelled to disown Weld, even as Weld had, for all intents and purposes, disowned him; he only held out faint hope that they might meet again at the feet of Jesus. But he could not part without a final blast. In a postscript, Stuart noted that the latest Eagleswood prospectus, while excellent in certain respects, displayed a "hostility to the holiest interests" of his students. "I pity them," he concluded, "and you."[44]

XIV

Wars, Civil and Familial

Charles Stuart had headed his final letter to Weld with a line from Psalm 11: "If the foundations be destroyed, what can the righteous do."[1] Though Stuart was referring to the deleterious effects of Weld's heresies, it is striking that he chose this Scriptural injunction but a few months before the outbreak of the Civil War. Ironically, this war, which shook the foundations of the American nation, allowed those righteous advocates of abolition an opportunity only dreamed of in peacetime. What Weld had predicted in 1842, a direct confrontation of the sections, had come to pass; it brought with it the real possibility of ending slavery as part of a Union victory. Indeed, veteran abolitionists had not felt such optimism about their cause since the heady days of millennial bliss in the early 1830s. Though Weld and others had moved theologically to liberal Christianity and Spiritualism, they returned to their evangelical roots in search of a language adequate to the dimensions of fear and hope that the War inspired. "How pregnant the signs of the times!" exclaimed Weld in 1862. "'For the oppression of the poor, for the sighing of the needy, now will I arise, saith the Lord.'"[2]

Though millennial in tone, Theodore's conceptions of the war showed the influence of a mature sense of history and society:

I profoundly believe in the righteousness of such a war as this is, on its anti-slavery side. You exult, as we do, in this mighty Northern uprising, notwithstanding its mixtures of motives, and base alloys and half truths, and whole lies, thrown to the surface, by the force beneath:—the elements of a vast moral Revolution are all aglow, in the surging mass of a national religious revival, better deserving the name, than anything that has preceded it— Simple right is getting such a hearing as never before on this Continent. Logic—Philosophy—political economy—moral suasion— fact—rebuke—and power of appeal, had done their uttermosts, and yet, all but a fraction of the North were profoundly infidel, on the subject of Slavery—Its sorcery had besotted them, till they "believed a lie"—But for this rebellion—just this, with all its diabolism, and nothing less, the maelstrom would have dragged us all down.[3]

Weld's recognition of this "national religious revival" reawakened the youthful reformer in him; he yearned to rejoin the cause he had abandoned fifteen years prior. In fact, the coming of the war threw into sharp relief that part of Weld's sense of a "higher sphere of experience" that had been a sophisticated form of resignation. Soon after the outbreak of hostilities, he asked Henry Bellows to make him an inspector for the newly formed United States Sanitary Commission. Bellows turned him down because he lacked the proper medical training, but he continued to search for a proper niche. He even began to heed the urgings of friends who hoped he would return to public speaking. In any case he was ready to give up Eagleswood. His beloved school, already plagued by chronic financial woes, had enforced upon the Welds what Sarah called a "penitentiary existence," imprisoning energies that might be unleashed to serve the Union cause.[4] Eagleswood graduated its last class in 1862.

Theodore's opportunity came soon after Lincoln issued his preliminary emancipation proclamation, when Garrison invited Weld to address a large meeting at Boston's Music Hall on November 9, 1862. Weld wrestled with his fears for some days, but finally decided to accept. Once having made the decision, he chose a topic—"The Conspirators: Their False Issues and Lying Pretences"—and launched into the writing of his address with a passion reminiscent of the old days. "When I began, I thought to bring what I wished to say *within* the allotted 'hour' but alas!" he wrote Garrison. "What I have already written will occupy *three* mortal hours! and the cry is 'still they come.' "[5]

Confidence did not come as easily as words. "I have not tested my voice either in a *long* talk or in a *large* house [for years]—It *may* fail me in [the] Music Hall," he warned Garrison. Nor would Weld risk speaking without a text. This past master of mnemonics felt so out of practice that he felt sure his mind "could not *traverse extemporaneously* with profit to [his] hearers." With the humorous chagrin of a youthful man grown old, Theodore exclaimed, "So I must read and *keep my finger on the line!!*" He would put up with these "distasteful" compromises, however, for nothing could get in the way of saying what must be said in such "teeming times."[6] On the appointed day, Weld projected his message to the far reaches of the Music Hall, and his voice lasted the full one hour and twenty minutes of a much-edited discourse. So successful was this initial venture that he planned an extensive speaking tour, one that could take him throughout New England and as far West as his old stamping ground, Ohio's Western Reserve.[7]

Theodore could have chosen no more important moment for a return to antislavery oratory. "Teeming times" he called them, and in fact these months between Lincoln's first message and that New Year's Day when the Emancipation Proclamation became official seemed as crucial to abolitionists as final victory itself. Would the President hold firm to his commitment? No one was sure. "Everything seems to depend upon what is done in the battle field and the lecture field before the 1st of January," wrote Angelina to Gerrit Smith in late November. It was "the accepted time and the day of Salvation from Slavery." She gloried, of course, in Theodore's contribution: "He is doing the very thing my heart wants him to do."[8]

And so for seven months Weld relived some part of his youth. First he toured Massachusetts towns—Danvers, Worcester, Lynn, Leominster, and others—sometimes alone and sometimes paired with the eccentric Parker Pillsbury. After a brief trip to Rhode Island, Theodore turned north toward New Hampshire, where he campaigned tirelessly for Republican candidates in gubernatorial and congressional elections to be held in March 1863. Always he had eschewed partisan politics, but never before had the stakes been so high. With the Union cause faltering from military reversals and a bad showing for the Republican Party in November 1862, it was no time to deny his energies to the party that so recently had raised the banner of emancipation.[9]

Theodore returned home for a few days in early March, and then moved west through Pennsylvania. In Ohio, he made one appearance in Cleveland before arriving at Oberlin, where he was treated to a hero's welcome and returned the kindness with five speeches in four days. This last feat brought out the screech in his voice and dictated a four-day rest. Memories stirred as he broke his silence to preach at James A. Thome's church in Cleveland. Then it was on to upstate New York for a few appearances, and finally home again to stay. He capped his speaking with a final major address, this to the American Anti-slavery Society's annual meeting in New York.[10]

Though more or less out of the lecture arena—Weld did address smaller audiences on occasion—he and the sisters remained active in other ways. For instance, they wrote a public letter to Garrison that forecast victory in imagery informed by the war itself:

> We see, in the blow about to fall, the bolt of God, striking Slavery dead, and burning up its corpse, leaving not a hair of the accursed thing to taint the air, or stain the ground, or bow down one free grass blade, or tether the tiniest rootlet in the soil.[11]

In another letter to Garrison, Sarah further developed the meaning of the war, in this case linking God, racial destiny, and the deliverance of the slave:

> This blessed war is working out the salvation of the Anglo-Saxon as well as of the African race. The eyes of the nation are being anointed with the eye-salve of the king of Heaven. . . . The war the holiest ever waged, is emphatically God's war, and whether

the nation will or not, He will carry it on to its grand consummation, until every American enjoys the rights claimed for them in
our Declaration of Independence. Will not some hero arise ere
this conflict closes, on whom will rest the mantle of Toussaint
L'Ouverture? Earnestly do I pray that from among the ranks of
our colored brethren a Savior will arise, who will make this war
resplendent with his deeds of valor, courage, wisdom and fortitude, and who will be deservedly hailed as the final Deliverer of
his people.[12]

It would be cheap irony to remind oneself that Sarah had once
been an ardent nonresistant to whom the phrase "blessed war"
would have been blasphemy. One need only quote Angelina on
the subject: "You see how warlike I have become—O yes—War is
better than Slavery. . . ."[13] However, it is sobering to observe
how Weld and the sisters distanced themselves from the carnage
of this bloodiest of American wars. Angelina had begun the process before the conflict commenced, resigning herself to the fact
that abolition might only come "thro' blood and insurrection." "I
feel willing it should come in my day," she added, "for the longer
it is put off, the worse it will be."[14]

Sarah, though no less ardent in her devotion to the Union
cause, was deeply shaken by the slaughter. "Would you believe
it," she wrote to a friend, "I still shun hearing the papers read—
All the sickening details of bloodshed and suffering I shrink
from." That was in early 1862. A year later, in February 1863,
she felt compelled to make her worst nightmare into a morality
play. She dreamed one night of a ball made of "human bones
and heads and shattered limbs and mutilated trunks of men"
cemented by filth and blood congealed, and as it rolled it grew
like a snowball. It rolled from the deep South to the Atlantic and
plunged into the ocean. Suddenly the waters became a mass of
foaming blood and flame, and lashed the European shore with
forked flames and "waves of gore." Sarah then heard the voice of
Heaven: " 'Behold the work of the slaveocracy should it succeed
in its rebellion.' "[15]

Weld himself never revealed his deepest reactions to the war's
carnage. Rather he spoke of the manly duties of soldiering, and

watched proudly as his students enlisted—and died—for the Union.[16]

If Weld steeled himself against the bloodshed of war, he had not lost his sensitivity to its inner costs. In this spirit he offered to his audiences not only rousing attacks on the Southern conspiracy, but also sobering, even touching, appraisals and criticisms of the reformers themselves. His most notable effort in this regard was a set of two lectures entitled "Cost of Reform," which Weld first presented in November 1863 before modest audiences at New York's Dodworth's Hall. In the morning address, he made sense of the sufferings of reformers of his own generation by linking them with sacrifices of past ages. It was a heroic picture, meant to inspire further commitment against the world's latest embodiment of evil, the Southern Confederacy. In his evening talk, however, Weld turned from the costs of martyrdom to those inner "perils to mind, soul, and spirit" that stunted the personal growth of reformers. He worried that the essentially negative, iconoclastic spirit of most reform, though necessary, might tend to make the reformer's "spirit as dry, as the husks he strips. Battering surfaces, rather than sounding depths, tends to draw him to the surface, and make *him* as superficial as the shallows he navigates." Thus the Reformer, a destroyer by profession, might accomplish his goals "without enlisting the higher functions of the soul; without love, without the spirit that forgives, that renders good for evil, that loves those who hate, sinks self and dies for enemies."[17]

This was an extraordinary message for a wartime audience. The Emancipation Proclamation was not even a year old and victory still seemed in doubt. Fear of internal subversion wracked the North. But four months earlier, violent riots against the draft had shocked New York. On the battlefield, the nation had been stunned by the slaughter at Gettysburg. A month later, Confederate guerrillas under William C. Quantrill had outraged the North by massacring one hundred and fifty men in Lawrence, Kansas. Was this the moment to speak of love for those who hated, of that spirit that died for enemies? It was precisely the right moment for Weld. Perhaps it was his way of holding out, in the worst of times, for a goal beyond military victory and Republican dominion. When most in the reform movement had put behind them the broadest and deepest visions of evangelical millennialism, those of universal Christian love, Weld tried to remind them of the loss involved.[18]

Despite pietistic qualms about reformers, Weld shared fully in the joy of the South's defeat. Angelina had hoped that he could celebrate the Northern triumph in her native city of Charleston, but he more appropriately took part in ceremonies at Oberlin. In the company of a number of Lane Rebels, Theodore held his audience "spell-bound" with a two-hour oration on the Higher Law.[19] And while he was at Oberlin, in communion with his own legendary past, he received a letter from his daughter that fused past and present:

> How nice it must be for you to go through the old places and see the people that used to hear your lectures. Have you seen any of the men that mobbed you . . . ? Have you been anywhere near Alum Creek? I think you said that the people who saved you were either dead or had moved farther out West. I wish I could be with you to see the ford you tried to cross and the bank you lodged upon. Do you suppose that the alder bushes are still there that you climbed up into?[20]

Sissy's letter may have been for Weld the most moving tribute to his long battle in reform, for evanescent public ceremonies could not compare with the love and admiration of one's own flesh and blood.

Theodore received no such reward from his sons. Both were of draft age, yet neither served. Charles (or Stuart, as he now preferred) insisted the North's cause to be "unjust," while Thody drifted through the war years in a profound melancholic stupor. Weld maintained a chilling silence on the matter of his sons and the war. What could he say? Yet as students and sons of friends marched off to war, hurt and disappointment must have run as deeply as his own commitment to the struggle.

Stuart's case was simple. In 1862, when talk first arose about a conscription act, he made it clear to his father that, on principle, he would not serve. When Weld offered to pay his son's substitute fee, Stuart angrily refused. If it came to that, he preferred jail. It was a question of his manhood. "To *my* mind the above statement is *perfectly clear* and *conclusive*," he wrote, "and I do *presume* it will be to you. . . . In short you have *no right* to [intervene in the matter]. By this time I shall be a perfectly *independent* man and not dependent upon you for support."[21]

Stuart's rebellion was built on a secure sense of self. The firstborn, a favorite of both Angelina and Sarah, closest to Theodore, Stuart might declare himself a man in strength. Indeed, he acted through strong identification with his parents. For instance, he had "not a particle of doubt, not a particle," that if Theodore believed as he did and were in the same situation, he would have taken a similar stand on principle. In defiance of his father, he remained his father's son. He even found room for compassionate understanding of the position in which he placed his parents.[22]

A different fate befell Theodore Grimké Weld. Significantly, while the family allowed little Charley to become the adult Stuart, they continued to call the younger son by his infant nicknames of "Thody" or "Sody." Distanced from Theodore by Stuart's presence, neglected by Angelina and smothered by Sarah, he entered his teens with an imperfect sense of love and belonging in the family. One can only imagine the shock when, at age thirteen, he witnessed Sarah's anguished leaving of home and the family's move to Eagleswood, where his parents would be ever busier catering to the needs of other parents' children. Who would love him then?

In these years, as she had always been, Sarah became the youth's source of love and support. Unfortunately, she gave him love colored by her own resentment toward his parents and her own wish to possess him as her own. Sarah wrote about his father's bad habits while Thody visited the Gerrit Smiths and suggested that he look to the Smith family for a model of proper manners. During her own painful sojourn in the winter of 1853–

54, she urged him to lay bare his needs before a neglectful Angelina: "You have a work to do with your dear mother. I think if you could ever feel like telling them how your soul yearns to enjoy the fulness of home love, they will feel it too and will be thankful for this incentive to make the circle of Home a temple of bliss." Yet Sarah truly thought that task to be her own. "O yes," she once wrote, "I will strive to bring back the winter home of your childhood."[23]

Telltale signs of trouble appeared in the 1850s. Thody began to stutter. At age eighteen, he abandoned Eagleswood School for a year to find work away from home. Reminiscent of Theodore's escape from Andover, the episode had a different outcome. Thody returned worse than ever, falling into inexplicable dreamy states. Seemingly exhausted, he would ruminate over deep philosophical questions or sit in silent torpor. In such a state, he claimed, one might possess the power to read minds and imbibe the wisdom of the world from unopened books. Perhaps Thody hoped to please Sarah with his claims of clairvoyance and profound thought, or mock her own interest with a caricature. In any case, she urged him to "swing loose instead of pondering questions of deep and eternal interest." The same advice came from one Mr. Cutler of Rome, New York, from whom the family sought advice.[24]

The real fear, however, was that Thody was going insane, and that this creeping madness had, at its root, willful sexual self-abuse. The experts agreed. They found semen in his urine specimens, and one savant bluntly stated that Thody suffered from debilitating nocturnal emissions. As for a cure, those whom the family consulted split into two basic camps. One recommended fresh air, carefully administered regimens of bathing and exercise, and mental relaxation. As a result, Thody was put under the care of Dr. Diocletian Lewis, a practitioner of the water-cure and gymnastics, and at times was sent to upstate New York to enjoy the fresh air and farm labor. Thus preoccupation with morbid sexual desire might be supplanted by natural outlets for energy. And at times, Thody showed some improvement.[25]

The other camp emphasized direct release of sexual tensions. One J. Peter Lesley recommended early marriage, which might give the youth both moral sexual focus and someone for whom to live and work. More fascinating was the advice of a Mrs. Coleman, a clairvoyant who had been recommended to Sarah for her peculiar talents. Coleman described Thody's condition as caused by the flowing of sperm back into the body and a resultant poisoning of energy and will. She recommended direct sexual stimulation by a moral woman—herself—so that he could become a "truly healthful man." The treatment was simple:

> It is only necessary to lay upon the small of the back the hand often, and at other times, it is simply necessary for the hand to be placed upon the ovarium. In this manner can the brain be affected to such a degree that the love element immediately commences passing down into the testicles, filling them, when again the brain acts upon the interior organs, and they transmute to the basilar portion a liquid which forms the proper fluid by which the whole system is cleared from the otherwise thickened mass of secretions.

Thody tried this treatment as well, and once again he showed at least temporary improvements.[26]

Temporary they could only be, for the family, in its extreme anguish, reinforced Thody's angry melancholia with a brand of caring tinctured by blame and threat. Sometimes the allusions were subtle—Sarah requesting that Thody ask Dr. Lewis if his therapy might have use "among lunatics."[27] And there is no question that the concern was sincere. "We have a little hope," wrote Weld to Martha Coffin Wright in 1862, "that it may yet not prove to be that *fatal* softening of the brain."[28] Yet injunctions to Thody often stressed the fact that *he* had inflicted pain on the family, and commanded *him* to change his ways. No one mixed messages better than Sarah:

> . . . no longer yield to the bodily and mental torpor which has so stealthily, so cruelly, so gradually taken possession of you—O think whether you are worthily using the talents committed to your care—You know with what intense interest I have watched

you, trying to persuade my aching heart that you might be under the preparing hand for some special work—Lately I have hailed with infinite pleasure the increase, or return of affectionate interest in us—Can you imagine the joy we feel when you say in action "I love you." Do not suppose I think you have been indifferent to our sufferings, I know you have participated in them to some extent—But has not the time come when by a noble effort you can make us all happy. . . .[29]

Theodore was more blunt. "You little know my dear son the distressing anxiety that we feel on your account," he wrote, "increased, as it is, by the fact, that we learn from Dr. Fowler—that you decline to use the means which he prescribed. . . . All authorities agree that this drain upon the seminal fluid will, if not stopped, lead ultimately to *insanity* or to *idiocy*."[30]

One wonders whether, in the midst of this twisted drama, Theodore remembered how Ludovicus had branded him a heretic and how he had embraced that identity as his own. One wonders because Thody, it would seem, made his father's warning a command. He embraced insanity. In profound melancholia he had found a means both for gaining long desired care and attention in the family and for punishing those who should have loved him more. It is sad to confront the fact that Theodore, who so sensitively shaped the characters of other men's children, helped devastate the character of his own son. It is sadder still to recognize that, though Weld might play Ludovicus to the child, Angelina seemed incapable of playing Elizabeth. And what hope was there for Thody without the strongest sort of maternal love? In a family that sent no soldier to Bull Run or Gettysburg, he was the pathetic casualty of an invisible war no less frightening, in its own way, than the one that ended at Appomattox in 1865.[31]

XV

Last Years

Sometime in 1863, after the demise of Eagleswood, the Welds moved to the outskirts of Boston. They boarded in West Newton until Theodore found more suitable quarters. In November he bought a "lovely little house" on the Neponset River in Fairmount, a new suburban development seven miles south of Boston. The Welds would live there the rest of their lives.[1] The migration symbolized Weld's changing religious and cultural allegiances. At Eagleswood and during the war, he drew closer and closer to the most distinguished members of Boston's Unitarian society; at the same time, his connections with the New York evangelicals ended. It seemed logical for the Welds to join the community in which they felt most comfortable.[2]

The move to Boston also helped to complete Weld's spiritual and familial odyssey. Once he had been a rebellious exile from his father's home and his family's region, a "backwoodsman" in the far reaches of the West. Slowly he began to face his New England self, his genealogy and its importance. This return to the country of his forebears was a slow one, but in the end he lived out the final thirty years of life only a few miles from the site of Thomas Welde's original Roxbury Church.

In this new setting, the Welds pursued traditional interests. They soon found teaching positions at Diocletian Lewis's newly opened Young Ladies' Boarding School in Lexington. Like Eagleswood, the school combined traditional studies with physical culture, attempting to right the "drooping shouders, weak spines and chests" that seemed endemic among "the most intelligent classes." Theodore lectured on mental and moral training; in addition, he supervised the composition and recitation classes, using Shakespeare and other "masters of thought and speech" as texts. Angelina taught modern history and Sarah helped as well, presumably as an instructor in French. They all worked hard, living at the school during the week and spending only Sunday at Fairmount. When the school burned down in 1867, however, the trio left full-time employment forever.[3]

It was just as well, for Theodore and the sisters felt themselves inexorably drawn to speak out on reform issues. Foremost were the problems of Reconstruction. Weld advocated federal laws to grant the freedmen equal rights and emphasized the need for strict enforcement. By 1870 he was bitterly attacking the government's negligence on this point. "The words of the A.S. amendments are dead words coffined up and buried in the statute book," Weld complained; "Nay Nay not *dead* for all dead things have lived, and these never drew a breath, those who made them left them in the clutches of a nurse who choked them instanter, before they could catch a living gasp." Left unenforced, such laws became taunts to the freedman. Unprotected liberty became protected slavery.[4]

Weld recommended extreme measures, including the use of federal troops. Having fought a bloody war to establish the Nation, that Nation must protect itself. To do so it must guarantee the rights of every citizen:

The United States is a nation, with *national* life, and national life carries with it self-defence, they are forever inseparable. Whether constitutions, laws and usages favor or frown, the *right* extends to the last man, the last dollar, the last ditch. . . . The *people*— they alone are the Nation's self. The Nation is its *citizens,* and the Nation's right and duty to protect and defend its citizens, all of them, is absolute and paramount.[5]

Weld's plea for military enforcement of civil rights was in striking contrast to original antislavery doctrines such as moral suasion and peaceful separation (though Weld himself was never a nonresistant). Yet his argument demonstrated a certain continuity as well, since the early abolitionists had had a nationalist vision of greatness for a slaveless America. They emphasized the *national* guilt and complicity in slavery. Now, after the war that freed the slaves, Weld stressed the national responsibility to protect their newly won rights.

Nor did the Welds stop with advocacy of black rights. They followed the freedmen's progress through the reform press, and when they could help directly they did. For instance, in the fall of 1871 Florida blacks found their homes and crops devastated by a tornado. Weld and the sisters immediately organized local collection of relief supplies, and the house at Fairmount became depot and way station for contributions.[6]

The Welds' deepest and most moving contact with the freedmen came, however, through totally unexpected circumstances. Reading the *National Anti-Slavery Standard* for February 8, 1868, Angelina noticed the name "Grimkie" in an article entitled "Negroes and the Higher Studies." This black Grimké had gained the attention of a faculty member at the all-black Lincoln University with an oration at a Literary Society exercise. Stunned by the mention of a freedman with her unusual family name, Angelina cloistered herself for a few hours to decide a course of action. She emerged resolved to find out about a possible family connection, and Sarah and Theodore supported her quest.[7]

Angelina wrote to Mr. "Grimkie" of Lincoln University assuming a relation—"you had been probably the slave of one of my brothers"—and indicating a desire "to know all about" him. She made clear her own antislavery record as well as those of Sarah and Theodore. She soon received a reply from Archibald Henry Grimké, one that contained the common courtesies and a statement causing her great distress: "I am the son of Henry Grimke, the brother of Dr. John Grimke, and therefore your brother. Of course you know more about my father than I do." This time she retired to her room for a few days, facing the reality of what was probably her worst fear. Abolitionists had long stressed the sordid sexual exploitation of slave women, and now Angelina had to face its existence in her own family. As it was, Henry Grimké's relationship with his slave Nancy Weston hardly fit the antislavery stereotype of unbridled lust. He began seeing her after the death of his legal wife, and provided a special cottage for Nancy and the three sons—Archibald, Francis, and John—which he had by her. Still, Henry would not free them and when he died they came under the indifferent ownership of Henry's legal son Montegue. Then followed escape attempts, reenslavement, separation, and finally freedom at the end of the Civil War.[8]

Knowing some of the truth, Angelina continued the correspondence to find out the rest of Archibald's story. More important, the Welds actively encouraged both Archibald and Francis to consider themselves kinfolk. Angelina saw to it that they had enough money to complete their educations. In June 1868 she and Stuart made the long journey to see the Grimké brothers at Lincoln University, thus cementing a relationship that continued to grow through the years. The brothers became regular visitors in the Weld home; with the help of Theodore and the sisters, Archibald and Francis became two of the most prominent blacks of their generation. Francis distinguished himself as a clergyman, while Archibald made his mark as a lawyer, writer, and diplomat.[9]

All the while, Theodore and the sisters continued to work in other reform areas. For instance, Theodore and other citizens urged limiting the sale of liquor in the light of several incidents of public drunkenness in Hyde Park.[10] Most of all, however, the Welds committed themselves to the women's rights movement. Each at one point or another served as an officer of the Massachusetts Woman Suffrage Association; Angelina and Sarah collected petition signatures for suffrage, while Theodore attended and spoke before suffrage meetings.[11] They even engaged in direct action. On March 8, 1870, the Welds, Lucy Stone, and fifty-seven other women marched through a bitter snowstorm to vote in the local Hyde Park elections. Once inside the town meeting, the Grimkés led their sisters in depositing illegal slips in the ballot box. The assembled crowd rushed forward to watch this novel event; too many stood on the platform, causing the wood to crack. Someone in the audience punned, "I think your platform is a very weak and shaky affair, after all." The crowd replied with hisses and cheers and general confusion.[12]

Marches in the snow, brave acts met with jeers and commotion—these scenes recalled earlier days in reform. Yet in his youth Theodore had literally been an outside agitator, one who set off antislavery sparks in a community and then left. Now, as he settled down to live out his life in Hyde Park, Theodore integrated reform concerns with a deep devotion to the institutional life of his town. He became a patriarch of this young Boston suburb, one of a number of notables who settled there and attempted to enrich the life of the community.

Theodore played varied roles in Hyde Park. He was elected to the school board by a margin of two to one over his closest rival. He spoke to local groups about the issues of the day. However, he was proudest of his part in founding two key institutions— the Hyde Park Free Public Library and the Second Congregational Church (Unitarian). Weld and others began fund-raising for the library in 1871; by April 1872 they had raised over four thousand dollars and collected almost one thousand books (one hundred twenty-five of which were from Weld's own shelves). It opened in March 1874. "The prime function of a public library," wrote the trustees, "is to quicken the desire to know and then to minister to the desire it has created, and nurse its growth from strength to strength."[13]

Such heady idealism soon found itself confronted by a question that would become a perennial for public libraries all over the country: Should they receive and circulate books advocating unpopular or controversial ideas? Hyde Park's new library became the center of a local tempest because its trustees pondered refusing a bequest that consisted of books by, of all people, Andrew Jackson Davis. Several members of the board found Davis's works blasphemous and lewd, though most admitted to not having read them. Soon after, they turned down the works of Thomas Paine. The *Norfolk County Gazette,* the area's most important newspaper, mocked the trustees and argued strongly that "the people who are taxed to pay for the support of a public library should not be deprived of the privilege of reading works upon ALL religions,—Orthodox or Heterodox."[14]

Such controversy upset Theodore, also a trustee, for a number of reasons. He feared that the library might be scuttled at its launching, and by its trustees' own stupidity. Furthermore, he was shocked that the works of his high-minded friend Davis could be the cause. Nonetheless a committee appointed to examine the books in question reported that they contained "matter decidedly objectionable for young people to read." Weld continued to defend Davis at trustees' meetings, and indeed took higher ground. "Any book," he told his colleagues, "in regard to God or Man, so long as it is worded in decent language, cannot be corrupting in its influence if read in the right spirit. We should be pleased to see even the strongest and most radical works on Atheism placed on the library shelves, so that all may have an opportunity of reading them if they chose so to do." Eventually the library voted to receive the works of both Davis and Paine.[15]

Theodore's other major endeavor in Hyde Park community life, the founding and maintenance of its Second Congregational (Liberal Christian or Unitarian) Society, signified a final synthesis of his ever-evolving views on the relation of man, church, and God. He and like-minded citizens met on June 1, 1867 to form a society that would serve the communal functions of a church while allowing the widest variety of religious expression among its members. This was perhaps why the founders mixed "Congregational," "Liberal Christian," and "Unitarian" in the name—their new society would give them the Congregational church's sense of social cohesion without dictating personal beliefs. More positively, it sought to promote within each individual that union with God that, but twenty years earlier, Weld thought possible only apart from organized religion. Now he believed that a church might serve both piety and community. The Preamble to the Society's Constitution, which Theodore may have helped write, explained how:

> We, the undersigned, inhabitants of Hyde Park and its vicinity, that we may quicken in ourselves and others the love of God and the love of man,—a reverence for the brotherhood of the race, for human rights, liberty, equality, and fraternity—irrespective of condition, language, sex, or national descent,—and that we may be helpers of one another in seeking for all, the largest growth in truth and goodness propose to associate ourselves together for the furtherance of the objects aforesaid. Conceding to all the same freedoms of conscience, thought and speech, that we claim for ourselves, we exact no sectarian or theological test of membership, and shall strive for no dead uniformity of speculative belief, as a means of obtaining that living unity with God, which first of all we should seek.[16]

Theodore typified a number of members of his reform generation in this spiritual journey from Orthodoxy to Liberal Christianity. The dark universe of Calvinism, its intricate theological systems and controversies, seemed to Weld and others unreflective of the times in which they lived, unsuited to the bright, harmonious world they liked to think would soon be brought into being. Yet in Unitarianism was to be found at least some continuity with Weld's older beliefs, that is the hope for a day when sectarianism would no longer separate Christians and, by extension, all humanity.

Ironically, when in 1879 the Hyde Park Church fell on hard times, it was the very ecumenicism of the preamble that some members of the church blamed for the trouble. One parishioner complained publicly of the "indeterminate, perhaps indefinable character of our faith." He asked, "What do we as a society believe? Can anybody tell? Are we certain that there exists as basis of our worship *any* distinctly defined idea?"[17]

Theodore, incensed by the attack, replied with a list of things in which the Society believed: God, the teachings of Jesus, the brotherhood of man, liberty and equality, truth, trust, and prayer.

Furthermore, he rebutted the charge that the Preamble was atheistic in spirit and therefore to blame for the Society's reduced membership and funds. Bursting through came the energy of Weld in his youth. His adversary had made a beast of the Preamble, so Theodore thought he might take his friend close in to survey this "Gorgon dire!": "Why! It neither belches thunder nor fire! It is no dragon! It looks just like a lamb! Its voice is neither a bellow nor a roar. Not even a hiss! Hark! It is only a bleat!"[18]

Theodore's jocular tone somewhat obscured his own continuing concern over issues of belief. In "Theism and Atheism," a lecture given before the Unitarian Society in 1876, he replied directly to the question: "Is there a God?" Countering crude evolutionary and materialist critiques of the idea of God, he insisted that the Deity's existence was as clearly demonstrable as man's own. When a man dies, he argued, we can no longer see the real man, only the body that was its home. But we know that the soul lives beyond our senses, and so does God. Weld asked his audience to imagine a man with only one of his six senses. "Add the senses, one at a time," he instructed, "and what new worlds of being, what new perceptions and notions of existence are revealed by each. What a world of light and beauty is revealed to the blind by the addition of the sense of sight. Who then, can conceive of the new realms of spiritual being that may be revealed to us by the addition of a new sense."[19]

It was, of course, an appropriate time for Theodore to contemplate realms beyond the senses, universes beyond death. He was seventy-three. His parents, brothers, and sister were all long dead. Periodically he would receive news of another antislavery comrade gone. Indeed, but two and a half years earlier, Sarah had died at the age of eighty-one. A service was held on December 27, 1873. Reformers from all over Boston gathered at the Weld residence to pay their last respects. The family sat clustered around an open coffin; according to Ellie Wright, Sarah's face displayed a "very natural, and placid" expression. There were eulogies by William Lloyd Garrison and Lucy Stone, then a hymn, and finally brief remarks by Theodore. "I wish I could say a few words," he began, tears streaming down his cheeks, "but I can't." Regaining his composure, he praised Sarah's self-denial, her tenderness and love for the family, and her simplicity —she had even requested that her coffin be of plain pine.[20]

In the presence of death, however, there appeared new generations of life. Sissy attended with her husband, the Reverend William Hamilton, and their nineteen-month-old daughter. Stuart, unmarried and now a writer on world affairs, was there as well. Indeed, in some ways he seemed the most stricken by Sarah's death. Thody was not present, presumably because his mental condition would not permit it.[21]

Soon after the funeral, Theodore revealed to the Gerrit Smiths that his tears had given way to a more profound understanding of Sarah's death. He refused to term her lack of physical presence a void, for the family still lived in the company of her spirit. "How true it is that when *such* spirits pass from our sight," he added, "we then know of a surety that *death* is only a name upon a little way-station on the eternal pathway which the car of life shoots swiftly by and never stops at. How soon we shall all pass it!"[22]

A year later Angelina suffered a paralytic stroke; however, the end came neither soon nor without pain. She endured a sometimes tortured existence for six years. During the final days, her generally peaceful mood was often punctuated by odd happenings. One night she began to hum and then stretched her arms around Theodore, kissing him as her humming grew more fervent. For three days and nights, during all her waking hours, she hummed the same tune. Only once did she stop, at that point to exclaim, "I'm singing to the dear Fa-ther, —hap-py, hap-py." She said it over and over again; even when she lapsed into silence, her lips continued to mouth "hap-py." Near the very end, she tossed and turned in what Theodore at first thought was physical pain but soon realized was "mental anguish." In her sleep she had transported herself back to childhood, and in "mingled tones of pathos and remonstrance" was preaching to the slaveholders

Angelina Grimké
(*Sophia Smith Collection, Smith College*)

around her on the wrongs of slavery. Finally, on October 26, 1879, death relieved her of her nightmares.[23]

Theodore mourned his wife's passing, but this death seemed different. At Sarah's funeral he could not hold back the tears; at a service for William Lloyd Garrison, feeling almost overwhelmed his words. However, for Angelina, death had been a deliverance from excruciating pain, from an agony Theodore had shared with her at bedside. "The waves that sweep over me do not whelm me," he wrote to Ellie Wright and her husband, "—though I buffet them with weary strokes. But I *cannot* mourn. Indeed I have *no sorrow!* It is all swallowed up in a great abounding joy— in *her deliverance.* Her exceeding gain is *all mine.*" Having witnessed her death throes, he felt the peace of having experienced a part of his own; he looked forward to joining her spirit.[24]

Theodore would have to wait over fifteen years. Meanwhile, he became something of a community elder, the relic of a past heroic age in the midst of genteel Boston. His sweet face, yellowed silver locks, and wild, straggly white beard stood out at the opulent social gatherings that marked that era. In 1890, for instance, Theodore, Stuart, and Archibald Grimké attended a Unitarian Club lawn party. Chinese lanterns, novel electric lights, and locomotive headlights illuminated the yard of a spacious Hyde Park mansion. On the Neponset River, which flowed by the house, a steam launch putt-putted guests on short cruises. Others danced to the music of the Acme Orchestra, while still others partook of a lavish spread in the dining room. One wonders how vividly Weld could recall the America of his pietistic youth as he took part in such galas.[25]

Of course, the past itself became the object of ceremony. Theodore celebrated his eightieth birthday in the company of nearly two hundred friends and admirers gathered at the New England Woman's Club in Boston. Among the guests were John Greenleaf Whittier, Samuel Seward, Samuel J. May, Henry Bowditch, William Lloyd Garrison, Jr., Thomas Wentworth Higginson, Henry Blackwell and Lucy Stone, Julia Ward Howe, Elizur Wright, and Gerrit Smith Miller. They represented a cross-section of Weld's life—childhood friends, antislavery comrades, students, and friends made since moving to Hyde Park.[26]

As was the custom, some contributed verse written for the occasion. William Lloyd Garrison, Jr.'s poem began:

> O, friend beloved, if aught that life holds dear
> Has been denied you in your long career,
> Not from your restful soul doth it appear.
> Therein is mirrored to us peace profound,
> The reflex of a depth we cannot sound,
> Shaming the shallow pools which all abound.

After brief words from others, refreshments were served and guests mingled for a few hours. Then, after a singing of "Auld Lang Syne," Theodore, laden with bouquets and baskets of flowers, took the train home to Hyde Park.[27]

No matter how touchingly memorialized, Theodore refused to become a passive observer. Throughout his eighties he continued to teach. He lectured on a variety of topics—Shakespeare, Byron, the lives of reformers such as William Lloyd Garrison, and the nature of religion. He presided over the "Weld Circle," an informal society that gathered to hear talks about art, religion, and literature. He helped found the Hyde Park Historical Society. And he even had time to play blind man's buff at the birthday party of Stuart's son, little Louis Weld. Theodore was eighty-eight at the time.[28]

Nor did age or the seductions of genteel society prevent Weld from speaking out on reform issues. He continued to campaign publicly for temperance and woman's suffrage. He also remained open to new ideas; at the age of eighty-six, for instance, he participated in a public debate over the merits of Bellamy's *Looking Backwards*, whose utopian ideas Weld apparently considered intriguing but impractical.[29] Occasionally he even mustered a prophetic fervor reminiscent of antislavery days. In a memorial address for Wendell Phillips, he compared Phillips's words to those of the Hebrew sage of old: "A horrible thing is committed in the land. The prophets prophesy falsely, and the priests bear rule by their means, and the people love it so; but what will ye do in the end thereof?" Theodore, speaking to an America scarred by public scandal and indifference, a North that had betrayed its victory against slavery, issued his own warning:

> Well may that same dread question pierce the deaf ears of our generation to-day. Yea, what will ye do in the end thereof? That is the question. What will ye do in the end thereof? Does no answer come? Hark! a burial ground that no eye can span is astir and tossing. Myriad graves break up their sods, and from out the heaving ground this answer comes: "Here moulder the bones of a million men, but not yet, no, not yet cometh the end thereof."[30]

Signs of Weld's end appeared just before the Phillips address. In June and July 1885, rheumatic attacks forced him to miss several meetings and lectures. That autumn he fell ill again, this time while visiting Sissy and her family in Michigan, though by October he had recovered. After that, he was plagued by chronic collapses. In December 1888, he suffered a seizure that left him helpless as a baby. Weld ate well, slept soundly, and experienced no pain; however, he could not dress or feed himself and could neither write nor stand without help. He credited his recovery to excellent nursing and "mind cure" therapy. By March 1889 he was able to attend church and by the following June he had resumed some teaching and lecturing.[31]

Even at age eighty-seven, spirit and body warred over the old issue of overwork. For instance, Sissy requested a letter stating his views of the two political parties and the work of the Women's Christian Temperance Union. Theodore took great pains to explain his recent illness so that she might accept only a short answer to her questions. He claimed, "I have learned the *length of my tether how far I can go and when to stop.*" Then he began a long treatise on the virtue of temperance and the evils of party loyalty; by now he had handed the pen to Anna Weld, his scribe and Stuart's wife. "But *stop!* here I am spinning out a yarn so long, when I was to be as short as possible," he complained. "Well you must set it down to *dotage.*" Anna added, "I write this sentence only under protest." Weld continued: "For you know if I live to November I shall then enter my 88th year." Anna coun-

Theodore Dwight Weld in his last years
(*Sophia Smith Collection, Smith College*)

tered: "There is no age to spirit and grandpa is *not* old." Weld then proceeded to dictate the rest of his long lecture on temperance and political parties.[32]

Theodore celebrated his ninetieth birthday at home, surrounded by Stuart's family and a small gathering of friends. Angelina Weld Grimké, thirteen-year-old daughter of Archibald Grimké, read a birthday poem, and General Henry Beebe Carrington, a Civil War hero and friend in Hyde Park, regaled the group with tales of antislavery days. This was to be Weld's last major social event.[33]

The year 1894 brought physical decline and Theodore spent his days quietly at home. In December, he may have ventured out for a court proceeding that marked the final event in Thody's dismal sojourn. The official notice in the *Norfolk County Gazette* read simply:

> Judge White, of probate court, on Wed. after hearing, found justifiable cause for restraining Theodore G. Weld of his liberty and as soon as the papers can be made out he will be sent to Westboro asylum.[34]

We do not know how the father reacted to his son's incarceration. We do not even know whether Theodore's fading mind could comprehend the event at all. Still, the final irony stands that he who had spent the better part of his life as an advocate of human freedom lived just long enough to see his namesake sacrifice that freedom to an elusive madness.

Theodore grew more feeble after the New Year, and died in his sleep during the night of February 3, 1895. Funeral services were held on Wednesday, February 7, at the Unitarian Society. Outside the sky was clear, the wind blew at twenty-five miles an hour, and the thermometer hovered around a chastening zero degrees. Inside the Society's minister presided over a celebration of Weld's life.

Several eulogies covered the highlights of his career. William Lloyd Garrison, Jr. recounted the story of Lane Seminary and stressed Weld's talents as a "persuader of men." He noted the publication and importance of *American Slavery As It Is,* as well as the great reform marriage of Theodore and Angelina. But all this was distant history. Garrison's words warmed as he described Weld's "striking and familiar figure as he wended his abstracted way through Boston streets, a contrast to the alert and nervous multitude." "A spiritual nature, a logical mind, a sensitive conscience, moral courage, an eloquent tongue," he remarked in summary, "these were the endowments of Theodore D. Weld."[35]

To the next speaker, Ednah Cheney, Weld symbolized "the whole spirit of this wonderful century." In particular she celebrated his support of women's rights, but it was the richness of the totality of Weld's life that deserved attention. "There will be no greater lesson for our young men and women to study," she concluded, "than the history of his struggles and of what he has accomplished."[36]

To the remarks of Garrison and Cheney, the modern observer can add that over eighty years after his death, we see even more clearly the sheer magnificence of the simplest dimensions of Weld's life and the transformations encompassed within it. We need only place side by side the Americas of Thomas Jefferson and Grover Cleveland to sense the changes he witnessed. He lived those years with a courage and strength extraordinary in any century. He helped shape his age by bravely championing unpopular causes, even risking life and limb in their service. And he displayed that rarer moral and emotional courage to face himself and his actions, to question his own beliefs, and to change.

But eulogies rarely come to the heart of the matter. Weld's life—so long, so complex, so interwoven with personal and public struggle, achievement, and tragedy—defies easy summary. In any case, the tribute he would have appreciated most was the very variety of people from all walks of life who braved the wind and cold to pay their respects. Black and white; anonymous citizens and famous reformers; a few old-timers who remembered the distant days and youngsters who knew only of Theodore's fondness for the Hyde Park Boys Union—for a few hours they mingled together. After a singing of "Nearer My God to Thee," Mr. Minnis, for years Theodore's favorite hackney driver, drove the hearse to Mt. Hope Cemetery. "It was time that the untrammeled spirit should be emancipated," Garrison had remarked in his eulogy. "He had no doubt that death was the threshold to a larger life and no man had more reason for the assurance."[37]

On the frozen, pristine day of his funeral, the sky offered no limit to the distance Theodore's soul might soar.

Notes

Abbreviations used in citations:

Birney Letters, Dwight L. Dumond, ed. *Letters of James Gillespie Birney, 1831–1857,* 2 vols. Gloucester: Peter Smith, 1966, or. ed. 1938.

Birney-Clements, Birney Manuscripts in the William L. Clements Library, University of Michigan, Ann Arbor.

Weld-Clements, Weld-Grimké Manuscripts in the William L. Clements Library, University of Michigan, Ann Arbor.

Weld-Grimké Letters, Gilbert H. Barnes and Dwight L. Dumond, eds. *Letters of Theodore Dwight Weld, Angelina Grimké Weld, and Sarah Grimké, 1822–1844,* 2 vols. Gloucester: Peter Smith, 1965, or. ed. 1934.

CHAPTER I

1. Weld to Lewis Tappan, May 2, 1836, MSS in New York Historical Society. The description of Weld on the *Oneida* is derived from details in this letter.

2. Weld to Anne Warren Weston, Rochester, March 26, 1836, in Weston Papers, Boston Public Library; Weld to A. A. Phelps, Troy, June, 1836, in Phelps Papers, Boston Public Library.

3. Weld to Sarah and Angelina Grimké, New York, December 28, 1837, in *Weld-Grimké Letters,* I, 508.

4. Malcolm Cowley, ed., *Walt Whitman's Leaves of Grass; The First (1855) Edition* (New York, 1959), 48. See Cowley's Introduction for a discussion of Whitman's persona; Garrison to G. W. Benson, Brooklyn, Conn., November 27, 1835, quoted in Wendell Phillips Garrison and Francis Jackson Garrison, *Wil-*

liam Lloyd Garrison, 1805–1879: The Story of His Life Told By His Children, 4 vols. (New York, 1885), II, 51.

5. A handy summary of Weld's quirks as they appeared to the man himself can be found in Weld to Angelina Grimké [New York], March 1, 1838, in *Weld-Grimké Letters,* II, 575–81; and Weld to Angelina Grimké [New York, March 12, 1838], in *Ibid.,* II, 592–99.

6. The only existing account of this trip is in Sarah Weld Hamilton, "Memories of Theodore Dwight Weld, The St. John of the Abolitionists," manuscript biography in Weld-Clements. My description of Weld in his old age is drawn from photographs of the period.

7. [William Andrus Alcott], *Forty Years in the Wilderness of Pills and Powders; or Cogitations and Confessions of an Aged Physician* (Boston, 1859), 2; see also Sidney Mead, *Nathaniel William Taylor: 1786–1858, A Connecticut Liberal* (Chicago, 1942), 58–59.

8. The literature on New England's brand of Calvinism, from its original Puritanism through later versions, is rich, complicated, and often highly contentious. The natural starting point for study is still the work of Perry Miller, particularly *The New England Mind: The Seventeenth Century* (Boston, 1961), and *The New England Mind: From Colony to Province* (Boston, 1961), though the flood of scholarship that has followed Miller often finds itself modifying or directly challenging many of his basic assumptions and findings.

9. For a detailed genealogy of the Weld family, see Charles Frederick Robinson, *Weld Collections* (Ann Arbor, 1938); for a useful portrait of Ezra Weld, Theodore's grandfather, see entry in *Biographical Sketches of the Graduates of Yale College with Annals of the College,* II, *May, 1745–May, 1763,* by Franklin Bowditch Dexter (New York, 1896), 631.

10. Sarah Weld Hamilton, "Memories of Theodore Dwight Weld," 33–34.

11. For information on Ludovicus at Harvard, see Harvard University, "Records of the College Faculty" (Harvard University Archives), V (1782–88), 233, 243, 257, 264, 283, 288, 313; VI (1788–97), 37–38; Harvard University, "College Records" (Harvard University Archives), III (May 5, 1788–August 31, 1795), 296, 320. For other biographical material about Ludovicus, see Robinson, *Weld Collections,* 123–24. For the Hampton Church and Weld's ministry, see relevant portions of First Congrega-

tional Church, Hampton, Connecticut, "Records, 1723–1897, 4v." (Bound manuscripts at Connecticut State Library, Hartford); and Sherrod Soule, "Historical Sermon," in *Services Commemorative of the Two Hundredth Anniversary of the Founding of the Church* (Danielson, Conn., 1923), particularly 13–14.

12. Ellen D. Larned, *History of Windham County, Connecticut* 2 vols. (Worcester, Mass., 1880), I, 417; Emma Lee Walton, comp., *The Clark Genealogy: Some Descendants of Daniel Clark, of Windsor, Connecticut, 1639–1913* (New York, 1913), 51, 66; Orlo D. Hine, *Early Lebanon: An Historical Address* (Hartford, 1880), 31; Robinson, *Weld Collections*, 123.

13. There is the intriguing possibility of a connection between Weld's later tendency toward what today would be called hyperactivity and unrecognized minimum brain damage, which may have resulted from the early bout with spasms. But the silence of the historical record and the inconsistency of contemporary medical usage precludes even a tentative surmise on this point. The account of these early months is in Sarah Weld Hamilton, "Memories of Theodore Dwight Weld," 27.

14. *Ibid.*, 27, 32; Weld to Angelina Grimké, New York, March 12, 1838, in *Weld-Grimké Letters*, II, 594.

15. Sarah Weld Hamilton, "Memories of Theodore Dwight Weld," 30–31. In later years he would feel deep ambivalence even about verbal aggression, of which he was a sometimes regretful master.

16. Unfortunately, there is precious little evidence concerning Weld's own sense of his relation to such illustrious ancestors as Thomas Welde on his father's side and Jonathan Edwards or Aaron Burr on his mother's.

17. Sarah Weld Hamilton, "Memories of Theodore Dwight Weld," 39–40. A brief and classic statement concerning the presence of hostility in this situation is Sigmund Freud, *Introductory Lectures on Psychoanalysis* (New York, 1966, tr. Strachey), 204–5.

18. Sarah Weld Hamilton, "Memories of Theodore Dwight Weld," 40.

19. *Ibid.*

20. *Ibid.*, 39.

21. *Ibid.*, 40–42.

22. *Ibid.*, 36, 45; Weld to Angelina Grimké, New York, December 15, 1837, in *Weld-Grimké Letters*, I, 493.

23. Sarah Weld Hamilton, "Memories of Theodore Dwight Weld," 42–43.

24. *Ibid.*, 29–30.
25. Alcott, *Forty Years in the Wilderness of Pills and Powders*, 4–5; Sarah Weld Hamilton, "Memories of Theodore Dwight Weld," 35–36.
26. Weld to Angelina Grimké, New York, March 12, 1838, in *Weld-Grimké Letters*, II, 594.
27. *Ibid.*, 593, 596–97.
28. Sarah Weld Hamilton, "Memories of Theodore Dwight Weld," 50.
29. *Ibid.*, 28–29.

CHAPTER II

1. A classic treatment of this theme is to be found in Alan Heimert, *Religion and the American Mind: From the Great Awakening to the Revolution* (Cambridge, Mass., 1966).
2. Charles R. Keller, *The Second Great Awakening in Connecticut* (New Haven, 1942), 12–35; R. J. Purcell, *Connecticut in Transition, 1775–1818* (Washington, D.C., 1918), 96; see also C. C. Goen, *Revivalism and Separatism in New England, 1740–1800; Strict Congregationalists and Separate Baptists in the Great Awakening* (New Haven, 1962); quotation is by Timothy Dwight and found in Keller, *Second Great Awakening in Connecticut*, 22.
3. Ellen D. Larned, *History of Windham County, Connecticut*, 2 vols. (Worcester, Mass., 1880); First Congregational Church, Hampton, Connecticut, "Records," I, entry for May 15, 1815, outlines visiting plan.
4. Ludovicus Weld, *A Sermon Delivered on the Day of the Annual Fast in Connecticut, March 30, 1804* (Windham, Conn., 1804), 11, 21, and *passim*.
5. Sarah Weld Hamilton, "Memories of Theodore Dwight Weld, The St. John of the Abolitionists," manuscript biography in Weld-Clements, 43–44.
6. Daniel Day Williams, *The Andover Liberals: A Study in American Theology* (New York, 1941), 2–7; [Andover Theological Seminary], *The Constitution and Associate Statutes of the Theological Seminary in Andover* (Andover, 1817), 9–10.
7. Theodore avoided the dorms by boarding at the house of John L. Abbot, according to *Biographical Catalogue of the Trustees, Teachers and Students of Phillips Academy Andover, 1778–1830* (Andover, Mass., 1903), 117; on living conditions, see

Henry K. Rowe, *History of Andover Theological Seminary* (Newtown, Mass., 1933), 29–31. For student letter, see *Ibid.*, 36–37.

8. "Mr. Theodore Dwight Weld," *Boston Herald*, September 15, 1889; Weld to Angelina Grimké [New York, March 12, 1838], in *Weld-Grimké Letters*, II, 598. The letter from Weld to Angelina Grimké emphasizes overwork, while the article lays blame more on the cold and exercise.

9. "Mr. Theodore Dwight Weld," *Boston Herald*, September 15, 1889.

10. *Ibid.*

11. *Ibid.*

12. Elizabeth and Ludovicus Weld to Weld [Hampton, Conn.], September 28, 1822, in *Weld-Grimké Letters*, I, 3–5. Ludovicus's letter is dated October 10.

13. Thomas Wentworth Higginson, *Cheerful Yesterdays* (Boston and New York, 1898), 71.

14. Erik H. Erikson, *Young Man Luther: A Study in Psychoanalysis and History* (New York, 1962), 43.

CHAPTER III

1. Theodore Erastus Clark to Theodore Dwight Weld, December 10, 1827, in Weld-Clements.

2. Elizabeth and Ludovicus Weld to Theodore Weld, Hampton, Conn., September 28, 1822, in *Weld-Grimké Letters*, I, 3.

3. For letter of resignation, see Hampton, Connecticut, *First Congregational Church, Records, 1723–1897*, 4 vols. (Bound Manuscripts, Connecticut State Library, Hartford), February 10, 1824, I, 145.

4. See Paul Alfred Carmack, "Theodore Dwight Weld, Reformer" (Ph.D., diss. Syracuse University, 1948), 18–19.

5. M[oses] M. Bagg, *The Pioneers of Utica: Being Sketches of Its Inhabitants and its Institutions, with the Civil History of the Place from the Earliest Settlements to the Year 1825—The Era of the Opening of the Erie Canal* (Utica, 1877), 62–65.

6. *Ibid.;* [Jonas Platt, Obituary of E. Clark], *Utica Christian Repository* 4 (December, 1825), 384.

7. Weld's own account is preserved in Barbara M. Cross, ed., *The Autobiography of Lyman Beecher*, 2 vol. (Cambridge, Mass., 1961), II, 232; Weld's nonenrolled status at Hamilton was brought to my attention by Mr. George Thompson, Reference

Librarian, Hamilton and Kirkland College Library. Weld's position among the Hamilton students has become part of the legend and seems logical when one considers his later leadership of students at Oneida Institute and Lane Seminary. In any case, Charles Finney refers to him as holding a "very prominent place" and having a "very great influence" among Hamilton's students; see Finney, *Memoirs of Rev. Charles G. Finney, Written by Himself* (New York, 1876), 184.

8. This account is based on previously oft-repeated stories that Weld recounted in Weld to Elizabeth Smith Miller, Hyde Park, June 30, 1888, in Weld-Clements.

9. Weld to Angelina Grimké [New York], March 1, 1838, in *Weld-Grimké Letters*, II, 577.

10. A basic though somewhat inaccurate account of Stuart's life is to be found in Dumas Malone, ed., *Dictionary of American Biography*, (New York, 1936), XVIII, 162–63. More detailed on his Indian years is Fred Landon, "Anti-Slavery Advocate Buried in Nearby Thornbury," *Collingwood Enterprise-Bulletin*, May 13, 1943 (Canadian newspaper), and Landon, "A Figure of Importance in Struggle over Slavery," *The Echo*, September 3, 1953 (Canadian newspaper), clippings in Weld-Clements.

11. Weld to Elizabeth Smith Miller, Hyde Park, June 30, 1888, in Weld-Clements.

12. *Ibid.*

13. Weld to Angelina Grimké, New York, February 18, 1838, in *Weld-Grimké Letters*, II, 562; Charles Stuart to Weld, New York, January 10, 1826, in *Weld-Grimké Letters*, I, 7; see an interesting discussion of the role of ego-ideals in the development of particularly narcissistic youths in Miles F. Shore, "Henry VIII and the Crisis of Generativity," *Journal of Interdisciplinary History*, 2 (Spring, 1972), 359–90.

14. On Beecher, see William C[onstantine] Beecher and the Reverend Samuel Scoville, assisted by Mr. Henry Ward Beecher, *A Biography of Rev. Henry Ward Beecher* (New York, 1858), 105–6; Charles Stuart to Weld, October 7, 1828, in Weld-Clements.

15. Stuart's comments reported in Weld to Angelina Grimké [New York], March 1, 1838, in *Weld-Grimké Letters*, II, 577.

16. "Thoughts on the Revival of Religion in New England," in Jonathan Edwards, *Works of President Edwards in Eight Volumes*, (Worcester, Mass., 1808), III, 225.

17. Elizabeth Weld to Weld [Apulia, New York], February 26, 1826, in *Weld-Grimké Letters*, I, 9.

18. The classic study of this region and its religious peculiarities is Whitney R. Cross, *The Burned-Over District; The Social and Intellectual History of Enthusiastic Religion in Western New York, 1800–1850* (New York, 1965).

19. [William Weeks] Bunyanus, *The Pilgrim's Progress in the Nineteenth Century* (New York, 1826), 10; I have used this reference for convenience. The original appeared in serial form in the *Utica Christian Repository* of 1825. Weeks also published [posthumously?] a much enlarged edition in 1848.

20. "Greenfield Hill," in William J. McTaggart and William D. Bottoroff, eds., *The Major Poems of Timothy Dwight* (Gainesville, Fla., 1969), 468.

21. [William Weeks] Bunyanus, *The Pilgrim's Progress*, 10.

22. *Ibid.*, 5–8.

23. "On the Manner in Which the *Millenium* is to be Introduced," *Utica Christian Repository* 4 (December, 1825), 371.

24. "Signs of the Times," *Utica Christian Repository* 2 (October, 1823), 307.

25. See Perry Miller, *The New England Mind: From Colony to Province* (Boston, 1961), 27–39, for a basic explanation of the jeremiad as a sermon form.

26. A fascinating but as yet unwritten history is that of the conversion experience, its changing nature and frequency in the Orthodox churches.

27. See especially Sidney Earl Mead, *Nathaniel William Taylor, 1786–1858, A Connecticut Liberal* (Chicago, 1942), *passim;* Cross, *The Burned-Over District*, 14–29 and *passim.*

28. Finney, *Memoirs of Charles G. Finney*, 59.

29. Henry B. Stanton, *Random Recollections* (New York, 1887), 40–42; Weld quoted in Cross, ed., *The Autobiography of Lyman Beecher*, 233. This is a standard description of a Finney performance, one used by practically all who have written at length about him. It dates from the 1830 Rochester revival, where Finney had already toned down his style from that evident in the Oneida revivals four or five years earlier.

30. Finney, *Memoirs of Charles G. Finney*, 4–6.

31. *Ibid.*, 7–10.

32. *Ibid.*, 10, 14.

33. *Ibdi.*, 12–23. My version of Finney's conversion is based entirely on Finney's own account. I have not done this because I believe it to be an "objective" account, but rather because I wished to preserve the integrity of a perfect specimen of a nineteenth-century conversion set-piece or moral tale. We will never know

enough facts about this particular incident of Finney's life to create a more historically accurate version. A different version, however, can be gleaned from the writings of George W. Gale. In particular, see "Oneida Institute," *The Quarterly Register and Journal of the American Education Society* 2 (November, 1829), 112. Gale's own account of his early relation to Finney differs greatly from the evangelist's own; it stresses the positive importance of the minister's teaching. See George W. Gale, "Autobiography of George W. Gale" (MS in Knox College, 1853), or Cross, *The Burned-Over District,* 151–59, for an account far more sympathetic to Gale. I have found Finney's, in general, the more convincing version, though in fact both Gale's and Finney's, self-justifying and written some years after the fact, are problematic.

34. Finney, *Memoirs of Charles G. Finney,* 16.
35. *Ibid.,* 16–17.
36. *Ibid.,* 19–20.
37. *Ibid.,* 20–21.
38. *Ibid.,* 24.
39. It is not clear whether Finney actually articulated this view before Gale and the presbytery; Cross claims that these views had not been formulated at the time; see Cross, *The Burned-Over District,* 158–59. I have included them as part of the account because they seemed implicit in Finney's revival technique and the wide impact he was able to make.
40. Like many theological terms, Arminian is one with many meanings in different periods and different books. At this point I merely am saying that for Finney the conversion experience of receiving grace was the first most important step to salvation, something Arminius would not have agreed with.
41. See the excellent reformulation of Mather's views in Robert Middlekauff, *The Mathers: Three Generations of Puritan Intellectuals 1596–1728* (New York, 1971), especially Chapter 13 ("The Psychology of Abasement"), 231–46.
42. No better example of this particular facet of Edwards's thought is to be found than the famous "Sinners in the Hands of an Angry God," most conveniently read in Clarence H. Faust and Thomas H. Johnson, eds., *Jonathan Edwards: Representative Selections, with Introduction, Bibliography, and Notes,* rev. ed. (New York, 1962), 155–72.
43. Finney, *Memoirs,* 52.
44. *A Calm Review of the Spirit, Means, and Incidents of the Late*

"Oneida Revival," as Exhibited in Various Presbyterian Societies (Utica, 1827), 21.

45. "A member of the late Church and Congregation," *A Brief Account of the Origin and Progress of the Divisions in the First Presbyterian Church in the City of Troy; containing, also, Strictures Upon the New Doctrines Broached by The Rev. C. G. Finney and N. S. S. Beman, with a Summary Relation of the Trial of the Latter Before the Troy Presbytery* (Troy, 1827), 19.

46. Beecher quoted in William G. McLoughlin, *Modern Revivalism: Charles Grandison Finney to Billy Graham* (New York, 1959), 36.

47. See Mead, *Nathaniel William Taylor*, 200–10.

48. *Letters of the Rev. Dr. Beecher and Rev. Mr. Nettleton, on the "New Measures" in conducting Revivals of Religion. With a Review of a Sermon, By Novanglus* (New York, 1828), iv.

49. Descriptions of the various "New Measures" can be found in the general accounts of Finney's activities provided by McLoughlin, *Modern Revivalism*, 85–100; Bernard Weisberger, *They Gathered at the River*, 87–126; Cross, *The Burned-Over District*, 173–84.

50. The quotation is from *Pastoral Letter of the Ministers of the Oneida Association, to the Churches under their Care, on the Subject of Revivals of Religion* (Utica, 1827), 14; the theme, however, is repeated in practically all the tracts written from all sides against the revival.

51. Cross, ed., *The Autobiography of Lyman Beecher*, II, 232.

52. *Ibid.*, 233.

53. Finney, *Memoirs*, 184–85.

54. *Ibid.*, 185; Cross, ed., *The Autobiography of Lyman Beecher*, II, 233.

55. Finney, *Memoirs*, 186; Cross, ed., *The Autobiography of Lyman Beecher*, II, 233.

56. *Ibid.*, 233–34.

57. Finney, *Memoirs*, 187.

58. Elizabeth Weld to Weld [Apulia, New York], February 26, 1826, in *Weld-Grimké Letters*, I, 9; Elizabeth Weld to Weld, Fabius, April 25, 1826, in *Ibid.*

59. Weld to Charles Finney, Fabius, April 22, 1820, in *Ibid.*, I, 17.

60. Memories from Labrador expedition in Sarah Weld Hamilton, "Memories of Theodore Dwight Weld, The St. John of the Abolitionists," manuscript biography in Weld-Clements, 43–44.

CHAPTER IV

1. Mention of the meeting and other details are from Weld's narrative in Barbara Cross, ed., *The Autobiography of Lyman Beecher*, 2 vols. (Cambridge, Mass., 1961), II, 234.
2. Whitney R. Cross, *The Burned-Over District; The Social and Intellectual History of Enthusiastic Religion in Western New York, 1800–1850* (New York, 1965), 163–64.
3. *Ibid.;* Barbara Cross, ed., *The Autobiography of Lyman Beecher*, II, 234.
4. See Lois Banner, "Religious Benevolence as Social Control: A Critique of an Interpretation," *Journal of American History* 60 (June, 1973), 23–41.
5. For a recent and perhaps the best detailed study of the revival and its opposition see Paul E. Johnson, *A Shopkeeper's Millennium: Society and Revivals in Rochester, New York, 1815–1837* (New York, 1978).
6. Lyman Beecher, "Resources of the Adversary and Means of their Destruction," in Beecher, *Sermons Delivered on Various Occasions* (Boston, 1828), 14. This particular sermon was preached on October 12, 1827, before the American Board of Missions.
7. Theodore D. Weld and Horace Bushnell in Oneida Institute of Science and Industry, *Second Report of the Trustees, Whitestown, March 20, 1830* (Utica, 1830), 6; see also the Reverend John H. Rice to the Secretary of the American Education Society, April, 1829, printed in *The Quarterly Register and Journal of the American Education Society* 1 (April, 1829), 210. This distinguished Southern Presbyterian was responding to a request for an essay on the "Ministerial character and preparation best adapted to the wants of the United States, and of the world, in the Nineteenth Century."
8. See, for instance, Lyman Beecher, *A Plea for the West* (Cincinnati, 1835), 9–10.
9. N. S. S. Beman, in *An Appeal to the Presbyterian Church, containing Three Numbers from the Christian Advocate, by the Rev. A[shbel] Green, D.D. also Review and Vindication, by the Rev. N. S. S. Beman. with Notes and Appendix* (New York, 1831), 52.
10. *Ibid.;* see also Whitney R. Cross, *The Burned-Over District*, 252–61.

11. Weld's address in *Hudson (Ohio) Observer and Telegraph,* November 15, 1832.
12. Indeed, a local tradition in Hampton had it that Ludovicus kept some rum in the cupboard under the stairs to give to those who shovelled snow at the homestead. This use of alcohol by the clergy was hardly unusual. Ludovicus's successor, however, was an ardent temperance man. See Susan J. Griggs, *Folklore and Firesides of Hampton and Vicinity* (Abington, Conn., 1941), 100.
13. Weld address in *Hudson (Ohio) Observer and Telegraph,* November 15, 1832.
14. Weld to Finney, Fabius, April 22, 1828, in *Weld-Grimké Letters,* I, 14–18.
15. George W. Gale to Finney, January 29, 1831, in Finney Papers, Oberlin College Library.
16. Extract from *Thirtieth Report of the Board of Directors of the American Education Society,* in *The Quarterly Register and Journal of the American Education Society* 1 (August, 1829), 18; see also Weld, Manual Labor Address in *Hudson Observer and Telegraph,* October 18, 1832.
17. Fellenberg would continue to have an influence on American educational reformers throughout the antebellum period; on Maine Wesleyan Seminary, see *Quarterly Register and Journal of the American Education Society* 2 (November 1829), 110–12; on Andover, see *ibid.,* 107–10, pages that also include material about other institutions.
18. Weld Manual Labor Address in *Hudson (Ohio) Observer and Telegraph,* October 18, 1832.
19. Green quoted in Theodore D. Weld, *First Annual Report of the Society for Promoting Manual Labor in Literary Institutions, Including The Report of Their General Agent, Theodore D. Weld, January 28, 1833* (New York, 1833), 111–13.
20. Frost quoted, *ibid.,* 114–15; Grimké quoted, *ibid.,* 117.
21. *Ibid.,* 111, 117.
22. *Ibid.,* 111.
23. *Ibid.,* 114.
24. *Quarterly Register and Journal of the American Education Society* 2 (November, 1829), 112.
25. *Ibid.,* 112.
26. For a sample of the reverence Weld's fellow students had for him, see the reminiscences of John J. Avery in Avery to Weld, Cleveland, December 12, 1893, in Weld-Clements.

27. Finney to Weld, Albany, July 21, 1831, in Weld-Clements.
28. Cross, ed., *The Autobiography of Lyman Beecher*, II, 234.
29. Oneida Institute, *Second Report of the Trustees*, 11; Chauncy K. Bushness to Weld, Norwich, Conn., December 5, 1883, in Weld-Clements; Cross, ed., *Autobiography of Lyman Beecher*, II, 234; Benjamin Thomas, *Theodore Weld: Crusader for Freedom* (New Brunswick, 1950), 19–20.
30. Robert S. Fletcher, *A History of Oberlin College from Its Foundation Through the Civil War*, 2 vols. (Oberlin, Ohio, 1943), I, 38; Thomas, *Theodore Weld*, 20; C. S. Renshaw to Finney, Oneida, July 15, 1832, Finney MSS, Oberlin College Library; there was a wider questioning of curriculum, the debate over which can be followed in the *Quarterly Register and Journal of the American Education Society.*
31. For a different and much more comprehensive look at the question of the changing nature of the ministry, see Donald M. Scott, *From Office to Profession: The New England Ministry, 1750–1850* (Philadelphia, 1978); the same author has produced a fascinating study of Weld and his cohort which should be compared with my presentation in this chapter and the two chapters on Lane Seminary which follow. See Donald Scott, "Abolition as a Sacred Vocation," in Lewis Perry and Michael Fellman, eds., *Antislavery Reconsidered: New Perspectives on the Abolitionists* (Baton Rouge, 1979).
32. John J. Avery to Weld, Cleveland, December 13, 1893, in Weld-Clements.
33. *The Elucidator* (Utica), March 30, 1830. Clipping in Weld-Clements.
34. Chauncy Bushness to Weld, Norwich, Conn., December 5, 1883, in Weld-Clements; Finney to Gale, Rochester, February 16, 1831, in *Weld-Grimké Letters*, I, 13n.
35. Alvan Stewart to Lewis Tappan, February 11, 1836, in the *Conglomerate*, excerpted in the *Norfolk County Gazette* (Mass.), August 13, 1892.
36. *Ibid.*
37. Charles Stuart to Weld, Apulia, July 8, 1828, in *Weld-Grimké Letters*, I, 22.
38. Elizabeth Weld to Weld, Apulia, July 5 [1828], in *Weld-Grimké Letters*, I, 20.
39. Ludovicus Weld to Weld, January 16, 1830, in *Weld-Grimké Letters*, I, 32.
40. Bertram Wyatt-Brown, *Lewis Tappan and the Evangelical War Against Slavery* (New York, 1971, or. ed. 1969), 98–99.

41. *Ibid.*, 99.
42. Weld to Finney, Oneida, March 2 [1831?], in *Weld-Grimké Letters*, I, 40–41.
43. Charles G. Finney to Weld, Auburn, March 30, 1831, in *Weld-Grimké Letters*, I, 45–46; Beman eventually founded, in 1833, the Troy and Albany School of Theology; see *ibid.*, I, 91.
44. T. Parmele to Weld, New York, May 12, 1831, in *Weld-Grimké Letters*, I, 46–47; G. Winslow to Weld, New Haven, June 30, 1831, *ibid.*, I, 47–48; Lewis Tappan to Weld, New York, October 25, 1831, *ibid.*, I, 50–52; Joel Parker to Weld, New York, November 9, 1831, *ibid.*, I, 54–56.
45. Weld, *First Annual Report of the Society for Promoting Manual Labor in Literary Institutions*, v–viii, 9–10.
46. *Ibid.*, 10.
47. *Ibid.*, 13.
48. *Ibid.*, 36.
49. *Ibid.*, 37.
50. *Ibid.*, 42.
51. *Ibid.*, 41.
52. *Ibid.*
53. *Ibid.*, 60.
54. *Ihid.*
55. *Ibid.*, 64.
56. *Ibid., passim.*
57. Elizabeth and Ludovicus Weld to Weld [Apulia], January 16, 1830, in *Weld-Grimké Letters*, I, 32; see Lois Banner, "Religion and Reform in the Early Republic: The Role of Youth," *American Quarterly* 23 (December, 1971), 677–95, for a similar though more general treatment of Weld and the Lane Rebels.
58. Weld to Henry B. Stanton, Mifflin Township, Ohio, February 15, 1832, in *Weld-Grimké Letters*, I, 60–65.
59. *Ibid.*, 60n, 64n–65n.
60. Lewis Weld to Weld, Hartford, April 12, 1832, in *Weld-Grimké Letters*, I, 73.
61. Elizabeth and Cornelia Weld to Weld, Apulia, April 9 and 12, 1832, in Weld-Clements.
62. *Ibid.*
63. Weld's letter is quoted in Ludovicus Weld to Weld, Fabius, June 17, 1832, *Weld-Grimké Letters*, I, 75, and in a portion of that letter deleted from the *Weld-Grimké Letters* but part of the original manuscript in Weld-Clements.
64. *Ibid.*
65. *Ibid.*, I, 76; the references to revivals and family prayer are

from the unpublished sections of Ludovicus Weld to Weld, Fabius, June 17, 1832, in Weld-Clements.
66. *Ibid., Weld-Grimké Letters,* I, 76–77.

CHAPTER V

1. J. L. Tracy to Weld, Lexington, Ky., to Oneida Institute, November 24, 1831, in *Weld-Grimké Letters,* I, 57.
2. F. Y. Vail to Weld [November, 1831], in *Weld-Grimké Letters,* I, 58–59.
3. Weld to Finney, March 19, 1827, in Finney MSS, Oberlin College Library.
4. Asa Mahan and T. D. Weld to Finney, Cincinnati, March 20, 1832, in Finney MSS, Oberlin College Library.
5. George H. Williams, *Wilderness and Paradise in Christian Thought: The Biblical Experience of the Desert in the History of Christianity and the Paradise Theme in the Theological Idea of the University* (New York, 1962), 18.
6. James Harris Fairchild, *Oberlin: Its Origins, Progress and Results* (Oberlin, Ohio, 1860), 6.
7. Catharine Beecher to former pupils in Hartford, Cincinnati, November 24, 1832, Ohio Historical Society MSS.
8. William Abell to Joseph Abell (1833), in Abell MSS, Cornell University Library.
9. Weld, *First Annual Report of the Society for Promoting Manual Labor,* 10.
10. G. C. Sellew to Jerusha Sellew, June 12, 1835, in Recent Acquisitions, 1969, Stowe-Day Foundation, Hartford, Connecticut.
11. Catharine Beecher to former school pupils in Hartford, Cincinnati, November 24, 1832, in Ohio Historical Society MSS.
12. Lyman Beecher Stowe, *Saints, Sinners, and Beechers* (Indianapolis, 1934); Lyman Beecher letter quoted on p. 55.
13. Beecher's farewell sermon in Boston, *ibid.,* p. 57.
14. Lyman Beecher, *A Plea for the West* (Cincinnati, 1835), 36–37.
15. *Cincinnati Pandect,* September 8, 1829, clipping in Lane Seminary MSS., McCormick Theological Seminary, Chicago.
16. *Ibid.*
17. Sereno W. Streeter to Weld, August 2, 1832, in *Weld-Grimké Letters,* I, 82.
18. *Ibid.*
19. *Ibid.,* I, 72–83.

20. Waterbury, Duncan, and Streeter to Weld, Lane Seminary, December 1832, in *Weld-Grimké Letters*, I, 92, 93.
21. *Ibid.*, I, 94.
22. Calvin Waterbury to Weld, August 2, 1832, in *Weld-Grimké Letters*, I, 82; George Bristol to Weld, Vicksburg, Miss., June 25, 1833, in *Weld-Grimké Letters*, I, 112–13.
23. *Ibid.*, 113.
24. Barbara Cross, ed., *The Autobiography of Lyman Beecher*, 2 vols. (Cambridge, Mass., 1961), II, 241.
25. *Ibid.*
26. Henry Beebe Carrington, *Theodore Dwight Weld and a Famous Quartette—In Memoriam 1903* (Boston, 1904), 3.
27. *Ibid.*
28. J. L. Tracy to Weld, November 24, 1831, in *Weld-Grimké Letters*, I, 56.
29. Calvin Waterbury to Weld, August 2, 1832, in *Weld-Grimké Letters*, I, 82.
30. Theodore Weld to Lewis Weld, Walnut Hills, Ohio, August 13 [1833], in Manuscript Collection of Mount Holyoke College Library.
31. *Ibid.*
32. Biggs to Vail, July 2, 1833, in Lane MSS and as quoted in Paul Alfred Carmack, "Theodore Dwight Weld, Reformer" (Ph.D. diss., Syracuse University, 1948), 223.
33. Barbara Cross, ed., *Autobiography of Lyman Beecher*, II, 232.
34. Heman Humphrey, *Parallel Between Intemperance and the Slave-Trade* (New York, 1889?), *passim.*
35. Weld to James G. Birney, Cincinnati, September 27, 1832, in *Birney Letters*, I, 27.
36. *Ibid.*
37. Professor [Benjamin] Silliman, "Some of the Causes of National Anxiety; An Address delivered in the Centre Church in New Haven, July 4th, 1832," in *The African Repository, and Colonial Journal* 8 (August, 1832), 167.
38. *Ibid.*, 166; the profound effect Nullification created in the North has not yet been adequately charted by historians.
39. Lewis Weld to Rev. Basil Manly, Hartford to [Charleston], October 23, 1834, in Letter Book III, files of American School for the Deaf, Hartford, Connecticut.
40. See William W. Freehling, *Prelude to Civil War: The Nullification Controversy in South Carolina, 1816–1836* (New York, 1966), 53–67, 109–12.

41. See Robert H. Abzug, "The Influence of Garrisonian Abolitionists' Fears of Slave Violence on the Antislavery Argument 1829–1840," *Journal of Negro History* 55 (January, 1970), 15–28.
42. Silliman, "Some of the Causes of National Anxiety," 170–72.
43. *Weld-Grimké Letters*, I, 48n.
44. Charles Stuart to Weld [London], March 26, 1831, in *Weld-Grimké Letters*, I, 44.
45. Charles Stuart to Weld [June, 1831], in *Weld-Grimké Letters*, I, 48–49.
46. Charles Stuart to Weld, Cotham Lodge near Bristol, April 30, 1832, in *Weld-Grimké Letters*, I, 74.
47. Thomas, *Theodore Weld: Crusader for Freedom* (New Brunswick, 1950), 80; Betty Fladeland, *James Gillespie Birney: Slaveholder to Abolitionist* (Ithaca, 1955), 52–53.
48. Weld to James G. Birney, Cincinnati, September 27, 1832, in *Birney Letters*, I, 27.
49. That the meeting of Green, Wright, and Storrs was the pivotal event in Weld's conversion to abolition is indicated by Weld's writing to Wright: "Since I saw you my soul has been in travail upon that subject. I hardly know how to contain myself." He then reports that he already has begun arguing with colonizationists; see Weld to Elizur Wright, January 10, 1833, in *Weld-Grimké Letters*, I, 99. Meanwhile, Arthur Tappan reported to Garrison Weld's conversion in a letter of December 12, 1832 (copy), in Garrison Papers, Boston Public Library.
50. Beriah Green focused on this point in *An Address, Delivered at Whitesborough, N.Y., September 5, 1833* (Utica, 1833), especially 6–7, 6n–7n, though he deals with slavery only tangentially and is more concerned with the generally demoralizing nature of human distinctions.
51. See Robert H. Abzug, "The Influence of Garrisonian Abolitionists' Fears of Slave Violence on the Antislavery Argument 1829–1840," *passim;* Tappan indicated to Garrison in his December letter that Weld "says he is prepared to prove the entire safety to the white population of giving instant freedom to the slaves." Tappan to Garrison, New York, December 12, 1832 (copy), in Garrison Papers, Boston Public Library.
52. Weld to Garrison, January 2, 1833, in *Weld-Grimké Letters*, I, 97–99.
53. *Ibid.*, I, 98.
54. Wright to Weld, Hudson, Ohio, February 1, 1833, in *Weld-Grimké Letters*, I, 104.

55. Weld to Wright, New York, January 10, 1833, *Weld-Grimké Letters*, I, 99.
56. *Ibid.*
57. *Ibid.*, I, 100.
58. Weld to A. A. Phelps, Lane Seminary, September 17, 1833, in Phelps Papers, Boston Public Library.
59. *Ibid.*
60. *Ibid.*
61. *Ibid.*
62. *Ibid.*
63. Cross, ed., *Autobiography of Lyman Beecher*, II, 241–242, Weld quoted.
64. [Henry B. Stanton], *Debate at the Lane Seminary, Cincinnati; Speech of James A. Thome, of Kentucky, Delivered at the Annual Meeting of the American Anti-Slavery Society, May 6, 1834; Letter of the Rev. Dr. Samuel H. Cox, Against the American Colonization Society* (Boston, 1834), 3.
65. Cross, ed., *Autobiography of Lyman Beecher*, II, 243.
66. [Stanton], *Debate at the Lane Seminary*, 3.
67. *Ibid.*, 4.
68. Speech of James A. Thome in [Stanton], *Debate at the Lane Seminary*, 7.
69. *Ibid.*
70. *Ibid.*
71. Recounted in Angelina Grimké to Sarah Douglass, New York, April 3, 1837, in Weld-Clements.
72. Speech of Thome in [Stanton], *Debate at the Lane Seminary*, 8.
73. *Ibid.*, 10.
74. *Ibid.*, 5.
75. *The Preamble and Constitution of the Anti-Slavery Society of Lane Seminary*, in *Cincinnati Journal*, March 28, 1834, as reprinted in the *Boston Recorder* (clipping, n.d.).
76. *Ibid.*
77. *Ibid.*
78. *Ibid.*
79. Weld to Lewis Tappan, Lane Seminary, March 18, 1834, in *Weld-Grimké Letters*, I, 133.
80. *Ibid.*
81. *Ibid.*, I, 133, 133n.
82. *Ibid.*, I, 134–35.
83. Huntington Lyman, "Theodore D. Weld," undated MSS, c. 1895, in Weld-Clements.

84. Weld to Lewis Tappan [Rochester, N.Y., March 9, 1836], in *Weld-Grimké Letters*, I, 273.
85. See, for instance, Birney's "Examination of the Objection of the Abolitionists," originally from the *Huntsville [Alabama] Democrat*, as reprinted in the *African Repository* 9.
86. See Weld to Birney, Lane Seminary, May 28, 1834, in *Birney Letters*, I, 112, 112–14; see also Elizur Wright to Beriah Green, New York to Oneida, June 19, 1834, in Elizur Wright, Jr. Papers, Library of Congress, Washington, D.C.
87. Weld to Birney, Lane Seminary, May 28, 1834, in *Birney Letters*, I, 112.
88. *Ibid.*
89. *Ibid.*, I, 113.
90. Weld to Birney, Lane Seminary, June 19, 1834, in *Birney Letters*, I, 119.
91. *Ibid.*
92. *Ibid.*, I, 120.
93. *Ibid.*, I, 120–21.

CHAPTER VI

1. This was a standard theological reference work.
2. Miscellaneous clipping in Weld-Clements.
3. Accounts of these events can be found in John Thomas, *The Liberator: William Lloyd Garrison* (Boston, 1963), 168–70, 190–93, 200–08; Wyatt-Brown, *Lewis Tappan and the Evangelical War Against Slavery* (New York, 1971, or. ed. 1969), 115–22.
4. The most complete account of the riots is Richard C. Wade, "The Negro in Cincinnati, 1800–1830," *Journal of Negro History* 39 (January, 1954), 43–57. Quotes are from pp. 55 and 50. Of course, as Wade contends and demonstrates, the causes of the riot and reactions were far more complex than I have described.
5. *Fifth Annual Report of the Trustees of the Cincinnati Lane Seminary: Together with the Laws of the Institution, and a Catalogue of the Officers and Students. November, 1834* (Cincinnati, 1834), 36.
6. *Cincinnati Journal*, May 16, 1834.
7. *Ibid.*, December 20, 1833.
8. *Ibid.*, May 16, 1834.
9. [James Hall], "Education and Slavery," *Western Monthly Magazine* [Cincinnati] 17 (May, 1834), 266–73.

10. *Ibid.*, 262–68.
11. *Ibid.*, 267.
12. *Ibid.*
13. *Ibid.*, 269.
14. *Ibid.*, 268.
15. *Ibid.*, 270–71; see Mary Douglas, *Purity and Danger: An Analysis of Concepts of Pollution and Taboo* (Baltimore, 1970), and *Natural Symbols: Explorations in Cosmology*, rev. ed. (New York, 1973), for stimulating discussions of the relation between pollution and the written and unwritten laws of social structure as well as novel assessments of the place of religion in social change.
16. [James Hall], "Education and Slavery," 269, 267, 270.
17. *Ibid.*, 268, 268–69.
18. *Ibid.*, 268; Miscellaneous clipping in Weld-Clements.
19. Theodore D. Weld to James G. Birney, Lane Seminary, May 28, 1834, in *Birney Letters*, I, 114.
20. Theodore D. Weld to James Hall in the *Cincinnati Journal*, May 30, 1834, in *Weld-Grimké Letters*, I, 136–46; only part of Taylor's disclaimer is reprinted in the above.
21. *Ibid.*, I, 139, 140.
22. Weld to William Lloyd Garrison, Hartford, January 2, 1833, in *Weld-Grimké Letters*, I, 98.
23. Theodore D. Weld to James Hall in the *Cincinnati Journal*, May 30, 1834, in *Weld-Grimké Letters*, I, 138.
24. *Ibid.*, I, 138–40.
25. *Ibid.*, I, 140.
26. *Ibid.*, I, 141.
27. *Ibid.*, I, 143.
28. *Ibid.*
29. *Ibid.*, I, 144.
30. *Ibid.*, I, 141.
31. *Ibid.*, I, 145.
32. *Ibid.*
33. *Ibid.*
34. *Ibid.*, I, 146.
35. *Ibid.*
36. *Fifth Annual Report of the Trustees of Cincinnati Lane Seminary*, 35.
37. *Ibid.*
38. *Ibid.*, 36.
39. *Ibid.*
40. *Ibid.*, 37.

41. The best place to begin with Lyman Beecher is Barbara Cross, ed., *The Autobiography of Lyman Beecher*, 2 vols. (Cambridge, Mass., 1961); a lively account of his life and significance is contained in Constance Rourke, *Trumpets of Jubilee: Henry Ward Beecher, Harriet Beecher Stowe, Lyman Beecher, Horace Greeley, P. T. Barnum*, ed. Kenneth Lynn (New York, 1963), 3–66.
42. Lyman Beecher Stowe, *Saints, Sinners, and Beechers* (Indianapolis, 1934), 60.
43. Weld to James G. Birney, Lane Seminary, May 28, 1834, in *Birney Letters*, I, 114; Weld later used this endorsement ironically in the student statement defending their leaving Lane, [Weld], *A Statement of the Reasons Which Induced the Students of Lane Seminary, to Dissolve Their Connection With That Institution* (Cincinnati, 1834), 7, 9.
44. Barbara Cross, ed., *Autobiography of Lyman Beecher*, II, 244.
45. *Cincinnati Journal*, June 13, 1834; a substantial part of Beecher's address was printed in the *African Repository* 10 (November 1834), 279–83.
46. *Cincinnati Journal*, June 13, 1834.
47. *African Repository* 10 (November 1834), 279.
48. *Ibid.*, 280 [misprinted as 272].
49. *Ibid.*
50. *Ibid.*, 281.
51. *Ibid.*
52. *Ibid.*, 282.
53. *Ibid.*, 283.
54. Charles Stuart to Weld, Apulia, New York, August 5, 1834, in *Weld-Grimké Letters*, I, 165.
55. Barbara Cross, ed., *Autobiography of Lyman Beecher*, II, 244–45.
56. Robert S. Fletcher, *A History of Oberlin College from Its Foundation through the Civil War* (Oberlin, Ohio, 1943), I, 154.
57. *Fifth Annual Report of the Trustees of Cincinnati Lane Seminary*, 38–41, quote is on p. 41.
58. Huntington Lyman to James A. Thome, Lane Seminary, August 17, 1834, in the Autograph File, Oberlin College Library.
59. Abraham T. Skillman to James G. Birney, Lexington, Ky., July 12, 1834, in the Birney MSS, Clements Library, University of Michigan.
60. Huntington Lyman to James A. Thome, Lane Seminary, August 17, 1834, in the Autograph File, Oberlin College Library.
61. *Ibid.*
62. *Ibid.*

63. Weld to James G. Birney, Lane Seminary, August 7, 1834, in *Birney Letters*, I, 127.

64. Weld to James G. Birney, Lane Seminary, August 25, 1834, in *Birney Letters*, I, 131.

65. Lewis Tappan to Weld [New York], July 10–11, 1834, in *Weld-Grimké Letters*, I, 155.

66. James G. Birney to Weld, near Danville [Ky.], July 17, 1834, in *Weld-Grimké Letters*, I, 158; James G. Birney to Weld, Near Danville, July 21, 1834, *Weld-Grimké Letters*, I, 161–62.

67. Elizur Wright, Jr. to Weld, New York, August 14, 1834, in *Weld-Grimké Letters*, I, 167.

68. Huntington Lyman to James A. Thome, Lane Seminary, August 17, 1834, in the Autograph File, Oberlin College Library.

69. For example, the letter of "A Ruling Elder" in the *Cincinnati Journal*, June 27, 1834.

70. Thomas Biggs to F. Y. Vail, July 23, 1834, in Vail Correspondence, Lane Seminary MSS, McCormick Theological Seminary, Chicago.

71. Thomas Biggs to Lyman Beecher, August 10, 1834, in Letters and Reports on Right of Students to Leave, Lane Seminary MSS, McCormick Theological Seminary, Chicago.

72. *Ibid.*

73. Executive Committee Minutes and Resolutions, August 20 and 23, 1834, Lane Seminary MSS, McCormick Theological Seminary, Chicago.

74. *Cincinnati Daily Gazette*, August 30, 1834.

75. Lewis Tappan to Weld, New York, September 29, 1834, in Slavery MSS, New York Historical Society.

76. *Ibid.*

77. Henry B. Stanton to James A. Thome, September 11, 1834, as quoted in Fletcher, *History of Oberlin College*, I, 160.

78. Huntington Lyman to James A. Thome, Lane Seminary, October 4, 1834, in Autograph File, Oberlin College Library.

79. Lyman Beecher to Weld, Frederic [Md.], October 8, 1834, in *Weld-Grimké Letters*, I, 172.

80. "Declaration of the Faculty of Lane Seminary," in *Fifth Annual Report of the Trustees of Cincinnati Lane Seminary*, 44–45. The accompanying statement is found on pp. 45–47; quotes on p. 47.

81. John Morgan to Weld, Huntington Lyman, Henry B. Stanton, L. Wells, E. Weed, A. A. Stone, and Andrew Benton, New York, October 30th, 1834, Mt. Holyoke College Library, South Hadley, Mass.

82. [Weld], *Statement of the Reasons*, 3.

83. *Ibid.*, 4–5.
84. *Ibid.*, 5.
85. *Ibid.*, 6–7.
86. *Ibid.*, 16.
87. *Ibid.*, 17.
88. *Ibid.*, 27.

CHAPTER VII

1. James A. Thome in H. Lyman, Sereno W. Streeter, H. B. Stanton, Wm. T. Allan, J. A. Thome, S. Wells, Benjamin Folts, and George Whipple to Weld, Cumminsville, January 8, 1835, in *Weld-Grimké Letters*, I, 190.
2. Weld to Rev. John J. Shipherd, Lane Seminary, June 21, 1834, in *Weld-Grimké Letters*, I, 152.
3. Birney Diary, October 23, 1834, James G. Birney Papers, Library of Congress.
4. Lewis Tappan to George Thompson, New York, January 2, 1835, in Garrison Papers, Boston Public Library.
5. Weld to Birney, West Union, December 11, 1834, in *Birney Letters*, I, 153.
6. *Ibid.*, I, 154.
7. *Ibid.*, I, 155; Weld to Birney, Ross County, January 23, 1835, in *Birney Letters*, I, 170–73.
8. Weld to Elizur Wright, Jr., Putnam, March 2, 1835, in *Weld-Grimké Letters*, I, 205–8; *ibid.*, I, 219n.
9. Emeline Bishop, M. R. Robinson, and Phebe Mathews to Weld, Cincinnati, May [6], 1835, in *Weld-Grimké Letters*, I, 218–21 [they sent the letter to Marietta]; Weld to Elizur Wright, Jr. [Pittsburgh, June 6, 1835], in *Weld-Grimké Letters*, I, 224–25; Weld to Birney, Pittsburgh, June 6, 1835, in *Birney Letters*, I, 194; Weld's greeting in the Western Reserve can be seen in Weld to Elizur Wright, Jr. [Elyria, October 6, 1835], in *Weld-Grimké Letters*, I, 236–40; the call to New York is to be found in Elizur Wright, Jr. to Weld [New York], Nov. 5, 1835, in *Weld-Grimké Letters*, I, 240–41.
10. Weld, quoted in Lewis Tappan to Finney, New York, August 17, 1832, Finney MSS, Oberlin College Library.
11. Weld to Sarah and Angelina Grimké, New York, December 28, 1837, in *Weld-Grimké Letters*, I, 508.
12. The routine varied widely and especially the number of lectures;

this estimate is Weld's own, from Weld to J. F. Robinson [Buffalo, N.Y., May 1(?), 1836], in *Weld-Grimké Letters,* I, 295.

13. Lewis Tappan to Finney, New York, March 22, 1832, in *Weld-Grimké Letters,* I, 68n.
14. Weld to Birney, West Union, December 11, 1834, in *Birney Letters,* I, 154.
15. Weld to E. Wright, Jr., Putnam, Ohio, March 2, 1835, in *Weld-Grimké Letters,* I, 206–7.
16. "Slavery Days—Sketch of Theodore Dwight Weld—Almost the Last of the Abolitionists—As a Boy He Championed the Colored Cause—And earned the Respect of Garrison and Phillips—A Tribute to Weld From the Poet Whittier," *Boston Sunday Globe,* January 6, 1889, 21.
17. Weld to Tappan, Utica, February 22, 1836, in *Weld-Grimké Letters,* I, 263–64.
18. Weld to Birney, Ross County, January 23, 1835, in *Birney Letters,* I, 172.
19. *Ibid.*
20. Weld to Birncy, Circleville, February 16, 1835, in *Birney Letters,* I, 181.
21. Weld to Tappan, Utica, February 22, 1836, in *Weld-Grimké Letters,* I, 265.
27. Weld, in Theodore D. Weld and H. C. Howells to Birney, Putnam, Ohio, August 4, 1835, in *Birney Letters,* I, 228.
23. *Ibid.*
24. Weld to Birney, West Union, December 11, 1834, in *Birney Letters,* I, 155.
25. See, for instance, "The Great Postal Campaign," in Wyatt-Brown, *Lewis Tappan and the Evangelical War Against Slavery* (New York, 1971, or. ed. 1969), 149–66.
26. Weld to Birney, West Union, December 11, 1834, in *Birney Letters,* I, 155.
27. American Antislavery Society. Commission to Theodore D. Weld: Particular Instructions, in *Weld-Grimké Letters,* I, 127.
28. The abolitionists shared this general sense with more conservative advocates of militant Christianity; the difference lay in the fact that antislavery advocates and others who proposed socially radical measures tended to place increasingly less importance on the essential role of the visible, earthly church.
29. Weld to Birney, Lane Seminary, June 17, 1834, in *Birney Letters,* I, 116.

30. Birney to Gerrit Smith, Danville, Kentucky, November 14, 1834, in *Birney Letters*, I, 150.
31. Weld to Elizur Wright, Jr. [Pittsburgh, June 6, 1835], in *Weld-Grimké Letters*, I, 224.
32. Sereno Wright to Joseph Gales [Treasurer of ACS], Granville, Licking County, March 23, 1836, in American Colonization Society Papers, Library of Congress.
33. See John Sessions to R. R. Gurley, Norwich, Chenango Co., N.Y., February 25, 1835; M. D. Mathew to Joseph Gales, Hillsborough, Ohio, March 3, 1835; [Milt Bierce?], Wells Clark, and David Beardsley to R. R. Gurley, Nelson, Portage Co., Ohio, January 8, 1836; George Sheldon to R. R. Gurley, Canton, Ohio, August 2, 1836; all in American Colonization Society Papers, Library of Congress.
34. John Sessions to R. R. Gurley, Norwich, Chenango Co., N.Y., February 25, 1835, in American Colonization Society Papers, Library of Congress.
35. Weld to Sarah and Angelina Grimké, New York, October 10, 1837, in *Weld-Grimké Letters*, I, 455.
36. The religious construction was probably more common among northern colonizationists in comparison to their southern counterparts.
37. The abolitionist intolerance of race prejudice was, of course, in many cases not absolute. See below.
38. This fear might not indicate proslavery feelings or even sympathy with extralegal means of dealing with antislavery advocates. It was, in fact, the disorder caused by abolitionist opponents that conservative critics feared most. Take, for instance, Phillip Hone's diary entry for November 17, 1837: "The terrible Abolition question is fated, I fear, to destroy the union of the States and to endanger the peace and happiness of our western world." See Allan Nevins, ed., *The Diary of Phillip Hone, 1828–1851*, 2 vols. (New York, 1927), I, 284.
39. For a fuller treatment of this theme, see Robert H. Abzug, "The Influence of Garrisonian Abolitionists' Fears of Slave Violence on the Antislavery Argument, 1829–1840," *Journal of Negro History*, 55 (January, 1970), 15–28. I no longer see a split between Garrisonians and western abolitionists and am now convinced that Weld and those around him were as much concerned with the issue as any of the other abolitionists mentioned. See below, the text.
40. Mrs. Sturges to Theodore Dwight Weld, Putnam, Ohio, March 19, 1835, in Weld-Clements.

41. *Ibid.*, as for all further references to the letter.
42. The quote is from James A. Thome to Weld, Augusta, Ky., April 17, 1838, in *Weld-Grimké Letters*, II, 642.
43. Sarah Carpenter to Weld, Ravenna, Ohio, October 22, 1835, in Weld-Clements.
44. *Ibid.*
45. One of the most interesting and recent examples of this point of view, with a twist, is Ronald Walters, "The Erotic South: Civilization and Sexuality in American Abolitionism," *American Quarterly* 25 (May, 1973), 177–201.
46. Theodore D. Weld to Birney, Lane Seminary, October 6, 1834, in *Birney Letters*, I, 138–40.
47. *Ibid.*, I, 139.
48. Weld to J. F. Robinson [Buffalo, May 1(?), 1836], in *Weld-Grimké Letters*, I, 296.
49. *Ibid.*
50. *Ibid.*
51. *Ibid.*, I, 297.
52. *Anti-Slavery Record* 1 (October, 1835), 110–13.
53. *Ibid.*, 110.
54. *Ibid.*
55. *Ibid.*, 111.
56. *Ibid.*, 112. So inspiring was this address to the young Joseph F. Tuttle, later President of Wabash College, Indiana, that he took notes and later worked them into a recreation of Weld's address for a historio-patriotic reader. See Henry Beebe Carrington, ed., *Beacon Lights of Patriotism; or, Historic Incentives to Virtue and Good Citizenship, In Prose and Verse, with Notes, Dedicated to American Youth* (Boston, 1895), 251–53.
57. *Anti-Slavery Record* 1 (October 1835), 112.
58. *Ibid.*
59. See Russel B. Nye, *Fettered Freedom: Civil Liberties and the Slavery Controversy, 1830–1860* (East Lansing, 1949).
60. Weld to Birney, Jefferson, Ashtabula County, Ohio, Sept. 26, 1835, in *Birney Letters*, I, 248.
61. Weld to Elizur Wright, Jr. [Elyria, Ohio, October 6, 1835], in *Weld-Grimké Letters*, I, 236–39; quote from Reminiscences of Huntington Lyman [Weld MSS], reproduced in *Weld-Grimké Letters*, I, 238n–39n.
62. *Ibid.*, I, 239.
63. Calvin Colton, *Abolition a Sedition. By a Northern man* (Philadelphia, 1839).
64. *Ohio Watchman* (Ravenna, Ohio), September 26, 1835.

65. *Ibid.*, August 29, 1835.
66. *Ibid.*
67. *Elyria Republican,* quoted in *Ohio Watchman,* October 31, 1835.
68. *Ibid.*
69. *Ibid.*
70. American Antislavery Society, "Commission to Theodore D. Weld: Particular Instructions," in *Weld-Grimké Letters,* I, 125.
71. Weld to Birney, Lane Seminary, July 8, 1834, in *Birney Letters,* I, 124.
72. See Abzug, "The Influence of Garrisonian Abolitionists' Fears of Slave Violence on the Antislavery Argument, 1829–1840," 24–26.
73. American Antislavery Society, "Commission to Theodore D. Weld: Particular Instructions," in *Weld-Grimké Letters,* I, 126.
74. *Ibid.*
75. Thome in J. A. Thome and J. W. Alvord to Weld, Middlebury, Ohio, February 9, 1836, in *Weld-Grimké Letters,* I, 257.
76. Mrs. [Lydia Maria] Child, *The Oasis* (Boston, 1834), xii.
77. *Ibid.*, ix.
78. See William H. Pease and Jane H. Pease, "Antislavery Ambivalence: Immediatism, Expediency, Race," *American Quarterly* 17 (1965), 682–95; Leon F. Litwack, *North of Slavery: The Negro in the Free States, 1790–1860* (Chicago, 1961), 216–30.
79. Charles Stuart to Weld, Whitesborough, N.Y., November 5, 1835, in *Weld-Grimké Letters,* I, 240.
80. Mathews in Phebe Mathews, Emeline Bishop, Susan Lowe, and Lucy Wright to Weld [Cincinnati, March, 1835], in *Weld-Grimké Letters,* I, 217.
81. See, for instance, Weld to Lewis Tappan [Rochester, March 9, 1836], in *Weld-Grimké Letters,* I, 273.
82. *Ibid.*, I, 270.
83. *Ibid.*, I, 271.
84. *Ibid.*
85. *Ibid.*, I, 271–72.
86. *Ibid.*, I, 273.
87. *Ibid.*
88. *Ibid.*, I, 274.
89. See above, note 78.
90. Weld to Lewis Tappan, Utica, February 22, 1836, in *Weld-Grimké Letters,* I, 263.
91. *Ibid.*
92. *Ibid.*
93. *Ibid.*, I, 128–29.

94. *Ibid.*, I, 265.
95. Though, as James Brewer Stewart has pointed out, some very basic philosophical factions were beginning to form below the surface. See Stewart, "Peaceful Hopes and Violent Experiences, the Evolution of Radical and Reforming Abolitionism, 1831–1837," *Civil War History* 17 (December, 1971), 293–309.
96. The schism may best be followed in Aileen S. Kraditor, *Means and Ends in American Abolitionism: Garrison and His Critics on Strategy and Tactics, 1834–1850* (New York, 1969).
97. Elizur Wright, Jr. to Weld, New York, May 26, 1835, in *Weld-Grimké Letters*, I, 221.
98. *Ibid.*
99. For details see Wyatt-Brown, *Lewis Tappan*, 167–71.
100. Weld to Lewis Tappan, Pittsburgh, December 22, 1835, in *Weld-Grimké Letters*, I, 247.
101. Weld to Lewis Tappan [Rochester, April 5, 1836], in *Weld-Grimké Letters*, I, 287.
102. Weld to Lewis Tappan, May 2, 1836, near Schenectady on Erie Canal Packet Boat, MSS in New York Historical Society.
103. *Ibid.*
104. *Ibid.*
105. Elizur Wright, Jr. to Weld, New York, April 21, 1836, in *Weld-Grimké Letters*, I, 291.
106. *Ibid.*, I, 291–92.
107. Weld to Lewis Tappan [Rochester, April 5, 1836], in *Weld-Grimké Letters*, I, 286.
108. Weld to Anne Warren Weston, Rochester, March 26, 1836, in Weston Papers, Boston Public Library.
109. *Ibid.*
110. Weld to A. A. Phelps, Troy, June, 1836, in Phelps Papers, Boston Public Library.
111. Henry B. Stanton to A. A. Phelps, Rochester, March 5, 1836, in Phelps Papers, Boston Public Library; Stanton to Phelps, York, Livingston Co., New York, April 13, 1836, in Phelps Papers, Boston Public Library.
112. Weld to Lewis Tappan [Rochester, April 5, 1836], in *Weld-Grimké Letters*, I, 286.
113. Weld to Phelps, Troy, June 1836, in Phelps Papers, Boston Public Library.
114. *Ibid.*
115. Elizur Wright, Jr. and Simeon S. Jocelyn to Weld, New York, May 19, 1836, in *Weld-Grimké Letters*, I, 304–5.
116. Rhode Island Anti-Slavery Society to Weld, Providence, May

29, 1836, in *Weld-Grimké Letters*, I, 306–7; quote is on p. 307.

117. Weld to Phelps, Troy, June 1836, in Phelps Papers, Boston Public Library; Weld to the Rev. Ray Potter, Troy, June 11, 1836, in *Weld-Grimké Letters*, I, 309.

118. *Ibid.*, I, 309–10.

119. Deborah Weston to Anne Warren Weston, June 10, 1836, in Weston Papers, Boston Public Library.

120. Weld to the Rev. Ray Potter, Troy, June 11, 1836, in *Weld-Grimké Letters*, I, 310; see William Lloyd Garrison to Samuel J. May, Providence, June 19, 1836, Garrison Papers, Boston Public Library, for on-the-scenes impressions of George Benson.

121. William Lloyd Garrison to William M. Chace, Brooklyn, Conn., June 11, 1836, in Garrison Papers, Boston Public Library.

122. *Ibid.*

CHAPTER VIII

1. Wright to Birney, September 15, 1836, in *Birney Letters*, I, 357.

2. Num. 11:16–17; Luke 9:1–2, 10:1–4; 10:12, 17; John Lytle Myers, "The Agency System of the Antislavery Movement" (Ph.D. diss., University of Michigan, 1961), 403–5.

3. Anne W. Weston to Deborah Weston, Groton, September 17, 1836, in Weston Papers, Boston Public Library.

4. Elizabeth Whittier Picard, September 2, 1836, attached to Samuel Thomas Picard to Weld, Portland, Me., March 1, 1894, in Weld Papers, Clements Library.

5. Anne W. Weston to Deborah Weston, Groton, September 17, 1836, in Weston Papers, Boston Public Library.

6. Myers, "Agency System," 361–62, 397–400.

7. Wright to Weld, September 22, 1836, in *Weld-Grimké Letters*, I, 338.

8. Wright to Weld, November 4, 1836, in *Weld-Grimké Letters*, I, 346–48.

9. Those who see Garrison as the supreme egotist will have to cope with such judgments on his part.

10. Garrison to Henry E. Benson, December 3, 1836, in Wendell Phillips Garrison and Francis Jackson Garrison, *William Lloyd Garrison, 1805–1879: The Story of His Life Told by His Children*, 4 vols. (New York, 1885), II, 116.

11. Sarah Grimké to Mary S. Grimké, Manlius, July 15, 1839, in Weld-Clements; Angelina Grimké to Jane Smith, as quoted in

Katharine DuPre Lumpkin, *The Emancipation of Angelina Grimké* (Chapel Hill, 1974), 96–97.
12. See Benjamin P. Thomas, *Theodore Weld: Crusader for Freedom* (New Brunswick, N.J., 1950), 117.
13. Lumpkin, *Emancipation of Angelina Grimké*, 161–62.
14. See, for instance, Weld to Lewis Tappan, Pittsburgh, December 22, 1835, in *Weld-Grimké Letters*, I, 249; Lewis Tappan to Weld, March 10, 1836, in *Weld-Grimké Letters*, I, 275; Weld to Lewis Tappan, October 10, 1836, in *Weld-Grimké Letters*, I, 344.
15. Weld to A. A. Phelps, Troy, June, 1836, in Phelps Papers, Boston Public Library.
16. Ludovicus Weld to Weld, July 18, 1836, in Weld-Clements.
17. Anne Warren Weston to Deborah Weston, September 17, 1836, in Weston Papers, Boston Public Library.
18. Weld to Elizur Wright, Jr., Putnam, Ohio, March 2, 1835, in *Weld-Grimké Letters*, I, 206–7.
19. Weld to James G. Birney, Jefferson, Ohio, September 26, 1835, in *Birney Letters*, I, 246.
20. Weld to Elizur Wright, Jr., June 6, 1835, in *Weld-Grimké Letters*, I, 225.
21. Lewis Tappan Diary, July 15, 1836, in Tappan MSS, Library of Congress, Washington, D.C.
22. Weld to Lewis Tappan, Oberlin, November 17, 1835, in *Weld-Grimké Letters*, I, 242–44.
23. *Ibid.*, I, 243.
24. *Ibid.*, I, 244.
25. Weld to Tappan, Oneida, May 2, 1836, in New York Historical Society MSS; see also Bertram Wyatt-Brown, *Lewis Tappan and the Evangelical War Against Slavery* (Cleveland, Ohio, 1969), viii, for a summary judgment of Tappan's personality.
26. Tappan, quoted in Weld to Tappan, May 2, 1836, in New York Historical Society MSS.
27. *Ibid.*
28. Charles G. Finney to Weld, Oberlin, July 21, 1836, in *Weld-Grimké Letters*, I, 318.
29. *Ibid.*, I, 318–19.
30. Sereno W. Streeter to Weld, Oberlin, July 20, 1836, in *Weld-Grimké Letters*, I, 317.
31. William T. Allan, Sereno W. Streeter, J. W. Alvord, and James A. Thome to Weld, Oberlin, August 9, 1836, in *Weld-Grimké Letters*, I, 324.

32. *Ibid.*, I, 323–27.
33. *Ibid.*, I, 327–29.
34. The most complete story of Charles's relation to Noyes is told, albeit from Noyes's point of view, in George W. Noyes, *The Religious Experience of John Humphrey Noyes* (New York, 1923), 126–135, 222–24, 292–98.
35. The term is used by Orson Fowler, the Phrenologist.
36. The best published introductions to Graham are Richard H. Shryock, "Sylvester Graham and the Popular Health Movement, 1830–1870," *Mississippi Valley Historical Review* 18 (September, 1931), 172–83; and Graham's own *Lectures on the Science of Human Life*, 2 vols. (Boston, 1839).
37. Graham to Gerrit Smith, March 4, 1840, as quoted in Ralph V. Harlow, *Gerrit Smith: Philanthropist and Reformer* (New York, 1939), 95.
38. Weld to Sarah and Angelina Grimké [New York], December 15 [1837], in *Weld-Grimké Letters*, I, 492.
39. The basic text of American Phrenology was Orson Squires Fowler, *Practical Phrenology: Giving a Concise Elementary View of Phrenology; presenting some new and important remarks upon the temperaments and describing the primary mental powers in Seven Different Degrees of Development . . .* , 10th ed., enlarged and improved (New York, 1842), available in many editions.
40. Angelina Grimké to Jane Smith, February 4, 1837, in Weld-Clements.
41. *Ibid.*
42. Fowler, *Practical Phrenology*, 5.
43. For general studies of the theory and practice of Phrenology, see John D. Davies, *Phrenology: Fad and Science, a 19th Century Crusade* (New Haven, 1955); and Madeleine B. Stern, *Heads and Headlines: The Phrenological Fowlers* (Norman, Okla., 1971).
44. O[rson] S. Fowler, *The Christian Phrenologist: or the Natural Theology and Moral Bearings of PHRENOLOGY; Its Aspect on, and Harmony with REVELATION* (Cazenovia, N.Y., 1843), 3–4, 10–11.
45. *Ibid.*, 11–15.
46. Weld to Sarah and Angelina Grimké, December 15 [1837], in *Weld-Grimké Letters*, I, 496.
47. Weld to Finney, Cincinnati, February 28, 1832, in *Weld-Grimké Letters*, I, 66–67.

48. Weld to Sarah and Angelina Grimké, New York, December 28, 1837, in *Weld-Grimké Letters*, I, 508–9.
49. Weld to Sarah and Angelina Grimké, December 15 [1837], in *Weld-Grimké Letters*, I, 496.
50. See William L. Garrison to Helen Garrison, New York, March 2, 1837, in Garrison Papers, Boston Public Library.
51. Weld to Anne Warren Weston, New York, May 1, 1837, in Weston Papers, Boston Public Library.
52. Elizur Wright to Weld, July 16, 1835, in *Weld-Grimké Letters*, I, 228; it appeared originally as "Is Slavery from Above or Beneath," *Quarterly Antislavery Magazine*, April 1837; and finally as *The Bible Against Slavery. An Inquiry into the Patriarchal and Mosaic Systems on the Subject of Human Rights*, 4th ed. enlarged (New York, 1838).
53. Weld, *The Bible Against Slavery*, 8.
54. William C. Wisner, *The Biblical Argument on Slavery, Being Principally a Review of T. D. Weld's "Bible Against Slavery"* (New York, 1844), passim. See also Caroline L. Shanks, "The Biblical Anti-Slavery Argument of the Decade 1830–40," *Journal of Negro History* 16 (April, 1931), 132–57, for a general discussion.
55. Wisner, *The Biblical Argument on Slavery*, 27–40.
56. Weld, *The Bible Against Slavery*, 6.
57. *Ibid.*
58. *Ibid.*, 7.
59. For the most insightful and wide-ranging as well as thorough discussion of the schism, see Aileen S. Kraditor, *Means and Ends in American Abolitionism: Garrison and His Critics on Strategy and Tactics, 1834–1850* (New York: 1969).

CHAPTER IX

1. Weld to Angelina Grimké, March 1, 1838, in Weld-Clements. Deleted from reprint of same letter in *Weld-Grimké Letters*, II, 575–85.
2. Weld to Angelina Grimké, March 1, 1838, in *Weld-Grimké Letters*, II, 579.
3. Weld to Angelina Grimké, March 1, 1838, in Weld-Clements. Deleted from reprint of same letter in *Weld-Grimké Letters*, II, 575–85.
4. Cornelia Weld's message to Weld, in Cornelia, Elizabeth, and

Ludovicus Weld to Weld, September 28, 1822, in Weld-Clements. "Windham alias Brooklyn" refers to Connecticut county and town names.

5. Charles Stuart to Weld, May 19, 1828, in *Weld-Grimké Letters*, I, 19; Charles Stuart to Weld, August 5, 1834, in *Ibid.*, I, 164–65.
6. John Morgan to Weld, January 13, 1835, in *Weld-Grimké Letters*, I, 199.
7. Weld to Angelina Grimké, March 1, 1838, in Weld-Clements. This part deleted from printed version. Weld to Angelina Grimké, March 4, 1838, in Weld-Clements.
8. Weld to Angelina Grimké, March 1, 1838, in Weld-Clements. This part deleted in printed version.
9. Cornelia, Elizabeth, Ludovicus, and Charles Weld to Weld, July 14, 1836, in Weld-Clements.
10. Weld to Angelina Grimké, March 1, 1838, in Weld-Clements. This part deleted in printed version.
11. Weld to Angelina Grimké, February 8, 1838, in *Weld-Grimké Letters*, II, 533-34.
12. Quotation from Catherine H. Birney, *The Grimké Sisters: Sarah and Angelina Grimké, The First American Women Advocates of Abolition and Woman's Rights* (Westport, Conn., 1969, or. ed. 1885), 39. I have depended on the interpretation of Katharine DuPre Lumpkin, *The Emancipation of Angelina Grimké* (Chapel Hill, 1974) for my general approach to Angelina's early years; see also Birney, *The Grimké Sisters;* and Gerda Lerner, *The Grimké Sisters of South Carolina: Rebels Against Slavery* (Boston, 1967).
13. Lumpkin, *Emancipation of Angelina Grimké*, 3–26.
14. *Ibid.*, 27–94.
15. Angelina Grimké to Weld, Brookline, February 11, 1838, in *Weld-Grimké Letters*, II, 536; Weld to Angelina Grimké, February 8, 1838, *Weld-Grimké Letters*, II, 534; Angelina Grimké to Jane Smith, November 18, 1836, as quoted in Lumpkin, *Emancipation of Angelina Grimké,* 97; Angelina Grimké to Jane Smith, November 19, 1836, as quoted in Lumpkin, 98.
16. Angelina Grimké to Jane Smith, December 17, 1836, in Weld-Clements.
17. *Ibid.*
18. Angelina Grimké to Jane Smith, quoted in Lumpkin, *Emancipation of Angelina Grimké*, 101.
19. Angelina Grimké to Weld, Groton, August 12 [1837], in *Weld-Grimké Letters*, I, 417.

20. Angelina Grimké to Weld, March 4, 1838, in *Weld-Grimké Letters,* II, 588.
21. Angelina Grimké to Weld, March 4, 1838, in *Weld-Grimké Letters,* II, 586.
22. Sarah and Angelina Grimké to Weld, New York, May 18, 1837, in *Weld-Grimké Letters,* I, 388.
23. *Ibid.*
24. Weld to Lewis Tappan, Hartford, June 8, 1837, in *Weld-Grimké Letters,* I, 397–400.
25. Weld to James G. Birney, Hartford, June 8, 1837, in *Birney Letters,* I, 386–87.
26. See Benjamin P. Thomas, *Theodore Weld: Crusader for Freedom* (New Brunswick, N.J., 1950), 129–31.
27. Angelina Grimké to Weld [Brookline], March 4 [1838], in *Weld-Grimké Letters,* II, 586.
28. Lumpkin, *Emancipation of Angelina Grimké,* 108–115.
29. See, for instance, even the relatively open-minded Samuel J. May's admission of conflict in *Some Recollections of Our Antislavery Conflict* (Boston, 1869), 233–34.
30. In addition to Aileen S. Kraditor, *Means and Ends in American Abolitionism: Garrison and His Critics on Strategy and Tactics, 1834–1850* (New York, 1969), see James Brewer Stewart, "Peaceful Hopes and Violent Experiences: The Evolution of Reforming and Radical Abolitionism, 1831–1837," *Civil War History* 17 (December, 1971), 293–309, for a sensitive appraisal of broader themes in the split.
31. Sarah Grimké to Weld, June 11, 1837, in *Weld-Grimké Letters,* I, 402.
32. George W. Noyes, *The Religious Experiences of John Humphrey Noyes* (New York, 1923), 126–35, 222–24, 292–98.
33. Sarah Grimké to Weld, June 11, 1837, in *Weld-Grimké Letters,* I, 402.
34. Weld to Angelina and Sarah Grimké, New York, July 22, 1837, in *Weld-Grimké Letters,* I, 412.
35. *Ibid.*
36. *Ibid.,* I, 413; the work in question was Catharine E. Beecher, *An Essay on Slavery and Abolition with Reference to the Duty of American Females* (Philadelphia, 1837); for more on Angelina's response, see Lumpkin, *Emancipation of Angelina Grimké,* 115–17.
37. Weld to Angelina and Sarah Grimké, New York, July 22, 1837, in *Weld-Grimké Letters,* I, 414.
38. Sarah and Angelina Grimké to Henry C. Wright, Groton, August

12, 1837, in *Weld-Grimké Letters,* I, 420; Amos Anson Phelps to Mrs. Charlotte Phelps, Boston, July 14, 1837, Phelps Papers, Boston Public Library.

39. Sarah and Angelina Grimké to A. A. Phelps, August 3, 1837; Angelina Grimké to Phelps, August 17, 1837; and Angelina Grimké to Phelps, September 2, 1837, all in Phelps Papers, Boston Public Library.

40. John Greenleaf Whittier to Sarah and Angelina Grimké, New York, August 14, 1837, in *Weld-Grimké Letters,* I, 423–24.

41. Weld to Sarah and Angelina Grimké, New York, August 15, 1837, in *Weld-Grimké Letters,* I, 425–26.

42. Angelina Grimké to A. A. Phelps, August 17, 1837, from Brookline, Phelps Papers, Boston Public Library.

43. Angelina Grimké to Weld and Whittier, Brookline, August 20 [1837], in *Weld-Grimké Letters,* I, 428.

44. *Ibid.,* I, 428–29.

45. *Ibid.,* I, 431.

46. *Ibid.,* I, 432.

47. Angelina Grimké to Weld, Groton, August 12 [1837], in *Weld-Grimké Letters,* I, 414–19; date of arrival of this letter mentioned in Weld to Sarah and Angelina Grimké, September 6, 1837, New York Historical Society MSS.

48. Weld to Sarah and Angelina Grimké, October 1, 1837, in *Weld-Grimké Letters,* I, 443.

49. Angelina Grimké to Weld [Brookline], August 27, 1837, in *Weld-Grimké Letters,* I, 441–42.

50. Weld to Sarah and Angelina Grimké, October 1, 1837, in *Weld-Grimké Letters,* I, 442–45 (letter misdated by editors).

51. Weld to Sarah and Angelina Grimké, September 6, 1837, in New York Historical Society Collections.

52. *Ibid.*

53. Weld to Sarah and Angelina Grimké [date given by editors as August 26, but obviously wrong from internal evidence; date on envelope September 6], in *Weld-Grimké Letters,* I, 432–36.

54. Sarah and Angelina Grimké to Weld, Fitchburg, September 20, 1837, in *Weld-Grimké Letters,* I, 446–50.

55. *Ibid.,* I, 450–52.

56. This letter is not extant, but the excerpts quoted and others are to be found in Weld to Sarah and Angelina Grimké, October 10, 1837, *Weld-Grimké Letters,* I, 452–59; and Weld to Angelina Grimké, New York, October 16, 1837, *Weld-Grimké Letters,* I, 459–67; quotes are on 465–66.

57. Weld to Sarah and Angelina Grimké, New York, October 10, 1837, *Weld-Grimké Letters*, I, 452–53.
58. *Ibid.*, I, 453.
59. *Ibid.*, I, 454–55.
60. *Ibid.*, I, 455.
61. *Ibid.*, I, 458–59.
62. Weld to Angelina Grimké, New York, October 16, 1837, in *Weld-Grimké Letters*, I, 459–64.
63. *Ibid.*, I, 464.
64. *Ibid.*, I, 466–67.
65. Weld to Sarah and Angelina Grimké, New York, November 6, 1837, in *Weld-Grimké Letters*, I, 475.
66. Sarah Grimké to Jane Smith, Boston, November 8, 1837, in *Weld-Grimké Letters*, I, 475–78; Weld to Sarah and Angelina Grimké, New York, November 21, 1837, *Weld-Grimké Letters*, I, 478–80; Sarah and Angelina Grimké to Weld, Brookline, November 30, 1837, *Weld-Grimké Letters*, I, 484–88; Weld to Sarah and Angelina Grimké, December 15 [1837], *Weld-Grimké Letters*, I, 490–96.
67. Weld to Sarah and Angelina Grimké, New York, December 28, 1837, in *Weld-Grimké Letters*, I, 504–10.
68. *Ibid.*, I, 507–9.
69. *Ibid.*, II, 514–15.
70. Angelina Grimké to Weld [January 7, 1838], in Weld-Clements.
71. Angelina Grimké to Weld, January 21, 1838, in *Weld-Grimké Letters*, II, 520–25.
72. Weld to Sarah Grimké, New York, February 8, 1838, in *Weld-Grimké Letters*, II, 531–32.
73. Weld to Angelina Grimké, New York, February 8, 1838, in *Weld-Grimké Letters*, II, 532–33.
74. *Ibid.*, II, 533.
75. *Ibid.*
76. *Ibid.*, II, 533–36.
77. Angelina Grimké to Weld, Brookline, February 11 [1838], in *Weld-Grimké Letters*, II, 536.
78. *Ibid.*, II, 536–38.
79. Weld to Angelina and Sarah Grimké, New York, February 16, 1838, *Weld-Grimké Letters*, II, 554–55.
80. *Ibid.*, II, 557–58; see Lumpkin, *Emancipation*, 163–64.
81. Weld to Angelina Grimké, New York, February 18, 1838, in *Weld-Grimké Letters*, II, 559–62.
82. *Ibid.*, II, 562–63.

83. Angelina Grimké to Weld [Boston, February 21, 1838], in *Weld-Grimké Letters*, II, 564–67.
84. Angelina Grimké to Weld, February 22 [1838], in *Weld-Grimké Letters*, II, 567–70.
85. Angelina and Sarah Grimké to Jane Smith, Brookline, February 22, 1838, in Weld-Clements.
86. Weld to Sarah Grimké, New York, February 24, 1838, in Weld-Clements; Angelina Grimké to Weld, February 26 and March 2, 1838, in Weld-Clements.
87. Angelina and Sarah Grimké to Weld, February 27, 1838, in Weld-Clements.
88. *Ibid.*
89. Weld to Angelina Grimké, March 1, 1838, in *Weld-Grimké Letters*, II, 575–80.
90. *Ibid.*, but deleted from printed version and only found in Weld-Clements.
91. *Ibid.*, *Weld-Grimké Letters*, II, 580–81.
92. *Ibid.*, II, 581–84.
93. Angelina Grimké to Weld, March 4, 1838, in Weld-Clements.
94. *Ibid.*
95. Weld to Angelina Grimké, March 7, 1838, in Weld-Clements.
96. *Ibid.*
97. *Ibid.*
98. Angelina Grimké to Weld, March 8, 1838, in Weld-Clements; for more on Angelina's first love, see Lumpkin, *Emancipation of Angelina Grimké*, 54–62, 66–70.
99. Weld to Angelina Grimké, March 12, 1838, in *Weld-Grimké Letters*, II, 593.
100. *Ibid.*, II, 594–96.
101. *Ibid.*, II, 596.
102. *Ibid.*, II, 596–98.
103. *Ibid.*, II, 599–601.
104. Angelina Grimké to Weld, March 15, 1838, in Weld-Clements.
105. Angelina Grimké to Weld, March 28, 1838, in *Weld-Grimké Letters*, II, 607; Weld to Angelina Grimké, March 31, 1838, in Weld-Clements.
106. Angelina Grimké to Weld, March 28, 1838, in *Weld-Grimké Letters*, II, 609; Angelina Grimké to Jane Smith, March 27, 1838, in Weld-Clements; Weld to Angelina Grimké, March 31, 1838, in Weld-Clements.
107. Mary Grimké quoted in Angelina Grimké to Weld, April 13, 1838, in Weld-Clements.

108. Angelina Grimké to Weld, April 11, 1838, in Weld-Clements.
109. Weld to Angelina Grimké [New York, March 12, 1838], in *Weld-Grimké Letters*, II, 603.
110. Weld to Angelina Grimké, March 20, 1838, in Weld-Clements.
111. Lewis Weld to Angelina Grimké, Hartford, March 28, 1838, in Weld-Clements.
112. Weld to Angelina Grimké, April 10, 1838; Ludovicus Weld to Angelina Grimké, April 3, 1838; and Elizabeth Weld to Angelina Grimké, April 3, 1838, all in Weld-Clements.
113. Charles Stuart to Weld, March 8, 1838, in *Weld-Grimké Letters*, II, 589–90.
114. Angelina Grimké to Weld, April 1, 1838, in Weld-Clements.
115. Ladd's remarks reported in A. W. Weston to Deborah Weston, Boston, March 7, 1838, in Weston Papers, Boston Public Library.
116. Tappan's comment discussed in Angelina Grimké to Weld [April 29, 1838], in *Weld-Grimké Letters*, II, 647.
117. Susan Taber to Debra Weston, New Bedford, Mass., May 23, 1838, in Weston Papers, Boston Public Library.
118. William Lloyd Garrison to George Thompson, May 7, 1838, in Garrison Papers, Boston Public Library; Garrison to Helen Benson Garrison, Philadelphia, May 12, 1838, in Garrison Papers, Boston Public Library.
119. Weld to Angelina Grimké, May 2, 1838, in *Weld-Grimké Letters*, II, 657; Weld to Angelina Grimké, May 9, 1838, in *Ibid.*, 673.
120. "Slavery Days—Sketch of Theodore Dwight Weld—Almost Last of the Abolitionists—As a boy he championed the colored cause— and earned the respect of Garrison and Phillips—A Tribute to Weld from the Poet Whittier," *Boston Sunday Globe*, January 6, 1889, 21.
121. *Ibid.;* Sarah Grimké to Elizabeth Pease, May 20, 1838, in *Weld-Grimké Letters*, II, 678–79.
122. *Ibid.*, II, 679.
123. James A. Thome to Weld, May 15, 1838, in *Weld-Grimké Letters*, II, 681.

CHAPTER X

1. Henry Blackwell to Lucy Stone [c. 1852], in Alice Stone Blackwell, *Lucy Stone: Pioneer of Woman's Rights* (Norwood, Mass., 1930), 126–29.
2. *Ibid.*

3. *Ibid.*
4. Weld to Angelina Grimké, New York, April 15, 1838, in *Weld-Grimké Letters*, II, 634–35.
5. *Ibid.*, II, 636.
6. *Ibid.*, II, 636–37.
7. *Ibid.*, II, 637–38.
8. *Ibid.*, II, 638–39.
9. *Ibid.*, II, 639.
10. Weld to Angelina Grimké, April 3, 1838, in Weld-Clements.
11. Weld to Angelina Grimké, New York, April 18, 1838, in *Weld-Grimké Letters*, II, 629.
12. *Ibid.*, II, 629–30.
13. *Ibid.*, II, 630.
14. Catherine H. Birney, *The Grimké Sisters: Sarah and Angelina Grimké, the First American Women Advocates of Abolition and Woman's Rights* (Boston and New York, 1885), 247–48.
15. *Ibid.*, 245–46; William Andrus Alcott, *The Young Housekeeper; or Thoughts on Food and Cookery*, 4th ed. (Boston, 1839). Some of this research on Alcott was originally done with David P. Handlin.
16. Alcott, *The Young Housekeeper*, passim and p. 23.
17. Birney, *The Grimké Sisters*, 245–46.
18. Angelina G. Weld to Anne Warren Weston, Fort Lee, July 15, 1838, in Weston Papers, Boston Public Library.
19. *Ibid.*
20. *Ibid.*; Angelina G. Weld to Jane Smith, Fort Lee, July 7, 1838, in Weld-Clements.
21. Angelina G. Weld to Anne Warren Weston, Fort Lee, July 15, 1838, in Weston Papers, Boston Public Library; Birney, *The Grimké Sisters*, 245–46.
22. Angelina Weld to Sarah Grimké, Fort Lee [September 3, 1838], in *Weld Grimké Letters*, II, 698.
23. *Ibid.*
24. *Ibid.*, II, 699.
25. *Ibid.*
26. *Ibid.*, II, 700.
27. Theodore Weld to Angelina Weld, New York [early June, 1839], in Weld-Clements.
28. Theodore Weld to Angelina Weld, New York, June 6 [1839], in Weld-Clements.
29. American Anti-Slavery Society, "Minutes of the Executive Committee," manuscript in Boston Public Library, Vol. 1, 149, May 2, 1939.

30. *Ibid.*, 156, May 14, 1839; 187, September 3, 1839.
31. Birney, *The Grimké Sisters*, 252; Angelina G. Weld to Anne Warren Weston, Fort Lee, July 15, 1838, in Weston Papers, Boston Public Library.
32. Theodore Dwight Weld, *American Slavery As It Is: Testimony of a Thousand Witnesses* (or. ed. 1839; reprint New York, 1969, ed. William Loren Katz); see Birney, *The Grimké Sisters*, 258–59, for the help of the sisters in compiling the book.
33. Weld, *American Slavery*, 53.
34. *Ibid.*, 54–55.
35. See, for instance, William Lloyd Garrison to Elizabeth Pease, November 6, 1837, in Wendell Phillips Garrison and Francis Jackson Garrison, *William Lloyd Garrison, 1805–1879: The Story of His Life by His Children*, 4 vols. II, 183–84; James Brewer Stewart, "Peaceful Hopes and Violent Experiences: The Evolution of Reforming and Radical Abolitionism, 1831–1837," *Civil War History* 17 (December, 1971), 293–309.
36. Weld, *American Slavery*, 7.
37. *Ibid.*, 7–8.
38. *Ibid.*, 9.
39. See introductory essay in Richard O. Curry and Joanna Dunlap Cowden, eds., *Slavery in America: Theodore Weld's American Slavery As It Is* (Itasca, Ill., 1972), xi–xxv.
40. *Weld-Grimké Letters*, II, 671n.
41. J. A. Thome to Weld, May 18, 1839, *Weld-Grimké Letters*, II, 765.
42. Sereno and Mary Streeter to Weld [Madison, Ohio, December 26, 1838], *Weld-Grimké Letters*, II, 732.
43. Birney, *The Grimké Sisters*, 243.
44. Anna Rutlege Grimké Frost to Angelina Weld and Sarah Grimké, Philadelphia, August 14, 1839, in Weld-Clements.
45. Angelina Weld to Anna R. Frost, Fort Lee, August 18, 18[39], in *Weld-Grimké Letters*, II, 789.
46. Lydia Maria Child to Angelina G. Weld, Northampton, October 2, 1838, *Weld-Grimké Letters*, II, 702.
47. Deborah Weston to Anne Warren Weston, New Bedford, April 1, 1839, in Weston Papers, Boston Public Library.
48. Lucia Weston to Anne Warren Weston, Boston, April 1839, in Weston Papers, Boston Public Library.
49. Deborah Weston to Ann Warren Weston, New Bedford, May 3, 1839, in Weston Papers, Boston Public Library.
50. Abby Kelley to Anne Warren Weston, East Hampton, May 28, 1839, in Weston Papers, Boston Public Library.

51. *Ibid.*
52. See John L. Thomas, *The Liberator: William Lloyd Garrison* (Boston, 1963), 264–77.
53. See Bertram Wyatt-Brown, *Lewis Tappan and the Evangelical War Against Slavery* (Cleveland, Ohio, 1969), 185–200.
54. Weld to Gerrit Smith, New York, September 16, 1839, in *Weld-Grimké Letters*, II, 796.
55. *Ibid.*
56. Weld to Gerrit Smith, Fort Lee, October 23, 1839, in *Weld-Grimké Letters*, II, 810.
57. Weld to A. A. Phelps, Fort Lee, July 23, 1839, in Phelps Papers, Boston Public Library.

CHAPTER XI

1. Catherine H. Birney, *The Grimké Sisters: Sarah and Angelina Grimké, The First American Women Advocates of Abolition and Woman's Rights* (Westport, Conn., 1969, or. ed. 1885), 260; Sarah Grimké to Jane Smith, Fort Lee, December 14, 1839, in Weld-Clements.
2. Angelina Weld to Jane Smith, Fort Lee, January 20, 1840, in Weld-Clements.
3. Andrew Combe, *The Physiology of Digestion considered with relation to the Principles of Dietetics*, 4th Amer. ed. (Boston, 1837), 213.
4. Gerda Lerner, *The Grimké Sisters of South Carolina: Rebels Against Slavery* (Boston, 1967), 279; Birney, *The Grimké Sisters*, 260–61.
5. Weld to Angelina Grimké, April 13, 1838, in Weld-Clements.
6. Angelina and Sarah Grimké to Jane Smith, Belleville, March 14, 1840, in Weld-Clements.
7. *Ibid.*
8. Sarah Grimké and Angelina and Theodore Weld to Gerrit and Anne Smith, Belleville, June 18, 1840, in *Weld-Grimké Letters*, II, 842.
9. Angelina and Sarah to Jane Smith, Belleville, August 8, 1840, in Weld-Clements.
10. Weld to Lewis Tappan, Belleville, September 15, 1840, in *Weld-Grimké Letters*, II, 850–51; Weld to Lewis Tappan, Belleville, October 3, 1840, in Weld-Clements.
11. *Ibid.*

12. Angelina Weld and Sarah Grimké to Jane Smith, August 8, 1840, in Weld-Clements; Angelina Weld to Jane Smith, September 8, 1840, in Weld-Clements; Sarah Grimké and Theodore D. Weld to Elizabeth Pease, December 20, 1840, in Garrison Papers, Boston Public Library.

13. Angelina Weld and Sarah Grimké to Jane Smith, Belleville, December 6, 1840, in Weld-Clements.

14. Ibid.

15. Angelina Weld to Jane Smith, Belleville, February 7, 1841, in Weld-Clements.

16. Joseph Sturge, A Visit to the United States in 1841 (London, 1842), 107–8.

17. Birney Diary, entry for March 14, 1840, in James G. Birney Papers, Library of Congress.

18. Lewis Tappan to Gerrit Smith, April 27, 1841, in Smith-Miller Collection, Syracuse University; see also James Sloan Gibbons to Maria Weston Chapman, New York, July 13, 1842, in Weston Papers, Boston Public Library.

19. Sarah Grimké to Theodore Weld, February 13, 1842, in Weld-Clements.

20. Weld to Angelina Weld [and Sarah Grimké] [February, 1842, though editors say January 15(?)], in Weld-Grimké Letters, II, 894.

21. Weld to William Lloyd Garrison II, March 14, 1875, in Garrison Papers, Boston Public Library.

22. See, for instance, Weld to Angelina Weld, Washington, January 18, 1842, in Weld-Grimké Letters, II, 897, for indirect evidence.

23. Weld to Gerrit Smith, June 30 [1841], in Weld-Grimké Letters, II, 866.

24. Ibid., II, 865–66.

25. Sarah Grimké to Weld, February 13, 1842, in Weld-Clements.

26. Beriah Green to Weld, Whitesboro, July 11, 1841, in Weld-Grimké Letters, II, 868–69; Weld to Lewis Tappan, Belleville, July 31, 1841, Weld-Grimké Letters, II, 870–71.

27. Weld to Lewis Tappan, Belleville, December 14, 1841, in Weld-Grimké Letters, II, 879–82.

28. Ibid., II, 882.

29. Weld to Angelina G. Weld, Washington, January 1, 1842, in Weld-Grimké Letters, II, 883–84; Weld to Angelina Weld, January 30, 184[2], Weld-Grimké Letters, II, 906.

30. Weld to Angelina Weld [February, 1842, though identified as January 15(?)], in Weld-Grimké Letters, II, 892.

31. "Slavery Days—Sketch of Theodore Dwight Weld . . . ," *Boston Sunday Globe,* January 6, 1889, p. 21.
32. Weld to Angelina Weld and Sarah Grimké, Washington, January 9, 1842, in *Weld-Grimké Letters,* II, 890.
33. *Ibid.,* II, 890n.
34. Weld to Angelina Weld, January 18, 1842, *Weld-Grimké Letters,* II, 897; Weld to Angelina Weld, January 30, 184[2], *Weld-Grimké Letters,* II, 906.
35. Weld to Angelina Weld [February, 1842, though identified as January 15 (?)], in *Weld-Grimké Letters,* II, 892.
36. Angelina Weld to Weld, Belleville, January 30, 1843, in Weld-Clements.
37. For more on Miller, see Whitney R. Cross, *The Burned-Over District: The Social and Intellectual History of Enthusiastic Religion in Western New York, 1800–1850* (New York, 1965, or. ed. 1950), 287–321; E. Douglas Branch, *The Sentimental Years 1836–1850* (New York, 1965, or. ed. 1934), 337–44.
38. See, for instance, Angelina Weld to Weld, January 3, 1842, in Weld-Clements; Weld to Angelina Weld and Sarah Grimké, Washington, January 9, 1842, in *Weld-Grimké Letters,* II, 888–89.
39. Angelina Weld to Weld, Belleville, January 3, 1842, in Weld-Clements.
40. Weld to Angelina Weld and Sarah Grimké, Washington, January 9, 1842, in *Weld-Grimké Letters,* II, 888–89.
41. Angelina Weld to Weld, January 23, 1842, in Weld-Clements.
42. Angelina Weld to Weld, Belleville, c. January 25, 1842 [though listed as c. Feb. 1], in Weld-Clements.
43. Weld to Angelina Weld, Washington, February 20, 1842, in *Weld-Grimké Letters,* II, 927.
44. Angelina Weld to Weld, Belleville, January 9, 1842, in Weld-Clements.
45. *Ibid.*
46. Weld to Angelina Weld [Washington, Feb., 1842, though identified as January 15(?)], in *Weld-Grimké Letters,* II, 892.
47. Weld to Angelina Weld and Sarah Grimké, Washington, January [23], 1842, in *Weld-Grimké Letters,* II, 898.
48. Weld to Angelina Weld [Washington, February, 1842, though identified as January 15(?)], in *Weld-Grimké Letters,* II, 892.
49. Angelina Weld to Weld, Belleville, January 9, 1842, in Weld-Clements.
50. Weld to Angelina Weld, January 30, 184[2], in *Weld-Grimké Letters,* II, 904.

51. Weld to Angelina Weld, Washington, February 20, 1842, in *Weld-Grimké Letters*, II, 926.
52. Weld to Angelina Weld, February 27, 1842, *Weld-Grimké Letters*, II, 935.
53. And, indeed, were old Puritan traits.
54. Weld to Angelina Weld, Washington, February 20, 1842, in *Weld-Grimké Letters*, II, 927.
55. Weld to James G. Birney, Washington, January 22, 1842, in *Birney Letters*, II, 663.
56. Weld to Angelina Weld and Sarah Grimké, Washington, February 17, 1842, in *Weld-Grimké Letters*, II, 923.
57. *Ibid.*, II, 923–24.
58. Weld and Sarah Grimké to Gerrit and Anne Smith, Belleville, April 11, 1842, in *Weld-Grimké Letters*, II, 941.
59. Weld to Birney, Belleville, May 23, 1842, in *Birney Letters*, II, 693–94.
60. *Ibid.*, II, 693; Weld to Lewis Tappan, Washington, February 3, 1843, in *Weld-Grimké Letters*, II, 974.
61. Weld to Angelina Weld, Washington, January 1, 1843, in *Weld-Grimké Letters*, II, 952; for an example of the cloud-kisses, see Weld to Angelina Weld, January 19, 1843, in Weld-Clements.
62. Weld to Angelina Weld, January 19, 1843, in Weld-Clements.
63. Angelina and Sarah Grimké to Weld, Belleville, February 2, 1843, in Weld-Clements.
64. *Ibid.*
65. Weld to Angelina Weld, Washington, January 9, 1843, in *Weld-Grimké Letters*, II, 959.
66. Weld to Angelina Weld, January 16, 1843, in Weld-Clements.
67. Angelina Weld to Weld [January, 1843, though identified as February, 1842], in Weld-Clements.
68. Sarah Grmiké to Jane Smith, Belleville, January 15, 1843, in Weld-Clements; Sarah to Weld, January 22, 1843, in Weld-Clements; Weld to Angelina Weld, Washington, January 22, 1843, in Weld-Clements.
69. Weld to Angelina Weld and Sarah Grimké, Washington, January 12, 1843, in *Weld-Grimké Letters*, II, 961–62; Weld complained of their incomplete reports in Weld to Angelina, Washington, January 22, 1843, in Weld-Clements.
70. *Ibid.*
71. Angelina Weld to Weld, Belleville, January 26, 1843, in Weld-Clements; Weld to Angelina Weld, January 29, 1843, in Weld-Clements.

72. Angelina Weld to Weld, Belleville, January 30, 1843, in Weld-Clements.
73. Angelina Weld and Sarah Grimké to Weld, Belleville, February 2, 1843, in Weld-Clements.
74. Angelina Weld to Weld, Belleville, February, 1843, in Weld-Clements.
75. Weld to Angelina Weld, February 1, 1843, in *Weld-Grimké Letters,* II, 971.
76. Joshua Leavitt to Angelina Weld, Washington, February 7, 1843, in *Weld-Grimké Letters,* II, 975.
77. Joshua R. Giddings to Weld, Washington, February 21, 1843, in *Weld-Grimké Letters,* II, 975–77.
78. Weld to Angelina Weld and Sarah Grimké, Washington, February 17, 1842, in *Weld-Grimké Letters,* II, 924; Weld to Angelina Weld, Washington, February 24, 1842, in *Weld-Grimké Letters,* II, 933.
79. Weld to James G. Birney, Belleville, May 23, 1842, in *Birney Letters,* II, 693.
80. Charles Stuart to Weld [Bath, England, January 31, 1843], in *Weld-Grimké Letters,* II, 968.
81. Angelina Weld to Jane Smith, March 15, 1843, in Weld-Clements; see also Angelina Weld to Sarah Grimké, January, 1845, in Theodore Weld and Mrs. Angelina Grimké Weld MSS., Library of Congress.
82. Angelina Weld to Jane Smith, March 15, 1843, in Weld-Clements.
83. See above, Chapter 4.
84. Quote from 1843 and found in Paul Alfred Carmack, "Theodore Dwight Weld, Reformer" (Ph.D. diss., Syracuse University, 1948), 443–44.
85. Weld to Prof. George Whipple, Belleville, December [17], 1843, in *Weld-Grimké Letters,* II, 985–88.
86. *Ibid.,* II, 985, and passim.
87. Weld to Lewis Tappan, Belleville, February 6, 1844, in *Weld-Grimké Letters,* II, 994.
88. Lewis Tappan to Weld, New York, February 1, 1844, in *Weld-Grimké Letters,* II, 992.
89. Weld to Lewis Tappan, Belleville, February 6, 1844, in *Weld-Grimké Letters,* II, 994.
90. Weld to Lewis Tappan, Belleville [December 29, 1843], in *Weld-Grimké Letters,* II, 989.
91. See, for instance, his side-by-side condemnation of the evan-

gelical churches and report that the antislavery "leaven" was working in New Jersey, in Weld to Lewis Tappan, Belleville, February 6, 1844, in *Weld-Grimké Letters*, II, 994–95.

92. Theodore Dwight Weld, "Truth's Hindrances," manuscript copy in Theodore Weld and Mrs. Angelina Grimké Weld MSS, Library of Congress.

93. *Ibid.*

94. *Ibid.*

95. *Ibid.*

96. Quote from "New England Reformers" in Mark Van Doren, ed., *The Portable Emerson* (New York, 1974), 131.

97. Weld to Lewis Tappan, Belleville, May 2, 1844, in *Weld-Grimké Letters*, II, 1004–5.

98. Anne Smith to Gerrit Smith, April 24, 1844, in Smith-Miller Collection, Syracuse University. I thank Art Makechnie for bringing this letter to my attention.

CHAPTER XII

1. Quoted in Bertram Wyatt-Brown, *Lewis Tappan and the Evangelical War Against Slavery* (Cleveland, Ohio, 1969), 249.

2. The significance and reality of these conditions has been discussed by Angelina's biographers; see Gerda Lerner, *The Grimké Sisters of South Carolina: Rebels Against Slavery* (Boston, 1967), 288–92; and Katharine DuPre Lumpkin, *The Emancipation of Angelina Grimké* (Chapel Hill, 1974), 193–94.

3. It might be added that such guilt led another nineteenth-century reformer, John Humphrey Noyes, to conceive of methods of birth control and "complex marriage" that allowed for safe and varied sexual experiences, and that became the hallmarks of the "free love" Oneida Community.

4. Charles Stuart to Weld, Toronto, November 2, 1845, in Weld-Clements; Weld to Lewis Tappan, Belleville, December 3, 1845, in Weld-Clements.

5. Stuart to Weld, Toronto, April 11, 1846, in Weld-Clements; Tappan to Weld, New York, March 18, 1846, in Tappan Letterbooks, 1846–1847, Lewis Tappan MSS, Library of Congress.

6. Stuart to Weld, Toronto, April 11, 1846, in Weld-Clements; Weld to Birney, Belleville, December 16, 1848, in *Birney Letters*, II, 1121; Weld to Birney, July 18, 1851, in Weld-Clements.

7. See Cross, *The Burned-Over District: The Social and Intellectual History of Enthusiastic Religion in Western New York*,

1800–1850 (New York, 1965, or. ed. 1950), 196, 343–44; for direct evidence of Swedenborgian interest in the Weld household, see Sarah Grimké to Jane Smith, Belleville, June 5 [1847 or 1849?], in Weld-Clements; some sense of the American understanding of Swedenborg can be gleaned from B. F. Barrett, *Life of Emanuel Swedenborg, with some account of his writings* (New York, 1841).

8. There is no modern biography of Andrew Jackson Davis. One must piece together an understanding of the man, and in that endeavor the following have been helpful: Robert W. Delp, "Andrew Jackson Davis: Prophet of American Spiritualism," *Journal of American History* 54 (June 1967), 43–56; "Andrew Jackson Davis," *Dictionary of American Biography*, III, Part 1, 105; Andrew Jackson Davis, *The Magic Staff; an Autobiography* (New York, 1857); "A Doctor of Hermetic Science," ed., *The Harmonial Philosophy; A Compendium and Digest of the Works of Andrew Jackson Davis, The Seer of Poughkeepsie . . .* (London, 1917). The famous Swedenborgian critique of Davis is George Bush and B. F. Barrett, *"Davis's Revelations" Revealed; being a Critical Examination of the Character and Claims of that Work in Its Relations to the Teachings of Swedenborg* (New York, 1847).

9. *Principles of Nature, Her Divine Revelations, and a Voice to Mankind. A Treatise in three parts. By and Through Andrew Jackson Davis, the Poughkeepsie Seer and Clairvoyant* (New York, 1847).

10. Joel Shew, *The Hydropathic Family Physician; A Ready Prescriber and Hygienic Adviser with Reference to the Nature, Causes, Prevention, and Treatment of Diseases, Accidents, and Casualties of Every Kind* (New York, 1854), 724–25; R. T. Trall, *The Hydropathic Encyclopedia: A System of Hydropathy and Hygiene in Eight Parts, Designed as a Guide to Families and Students, and a Text-Book for Physicians* (New York, 1854), II, 293–96. Both Shew and Trall attest to the extreme discomfort of the condition of *prolapsus uteri*. Shew notes: "This may be said to be one of the fashionable diseases of the day; that is, a great many persons suppose they have it when no such trouble actually exists" (p. 724). Thus another interpretation of Angelina's condition might describe it as a hysterical symptom. No strong evidence exists one way or the other. We do know, however, that she used a self-devised supporter, a practice condemned by both Shew and Trall, but at least indicative that she may have had a genuine prolapsed uterus.

11. Quotation from an advertisement for Orange Mountain in *Water-Cure and Herald of Reforms* 6 (November, 1848), 158; for a complete description of this particular establishment, see *Orange Mountain Water Cure; with Illustrations* (New York, 1851), a pamphlet advertising its wonders; see also Harry B. Weiss and Howard R. Kemble, *The Great American Water-Cure Craze: A History of Hydropathy in the United States* (Trenton, 1967), 139–41, and passim; on Angelina's use of the bowling alleys, see Angelina to Weld [South Orange, Sept., 1849], in Weld-Clements.

12. Andrew Jackson Davis, *The Magic Staff*, 428; Angelina to Sarah Grimké, Weld, and Thody [September, 1849, though dated by Weld, years later, as August 17], in Weld-Clements.

13. *Ibid.*; chart in Davis, *The Magic Staff*, 372–81.

14. Angelina to Sarah Grimké, Weld, and Thody [September, 1849, though dated by Weld, years later, as August 17], in Weld-Clements.

15. The Spiritualist trivialization of judgment caused the most anguish among evangelicals. The implication to Charles Stuart, for one, was that this "sin-refining school" made God, "at last and for ever, as really the friend, of the tyrant, the oppressor, the hypocrite, the liar, and libertine, the murderer, as of the innocent, virtuous and helpless sufferer." Stuart to Weld, Lora, Canada West, January 14, 1860, in Weld-Clements.

16. Quotations from Davis's attempt to define the true reformer, in Andrew Jackson Davis, *The Great Harmonia; being a Philosophical Revelation of the Natural, Spiritual, and Celestial Universe,* Vol. II: *The Teacher* (Boston, 1851), 103.

17. Angelina to Theodore [1849], in Weld-Clements. This letter must have been written in September 1849, since it is from the water-cure.

18. *Ibid.*

19. Weld to Birney, Belleville, July 18, 1851, in Birney-Clements.

20. Sarah Grimké to Harriot Hunt, Belleville, August 22, 1848, in Weld-Clements; Henry Stanton to Weld, September 22, 1848, in Weld-Clements; for names of students, see Theodore Dwight Weld account books, New York Public Library.

21. Weld to Samuel Allinson, Jr., Belleville, January 7, 1848, in Haverford College Library, Haverford, Pa.; Angelina to the Gerrit Smiths, May 1 [1852], in Gerrit Smith Collection, George Arents Research Library, Syracuse University, Syracuse, N.Y.; Sarah Grimké to Elizabeth Smith Miller, Brookline and Belleville, Sept. 18–27, 1852, in Weld-Clements.

22. Weld to Gerrit Smith, added to Angelina to Smith, Belleville, January 6, 1854, in Smith Collection, Syracuse; see also Weld to Smith, March 4, 1852, and Weld to Smith, December 1, 1852, in Smith Collection, Syracuse.
23. For Alcott, see Robert H. Abzug and David P. Handlin, "William Andrus Alcott and the Search for a Natural Order" (unpublished paper); Horace Bushnell, *Views of Christian Nurture, and of Subjects Adjacent Thereto* (Hartford, 1847).
24. Two broad treatments of order and disorder in this period are to be found in John Higham, *From Boundlessness to Consolidation: The Transformation of American Culture 1848–1860* (Ann Arbor, 1969), and Rowland Berthoff, *An Unsettled People: Social Order and Disorder in American History* (New York, 1971).
25. Weld to Angelina, Belleville, June 5, 1846, in Weld-Clements.
26. Theodore Dwight Weld account books, New York Public Library; Sallie Holley to Caroline F. Putnam, Worcester, December 19, 1852, quoted in John White Chadwick, *A Life for Liberty; Anti-Slavery and other Letters of Sallie Holley* (New York, 1899), 107–8.
27. Ellie Wright to Hether Wood, Belleville, April 26, 1854, in the Garrison Family Papers, Sophia Smith Collection, Smith College Library.
28. *Ibid.*
29. Ellie Wright to Hettie Wood, Belleville, May 5, 1854, in the Garrison Family Papers, Sophia Smith Collection, Smith College Library.

CHAPTER XIII

1. See Maud Honeyman Greene, "Raritan Bay Union, Eagleswood, New Jersey," *Proceedings of the New Jersey Historical Society* 68 (January, 1950), 1–20, for the best introduction to the Union.
2. *Ibid.*, 6.
3. Angelina to Harriot [Hunt?], April 10 [1854?], in Theodore Weld and Mrs. Angelina Grimké Weld MSS, Library of Congress.
4. Sarah Grimké to Harriot Hunt, Raritan Bay, December 20, 1854, in Weld-Clements.
5. Greene, "Raritan Bay Union," 18; Benjamin P. Thomas, *Theodore Weld: Crusader for Freedom* (New Brunswick, N.J., 1950), 228–29.

6. *Ibid.*, 228.
7. Weld exchanged letters with Adin Ballou of the Hopedale Colony on the subject of communal experiments. See Adin Ballou to Weld, December 23, 1856, in Weld-Clements.
8. Thomas, *Theodore Weld,* 229–30.
9. "Eagleswood School, Perth Amboy, New-Jersey," circular for school in Garrison Family Papers, Sophia Smith Collection, Smith College Library.
10. *Ibid.*
11. *Ibid.*
12. *Ibid.*
13. Greene, "Raritan Bay Union," 11; for Peabody's work with Alcott, see Odell Shepard, *Pedlar's Progress: The Life of Bronson Alcott* (Boston, 1947), 164–90.
14. See Weld to Birney, March 8, 1854; Weld to Birney, May 11, 1853; and Weld to Birney, May 26, 1854, all in Birney-Clements.
15. Stuart to Weld, July 20, 1856; Stuart to Weld, June 30, 1854, both in Weld-Clements.
16. Charles Stuart to Birney, Lora, March 6, 1855, in *Birney Letters,* II, 1170.
17. Martha Coffin Wright to David Wright, Philadelphia, October 26, 1854, in Garrison Family Papers, Sophia Smith Collection, Smith College Library.
18. Except, perhaps, for exceptional researchers and theorists.
19. Weld, "Shakespeare," unpublished manuscript in Weld-Clements; see also unidentified newspaper clipping describing Weld's lectures on Shakespeare at the Unitarian Parish Hall, Hyde Park, Mass., in scrapbook in Henry A. Rich Collection, Hyde Park Branch, Boston Public Library (courtesy Hyde Park Historical Society).
20. Weld, "Shakespeare."
21. Programs in the Garrison Family Papers, Sophia Smith Collection, Smith College Library.
22. O.S.N., miscellaneous clipping of letter to the editor of the *Evening Post,* in Gerrit Smith Collection, Syracuse.
23. Gerda Lerner, *The Grimké Sisters from South Carolina: Rebels Against Slavery* (Boston, 1967), 330; Thomas, *Theodore Weld,* 231–34.
24. Thomas, *Theodore Weld,* 234; Thoreau to Sophia Thoreau, November 1, 1856, in F. B. Sanborn, ed., *Letters of Henry David Thoreau* (Boston, 1894), 335–39.
25. For instance, there is Ellie Wright's observation of Angelina,

"What I care for most is to keep out of Mrs. Welds way; keep her out of mine, for she is an awful bore. . . . Mrs. Weld is out in the entry firing away at 'Lena,' one of the girls chambermaid, I believe, because she didn't happen to do her work according to her 'ideas' . . . ," in Ellie Wright to Martha Coffin Wright, April 11, 1855, in Garrison Family Papers, Sophia Smith Collection, Smith College Library.

26. See Lerner, *Grimké Sisters*, 13–182; Katharine DuPre Lumpkin, *The Emancipation of Angelina Grimké* (Chapel Hill, 1974), 3–77.

27. Lerner, *Grimké Sisters*, 318–19; Lumpkin, *Emancipation of Angelina Grimké*, 185–203; quote from Angelina to Sarah [c. 1853], in Lumpkin, 202.

28. Lerner, *Grimké Sisters*, 319–20.

29. *Ibid.*, 335–36; Lumpkin, *Emancipation of Angelina Grimké*, 206–7.

30. Maria Weston Chapman to "Dear Folks," Weymouth, December 30, n.d. [c. 1857], in Weston Papers, Boston Public Library.

31. Sarah Grimké to Sarah Wattles, Eagleswood, February 13, 1856, in Weld-Clements. Though this letter comes after Sarah's crisis, it certainly indicates a conflict she had faced for years.

32. Quoted in Lerner, *Grimké Sisters*, 323.

33. *Ibid.*, 320.

34. For Sarah's description of a seance, see Sarah Grimké to Harriot Hunt, Belleville, December 16 [1850–1?]; on her research journey see Lerner, *Grimké Sisters*, 320–21; see also Gerda Lerner, ed., "Sarah M. Grimké's 'Sisters of Charity.'" *Signs: Journal of Women in Culture and Society* 1 (Autumn, 1975), 246–56, for extracts from Sarah's unpublished manuscripts of this period; from Washington, Sarah described an incident of her journey that gives one some idea of her frustrations: "Yesterday [I] visited the Capitol went into the Supreme Court, not in session, was invited to sit in the Chief Justice's seat. As I took the place I involuntarily exclaimed Who knows but this chair may one day be occupied by a woman. The brethren laughed heartily, nevertheless it may be a true prophecy." Sarah Grimké to Sarah Wattles, Washington, December 23 [1853].

35. Lerner, *Grimké Sisters*, 325.

36. *Speeches of Gerrit Smith in Congress* (New York, 1856), 113.

37. Weld to Gerrit Smith, May 1, 1852, in Weld-Clements; Weld to Gerrit Smith, June 10 [1854].

38. Diary of Ellie Wright, Book Six, Loose Entry for July 3 [1857],

should be in Diary Book Eight, in Garrison Family Papers, Sophia Smith Collection, Smith College Library.
39. Sarah Grimké to Augustus and Sarah Wattles, March 23, 1857, in Weld-Clements.
40. Sarah Grimké to Augustus Wattles, June 10, 1854, in Weld-Clements.
41. Thomas, *Theodore Weld*, 237; quote from Annie [McKim?] to Ellen Wright, Eagleswood, November 16 [1859], in Garrison Family Papers, Sophia Smith Collection, Smith College Library.
42. Thomas, *Theodore Weld*, 237–38.
43. Charles Stuart to Weld, August, 1859, in Weld-Clements.
44. Charles Stuart to Weld, Lora, Canada West, January 14, 1860, in Weld-Clements.

CHAPTER XIV

1. Charles Stuart to Weld, Lora, Canada West, January 14, 1860, in Weld-Clements.
2. Weld to [Martha] Wright, Perth Amboy, June 2, 1862, in Garrison Family Papers, Sophia Smith Collection, Smith College Library.
3. Weld to Martha Coffin Wright, March 23, 1862, copied in Mrs. Wright's hand, Garrison Family Papers, Sophia Smith Collection, Smith College Library.
4. Benjamin P. Thomas, *Theodore Weld: Crusader for Freedom* (New Brunswick, N.J., 1950), 239–40; quote from Sarah Grimké to Elizabeth Smith Miller, June 19, 1861, in Weld-Clements.
5. Weld to William Lloyd Garrison, Perth Amboy, October 8, 1862; Weld to Garrison, Perth Amboy, October 30, 1862, both in Garrison Papers, Boston Public Library.
6. Weld to William Lloyd Garrison, October 8, 1862, in Garrison Papers, Boston Public Library.
7. Thomas, *Theodore Weld*, 244.
8. Angelina to Gerrit Smith, November 10, 1862, in Gerrit Smith Papers, Syracuse University.
9. Thomas, *Theodore Weld*, 244–48.
10. *Ibid.*, 248–49; Weld to James M. McKim, February 14, 1863, in McKim Collection, Cornell University Library; Garrison to Weld, Boston, April 6, 1963, in Theodore Weld and Mrs. Angelina Grimké Weld MSS, Library of Congress; William Lloyd Garrison to [Oliver] Johnson, Boston, May 5, 1863, in Garrison Papers, Boston Public Library.

11. Weld, Angelina, and Sarah to William Lloyd Garrison, December 1, 1863, in Garrison Papers, Boston Public Library. Marked *Public*.
12. Sarah Grimké to William Lloyd Garrison, West Newton, November 30, 1863, Garrison Papers, Boston Public Library. Letter meant for Anniversary Meeting.
13. Angelina to Gerrit Smith, November 10, 1862, in Gerrit Smith Papers, Syracuse University.
14. Angelina to Thody, December 1860, in Weld-Clements.
15. Sarah Grimké to Catherine Brooks Yale, Perth Amboy, March 15, 1862, in Weld-Clements; dream described in letter fragment from [February, 1863], with sections of letters from Theodore and Sarah to "Dearest Friends," in Weld-Clements.
16. On a surviving letter of one pupil, Weld later inscribed: "A little florid but most interesting. O, the enthusiasm of youth! The dear boy gave his life in the next battle." N. Hallock Mann to Weld, December 31, 1863, in Weld-Clements.
17. Theodore Weld, "The Cost of Reform," unpublished manuscript, in Weld-Clements.
18. I have discussed this address and its implications in depth in "Theodore Weld's 'Cost of Reform'—A Pietist Views Means and Ends in American Abolitionism," a paper presented May 26, 1976, at the University of California, Berkeley, Department of History Colloquium.
19. Thomas, *Theodore Weld*, 251–52.
20. Sarah Weld to Weld, n.d., in Weld-Clements; Thomas, *Theodore Weld*, 252.
21. Charles Stuart Faucheraud Weld to Weld, June 2, 1862, in Weld-Clements. Stuart was no pacifist. In fact, he later became a champion of Maximillian in Mexico. See Stuart Weld to Gerrit Smith, Hyde Park, February 24, 1868, in Smith Collection, Syracuse University.
22. Stuart Weld to Weld, Cambridge, September 25, 1862, in Weld-Clements.
23. See Katharine DuPre Lumpkin, *The Emancipation of Angelina Grimké* (Chapel Hill, 1974), 197–99; quotes are from these pages.
24. See Gerda Lerner, *The Grimké Sisters from South Carolina: Rebels Against Slavery* (Boston, 1967), 345–49, for the most complete narrative of Thody's demise and the various therapies tried. Lerner chooses to see his illness as a mystery, though she concedes that it might be "of a psychosomatic nature" (p. 345). Lumpkin, who sees so clearly the warped nature of at least Sa-

rah's relationship to Thody, makes no connection between the psychodynamics of the family and his illness. See Lumpkin, *Emancipation,* 215; Thomas buries the problem by calling Thody, incorrectly, "almost an invalid from birth"; Thomas, *Theodore Weld,* 240. Quotation from Sarah in Sarah Grimké to Theodore Grimké Weld, Eagleswood, May 21, 1860, in Weld-Clements.

25. Details in Lerner, *Grimké Sisters,* 345–49.
26. *Ibid.* On the important point of whether Thody utilized Mrs. Coleman's services, Lerner rules out the possibility that he did. She states: "Considering Sarah's primness and the nature of Mrs. Coleman's treatment, the image of Sarah considering this letter staggers the imagination" (pp. 347–48). And: ". . . there is no evidence of any further correspondence with Mrs. Coleman" (p. 348). Almost two years after the correspondence with Coleman, Sarah mentions in a letter to a friend that Thody is being treated by the woman and is doing better. See Sarah Grimké to Catherine Brooks Yale, Perth Amboy, March 15, 1862. As for the early marriage treatment, see J. Peter Lesley to Weld, September 17, 1859, both letters in the Weld-Clements.
27. Sarah Grimké to Thody, Eagleswood, May 21, 1860, in Weld-Clements.
28. Weld to [Martha] Wright, Perth Amboy, June 2, 1862, copy in Martha Wright's hand, in Garrison Family Papers, Sophia Smith Collection, Smith College Library.
29. Sarah Grimké to Thody, April 11, 1860, in Weld-Clements.
30. Weld to Thody, Eagleswood, July 26, 1860, in Weld-Clements.
31. Thody seems to have won on one point. His fate was a chronic topic of thought and action for the entire family throughout the postwar years. As for Angelina, it is indeed extraordinary that she was hardly active at all in seeking a cure or caring for her son, certainly when one compares her actions with Sarah.

CHAPTER XV

1. Sarah Grimké to *Ma bien aimée,* West Newton, November 14, 1863, in Weld-Clements.
2. One important pivotal symbol to Weld's evangelical friends was Theodore's decision to send his son Stuart to Harvard, that den of Unitarian heresy. See Beriah Green to Weld, January 6, 1860, in Weld-Clements.
3. See the circular for "Young Ladies' Boarding School, Lexington,

Mass.," in Weld-Clements; Gerda Lerner, *The Grimké Sisters from South Carolina: Rebels Against Slavery* (Boston, 1967), 357–58; Benjamin P. Thomas, *Theodore Weld: Crusader for Freedom* (New Brunswick, N.J., 1950), 253–56.

4. Signs of this position appear in "Dead Issues-Alive," manuscript in Weld-Clements, which probably dates from just after the war; quotations and main argument from "The Nation. Its Rights and Duties" [c. 1869–70], manuscript in Weld-Clements. The interpretation in this and subsequent paragraphs directly contradicts that of Benjamin Thomas; see Thomas, *Theodore Weld*, 255. The latest work on antislavery activists after the war ignores Weld entirely; see James M. McPherson, *The Abolitionist Legacy: From Reconstruction to the NAACP* (Princeton, 1975).

5. "The Nation. Its Rights and Duties."

6. Sarah Grimké, "An Appeal," in *Norfolk County Gazette*, January 6, 1872; Sarah Grimké to William Lloyd Garrison, Hyde Park, October 30, 1871, in Garrison Papers, Boston Public Library.

7. The story of the black Grimké brothers as told here is a composite of more complete versions in Lerner, *Grimké Sisters*, 358–66; Katharine DuPre Lumpkin, *The Emancipation of Angelina Grimké* (Chapel Hill, 1974), 220–27.

8. *Ibid.*

9. *Ibid.*

10. See *Norfolk County Gazette*, September 20, September 27, and October 4, 1873.

11. See Lerner, *Grimké Sisters*, 366; Lumpkin, *Emancipation of Angelina Grimké*, 227; examples of Weld's participation appear in the *Norfolk County Gazette*, February 10, 1877, and October 13, 1876.

12. For a somewhat different account, see Lerner, *Grimké Sisters*, 366–67; my account is based on a story in the *Boston Evening Traveller*, March 8, 1870.

13. For school board election, see *Norfolk County Gazette*, March 3, 1873; for his resignation, see *ibid.*, September 26, 1874; for public library, see "Report of the Trustees," in *Norfolk County Gazette*, April 3, 1875; for a general sense of community life in Hyde Park as contemporaries perceived it, see Edmund Davis, Henry B. Humphrey, and Jos. King Knight, compilers, *Memorial Sketch of Hyde Park, for the First Twenty Years of Its Corporate Existence* . . . (Boston, 1888), passim.

14. See the *Norfolk County Gazette*, April 4, July 11, September 19, 1874, and April 27, 1875; quotation is from the July 11, 1874 issue.
15. *Ibid.*, September 19, 1874, and April 27, 1875.
16. For founding of church, see clippings in Scrapbook I of Henry A Rich Collection, Hyde Park Branch, Boston Public Library (courtesy Hyde Park Historical Society), and [E.Q.S.] Osgood, "Twenty-Fifth Anniversary Sermon—Unitarian Church," in *Norfolk County Gazette*, June 10, 1893; for Preamble, see *ibid.*
17. Weld, "Letter" to W. S. Everett, in *Norfolk County Gazette*, June 21, 1879.
18. *Ibid.*
19. *Norfolk County Gazette*, June 10, 1876.
20. In spirit communications, Sarah's father assured her that he would take care of her after death. See [John Faucheraud Grimké's spirit] to Sarah Grimké, March 12, 1865 and May 27, 1866, in Weld-Clements; for details of the funeral, see Ellen Wright Garrison to Eliza Wright Osborne, December 29, 1873, and Ellen Wright Garrison to Martha Coffin Wright, December 30, 1873, both in Garrison Family Papers, Sophia Smith Collection, Smith College Library.
21. *Ibid.* Ellen Garrison did not like William Hamilton, Sissy's husband. She described him as "a forlorn lugubrious young man—with a horrid stubborn looking jaw and skull." See Ellen Wright Garrison to Martha Coffin Wright, December 30, 1873, *ibid.* Stuart's sense of mourning lived far beyond the funeral, despite the best attempts of his father and William Lloyd Garrison to persuade him that Sarah lived on in the spirit world. See William Lloyd Garrison to Stuart Weld, Roxbury, September 28, 1875, in Miscellaneous MSS, New York Historical Society.
22. Weld to Gerrit Smiths, Hyde Park, January 25, 1874, in Gerrit Smith Collection, Syracuse University.
23. [Weld], *In Memory Angelina Grimké Weld* (Boston, 1880), 59–61; see also Catherine H. Birney, *The Grimké Sisters: Sarah and Angelina Grimké, The First American Women Advocates of Abolition and Woman's Rights* (Westport, Conn., 1969, or. ed., 1885), 311–13.
24. Weld to William and Ellen [Garrison], Hyde Park, November 10, 1879, in Sophia Smith Collection, Smith College Library.
25. *Norfolk County Gazette*, September 27, 1890; see *ibid.*, August 25, 1883, for a description of a similar reception for Andrew Jackson Davis.

26. *Ibid.*, December 1, 1883; *The Woman's Journal* (Boston), December 1, 1883.
27. *Norfolk County Gazette*, December 1, 1883; *The Woman's Journal* (Boston), December 1, 1883.
28. On his lecturing, see *Norfolk County Gazette*, June 25, 1881. October 6, 1883; Weld to William Lloyd Garrison, Jr., September 22 [1880], and Ellen Wright Garrison to Eliza Wright Osborne, January 11, 1881, both in Garrison Family Papers, Sophia Smith Collection, Smith College Library. On "Weld Circle," see *Norfolk County Gazette*, December 8, 1883. On Historical Society, see Scrapbook III, Henry A. Rich Collection, Hyde Park Branch, Boston Public Library. For "blind man's buff," see *Norfolk County Gazette*, April 30, 1892.
29. *Norfolk County Gazette*, February 2, 1890. This opinion, in fact, was reported as being the "sentiment of the gathering," and we know no more about Weld's particular view of Bellamy.
30. Weld, "Lessons from the Life of Wendell Phillips," in *Memorial Services upon the Seventy-Fourth Birthday of Wendell Phillips, Held at the Residence of William Sumner Crosby . . . Nov. 29th, 1885* (Boston, 1886), 7–38; quote is on 37–38.
31. One can follow the course of Weld's health in *Norfolk County Gazette*, June 27, 1885, July 4, 1885, September 19, 1885, October 3, 1885, and March 30, 1889; in addition, for his breakdown of 1888–1889 see Weld to Sarah Weld Hamilton, Hyde Park, June 26, 1890, in Schlesinger Library, Radcliffe College.
32. Weld to Sarah Weld Hamilton, Hyde Park, June 26, 1890, in Schlesinger Library, Radcliffe College.
33. *Norfolk County Gazette*, November 25, 1893, for details of birthday celebration, including poem by Angelina Weld Grimké, and a note that one of the visitors was the daughter of John Brown.
34. *Norfolk County Gazette*, December 29, 1894; it should also be noted that in his last year Stuart Weld and his wife Anna attended to Theodore's every want, thus in some sense repeating the final nursing of Ludovicus by his own rebellious son.
35. *Boston Herald*, February 7, 1895; *Hyde Park Times*, February 8, 1895. For weather conditions, see *Boston Evening Transcript*, February 7, 1895.
36. *Hyde Park Times*, February 8, 1895.
37. *Ibid.*

Bibliography

MANUSCRIPT SOURCES AND LOCATIONS

American School for the Deaf, Hartford, Connecticut
  Lewis Weld Notebooks
Boston Public Library, Boston, Massachusetts
  American Antislavery Society Official Records
  Chapman Papers
  Child Papers
  Garrison Papers
  Grimké Papers
  May Papers
  Phelps Papers
  Weston Papers
  Wright Papers
Connecticut Historical Society, Hartford, Connecticut
  Wolcott Papers
Connecticut State Library, Hartford, Connecticut
  Records of First Congregational Church, Hampton
Cornell University Library, Ithaca, New York
  Collection of Regional History
  Abell Family Papers
  Fowler and Wells Family Papers
  Hazzard Papers
  McKim Collection
  White Papers

Bibliography

George Arents Library, Syracuse University, Syracuse, New York
  Gerrit Smith Papers
Haverford College Library, Haverford, Pennsylvania
  Allinson Family Papers
  Nathaniel Peabody Rogers Papers
Houghton Library, Harvard University, Cambridge, Massachusetts
  Whittier-Pickard Manuscripts
  Abolition Collection
Howard University Library, Washington, D.C.
  Francis James and Archibald Henry Grimké Papers
  Abolition Collection
Hyde Park Public Library, Hyde Park, Massachusetts
  Henry A. Rich Collection
Library of Congress, Washington, D.C.
  American Colonization Papers
  American Antislavery Society Papers
  Birney Manuscripts
  Giddings-Julian Manuscripts
  Leavitt Papers
  Tappan (Benjamin and Lewis) Manuscripts
  Weld Manuscripts
  Wright Manuscripts
  Gerrit Smith Personal Papers
  Gallaudet Papers
McCormick Theological Seminary Library, Chicago, Illinois
  Lane Seminary Manuscripts
Mount Holyoke College Library, South Hadley, Massachusetts
  Manuscript Collections
New York Historical Society, New York, New York
  Child Papers
  Clarke Papers
  Garrison-McKim Papers
  Slavery Manuscripts
New York Public Library, New York, New York
  Weld Account Books
Oberlin College Library, Oberlin, Ohio
  Antislavery Collection
  Cowles Collection
  Finney Papers
  Oberlin College Library Autograph Letters
  Thomas Manuscripts

Bibliography

Ohio State Historical Society, Columbus, Ohio
  Giddings Collection
  Tappan Correspondence
  Miscellaneous File
Phillips Andover School Archives, Andover, Massachusetts
  Archives and Student Records
Schlesinger Library, Radcliffe College, Cambridge, Massachusetts
  Beecher and Stowe Papers
  Loring Family Papers
Sophia Smith Collection, Smith College, Southampton, Massachusetts
  Garrison Family Papers
Stowe-Day Foundation, Hartford, Connecticut
  Beecher Collection
  Miscellaneous Papers
Swarthmore College Library, Swarthmore, Pennsylvania
  Whittier Papers
Western Reserve Historical Society, Cleveland, Ohio
  Marius Robinson Manuscripts
  Wright Manuscripts
  Miscellaneous Manuscripts
William Clements Library, University of Michigan, Ann Arbor,
  Michigan
  Birney Papers
  Theodore Dwight Weld, Angelina Grimké Weld, and Sarah Grimké
  Papers
Yale University Library, New Haven, Connecticut
  Beecher Papers
  Lewis Weld Family Papers

PRINTED PRIMARY SOURCES

Every student of Weld or of the Grimké sisters owes an enormous debt to the editors of two sets of transcripts of Weld, Grimké, and Birney letters at the William Clements Library and elsewhere: Gilbert H. Barnes and Dwight L. Dumond, eds., *Letters of Theodore Dwight Weld, Angelina Grimké Weld, and Sarah Grimké, 1822–1844*, 2 vols. (Gloucester, Mass., 1966, or. ed. 1934), and Dwight L. Dumond, ed., *Letters of James Gillespie Birney, 1831–1857*, 2 vols. (Gloucester, Mass., 1966, or. ed. 1938). Though its title page and preface are inaccurate, Weld's *American Slavery As It Is* (New York, 1969, ed. Katz, or. ed. 1839) does provide a facsimile edition of the original text. The best modern collection of antislavery source

Bibliography

material is William H. Pease and Jane H. Pease, eds., *The Antislavery Argument* (Indianapolis, 1965).

SECONDARY SOURCES

Weld first came to the attention of historians as the main actor in Gilbert Hobbs Barnes, *The Anti-Slavery Impulse, 1830–1844* (New York, 1964, ed. McLoughlin, or. ed. 1933). Barnes sought to reinterpret antislavery history by putting Weld and revival-based abolition at the forefront of the movement, thus denying the preeminence of William Lloyd Garrison. The book has great historiographical importance, but at this date must be considered distorted in its characterization of Weld and his importance. Written in the Barnes tradition, Benjamin P. Thomas, *Theodore Weld: Crusader for Freedom* (New Brunswick, New Jersey, 1950), gives us a livelier, more humane, and more comprehensive view of Weld than Barnes. Still, Thomas's book lacks depth and is not really a complete account of Weld's life.

The Grimké sisters are served by three works of different eras: Catherine H. Birney, *The Grimké Sisters* (Westport, Connecticut, 1969, or. ed. 1885); Gerda Lerner, *The Grimké Sisters of South Carolina* (Boston, 1967); and Katharine DuPre Lumpkin, *The Emancipation of Angelina Grimké* (Chapel Hill, 1974). Birney is notable chiefly for her extensive quotations of primary source materials. Lerner's is an excellent introduction to the public life of the sisters. Lumpkin treats Angelina's inner life with great sensitivity, though she has found it necessary to diminish Weld and Sarah Grimké in the process.

There is no need to list here all the many primary and secondary works on abolition and reform that I have consulted for this study. Many appear in the footnotes, and the reader can get basic (though somewhat dated) introductions to this material in the bibliographies of Thomas, *Theodore Weld*, and Louis Filler, *The Crusade Against Slavery, 1830–1860* (New York, 1960). The best list of antislavery primary source material in printed form is Dwight L. Dumond, *A Bibliography of Antislavery in America* (Ann Arbor, 1964). Some recent works of particular interest include Lewis Perry, *Radical Abolitionism: Anarchy and the Government of God in Antislavery Thought* (Ithaca, 1974); Ronald G. Walters, *The Antislavery Appeal: American Abolitionism After 1830* (Baltimore, 1976); and Peter F. Walker, *Moral Choices: Memory, Desire, and Imagination in Nineteenth-Century American Abolition* (Baton Rouge, 1978). A recent article by Lewis Perry, " 'We Have Had Conversations in the World': The

Bibliography

Abolitionists and Spontaneity," *Canadian Journal of American Studies* 6 (Spring, 1975), 3–26, discusses the theme indicated in the title largely through the life and romance of Weld. His interpretation is for the most part compatible with mine, though a comparison of the present work and Perry's article will reveal some contrasts. Two biographies of significant abolitionists have been quite useful: Bertram Wyatt-Brown, *Lewis Tappan and the Evangelical War Against Slavery* (New York, 1971, or. ed. 1969), and John L. Thomas, *The Liberator: William Lloyd Garrison* (Boston, 1963). I might add that Wyatt-Brown, in articles and papers too numerous to list here, has been quite important in shaping my vision of antebellum reformers and abolitionists in particular.

Index

Index

Index

Index

Index

Index